Family
HUYBERTIE LANSII

This genealogy represents those ֽ
who figure prominently in the text. In general it includes
only children who survived into adulthood.

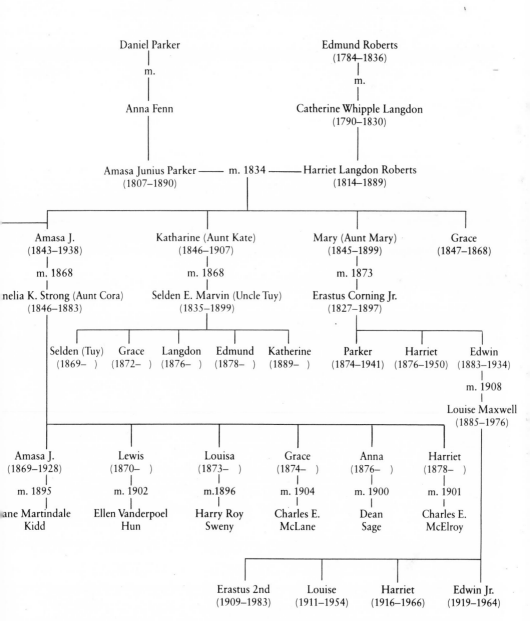

Daniel Parker
|
m.
|
Anna Fenn

Edmund Roberts
(1784–1836)
|
m.
|
Catherine Whipple Langdon
(1790–1830)

Amasa Junius Parker —— m. 1834 —— Harriet Langdon Roberts
(1807–1890)   (1814–1889)

Amasa J.
(1843–1938)
|
m. 1868
|
nelia K. Strong (Aunt Cora)
(1846–1883)

Katharine (Aunt Kate)
(1846–1907)
|
m. 1868
|
Selden E. Marvin (Uncle Tuy)
(1835–1899)

Mary (Aunt Mary)
(1845–1899)
|
m. 1873
|
Erastus Corning Jr.
(1827–1897)

Grace
(1847–1868)

Selden (Tuy)
(1869–)

Grace
(1872–)

Langdon
(1876–)

Edmund
(1878–)

Katharine
(1889–)

Parker
(1874–1941)

Harriet
(1876–1950)

Edwin
(1883–1934)
|
m. 1908
|
Louise Maxwell
(1885–1976)

Amasa J.
(1869–1928)
|
m. 1895
|
ane Martindale
Kidd

Lewis
(1870–)
|
m. 1902
|
Ellen Vanderpoel
Hun

Louisa
(1873–)
|
m.1896
|
Harry Roy
Sweny

Grace
(1874–)
|
m. 1904
|
Charles E.
McLane

Anna
(1876–)
|
m. 1900
|
Dean
Sage

Harriet
(1878–)
|
m. 1901
|
Charles E.
McElroy

Erastus 2nd
(1909–1983)

Louise
(1911–1954)

Harriet
(1916–1966)

Edwin Jr.
(1919–1964)

Pruyn

AN ALBANY GIRLHOOD

HUYBERTIE PRUYN HAMLIN

Edited by Alice P. Kenney

Washington Park Press Ltd.
Albany, New York

Washington Park Press Ltd.
7 Englewood Place
Albany, NY 12203
(518) 438-5391
(518) 465-0169
95 94 93 92 91 90 5 4 3 2 1

Hamlin, Huybertie Pruyn, 1873–1964.
   An Albany girlhood / Huybertie Pruyn Hamlin;
edited by Alice P. Kenney.

   Includes index.
   Includes bibliographical references.
   ISBN 0-9605460-9-X: $25.00
   1. Hamlin, Huybertie Pruyn, 1873–1964 — Child-
hood and youth. 2. Albany (N.Y.) — Biography.
3. Dutch Americans — New York (State) — Albany
— Biography. 4. Upper classes — New York (State)
— Albany — History. 5. Albany (N.Y.) — Social life
and customs. 6. Dutch Americans — New York
(State) — Albany — Social life and customs.
I. Kenney, Alice P., 1937–1985. II. Title.
F129.A353H35   1990
974.7'43041'092 — dc20
[B]   90-37455
                                                          CIP

All photographs are drawn from the private papers
of Huybertie Pruyn Hamlin, now in the collection
of the McKinney Library of the Albany Institute of
History and Art.

Book Design: Mount Ida Press
Typography: The Letter Shop
Printing: Thomson-Shore, Inc.

CONTENTS

In Memoriam

ALICE P. KENNEY

ALICE P. KENNEY WAS THE IDEAL person to undertake study of the extraordinary bequest of Huybertie Pruyn Hamlin — the Hamlin Papers, catalogued in the McKinney Library of the Albany Institute of History and Art in 65 boxes, 401 folders, and 13 packages.

Herself a native of Albany, Dr. Kenney had, from her earliest days, shown special aptitude in history. After graduating with honors from Middlebury College, she completed a masters and doctorate at Columbia in three years and joined the history faculty of Cedar Crest College. In addition to teaching and chairing the department, she undertook scores of research projects, developing particular expertise in the early Dutch settlers of the Hudson Valley. She became known widely as an inexhaustible scholar and an indefatigable researcher, and she published in a broad range of subjects.[1]

In 1979, she turned her attention to the Hamlin Papers at the McKinney Library of the Albany Institute of History and Art. Dr. Kenney, who suffered from a variety of disabling conditions, including impaired vision, displayed such dedication that she earned the willing assistance of a cadre of volunteers. Aided also by her family, her secretary, and the staffs of the Albany Institute of History and Art and the Albany Public Library, she began research on the life and work of Huybertie Pruyn Hamlin with an eye to publishing the most important texts.

Once she was familiar with the full body of the work, Dr. Kenney chose *An Albany Girlhood* for detailed study. She broke the continuous text into manageable sections and enriched the whole with copious notes. Bringing to bear her formidable knowledge of American history of the last quarter of the nineteenth century, Dr. Kenney investigated the architectural essence and history of each building mentioned; she traced the genealogies of the families described; she researched the social, political, and economic significance of relevant citizens on both sides of the Atlantic; she studied the forms of food, drink, dress, transportation, home decoration, and entertainment prevalent at the time. With incomparable zeal she traced the work of writers, dramatists, artists, actors, athletes, educators, and scientists; and she analyzed the contributions of government officials, business leaders, engineers, clergy, even fashion designers who came into Mrs. Hamlin's young life. She wrote summary outlines of each chapter, prepared a genealogy of the family and the neighbors on Elk Street, and compiled a bibliography of hundreds of items. In notes throughout the text, she explained the now-obscure, identified the now-forgotten, and surrounded events with their historical context. The notes display what William Rowley identified as Dr. Kenney's "tireless character and almost unbelievable grasp of mind."[2]

Her work came to an abrupt end with her unexpected death in February 1985, at the age of forty-seven. Her mother, her secretary, and her research associates completed unfinished pieces of research and compiled the many pieces of the project, which then totaled over 800 pages. (Copies of the unabridged text have been placed in the Pruyn Room of the Albany Public Library and the McKinney Library of the Albany Institute of History and Art.)

This work would not have come into being without the persistent commitment and unflagging faith of Dr. Kenney's mother, Marjorie Kenney, and the generous support of the Alice P. Kenney Memorial Trust. It is published in recognition of Dr. Kenney's excellent scholarship, in admiration for her inspiring courage, and in gratitude for her intelligent, generous, and heroic contribution to the essential culture of Albany.

S.D.

ACKNOWLEDGEMENTS

WHEN ALICE KENNEY came to the sudden ending of her own story in February 1985, it became the task of those who had worked closely with her to finish the book on which she and so many others had spent countless hours. *An Albany Girlhood* is a tribute to all of them.

At the time of her return to Albany from her teaching in Pennsylvania, she met Gloria Freedman, Special Services Librarian of the Albany Public Library, and her group of volunteers who read books onto tapes for the sight-impaired. Their reading gave Alice access to the manuscripts and books she needed. Space does not permit mentioning the names of all who helped, but a few read many books — Sue Britten, Ruth Johnson, Vincent Trimarchi, James Leonard, Fred Childs, Evelyn Bernstein, Pat Caccomo, Marcia Perry, Sister Paul Dupré, Sister Anne Kelley, David Bennett, and Elton Butler.

Much research in Albany history and genealogy was done by Norman Rice and Roderick Blackburn and the staff of the Albany Institute of History and Art, by Gloria Freedman and James Hoban of the Albany Public Library, by Lee Johnson of the New York Public Library, and by Kenneth MacFarland, Martha Noble, William Rowley, and Robert DeVito.

Janet Rose, Esther Phinny, and members of the staff of the Bethlehem Public Library provided invaluable service in making materials available.

Mildred Zimmerman read all of Mrs. Hamlin's manuscript onto tape and assisted in research for notes.

Edith DeGiulio, who started as a reader, later became secretary for Alice. Her loyalty and expertise made possible this book and many articles which were in progress.

Charlotte Wilcoxen served first as reader, then research associate for genealogical and historical facts, and finally as custodian into whose care was entrusted the unfinished manuscript.

More recently, James Hoban helped to expedite the publication, Margaret Mirabelli provided keen insight into the overall value of the project, and Susan Safford assisted with research into the genealogy and photograph collection. Susanne Dumbleton edited the text, notes, and photographs to bring the whole into publishable form.

My sincere appreciation to each and every one, whether named or just remembered.

MARJORIE W. KENNEY

INTRODUCTION

HUYBERTIE PRUYN HAMLIN

H UYBERTIE LANSING PRUYN HAMLIN (pronounced Hī′ berty Lan′ sing Prīne Ham′ lin) lived an extraordinary life.[1] Her parents were esteemed and wealthy members of the Albany community, and her childhood home at 13 Elk Street was one of the most architecturally elegant and socially active in the city. Though her father, J. V. L. Pruyn, died in 1877 when Huybertie was only four, her childhood and youth were filled with activity and opportunity.

With her mother (Anna Parker Pruyn), her half-brother John, and her sister Harriet, Huybertie spent her childhood surrounded by the larger family, including sixteen first cousins, all grandchildren of Harriet Langdon Roberts Parker and Judge Amasa J. Parker. She was immersed in traditions of elegance and style prevalent at the time and in the assumptions of Democratic politics and Episcopal religion. The house was filled constantly with distinguished visitors from around the world.

From her eighth birthday until well into her seventies, Huybertie followed the Pruyn family tradition of keeping a diary (1881–1956). Entries of the early years savor life at home and focus with affection on family, school, church, friends, and the persons and activities of the neighborhood. As she entered her youth, Huybertie travelled frequently, moving easily amongst the "Quality" in Europe and other American cities, recording her encounters in detailed notes. In 1895, she complemented her Albany debut with presentation at court in London. But she always returned to Elk Street with enthusiasm and deep affection, racing up the hill from Union Station to greet her beloved poodle Fromo and to settle into the warm routine maintained in her absence by an attentive household staff.

Albany was not to be her constant home, however. In 1898 she married Bostonian Charles Sumner Hamlin, an attorney who served as Assistant Secretary of the Treasury under Cleveland and Wilson and as long-time member of the Federal Reserve Board. Huybertie therefore spent her married life as a socially prominent member of government circles in Washington and Boston, summering at Mattapoisett on Cape Cod. In the early years of the century, she made frequent trips to Albany to visit with her mother. When Anna Pruyn died in 1909, Huybertie and Harriet (John had died in 1902) decided to sell the house. Huybertie's journals record the day of her last visit to the house, June 20, 1910, as an occasion of great sadness.

Throughout the forty years of marriage, Huybertie moved energetically about in political life, entertaining at the Hamlin homes in Boston, Washington, and Mattapoisset, visiting, traveling, and keeping notes. She and Charles Hamlin had one child, a daughter Anna, born in 1900. Anna was described everywhere as a splendid girl — lively, bright, affectionate, and thoughtful. Letters to her parents show her to be loving and devoted. In 1921, Anna had serious surgery for an intestinal thrombosis, from which she appeared to have recovered thoroughly. In 1925, however, while vacationing in Bermuda, Anna was suddenly taken ill, and before her parents could reach her side, she died of complications following surgery for intestinal lesions. Her parents were desolate.

In all probability, it was this tragedy which led Mrs. Hamlin to transform the jottings written for her own amusement into prose pieces for a general audience. Remembering Anna's love of Albany stories, perhaps wanting to overcome her own grief, Mrs. Hamlin began, in about 1926, to write. She dedicated an early draft, "Purely Personal and 13 Elk Street," to her daughter: "In loving memory of Anna Hamlin, who also played in the nursery and garden at 13 Elk Street for the first ten years of a short and happy life, and who asked me to write these reminiscences."

With her journals as primary sources, Huybertie rendered again and again the stories of her childhood and her young adulthood. She added narratives about her experiences in Washington and in Europe. "I once counted that I typed something like two thousand pages a year," she said in an interview with William Kennedy in 1963.[2]

When her husband died in 1938, she was cut off from public life but maintained active correspondence with scores of friends and associates, many of them influential members of state. Among those with whom she sustained long-time relationships were the Wilsons and the Roosevelts.

Mrs. Hamlin returned to Albany in the early forties — alone. She had suffered great loss: her family, her home, her wealth, and her access to persons of power were all gone. She moved into a small apartment at 352 State Street and settled into a life marked by conscious attention to both the past and the present. She continued to participate actively in the efforts of the national Democratic Party. She readily provided consultation to researchers at the Albany Institute of History and Art and to authors in search of the past — Edgar Van Olinda, C. R. Roseberry, Charlotte Wilcoxen, and William Kennedy. She also continued to write on her own. She prepared full-length manuscripts and essays, some of which were published in the *Times Union*, in Cape Cod newspapers, and in regional magazines and journals.

One of the last book-length pieces she completed was *An Albany Girlhood*, dated 1948. This was most likely the culmination of other approaches to the subject, a synthesis of the best of many attempts. The proposal was repeatedly rejected by book publishers as being interesting and valuable but not commercially viable. But Mrs. Hamlin seems not to have lost hope. Confident of the ultimate value of her work, she assigned the task to posterity, closing the manuscript with words from Virgil which had been stitched by a friend on the baby book she kept for Anna: "Perhaps sometime it will be a pleasure to recall these things." She was correct. Her papers have become a matter of serious interest to scholars of social and political history, urban and social studies, architecture and design, and women's studies.

THE NATURE OF *AN ALBANY GIRLHOOD*

An Albany Girlhood is a fascinating text from a variety of perspectives. It possesses historical value in the abundance of details of the daily life of the wealthy and powerful families of Albany at the end of the nineteenth century. With her direct and simple narrative, Mrs. Hamlin presents a clear view of the cosmopolitan style prevalent at the time, for provincial as Mrs. Hamlin seems in her chauvinistic affection for Albany, she, like many of her contemporaries, was a skilled citizen of the larger world, as comfortable in European capitals as in Albany.

But *An Albany Girlhood* is of historical interest also for the tension underlying the text. Huybertie Pruyn Hamlin presents a fascinating dialectic. The young woman she describes bursts with enthusiasm for life, eager to dispatch with her restrictive clothing and the labyrinth of rules guaranteed to subdue her. How ridiculous, she writes from her middle years, to have hiked, bicycled, tobogganed, canoed, and iceskated in floor-length skirts and crinolines. How foolish, she implies, to have been expected to "call on" houses whose residents would have preferred that she go away. How absurd, she notes, from her post-World War II vantage point, to have professed democratic principles and yet bowed to the rude backs of European royalty — who, she believes, would have preferred life without the awkward courtesy of Americans. The text fairly bristles with gleeful reports of breaches of etiquette, acts of mischief, witty affronts to the denizens of Quality Row.

It appears at times that the author champions nonconformity and secretly prefers "characters" to paragons of virtue and propriety.

Yet it is to the life of elegance and privilege, with its rules designed to exclude the uninitiate as well as to embellish existence, that Mrs. Hamlin casts her longing backward look. Though she claims to disdain the clothing of the period, she describes each item in loving detail. Though she mocks the rules in reports of rebellions she led or inspired, she transcribes the expectations with exactness and condescends to those who transgressed through ignorance or carelessness. Though she seems aware of the lesser education available to those less privileged, she accepts the legitimacy of her right to be served and presumes an inherent inferiority of those she calls "ordinary people," describing their activities with a patronizing tone. Moreover, though aware of the limitations on the aspirations of women, and though writing from a post-World War II perspective, she reports her mother's energetic anti-suffrage activities without comment.

This last paradox is ironic, for Huybertie's personal integrity and hard-to-bridle enthusiasm put her at risk in the repressive way of life for which she is so nostalgic; that is, Huybertie, having finished school, made her debut, and been presented at court, had no suitor! It was no surprise. With her forthright speech, high energy, and robust manner, she must have seemed a formidable match in a time in which women were, above all, to be demure. According to Huybertie herself, she was more interested in having fun than in wooing a mate, and if newspaper reports are to be believed, she was the catalyst of many of the social community's most adventurous undertakings: *The Boston Globe* noted in its coverage of her eventual wedding: "She is of a vivacious disposition and possesses a refreshing indifference to some of the stilted conventions of 'Society.' "

In this and other ways the text shows Huybertie as having an ambivalent relationship with the life she was on the one hand *privileged*, and on the other hand *forced* to live.

An Albany Girlhood reflects, too, the historic tension between the verbal restraint characteristic of the Dutch upper class culture in the nineteenth century and the non-reflective forthrightness which marks American culture, particularly with the heightened social activism for democratization following World War II. Even for a renegade such as Huybertie, there were subjects and styles which were clearly not acceptable. A writer of Mrs. Hamlin's background might, for example, discuss the accoutrements of a life — its objects and events — but not its essence — its feelings and ideas. Thus, in one chapter Mrs. Hamlin presents lengthy details on parties in Albany and arrangements for an upcoming trip to Europe. Tucked amidst the descriptions of food and clothing and reservations is a scant paragraph noting the death of her brother's child — her godson. "We were greatly saddened by the death, after weeks of illness, of little John V. L. Pruyn. His illness was at first thought to be from his teeth, but complications arose. There were no baby specialists in Albany at that time. I always thought that if he had been hurried to Dr. Holt in New York, he would have been saved." In the next sentence she proceeds breezily, "Mother and I sailed on the *Majestic* again...."

Even acknowledging the more frequent death of children at that time, the modern reader might be offended by the casualness with which this information is presented and dismissed. The writer seems callous and self-righteous. But for Mrs. Hamlin, the suppression of emotion was a matter of propriety. Grief, like love, doubt, longing, and other powerful components of the inner life, were to be repressed. They certainly were not to be paraded in public.

This tendency to repress is no more touchingly evident than in the descriptions elsewhere of the death of her daughter. In the dozen or so typescripts treating Anna's death, Mrs. Hamlin, her husband, and others painstakingly note what Anna wore, what games she played, what she said and wrote in the days just before her illness and death. They describe events — medical procedures, memorial services, funeral eulogies. But when Mrs. Hamlin embarks upon commenting what Anna's death means, how it feels to have lost her child, she breaks off, "I cannot continue with this."

It is probable that the restrictions applied to some degree to living as well. In the final pages of *An Albany Girlhood*, Mrs. Hamlin describes her last discussion with her mother on the night before her marriage to Charles Hamlin. It is 10:20; Huybertie is in her room:

"Just as I was settled, Mother came in and sat down in the little white rocker and began to cry. This frightened me. The only time I had seen her really cry was when Aunt Cora died, many years ago. She said I had been all the world to her, that no one was good enough, even Charlie, whom she liked so much.

"I laughed at that, but she did not smile. She felt life alone in that big house was not worth living. I was sorry. I did not know what to say to comfort her. I was afraid I might cry too, and that would be so dreary, and anyway it was very late in the day.

"Fromo solved the problem. He gave a wide and noisy yawn, and then rolled over and fell out of bed with a thump. Then he ran off and curled up on a rug in the nursery.

"I slept well that night. . . ."

Here, in one of the few instances of dramatic interchange in the thousands of pages of manuscript, Mrs. Hamlin is clearly uncomfortable with her mother's rare expression of deep feeling. She appears not only unable, but also unwilling to respond.

As these excerpts indicate, then, the Hamlin papers, *An Albany Girlhood* in particular, are of value both for what they tell and what they withhold.

Together this text and subtext reproduce a way of life. For in addition to presenting a richly detailed portrait of daily life, the Hamlin papers provide access to a broad array of cultural assumptions — attitudes and aspirations of a generation and a class. Moreover, the nostalgia which permeates the text testifies as powerfully as the facts to the enormity of change the twentieth century brought to Mrs. Hamlin and those with whom she had shared her privileged days.

In this context the work of Huybertie Pruyn Hamlin merits a place beside the texts of Cuyler Reynolds, Arthur James Weise, and Codman Hislop both as primary source and as commentary on the history of Albany during her lifetime, 1873–1964.

SUSANNE DUMBLETON

NOTE ON THE EDITED TEXT

THIS VOLUME WAS EDITED by several hands. Alice P. Kenney and her assistants at the Albany Public Library and the Albany Institute of History and Art were concerned primarily with the historical authenticity and fullness of the text and notes. Susanne Dumbleton at Washington Park Press was concerned primarily with the accuracy, coherence and style of the text and the appropriateness of the notes. Whenever possible, she has respected the wishes of Dr. Kenney. No effort has been made within the volume to differentiate the work of the various editors.

In the primary text (Hamlin), the spelling has been regularized, the material has been divided into chapters and paragraphs, and punctuation has been modernized. However, the antiquated use of formal titles has been retained to indicate the author's conscious attention to age and social class. Errors in word choice, usage, or the mechanics of style have been eliminated. When the change is substantive, it has been indicated with brackets.

Also in the primary text, repetition of material has been reduced, the abridgements being signaled by ellipses. In the several instances in which digressive passages have been eliminated, a description of missing material has been inserted into the text in brackets. Information essential for the reader to comprehend the text has also been inserted in brackets.

Where the author has made an error — as in identifying a person or giving a date, for example — the problem has been identified and corrected in the notes.

Unless otherwise indicated, biographical data has been drawn from three sources — *Dictionary of American Biography, Dictionary of National Biography,* and *Albany City Directory.*

PART ONE

EARLIEST MEMORIES

1873 ❦ 1885

PROLOGUE

I BELIEVE THE CORRECT WAY to begin one's reminiscences is to give one's birth date — mine was April 8, 1873, a Tuesday — then say what you first remember, but the trouble is that I remember so many things first all in a heap, that I cannot say surely which comes ahead. [†]

Later in my life I [was][2] told there had been a great discussion about my name. Ariantje Ver Planck, Alida Van Slichtenhorst and Catalyna Schuyler were gravely considered, but these were discarded in favour of Huybertje Lansing, the name of my father's mother [also spelled Hibertje], who was born in 1773. [The author's full name would thus be pronounced He ber' ja Lan' sing Prīne. Her first name was often written as Huybertie, pronounced Hī' berty.] This idea was Mother's. She argued that as I was the youngest of father's five daughters, and none of them had been named for their grandmother, the choice was obvious. In spite of many protests, Mother carried the day. I had a strong Dutch constitution, so I survived it. But of course such a name, forgotten during the Yankee invasion of Albany, led to many nicknames. It had been intended to call me by the last half of the name, "Bertje," which was the diminutive brought over from Holland and used in the Dutch colonies. But this soon ran into "Bertie" (a boy's name, short for Herbert, Albert or Robert), "Bertchen," "Butter," "B," and "Beppo," to give some samples.

I seem to have been a buxom, healthy baby, and the only one of our family with brown eyes. My cousin Louise Parker was six weeks older, and we were baptized together by Bishop Doane at St. Peter's Church at noon on Saturday, May 3rd, 1873, with water from the Jordan brought home by Father many years before. Aunt Kitty Gansevoort, at that time only engaged to patient Uncle Abe Lansing, handed me up. Aunt Cora Parker was the other godmother, and my [step-]brother Jack, then only fourteen and a student at St. John's School, Ossining, was my godfather.

An Albany custom of Dutch origin is for one of the godmothers to give

---

[†] *The first thirteen pages of the manuscript are missing. Though what H.P.H. intended as her beginning is unclear, selected passages from "Purely Personal and Thirteen Elk Street," an essay she had begun earlier but not completed, give an excellent introduction to her early years at home on Elk Street.*[1]

a baby girl a string of gold beads. Aunt Kitty gave me mine. They were bought at Howard & Co. in New York, and were in a red satin box. I gave them later, in the same worn old box, to my great niece, Carolyn Pruyn, when I was her godmother in 1930. Aunt Cora gave me a pair of gold bar pins. One was lost in Newport when I was ten, and the mate I have now given to her great-granddaughter, Cornelia Kane Merritt. Jack gave me a set of mug, knife, fork and spoon, in an enormous box lined with blue silk. Mother started to keep a diary for me, but only wrote a few pages, in a charming red leather book with my name on it in gold tooling. I have taken from it the details of my christening.

Perhaps the nursery table might take precedence among my memories. It is here in the dining room at Mattapoisett [Mrs. Hamlin's summer home]. Everyone admires it, which pleases me. It is a fine example of American Empire, and I have always loved it very much. Its claw feet were great giant paws to me, as I crawled underneath it or sat open-mouthed, listening to Maggie Gleason singing "Gaily the troubadour plays his guitar" or "Darling, I am growing old." Tunes, more than anything else, have the power to recall certain days, or rooms, or people long forgotten. . . . There was a hiding place under the table which endeared it to me, and many precious possessions belonging to Jack, or Hattie [Bertie's older sister] or the nurse were tucked in there, and nobody was any the wiser. To this day, I think I am the only one who knows about that nook.

Our nursery life centered around that old table. We started the day by having breakfast on it at 8:15 every morning, when Delia O'Herran, the long-suffering kitchen maid who aided Bridget [Biddy] the cook, carried it up on a large tray. Delia was a great friend of ours. She helped us play tricks on our nurse, or steal from Biddy, or make molasses candy in the kitchen while Biddy took her nap. We in turn were thrilled to listen to her troubles over her love affair with Emil Grame, the baker. Biddy, she complained, was most impolite to him when he came to see her because he was not Irish, and she made a fuss whenever Delia tried to walk out with him. But love found its way, and Delia and Emil were finally married and lived happily ever after.

My first spanking was on account of Delia. She came up as usual one morning with the tray, and as I ran out to greet her, I insisted that if she had not brought up hominy in our porringers, I would kick. She said that I must have gotten out of bed the wrong way, as I had particularly asked for oatmeal. True to my promise, I began to kick Delia, and everyone else.

My legs were strong and hard, and I roared in loud accompaniment. Frieda protested, and Hattie lectured me from the bathtub. Suddenly the door to Mother's room flew open, and without any questions Mother, with her slipper in hand, proceeded to give me a good licking. She told me to tell Delia I was sorry, and left me to roll disconsolately under the table, hugging a claw foot.

The table had a dark green cloth cover with a scalloped edge, and figures from "Under the Window" stitched around it. A low gas lamp with a vivid glass shade with black flowers on it hung over the center, and in the late afternoons we did our lessons there. What joy it was, when Hattie was deeply absorbed in really trying to learn something, to slip down under the table, push in the support of the drop leaf, and see everything fall Bang! on the floor. . . .

Hattie and I shared the nursery bedroom until she was grown up. For many years there were two beds for Hattie and the nurse, and the old-fashioned crib for me. It was made of walnut and had carving at the head. The sides had brass hooks to hold them up, and on those I learned to vault. If we woke up early enough in the morning or could work it at night, we played a game of Hattie's invention called "Mrs. Come-tickle-me." Or we went travelling down the sides and across the bottom of the beds under the bedclothes, where it was all dark and you might smother if you got lost. Sometimes at night we carried all the fire irons from the nursery into the bedroom very quietly. Then when we were supposed to be asleep, we would gather them together, hold them up as high as possible, and let them drop with such a smash that everyone came running to find out what had happened.

Hattie taught me many things on those early mornings, especially Saturdays and Sundays. . . . [It was also in bed that] she initiated me into the card trick of three robbers who came to rob the house and were followed into the cellar, the bottom of the pack, by Jack, who was a policeman. After endless patience on her part, I finally managed to bring about the meeting of the robbers and the lone policeman in the center of the pack. It was the only trick I ever mastered. We had great competition over "Father and Mother have gone to bed and left me alone to make gingerbread," where I excelled. I could pull myself up without uncrossing my legs, while Hattie rolled over completely. I must not forget "Thirty days hath September, April, June, and November," but any explanation of leap year passed over my head. It simply did not register. I was overcome with my own brilliance when I learned with my fingers "Here is the church, and here is the steeple.

Open the door and see all the people. Here is the minister walking upstairs, and here he is saying his prayers." The last part, where by a twist of the thumb the minister is in the pulpit, was a veritable triumph for Hattie as well as for me, for it seemed that we never would master it. . . .

The six-weeks' advantage that Louise Parker had over me in age was a terrible thorn in the flesh. She and Harriet Corning were both born on Washington's birthday and celebrated their birthdays together, usually at the Cornings. All that seemed enough without rubbing it in on me. On February 23rd, Louise would tell the other girls in school, "I was seven yesterday, and yet Mama wants me to play with Bertie, who is only six, and sleeps in a crib, and I just won't do it. She can play with the little girls." This last meant her sisters, Grace, Anna, and Harriet Parker, and our cousin Harriet Corning. I associated those six weeks with Lent, when we swore off cakes, candies, and soda water and ate only stewed prunes or baked apples for dessert every night except Sunday, when we were allowed Biddy's ice cream for the midday dinner. . . . The birthday of Louise and Ash Wednesday usually about coincided and seemed to fit in with my gloom, while my birthday on April 8th was apt to come along with Easter and the joy of the season and [of] being the same age again as Louise.

Mother always came into our bedroom with a glass-shaded candlestick before she went to bed, and looked carefully at our coverings. Hattie had light blue blankets with white bars, and mine were pink. For cold weather we had pink and blue puffs, tufted with small bows, and our winter wrappers were pink and blue eider, bound with ribbon. Generally we did not wake up, but when I did I would murmur "Cuckoo! Cuckoo!" like the hall clock and roll over with a feeling of peace and contentment. . . .

In the morning Frieda made the fire in the nursery by seven o'clock, and at 7:15 I had to turn out in the cold to take my bath, for we had no furnace heat in those rooms until many years later and never missed it. At 7:30 Hattie turned out. I never could make her get up first. She said she was the oldest and could choose, though I said that being the youngest I needed more sleep.

For many years we had prayers every morning at 8:15 in the "Oratory," which was a bow window opening out of the extension library. It had four windows facing north, and in the four lower sashes were the four winds done in stained glass by Clayton & Bell of London. Old Boreas was a champion prize blower, with his cheeks full of what was supposed to be wind, but which made him look more like a Chinese laundryman squirting water, a pastime in which we loved to indulge. There was a charming little altar of carved black oak, with a kneeling stool in front, and on the altar a small crucifix and two dark blue Limoges enamel vases and two old brass candlesticks. The walls were paneled wood, and on them hung several ikons brought from Russia by Father, and there were also two heads of Russian saints in interesting old settings. There were two lecterns, one made of olive wood from the Mount of Olives and one of oak from the Abraham tree at Horeb. Hattie knelt at a prie-dieu and Jack and I knelt at chairs close by, while Mother read the morning prayers. I can hear her voice now. . . .

❧   ❧   ❧

The black cloud that hung over my childhood for many years was my winter underclothes. They nearly drove me crazy, and as I look back, I cannot blame myself. Great heavy clumsy things, they became like boards after two or three washings. As I was very warm-blooded, and on the move all day, they clung closely and scratched me to distraction, especially the day they were clean. Hattie did not mind them, which made my case more hopeless, as I was thought just a crank. The first cool night in the fall would bring Mother into the nursery early in the morning, and I was doomed. We had medium weight, winter weight, and delicious gauze for summer, with low necks and no sleeves. I could have worn these all year and been comfortable. Even the medium weight would have been tolerable. But such an idea was simply relegated to the country of useless dreams.

Sundays and Thursdays were clean underclothes days. The previous nights, I decorated the backs of the lovely nursery chairs with a clean shirt stretched over one and the drawers over another, to make them stick less closely to my squirming skin. I quivered as they were drawn on, and for hours I could not bear for anyone to touch me, as they would press the wool against me. I was often considered cross when I was really a martyr. Finally, dear old Dr. Cox came to the rescue. I sobbed out my woes, and to my joy he sided with me, my first ray of hope. Mother had thought it was a mania of mine, and that I would come to my senses, as Hattie got over her mania for washing her hands every time she touched a door handle or anything else. So the nightmare underclothes were discarded forever, and Mother took me downtown to buy the silk ones. My end of the bargain was to remember to pull on red Canton flannel bloomers when I skated or coasted. They were as full as the traditional Dutchman's trousers and all my petticoats were stowed in them, so I fairly rolled along. I often wonder what Mother, Mrs. Chandler, or Frieda would say to the present light attire.

We had winter- and summer-weight flannel petticoats. They had three tucks too, for letting down, so they were even clumsier. We wore cotton "Tommies" for summer, and flannel ones in winter, and undershirts at night too, while in very cold weather we wore crocheted bed socks. I had a pair of variegated ones. Our stockings, too, were graded. In summer for best, we wore fine gray French lisle thread ones, and gloves to match. Both the black and colored stockings came off when we got hot. There were no fast colors, and people were often poisoned by the dyes. We all wore far too many clothes, and they were hot and cumbersome to run about in. Our white petticoats were stiff with starch, and the Hamburg edgings [on the drawers] had sharp points which were particularly scratchy. . . .

First we put on our shirts. They had heavy cotton waists which buttoned in the back and were stitched in groups of rows to give them strength. Drawers and petticoats were buttoned onto this waist behind, before, and on both sides. Also, the side garters buttoned on. Round garters were supposed to interfere with circulation. All this made quite a weight hanging from the waist and not from the shoulders. It gave a clumsy waist line, as the skirts were gathered onto bands. When we were little, the white skirts had tops, which also buttoned behind, but they were considered childish. Like cribs, we begged to discard them. Then later came the Balmoral skirts for winter. They were very stylish, and also very heavy, as they were of wool in squares or plaids with a ruffle around the bottom. They took the place of white skirts, and were considered a great help in winter, for warmth and also for saving laundry. But on Sundays, everyone came down in a fresh and much starched white ruffled skirt. You could hear all the servants as they rattled about the house after their return from Mass.

Mother provided nightgowns for me when I was about twelve, but I scorned them until I was almost sixteen, as "Tommies" could be stuffed out with pillows, and things could be conveniently stowed in the legs. The nightgowns were high neck and had long sleeves, even in summer. They usually had much tucking each side of the front buttons, and often a collar, sometimes a sail or collar which tangled about the neck. Ribbons were strung through the lace on the cuffs, and often there was a large bow of one's favorite color at the neck. In fact, ribbons were strung through everything, and corset covers, which came with the grownup stage, were most elaborate.

❦   ❦   ❦

Our nursery opened from the bedroom, and also into the hall and into a small room next to Mother's room. The nursery was a lovely large room, sunny all day. The front windows were really doors which slid back into the wall, and the blind doors or shutters inside did the same. In the winter we had gay red chintz curtains with green leaves and yellow birds; gilt cornices held them. White net curtains were next to the windows. In the winter, sand bags were laid at the foot of every window in the house, to keep out the draughts. The sand was poured into long unbleached bags which were stitched tight. Then another bag to harmonize with each room was pulled over the cotton ones. In the nursery they were covered with red felt, in the library with brown velvet, etc. If nobody was looking and you had a stolen penknife or scissors, it was so nice to cut a hole and see the sand leak out.

Outside the glass doors of the nursery, there was a little piazza with an iron railing and a tin-covered floor. This piazza looked all over Elk Street, a vantage point rivaling any neighbor's view. A lovely Linden tree grew right against the piazza and reached to the rooms above ours. How I loved that straight friendly tree, which seemed to protect us, and to look in the windows and laugh or cry with us, or long to join us on winter mornings as we dressed before the open fire. All good Dutchmen plant a Linden in front of their houses. . . .

When I was very small, I had my bath in a tub in front of the nursery fire. This had tiles all around the border, painted by Daisy Doane, the Bishop's daughter, and sold for the benefit of the new Child's Hospital.

There was a high wire fender to protect us from falling into the fire, and if we had colds, square patches of flannel were hung on the fender to heat. Nutmeg was peppered over them, and they were tied around our necks with tapes, while our feet were boiled in a foot tub of hot water and mustard, and a heavy blanket covered tub and legs. To add to the indignity, medicine was administered at intervals, and mutton tallow was smeared over our noses and chests. If we had sore throats, we loved to chew slippery elm, and horehound drops were essential to our welfare. . . .

A beautiful tall clock made in Amsterdam stood in a corner. . . . I used to sit on the floor, watching the tiny ships moving incessantly at the top, to and fro with the ticking. The harbor of Amsterdam was painted on the background, and miniature docks, warehouses, and church steeples could be seen behind Father Time, who, hour glass in hand, surmounted all, popping up between the ships and mermaids and sea serpents. The moon, too, appeared in all of her phases, and the date was invariably correct, a perfect conundrum to me. The top of the clock was decorated with three gilt plumes, and below was the door with the brass figure of Old Time again; you never could forget him. When the door was opened in its stomach, as I called it, the pendulum and weights were revealed, a mysterious display too. Every night I kissed the clock before going to bed. It was surely alive to me, and like any of the family. Of course I learned to tell time by it. Christmas Eve I tied a present to the key. The present was removed by Mother, but I was perfectly content to believe it had been gathered in by Dutchy [the name the children gave the clock] and stowed in a secret spot. . . . That clock was as much a part of our lives as eating or sleeping. . . . In my prayers I said, "God bless Papa, Mama, Sister, Brother, Dutchy, the cats, canary, and horses."

On the wall by the clock hung a small walnut cupboard with two shelves. On the top shelf was kept Arabian balsam for cuts and bruises, mutton tallow in a china jar, camphor ice for our lips, and glycerine or Mr. John Townsend's magic lotion for chapped hands, and several kinds of plasters. In the lower shelf was the birdbath tub, with sand and seeds. We often put cotton batting in a tumbler, wet it, and sprinkled birdseeds on it, and soon the glass was full of green. We also had an earthenware pig which could be filled with water. This soaked through, and birdseed stuck to the outside and soon grass bristled all over him. Then sepia ink was kept there. We used this for spatter work on Sunday afternoons when we had ferns from the Corning farm or our garden. And there too in that small cupboard, Frieda kept her secret, a Holman's Liver Pad with the picture of the inventor stamped on it. One day we pulled it out and threw it over the bannister for Frank the butler to see what Frieda wore. Then we were sorry when she cried all night.

Mother generally heard our prayers. We said "Now I lay me." Dr. Cox had a version, "When I get up and go to work, I pray the Lord I will not shirk. If I should die before the night, I pray the Lord I did all right." We also learned German prayers, and of course the Lord's Prayer, as we grew older. . . .

There was a pretty Swiss chalet on the bookcase, but we were forbidden to touch it, and I cannot remember that we ever disobeyed, but it was a temptation. The chalet had belonged to Jack's own sister, Kitty Pruyn, who had died of scarlet fever in the nursery when she was eight. I felt sorry for her, and wondered why she had had to leave such a lovely life and go out into the cold and dark. But she was not alone, for her two little sisters, Mary Weld and Harriet Corning, had also died. There was no one to tell us about them either, for Jack was born after they all died. I often wished Kitty could come and play with me, entirely forgetting that if Kitty had lived, she would have been grown up. I wondered what she liked to eat and if she had minded winter underclothes, and if she was ever naughty and had to stand behind the little green baize screen close to "Dutchy" for three minutes, with an added minute for each time [she was] caught peeking through the cracks.

There was a lovely full length marble of Kitty downstairs, done by M. E. D. Palmer, the sculptor and our near neighbor. Once on a very cold day when Mother had guests at luncheon, I stole downstairs and dressed Kitty and "Will O' the Wisp" in my doll's warmest coats and blankets. I had to drag up chairs to reach them, and one foot of "Will's" was the only one that could wear a sock. I was pleased with my thoughtfulness in such biting January weather, and bewildered by a burst of laughter which came upstairs, and the clear voice of a guest saying, "That Bertie of yours is a little pickle. She will probably run down herself with no clothes on!" My reward for thinking of others was three minutes again behind the screen, while Frieda grumbled to Maggie that she had left me taking a nap, and now I had gone and gotten her well into trouble. Such was the reward of virtue.

I have read in the newspapers recently that the discovery has been made that purple glass in windows makes children grow. That is old news, for there was a mania in my youth for having a sheet of purple glass mounted in a narrow moulding and hung in the window against the ordinary white glass. We had one in our nursery, and perhaps that was another reason why I grew fat and stocky. Grandmother had one too, set in one of the third [floor] room windows, but it could not do any good as that room was generally used at night, so it made it very gloomy. Ours was soon cracked. I threw a hairbrush at Hattie because she had said my face was dirty, and it hit the glass instead of her.

My first nurse was Mrs. Dormer. She was so devoted to me that she was very unfair to Jack and Hattie, and sometimes ordered them out of the nursery which belonged to all of us. I can remember sitting on her lap in front of the nursery fire and seeing Hattie in a gray suit come to the door, and Dormer telling her to "go and leave me alone in my own room." She had a son named Richard, and one day he came to see her in the nursery. She got very mad at him because he asked for money, and [she] took him by the shoulders and shook him until his teeth rattled. I screamed so loud that everyone rushed to see what the trouble was, and that ended poor old Dormer. A few days later she kissed me very often as she tied my bonnet, and Hattie and I started off with our dear old Mrs. Chandler to play . . . with the Marvin cousins, who then lived at 54 South Swan Street. When we returned home, there was no Dormer. I howled my head off, refused to eat, fell asleep from exhaustion in Mrs. Chandler's arms, and then never asked for Dormer again. The next day Frieda Wagner, a pretty German girl, came to take care of us and teach us German.

CHAPTER 1

L IKE ALL CHILDREN I had my favorite stories and I wanted them told in the same way.[†] If other than the usual words were used, I wanted them corrected. I liked the story about Great Aunt Alida Lansing. She was about nine when General Burgoyne threatened Albany in the summer and fall of 1777. She lived in a house built in 1766 near the lovely Patroonskill by the "Kissing Bridge."

Father described the Hessians who were fighting along with the British — their enormous size, their enormous head gear, and the story that they were so large because they each ate a baby a day. Albany was frightened and had boats ready by the river to leave the city if the army got nearer than Saratoga. Then he would tell about Aunt Kitty Lansing's brave grandfather, General Gansevoort, who held Fort Stanwix so the British were kept from joining Burgoyne. Then, when everyone was in a state of terrific excitement, Great Aunt Alida heard faint hoof beats clattering down the King's Highway. As the noise drew nearer, she ran out and saw an officer on horseback beating his horse with a stick.

"What news — what news?" shouted Great Aunt Alida and everyone else.

"Burgoyne and his army are our prisoners!"

This was too much to believe. Great Aunt Alida and everyone else shouted in Dutch, "You lie! You lie!"

This in turn was too much for [the rider,] Colonel Nicholas Van Rensselaer, who had been sent by General Gates to carry the good news to Albany. He threw his stick at her, and she picked it up, and it was planted on the present corner of Broadway and North Lansing Street, which is almost under the viaduct.

"And did it really grow, papa?" I always asked, as if I had never heard it before.

"Yes," he said, "It grew. The stick grew up into the Burgoyne Elm."

As a matter of fact, I remember seeing this tree just before it died. We had a stump of it in the Elk Street garden as well as a stump of the Elm from the "Slippery Elm" corner of State and Pearl Streets, planted by Philip Livingston.

---

† *This is the first extant page of the manuscript, "An Albany Girlhood."*

Another often repeated story was about the baker and his wife and the witch who blew into the little bakery in a storm on New Year's Eve. "Was it a snow storm, papa?" Father would patiently say he supposed it was snow and wind, but I had to be sure. The witch wanted a dozen "Nieuw-jaarskoeks," and the baker counted out twelve.

"I wanted thirteen!" shouted the witch. "You gave me only twelve!"

The baker's name was Volckert Jan Petersen Van Amsterdam, and his wife was Maritje. "You wanted a dozen, and twelve are a dozen." The baker was very angry and told her to "go to the Duyvel to get the thirteenth."

The witch blew out again but told the unfortunate baker that everything would go wrong with him during the next year, and it did. He and his wife were both ill, the roof fell in, and when New Year's came around again, they were very gloomy.

Then the witch returned on New Year's Eve and asked for a dozen cakes. The baker had learned his lesson, and he counted out thirteen, and to this day thirteen are a "baker's dozen."

Father had gone to the Boy's Academy, and he liked to look out at the boys playing in the large yard opposite the nursery windows on Elk Street. . . . In some receipted bills I have, the cost of tuition for a year is "For language $31.00 and for all other studies $23.00." Among the rules printed on the back of the bill is:

> Every student brings twenty-five good writing quills at the com-
> mencement of the quarter or the sum of two shillings which he
> hands to the Writing Master. If the latter, he is furnished with
> Pens during the Quarter. The former however is preferred if it is
> equally acceptable to Parents. Ink is furnished by the Academy.[1]

Another favorite story was about [Father's] waving a little flag for a procession in honor of Jackson's victory at New Orleans. He was down on the waterfront when the canal boat "Seneca Chief" arrived with Governor De Witt Clinton and his party on their way down to New York for the ceremony of the "marriage" of the waters of Lake Erie with the Atlantic Ocean.

Father lived from the stage coach era to the time of the invention of the telephone.[2] [He kept diaries from about 1828 up to his last illness. . . .] His family all spoke Dutch at home, and he liked us to learn the nursery rhymes in Dutch, and his diaries allude often to the "Yankee invasion" of Albany soon after the Revolution. He considered Elkanah Watson as the leader of this invasion. Poor Elkanah had the housewives chasing him with brooms for trying to have big State Street graded and paved.[3] Father was a great admirer of Harmanus Bleecker and, like him, tried to have the foot of State Street kept open and preserved as a park on the river front.[4]

Always a Democrat, he had inherited his principles of Jeffersonian Democracy from his great-uncle, Mayor Abraham Yates Jr. He served in the State Senate and for two terms in Congress. In those days Albany and Schoharie alternated candidates, as they were in the same district. This was very unsatisfactory, as you had to drop the measures in which you were interested, and be out for two years, and then start all over again for another term, if you got the nomination.

In 1840 he married the niece and namesake of Mrs. Erastus Corning of 102 State Street, Harriet Corning Turner, and in that way he became interested in the great railroad developments in which Mr. Corning was interested. He was a director of the Mohawk and Hudson River Railroad in 1835, and the consolidated agreement of the ten railroads of the state was drawn by him. Thus was formed the great New York Central Railroad in 1853.[5] He was one of the three original Capitol Commissioners and laid the first stone in 1869.[6]

Father was appointed a Regent of the University of the State of New York at the age of 33, and in 1862 he was chosen chancellor and served until his death. He started the custom of having a convocation in the summer, in Albany, of the heads of colleges, schools, and other institutions connected with the work of the Regents.[7] During one evening, he gave a reception at 13 Elk Street, and the ten gallon East India china punch bowl was filled with the seemingly innocent but potent Albany punch, a very famous brew. We were told that those learned men almost scraped the flowers off the china in their enthusiasm for more. The bowl is now used in the Institute. Father was for twenty years president of the old Albany Institute.[8]

The St. Nicholas Society was one of his greatest interests.[9] In 1875, on his last trip to Europe, he was a member of the conference held at The Hague on the Codification of International Law. At the close, he offered a resolution of thanks for hospitality received, first in English, and then in the old Dutch which his family had spoken in Albany. This was received with immense applause when it was realized it was the survival of over two hundred years.

The last time I saw my father was on the dining room piazza when he came out to wish us good-bye. He was very ill, and it was thought the cure at Clifton Springs might help him.

CHAPTER 2

AFTER MY FATHER'S LONG ILLNESS and death, Mother was rather an invalid for several years. The "Chars" really ran the house and family. They had been with us for about seven years before I was born. The Chars were Mr. and Mrs. William Chandler, late of London, where he had been a bill-broker. They were well educated, with no trace of Cockney accent. Char got into difficulties by lending money to young Lord Huntingtower, who was unable to repay it. So they had to start life all over again, and with their four children came to New York.[1]

Char found that he could not take up the kind of work he had done in London, as conditions were different, so they made arrangements for the children and took places in households. But they disliked being separated. In some way Mother heard of them through Mrs. Woolsey. She went to New York, liked them both, and engaged them as butler and housekeeper. They were a godsend to us all for many years.

Missie Char, as we called her, gave Hattie her first music lessons and supervised her other lessons, as she went to St. Agnes, then on Columbia Place. Before I went to the Kindergarten, at the then new St. Agnes on Elk Street, she taught me to read stories with two syllable words and to print letters, and she gave me six little silver spoons with my name on them.

The Chars had a large room in the basement with a bath close by, and Char presided at the head of the maids' dining room table. Char had reddish hair and a short beard, and a rather reddish temper at times. We were never tired of hearing about their wedding at St. Helen's Bishopsgate, and whenever we went to London we always made a pilgrimage down there for the sake of our kind old friends. In later years, the grandson of Lord Huntingtower, Lord Dysart, undertook to repay his grandfather's debts. The Chars went to London in 1885–86, but they had to spend so much money on the trip and living there that it hardly repaid them.

Good old Char had no sense of humor. He could not understand Dr. Cox and his "queer ways." The doctor had a certain way of jerking the front door bell which annoyed Char's sense of dignity. The doctor would say, "Good morning, Chandler. I'm awfully sorry about it all. It's terrible."

"Oh! What sir? What has happened?"

The doctor would hand Char his hat and coat and shake his head sadly.

Then he would suddenly leap for the stairs and run up two steps at a time shouting, "Hail the forks! The knives are coming! Spoons get out of the way! Slap the dishes on the table! We have hash today!" Char would stand at the foot of the stairs looking very solemn. When the doctor came down, Char would wait respectfully, holding the doctor's coat, hand him his hat, bow stiffly as he held the door open, and sigh deeply as he closed it.

One morning Mother gave Char a note for Dr. Cox and said to bring back an answer. Char walked down to the doctor's house at 109 State Street and found the doctor just about to drive off in his buggy. Char gave him the note and said in his respectful way, "There should be an answer, sir."

The doctor read the note, looked sadly at Char, and said, "Chandler, I never thought it would come to this. Mrs. Pruyn says, 'Please give the bearer of this note a sound whipping,' " and the doctor reached for the buggy whip.

Chandler gave one incredulous look, turned on his heel, and ran up State Street. He arrived breathless at our house and announced to Mother, "That poor doctor has gone clean daft," and told her what had happened.

We loved the doctor and his tricks.[2] He had a wonderful way of finding out by his nonsense how ill the patient really was, and he knew small ways of making a patient more comfortable. There were no clinical thermometers, but he could tell by holding his hand on the forehead just what temperature you had. He carried his leather case of bottles, with the liquids on one side and powders on the other, and little squares of paper in a side pocket. The liquids were measured out in drops into tumblers half full of water. We had special medicine glasses numbered one and two, with metal covers and silver spoons. "Take a tablespoon alternately every hour." We never knew what medicine he gave us. [Pulsatila, Bryonia, Nux Vomica, Belladonna all tasted more or less alike.] His theory was that if patients knew what medicine he had given, they might take it themselves [on other occasions], when the cause of their illness perhaps arose from totally different reasons.

There were two schools of medicine in those days, and whether you were a Homeopath or an Allopath was a matter of serious discussion. Dr. Cox was a Homeopath, though he called himself "eclectic" — that is, he gave whatever cure he thought was needed. There were fewer Homeopaths in Albany, and they were not allowed at the City Hospital. They had for years a small hospital on North Pearl Street at Clinton Place, but later they built their own hospital. It is now called "Memorial," and one does not hear any more of the endless disputes between disciples of the two schools. Bishop Doane wrote a rhyme about the Homeopaths.[3]

> Stir the mixture well
> Lest it prove inferior,
> Then put half a drop
> Into Lake Superior.
> Every other day
> Take a drop of water —
> You'll be better soon,
> Or, at least you oughter.

Dr. Cox taught us to ride horseback. He had a gray horse named Bob, who lived in the doctor's stable on Maiden Lane at the rear of his house. This stable was opposite the city jail, with the terrifying "Bridge of Sighs" connecting the City Hall with the jail. When we were sent down to Maiden Lane to make our duty calls on Aunt Catherine Pruyn, I was torn between the pleasure of giving sugar to Bob and my fear of the inmates of the jail, who looked out of the barred but open windows at us and made faces, and often called out jovially, "You ought to be inside too."[4]

At one time we had Bob in our stable for about two years, and there is a photograph of us taken in the garden. Hattie is on her horse and I am on Bob. He was a stubborn little fellow and could take the bit in his teeth and go his way. When I first rode Bob, he was on a leading rein. The doctor held the rein until I got used to riding. He broke in many little girls in this way on Bob, and we made quite a cavalcade when perhaps eight or ten of us went out together with the doctor. He often had patients at the convent, or even up in Troy, and we never had any accident.

Sometimes in the south end of the city, boys would fire something at us and sing out, "Lady on a horseback; lady on a flea; lady on a codfish; can't catch me." In the fall boys made bonfires of the leaves, and often the horses shied at the flames. When a dog ran out and barked at us, the doctor would take off his hat to the dog and say, "How do you do?" Strangely enough, the dog would slink off. The doctor said dogs enjoyed being treated politely. . . .

In the fall of 1881 our Uncle Amasa Parker Jr. had a frightful runaway, from the corner of State and Willett Streets down State Street until the horses were stopped near the Capitol. I think one of them fell down, but I am not sure. It was a double carriage called a "cut-under." My uncle [was] driving and his wife, Aunt Cora, [was] sitting beside him. In the rear seat were Aunt Cora's aunt, Mrs. Louis Rathbone, and her sister-in-law, Mrs. Charles Strong of Savannah. They had been to the Corning farm and had returned by Delaware Avenue.

The Presbyterian Church on the corner of State Street was being built, and some boys threw small pieces of stone and mortar at the horses, with the consequence that the horses plunged. A piece of harness broke, the traces fell and knocked [the horses'] heels, and off they ran down State Street. Mrs. Rathbone was thrown and killed. Aunt Cora, who [was] also thrown, was picked up for dead and carried into Mrs. McClure's house at 238 State Street. Mrs. Strong was thrown but not injured. My uncle was thrown, but he hung on to the reins and was dragged for two blocks. His leg was broken in several places, and he was a mass of cuts and bruises. Aunt Cora had been knocked unconscious, but no bones were broken.[5]

It was a terrible catastrophe, and to keep the house quiet, the four little Parker girls, with Mammy, came down to stay with us for two months. They were in the two rooms over the nursery rooms, and at bed time I went up to play with them. The games were very noisy, and were invented mostly by Grace. We played "Grandpa Scuttle" and "Holy Bishop," and if the windows were open the whole street must have heard the noise. One night I hid under Grace's bed, and when the lights were out, I gently pushed up the mattress. I never heard such screams in my life. Grace was sure it must be a burglar. For several nights I was kept from going upstairs. Sometimes Harry Pierson would come over and play the zither. Jack timed us to see how long we could stop talking, and he gave prizes.

Mother liked to read aloud, and she often read to us in the late afternoon before dinner. Many of the books were by English authors, as my father had a book agent who lived in London, Mr. B. F. Stevens.[6] He was also a great collector, both for himself and for other collectors, like Mr. James Lenox in New York and Mrs. John Carter Brown in Providence. He came from Vermont, and always wrote after his name, "G.M.B." — Green Mountain Boy. It was through him that father bought the Robert Burns manuscript of "Auld Lang Syne." Mother subscribed through him to *Punch*, the *Guardian*, and the weekly *London Times*.

Mr. Stevens sent over any new books that he thought were of interest to her or to us, and we had *Black Beauty* and Stella Austin's books soon after their publication. We cried over Dicky in *For Old Sake's Sake*, and the lost children in *Somebody*, and for Pat, we laughed over his doings, and we often tried to imitate the performances of some of them. Miss Edgeworth's

Parent's Assistant was a favorite of Missie Char, who liked us to take to heart "Simple Susan," "Lazy Lawrence," and "Waste not Want not." She [read] to us when we had contagious diseases and introduced us to *Chatterbox, Every Girl's Annual*, and a *Life of Queen Victoria*.[7]

Other books we liked to hear over and over were *Alice in Wonderland, Ronald Bannerman's Boyhood, Lady Green Satin and Her Maid Rosette, Children of the New Forest*, all of Mrs. Ewing's books, and of course, *Robin Hood*. Later I was completely fascinated by Miss Yonge's books, and I knew some of them almost by heart. There were two English books that I have never seen elsewhere, and the author is not given, *The Queen of the County* and *Margaret and Her Bridesmaids*. This latter is lost, but I still cherish *The Queen*.[8]

We loved Jacob Abbott's *Franconia Stories*, and once we acted scenes from them — Beechnut, Phonny, Wallace the Harvard student of 14 — we loved all [these characters]. *The Story of a Bad Boy* was particularly interesting, as "Tom Bailey," Thomas Bailey Aldrich, was the author. Grandmother knew the Aldrich family in Portsmouth. We thought *The Wide, Wide World* and *Queechy* very dull, but we agreed on Louisa Alcott's books and read each one.[9]

My father had been especially anxious that we must read all the books that would help us to love and understand local history, and my mother was careful to carry this out. So, we were early introduced to Mrs. Grant's famous *American Lady*. The last two editions had been dedicated to my father and mother by General James Grant Wilson, a godson of Mrs. Grant. Cooper's *Satanstoe* and *The Chainbearer* are among his best stories, and also are least known here. There was Domine Frelinghuysen, and then there was Joel Munsell, with all his volumes for reference. Our library had a great many local histories, and some were especially bound by Munsell himself.[10]

My sister wanted to read *Jane Eyre*, but she was almost grown up before this was allowed. She carried everywhere in her travelling bag *The First Violin*, and was romantic over the adventures of the English heroine.[11]

May Cooper was a wonderful neighbor and she came over often and helped us with the daubing that we called painting. We took tracing paper and put it over some picture we liked in a book like "Pretty Peggy" or "Little Anne" [and traced a figure]. Then we put this paper over one of the white wood objects then in vogue for "real hand painting." Sometimes it was a wooden plate, or a tray, or even an imitation iron stood on one end, and we traced the figure on to that and then daubed on the colors. Hattie colored a pair of white china vases for mother, and May had them baked, and they ornamented mother's bureau for years. We also did "Spatter work." We picked ferns in the garden and then laid them on white paper, and with a brush dipped in sepia, we had a great time spattering the ferns and everything else.

May played games with us. "Dr. Busby" was a favorite, and "Parcheesi," and the card game of "Nig" — the one who cheats the most wins — and endless games of "Geography," in which a letter is chosen and everyone writes in two minutes all the names they can remember with that first letter. May introduced us to paper-doll books, and these were a great help on rainy days. We cut figures out of magazines and then made them extra dresses of tissue paper.

Hattie did not care much for sewing, but I made quantities of clothes for the dolls and later had a small sewing machine called "The Daisy." Everything was a daisy in those days. To say a girl was "A Daisy" was the highest praise. Hats and dresses were called "Daisy." Those years were the era of Oscar Wilde and his sunflowers, and of Kate Greenaway, and of the Gilbert and Sullivan light operas, and also of Huyler's candy stores with candies called Buttercups, which I wish they made now, and the wonderful ice cream sodas. A soda at Townsend's was five cents, but with ice cream at Huyler's it was ten cents. The shop was on Pearl Street, close to Maiden Lane, and it had bright red window shades.[12]

It is interesting to look back and see how all these irrelevant things entered into our nursery life in one way or another. Hattie took the tunes of the new operetta *Patience* and several others from *Pinafore* and *Iolanthe* and wrote German words for them. They were used in German plays at St. Agnes, in which we took part. Frau zum Busch wrote the little plays. In "Das Millmädchen" Louise and Grace Parker drove onto the stage in their brother's cart, with two St. Bernard dogs to pull it. The cart was full of milk cans we then used.[13]

Hattie could do wonderful tricks with cards, and every now and then she and the boy cousins gave a trick show at grandfather's. One year Louis drove down to take her in his little sleigh with bells, and the two dogs to pull it. The dogs ran away and turned the sleigh over in a drift on Washington Avenue. Hattie lost or broke many of her new tricks, just arrived from Hart's trick shop in New York for her birthday.

Returning to the nursery, when we had any contagious diseases that might involve our eyes or ears if we caught cold, Mother had the bedrooms darkened, but of course then she could not see to read. So, she used to tell us stories, and we liked them just as well. We wanted to hear over and over about the French school to which she went after graduating at the old Female Academy.[14] The school was on Park Place, very near us. She was a boarder, though only two blocks from her own home. It was a famous school kept by M. and Mme. Mollinard and their niece. Four girls slept in a room, and the heat was only on one floor. Everything was studied in French, and no English was allowed. Then she went to a French boarding school in New York. [We also used to ask her to tell about when] she had heard Jenny Lind and gone to the Opera.[15]

Then there was the story of Mme. Jumel. "Tell us about the crazy old lady near New York." That was how we thought of the famous Mme. Jumel, who lived in the house which had been Washington's headquarters for a time. Mother had cousins, the Appleton Havens, who lived in the country out at Fort Washington, and she went to stay with them. Mr. Haven took her to call on Mme. Jumel, who had married Aaron Burr in her old age, but [had not stayed] married to him for very long.

Mother told us of the dinner table all set for a dinner given long years before for Joseph Bonaparte, ex-King of Spain. He praised the table so much that Mme. Jumel had kept it just as it was that night — china and glass, gilt ornaments, confectionery all crumbled and moldy — probably at least thirty years old. Dickens had been taken out there to see her, and he had brought it into his book *Great Expectations*. We were never tired of this tale, and of Mme. Jumel's trip to Europe as Vice-Queen of America. Was not Burr Vice-President, and though she had resumed her name of Jumel, still there were advantages of being Vice-Queen.[16]

Mother kept a diary up to the time she came out, but not after that, which is too bad. Besides this account of Mme. Jumel, she wrote about the visit to the White House with her parents when James Buchanan was President and Miss Harriet Lane, his niece, was first lady.

"Tell us about how you almost did not have a wedding dress!" [we would say]. Mother would tell us how anxious they were, as the dress never came until late in the afternoon before the wedding, when a special messenger brought it up himself in the train from New York.

I have several newspaper accounts of the wedding, on September 7th,

1865, at St. Peter's at noon, with Bishop Horatio Potter of New York officiating. He had been rector of St. Peter's for many years, and a close friend of Father's. We were still part of the diocese of New York at that time. Apparently a great sensation was created, as there was Communion service for the bride and groom. Bishop Potter was taken to task in a New York paper.

"We therefore would like to know whether it is true that this same prelate [Bishop Potter], when officiating at the wedding of a prominent individual in a neighboring city, adopted the form of the English liturgy, instead of that ordered and provided by the Protestant Episcopal Church of the United States, and, if so, whether he did not violate the prescribed rules of his own church? Whether also, when administering the Eucharist to the newly wedded pair, he did not in the presence of the congregation there assembled, elevate the sacred elements after the manner adopted in the Roman Catholic Church?"

There is no record of any reply from Bishop Potter.

We loved, too, to have her tell about her life before she married, and what she and her three sisters and brothers did, and the games they played, and how they raised fruit in the garden. But, invariably, we returned to her wedding, and endless questions. "What did the four bridesmaids wear, mother?" and "What kind of flowers did you carry?" Her bouquet was of real interest, as the flowers were the "Holy Ghost Orchid." This rare orchid symbolized "the Heavenly Dove that descended on the Son of God." I have never seen one.

"And, what did he give you?"

"A single string of pearls with a diamond and enamel pendant."

"And what did the bridesmaids have?"

"Rings with an amethyst and the letter 'P' set in diamonds. Yes there were ten ushers, mostly our relatives."

In the darkened room we asked over and over, and she was endlessly patient. . . .

My father was twenty-nine years older than my mother. In fact my father and my grandfather, Judge Parker, were close friends, as there was only four years difference in their ages. The twelve years of my parents marriage were full of interest, and above all, ideally happy. Father was again elected to Congress, and my sister Hattie was born in Washington in January, 1868. They made three trips to Europe. The wedding trip was on a paddle wheel, the *Scotia*.

Father had many delightful friends in England, and his interest in church matters brought him close in touch with Dean Stanley of Westminster Abbey, with the Master of the Temple, with Archdeacon Sinclair and many more. Mother was presented to Queen Victoria, and also at the Court of The Hague, where our cousin was a Lady in Waiting. They were at a weekend house party at the Duke of Argyle's at Inverary Castle, when Lord Lorne and Princess Louise, just married, were also of the party. They were particularly interested in a long talk with the historian Carlyle, in his home in Cheyne Walk.

I could never give a true story of our nursery life unless I told about the Linden tree. It was tall and straight and healthy. It stood in front of the little iron balconies at the front of the house. It shaded us in summer heat, and its foliage was a screen so that when we were on the balconies, no one could see us but we could see everything. I loved that tree. I believe that my father planted it when one of us was born — I do not know which it was, but it was not I, as it was a large tree when I first remember it. It must have been for my brother, born in 1859. In spring we watched the leaves come out, and we called it "Lindy." Like "Dutchy," the clock, it was part and parcel of the family. I used to earn pocket money by sweeping the balconies at five cents each. It was considered good exercise for a growing child, and expanded the chest.[17]

Our Aunt Catherine Pruyn was what might now be called a "problem child." She was one all through her life, and lived to be eighty-three. At the same time, I wish now that I had been more patient with her, as she had many stories to tell. She was born on Valentine's Day in 1803. "What a valentine for her family," we used to say as we walked away after a visit. The Revolution was not so far behind her as World War I is for us today. Her family talked about it, so she liked to pass on the tales, but we did not always appreciate them. She was a tall, fine-looking woman and held herself with great distinction, but she did love to wear jewelry.

She lived where the Pruyn Library stands now.[18] There was a garden back of the house, about where the children's room of the library is. There was a tall, wooden fence, on the Patroon Street side (as she continued to call Clinton Avenue, just as Central Avenue was always the "Bowery" to her). Boys in the neighborhood loved to pelt the fence with mud, just to make Aunt Catherine come out on her stoop and scold them, which she did with vigor. She would superintend the colored man as he mopped off the mud, but as soon as he finished, the boys returned.

Aunt Catherine felt lonely down on Clinton Place. She complained that her friends were moving up town, so for a time she lived with her niece, Emma Pruyn, Mrs. Girard Wood, on Lancaster Street. When we went to see her and cousin Emma, we walked along Pill Row, as Eagle Street from State Street to the Medical College was called because so many doctors lived there. Aunt Catherine liked to read us the story of "Goody Two Shoes," from a book with pretty colored illustrations.

Later she went to live with the two Miss Pierces on Maiden Lane and stayed there the rest of her life. . . . At one time she threatened to leave there on account of the name. She said it was embarrassing to her, as well as to the Pierces, to have to tell the clerks in shops that their address was on Maiden Lane, that they began to laugh. She asked Mother to see the Mayor and try to have him change it. She even suggested that "Flower Lane" would be an acceptable substitute. Mother thought that, as there had been no flowers on Maiden Lane for many years, another name would be more appropriate. Fortunately, Aunt Catherine did not press the matter.

She felt it deeply that my father had left the Dutch Church in 1859, and had joined St. Peter's. "The Dutch Church was always for our independence," she would tell us. "It was St. Peter's that was full of Tories, and the Sons of Liberty imprisoned the rector, Mr. Munro, in Fort Frederick." She would look at us as if we were personally responsible for the Tories.[19]

She would lower her voice and whisper, "I know what became of Chancellor Lansing. He never went to New York. That was a made-up story. He was here in his own house, and, . . ." Then her voice would sink lower, "he hanged himself in his attic. Of course, his family wanted to keep it quiet, so they buried him at night. I know what I am saying. I am his relation, and I cannot be deceived. He hanged himself in his attic. Remember what I say!"

This was about the famous case, still unsolved, of the disappearance of one of the most prominent men in the state, in December, 1829. But the Chancellor did go to New York, in spite of Aunt Catherine's tale. He left the City Hotel with letters to mail, and the doorman is the last person to have seen him alive. It was a rainy night, and he carried an umbrella. He was to dine with friends, and it is supposed he planned to carry the letters first to the Albany night boat, as it was the custom to use boats as carriers for mail. The letters would be mailed in Albany the next day.

The usual theory is that in the dark and rain, he fell off the gang plank and was drowned. He never appeared for the dinner at the house of a friend who was expecting him. Many insisted he had been kidnapped and killed by medical students, as he was an unusually well-built and well-proportioned man. (They wanted his body for their dissecting.) Others were sure it had to do with the tremendous anti-Masonic condition of the state.

These ideas have been discarded. Nothing is really known, but in his autobiography Thurlow Weed tells a strange story about it. He says that years later a well-known man came to him and told him the story of the murder of the Chancellor, why it was done, who did it, and how the body was disposed of. He was asked to make this story public after the deaths of those involved. When it happened that all three of the men were dead, Mr. Weed was distressed to think of the families left to face the story, even after the lapse of almost fifty years. He decided to call in two intimate friends for a conference; R. M. Blatchford was one and Hugh Maxwell the other. After telling them the story as told to him, they talked it over for several hours and decided to let the secret die rather than involve the descendants. Mr. Weed outlived both these men, and when he died in 1882, all knowledge of this tragedy died too. Missie Char usually came with us when we made our duty calls on Aunt Catherine, and she tried to keep off this gruesome tale, but we rather encouraged it.[20]

Aunt Catherine had strong ideas about the "Yankees." She would start off with the assertion that "I am always polite to everyone." We privately rather doubted that. "But, I never could receive anyone in my house from Massachusetts. They are as tricky as Boston."

This was on account of the long drawn-out boundary dispute about the location of the Yankee border line. The Dutch had claimed to the Connecticut River and had made settlements and built forts. The "Yankees" claimed to the western ocean, whatever that meant. Aunt Catherine said the Yankees had plundered the Dutch settlers between the Connecticut and Hudson Rivers and had sold their loot in Boston. The Yankees claimed the Dutch had stolen from their settlers and had sold plunder, through the Indians, at Montreal, as they paid better prices. "Do you know what the Iroquois called the Yankees?" "They called them 'Kinshon,' which meant the codfish people." I have often wondered what Aunt Catherine would have said years later, if I had told her that I was going to marry one of the "Kinshon," a Yankee from Boston. How would she have treated him?[21]

"What are you learning in school?" said Aunt Catherine to Hattie one day.

"Paul Revere's ride," said Hattie promptly.

"There," said Aunt Catherine. "That's just what I mean. They fill the poetry and school books with stuff and nonsense about a man whose name made easy rhyming, and a Yankee rhymester did the rest. It was the luck of having such a name that turned him into a hero and nothing that he did. He rode out on a mild April night, on a good road, and he had not been wounded.

"Our Symon Schermerhorn carried the news of the French and Indian massacre at Schenectady in 1690, on a bitter night in February when the snow was deep. He had been wounded seriously. His son had been killed, and his house burned. In spite of that he went out of his way to warn settlers at Niskayuna. When he reached the gate at Albany, he fell from his horse with exhaustion, and the horse died. That's being a hero. But, he is unknown because his name is hard to rhyme with, and we had no Longfellow."[22]

In later years Aunt Catherine became more and more unaccountable. She would invite someone to drive to church with her, but when service was over, she would drive off and leave them. "She bored me, and anyway, one way is enough." She had a story we loved about a large muff of dyed fox fur with a pink ribbon at one side.

She would begin, "Children, I must warn you that Pride always has a fall. I had one. My two brothers, your father and your uncle Lansing, gave me a muff for the New Year in 1830. We started for Church, and I walked between them carrying the muff, and I was very proud. In those days the pigs ran loose in the streets. One of them ran into me and tipped the muff, and me, into the gutter. You take warning. I was proud, and that was what happened to me." [23] . . .

Aunt Catherine left me a very handsome silver teapot with her name on it, also the muff, and the embroidered white dress she wore at the Lafayette Ball in the old Capitol. Both the dress and muff are in the Institute. Peace be to her troubled head, but all the same, I think she had quite a happy life in her own strange way.[24]

CHAPTER 3

I HAVE SPENT MANY YEARS of my life in other cities, but I have never seen in any of them such a unique and interesting family as that of Bishop and Mrs. Doane at 29 Elk Street.[1] As I first remember them, the bishop's old aunt, Miss Mary Doane, was living with them. She was a quaint-looking little soul and was generally in the background, busy with her knitting. She had coal black hair parted in the middle and dropping over her ears. We were sure it was a wig.

Mrs. Doane's sister, Miss Margaret Condit, also lived with them. She was variously addressed as "Maggie," "Smiggie," or "Nimmie." There were also two daughters, Miss Lizzie and Miss Daisy. Not the least of that household was Maggie Brady, a large Irish woman who bossed everything. Then there was old Michael Dunn, who was butler and valet until he grew so old and shaky that he had to be retired to light work outside. As we speeded to school, we would be sure to see old Michael leaning on a broom, in deep conversation with the passers-by.

In the early days, the dogs were Morley and then Morley Jr. The latter, a black and white spotted dog, bore no resemblance to his tan father. After Morley died, they had a beautiful Collie named "Laddie" from the Corning farm. The bishop was never happy without a dog. They were part of the family life, sitting on the landing, stretched by the library fire, or waiting for the bishop on his daily rounds of the chapel, hospital, or school.

The bishop was born in Boston where his father had been rector of Trinity Church at the time of his birth. His mother had been a widow, Mrs. Perkins, with a daughter and two sons. When our bishop was a baby, his father became bishop of New Jersey, and they all went to live in Burlington. Our Bishop Doane had one brother, George, who had joined the Roman Catholic Church. When I first remember him, he was a monsignor and a member of the Pope's household. At Christmas, most of this large family met at the bishop's house for the holidays. They made quite a party on Christmas Eve, when the choir boys sang carols. Often I have watched the household as they passed up and down the street, or the bishop as he passed alone with his dogs on his varied ways.

Miss Daisy Doane died at North East Harbor [in 1883], when I was still a child. She had painted the tiles for our nursery fireplace. In each corner were the words of the rhyme:

> Boys and girls come out to play.
> The moon doth shine as bright as day.
> Come with a whoop and come with a call;
> Come with a good will or not at all.
> Up the ladder and down the wall;
> A penny loaf will serve you all.

On the tiles the children looked gay and happy as they ran hand in hand. . . .

Bishop Doane wore the gaiters and shovel hat of an English bishop. In the winter, he wore a heavy coat with a fur collar and carried a leash for the dog, in later years the St. Bernard, "Tiber" or "Cluny." On holidays, the whole family took a walk, unless the weather was too stormy. These walks brought everyone to the windows to see the unusual spectacle.

The bishop's half-sister, Mrs. Cleveland, looked and dressed like Queen Victoria. As she was quite lame, a wheelchair was borrowed from Child's Hospital, and her faithful maid, MacNaughton, known as "Norty," pushed it. Miss Lily Cleveland, was she not as round as an apple? She wore a sealskin coat over a cardigan jacket, with a Shetland shawl wound about her neck. She was topped with a small English walking hat. Mr. Edward Perkins, the bishop's half-brother, known to all as "Uncle Edward" or "Nunky," was very proud of the fact that for over thirty years his measurements, at his London tailor's, had not changed. He was a rather slim man, who wore a fur cap with ear tabs, also English, and carried a gold-headed cane.

Monsignor Doane was very striking, tall and large and very jolly, given to joking at his more serious relatives and at Uncle Edward's endless puns. The Monsignor was naturally nervous about falling on the icy pavements, so old Michael walked backwards in front of him, carrying a hod of ashes over his left arm, and in his right hand a small shovel with which he scattered the ashes. The Monsignor had white hair and wore the vivid purple collar of his office. He rolled along in his jolly way, his voice penetrating the thickest walls.

In the meantime, Mrs. Doane and her sister, Miss Condit, clung together on the inside of the group. They did not like to leave the warm library fire and were only induced to join the family consitutional by the necessity of getting fresh air and by the persuasion of the bishop. Dressed almost alike, the sisters usually wore Dolmans, three-quarter length coats trimmed with a great deal of braid, which were fashionable at that period. Their small bonnets were tied with ribbons under the chin, at one side. Mrs. Paul Fenimore Cooper, at "Cape Lookout," always insisted that Mrs. Doane and Smiggie wore bits of the seasonal colors of the Church in their bonnets and about their necks. Mrs. Gardiner, the Doanes' daughter [Lizzie], was the soul of energy, and she set the pace, marching ahead with Mr. Gardiner. . . . Mrs. Gardiner wore unusual clothes too, but Mr. Gardiner was warmly clad in a fur-lined coat and cap.

The Doane-Perkins family had tender bronchial tubes and so, to prevent the cold air from getting into them, they wore "respirators." . . . They were oval, and made of heavy black silk with some wire or copper between, I think. They fastened around the head with a thin black elastic, and closely over the mouth. . . . If any of them wished to speak, they had to push up the oval and quickly replace it.

Clinging to the bishop's arm would be several Gardiner grandchildren [delineated in the bishop's rhyme]:

> There were Mary and Margaret and Anne Terry
> With Doane the man of the *familee*
> And dear little Betty, the last on the tree.

When the cavalcade reached the street crossing in front of the Van Benthuysens at No. 8, they would pause to have a discussion as to which way they would go next. Crossing the street to the park at that point meant a shortening of the walk. Mrs. Doane and Smiggie favoured that, and so did Mrs. Cleveland in her wheelchair. But most of the others liked to go to the lower crossing at Eagle Street and walk along beside the park, and so up around Washington Avenue, and home sweet home by Hawk Street. It was largely a question of the dog and what was best for him. He would enjoy rolling in the heavy snow of the park, and the longer the better. The discussion occupied about ten minutes, and Miss Albina Bulkeley at No. 9, the Van Benthuysens at No. 8, and Mrs. James Kidd at No. 7, had time to get a full view of the party, while the Fenimore Coopers across the street crowded the windows and made mental notes of them all. It was a debated question in Albany as to how many wives the bishop had, as very few people could untangle this unusual family. . . .

In the evenings, Mrs. Doane and Smiggie usually played some card game at a table close to the fire, while the bishop, with his pipe, rested from the long day and talked on all kinds of subjects. He had a wealth of anecdotes and history and incidents from his many trips to Europe. He had charge of the American churches, and [greatly enjoyed] the change and rest his

European travels [afforded him]. The bishop's desk in the library gave him the same view over the river that we had from the nursery window, but he had the advantage of being higher up.

☙   ☙   ☙

Although I am ahead of the time, I will tell of Mother's and my trip to the Adirondacks in July, 1894. Mother had never been to the Adirondacks, and she was anxious to see some parts of them. The bishop always returned ... in order to make his visitations in that part of the diocese in summer weather, as in winter the roads were almost impassable.[2]

Mother and I met the bishop at the Sagamore Hotel on Lake George, where we joined General and Mrs. Robert Lenox Banks, Lenox Jr., and little Mary, who spent the summers there. From there we drove to Ticonderoga village over a frightful road. While the bishop had service and later lunched with the rector and his wife, Mother and I went to see the ruins of Fort Ticonderoga now so wonderfully restored. The bishop always had trouble on these trips, because the wives of the rectors went to great pains to provide him with ice cream and canned lobster salad, and he disliked both very much.

By carriage and railroad we reached Blue Mountain Lake, and from there went to the Durant's camp, "Pine Knot," on Raquette Lake. They had sent their launch for us, and we passed through fascinating Eagle and Utowanna lakes. That evening they illuminated the lake where their houseboat was anchored. At St. Hubert's Inn we were joined by the Rev. Mr. Larom, the rector of St. Luke's at Saranac Lake, known as the "Rector of all out doors."[3]

As I look back on the clothes we wore, we must have been a funny sight. There were no so-called sport clothes anywhere. Mother wore a black silk dress with a slight train. All her summer dresses were silk or nun's veiling. The leg-o-mutton sleeves were enormous, the collars were high and tight, and the skirts fell long and full. As a concession to the rural aspect of this trip, Mother had discarded her usual little bonnet and 'wore a black straw hat with a small brim, pinned on with several black-headed hat pins. Her shoes were then a popular kind called "Congress Shoes." They had elastic sides and no buttons or laces, so were easy to pull on and off. She wore gloves with two buttons, *gants de suede* of the period, which pulled on loosely.

I, too, had long dresses that needed to be held up in the back, as they were lined and boned. My hat was white and large. We were restricted to one suitcase of a certain weight each. That does not sound difficult now, when we can go off for a week and get everything in, but in those days this was a problem, as one dress with its sleeves and bustle would take up a whole suitcase. The only sensible article with me was a blue cape of water-proof material bought in London.

When we left Raquette for the Fulton Chain, Mother had not the dimmest idea what lay ahead with the long carries. Each of us was in a separate light Adirondack boat with a guide, and the bags were distributed. We had a carry to walk between each lake, and several carries were long and steep. Mr. Larom and I often walked ahead and waited for Mother and the bishop to catch up. It was funny to see the bishop's shovel hat and gaitered legs in the wilderness, while Mother, in her city clothes, looked completely out of the picture.

In the middle of the longest carry, a terrific thunderstorm overtook us, and the walking became very slippery. Mr. Larom and I easily reached the little cabin shelter, but Mother and the bishop got the full storm and were soaked. . . . [They were a picture, proceeding at snail-like pace,] Mother leaning on the bishop's arm, rain pouring from their hats.

When they reached the shack, Mother said to the man in charge that she would like hot water and a bath. The man pointed at the stove and said, "There's the kittle. Take that!"

The bags had to be unpacked to find dry clothes. All this took time, and we had some distance to go. However, the storm cleared, and we just made the station and caught the train to Paul Smith's. I never saw anyone more relieved than Mother when she got on the Pullman and had the morning papers and afternoon tea.

At Saranac we were in a cottage near the hotel, and we sat in the dining room at Dr. Trudeau's table with Mrs. Trudeau, their son Ned, and the little boy Francis. The bishop had services at St. John-in-the-Wilderness, and after two days there we went to Saranac Lake and saw the wonderful sanitarium built by Dr. Trudeau. We drove out to the Ampersand Hotel, so soon burned down, and after that went to Lake Placid where the bishop left us, and we took the Chateaugay railroad to Plattsburg and then home. I think Mother was delighted to feel that at last she had accomplished the Adirondack trip, but I am also sure that it was a great relief to have it well over.[4] . . .

       ❧   ❧   ❧

I cannot imagine a more charming personality than the bishop, always a most delightful companion to young and old. I often think of the years when he made our house his headquarters, before his house was opened each fall. . . . I can easily recall our dinner table, the bishop just back from a visit and having some amusing experiences to tell. Perhaps we would be alone, or perhaps he had brought back some stray clergyman. Whoever dropped in, there was always interesting talk, vital, witty, full of anecdote and information. . . .

Upstairs in the library the bishop made himself particularly delightful. Comfortably seated with a cigar, he would start on a train of reminiscences and stories about old days in Burlington, his rectorship at Hartford before he came as rector of St. Peter's, and his visits to Lambeth or Fulham. He might read some story or poem, or perhaps a rhyme he had scribbled on the back of an envelope on the train. It was often hard for him to decipher his own hopeless writing. The Doanes always gave us Christmas presents, and the bishop wrote little rhymes or jingles to go with them.

Rev. Edward Tibbits was the head of the Hoosac School and also a canon at the Cathedral. The bishop invited him to go to Europe with him on one of his visitation trips, as his chaplain. When they returned, he was asked about the trip, and the canon said, "It was a grand success. Everything went right. I was chaplain and could pay my own way, and I acted also as maid to Mrs. Doane."

When Dr. Doane was rector of St. Peter's, the Onondagas sent several of their Sachems to St. Peter's to lay claim to the Queen Anne Silver. My mother and brother were in church and saw them in their modern Indian clothes with bead embroidery and one feather as head-dress. After service Dr. Doane invited them to come to the old rectory on Lodge Street. Mrs. Doane, in an effort to entertain them, remarked that she had never seen any Indian dances. They danced at once and almost shook down the rectory. One of them threw a tomahawk close to Mrs. Doane's head, but fortunately his aim was perfect, and it struck safely in the wall. Perhaps her bonnet represented the head-dress of an enemy nation.[5]

After Grandfather died, Mother had the Sunday night suppers. The only difference between a dinner and a supper was that soup was served at dinner, while at supper, we had tea and coffee. At the end of the table I poured chocolate. Usually the Doanes came, and sometimes there were as many as eight or ten of them including the German governess, Fraulein Jessen. . . .

The bishop sat on Mother's right. He was of course very tired after his long day, and he did not care for tea. He was afraid of coffee at night, and chocolate was not much in the way of bracing anyone. So Mother used to have a pint of champagne for him, but none for anyone else. We never could persuade her that when older men came, they also often felt as tired as the bishop and did not care for tea or coffee but would welcome champagne, but it was no use. The bishop enjoyed the champagne, of course, and did not seem to realize how funny the situation was. . . .

The bishop enjoyed stories on himself. One that he told [concerned plans] being made for the Cathedral; he had a bill introduced in the Legislature granting him permission to inter three bodies in a sealed vault under the altar — himself, Mrs. Doane and Miss Condit. The bill passed promptly and was signed by the Governor. The last sentence read: "This Act to take effect immediately."

Another story he enjoyed was about a small boy at North East Harbor who had swallowed a penny. His family was much worried, but the boy said, "Send for Bishop Doane. He can get money out of anyone."

On Easter Sunday, the bishop stood at the door of the old chapel, and later of the cathedral, and greeted everyone with the old salutation used by the Eastern Church, "The Lord is risen!" To which the reply is: "He is risen indeed!" Strangers were rather bewildered by this greeting, and when it was given a second time to a stranger, she replied, "Yes. So General Marvin told me." About every six months of my life I have heard a different [anecdote involving] this [Albany] greeting. Though [some have been] garbled and utterly untrue, [they] have been funny. . . .

The three houses above the bishop's house belonged to the Huns.[6] In the one next door, No. 31, lived old Dr. Thomas Hun, a very noted doctor in his time. He and my father used to talk Dutch together, for they were about the last ones left here who remembered any of it. As we ran up to school, we often met him as he came slowly down his steps by the metal lion that stood on the stone between the houses. He wore a heavy cape and carried a heavy cane.

His son, Mr. Marcus Hun, and his family all lived there too. The doctor's offices were in the lower part of No. 33, but above them the family had bedrooms. Mr. Leonard Gansevoort Hun was unmarried, and he also lived there. He was a lawyer. Mrs. Marcus Hun (Mary Vanderpoel) was very witty. There were in time five little Huns, all younger than I was. We coasted together, as we did also with the four children of Mrs. Edward Hun at No. 35. . . . The Hun doctors were allopaths, and their followers were known as "Hunites," while Dr. Cox's were called "Coxites."

CHAPTER 4

W HEN THE TELEGRAM CAME to Char, telling of Father's death at Clifton Springs [1877], Missie Char was much distressed and wept, exclaiming sadly as she folded me in her arms, "You poor little half orphan!"

I was indignant, "I won't be a half of anything!" I shouted. "I'm a whole one or nothing!"

Children that we were — I was under four[1] — we were dressed in black. We had black ulsters and felt hats, as it was November, and black gloves and stockings. We must have been rather a pathetic sight. There was a house service in the music room, and it is there that I first remember Dr. Battershall. Jack carried me in his arms, and I clung to his hand at St. Peter's, as the crowded church frightened me. After that, we were sent down to the Cornings, and were not taken to the cemetery. It was a cold day, and as we were driven home in the Cornings' carriage, the wind and dust blew about the old City Hall, and I looked up to see how my friend "Themis" was doing on the dome of the Capitol in the wind.[2]

I am glad that the custom of putting children in mourning has passed away with the many changes that come with time. The old rules for mourning were very strict, and our family carried them out rigidly. My sister and I wore black in winter for three years. In summer, we wore white with black sashes and hair bows. Most of my dresses were of French piqué with Hamburg embroidery flounces.

After three years, we had mixed black and gray dresses, made at Swears and Wells in London, with hats to match. We also had the black velvet dresses made there. We hated them. They were so hot. After they were outgrown, I had one made of the two together, so I had a black velvet dress to wear until I was twelve. In summer, we had lilac and white dresses with lilac sashes.

I remember seeing Mother in colors only once. It was a beige summer dress with beige lace and there was some red about it. The hat was lace too, with a red bow. I never saw her in colors again. After Father's death, she wore the heaviest kind of mourning, with a long crepe veil. After two years of wearing it over her face, Dr. Cox protested, and she wore it down the back.

The rule for the death of a grandparent was six months of heavy mourning, and six months of graduating into grays and lilacs. For an aunt or uncle, it was three months. There were rules, too, for first cousins and second cousins and great-aunts and uncles. We carried out every one of these regulations, and by the time I was eighteen, we had worn mourning for seven relatives.

One September evening in Newport, when I was nine, Mother told me that there were two boxes in the hall, and that she wanted me to open them. They came from Hollanders and when I opened the large one, there lay in tissue papers a red dress with a red and white vest, and in the other box a red turban with red and white trimming.

"How beautiful", I exclaimed. "But who is going to wear them?"

Mother said, "They are for you to wear."

"For me?" I exclaimed incredulously. "For me really?" Then I burst out crying, sobbing. I had never thought that I would have a red dress like all the other girls in Newport.

It seemed a dream come true, and I tried on the dress and hat and went from room to room looking in all the mirrors. When I went to bed, kindly Mary hung the dress where I could see it the moment I woke up. Oh to be like Sallie and Gertrude and all the rest!

Then I said, "Mother, could I have a pink sash to wear with my white dresses for dancing class?"

Mother took me to Thames Street that very day, and we bought a pink sash, and the hated lilac sash was discarded. In later years Mother told me that she had been much upset the evening she gave me the red dress, as she realized that I had been starved for colors. Perhaps unconsciously the longing had shown itself in the too gay combinations in which I dressed my dolls. . . .

But alas; after several months of wearing the treasured red dress, I came home from school and ran into Mother's room. She was to have had a large dinner that night for Governor and Mrs. Cornell, but a letter had come from Mr. Dabney of Boston, the American Consul in Teneriffe in the Canary Islands, to tell Mother that her oldest stepson, Erastus Corning Pruyn, had died at Orizaba. There was no cable, and it had taken a month for the letter to come. The dinner was cancelled at once.[3]

Then came a real tragedy for me. The red dress was sent with other dresses to be dyed black. We were to wear mourning again for a year. I had never seen my half-brother. He was a romantic figure, who sent us boxes of presents from the various places he lived. He had married a Spaniard named "Lolita." A year of mourning was more than I could face. I sobbed over the red dress again, that lovely beautiful dress of which I was so proud.

The reaction was that my dolls all went into mourning too.

I have run ahead and must return to our nursery days and our pretty young German nurse, Frieda Wagner. She had charge of our baths and dressing and the two nursery rooms. She made the fire in the early morning and took charge of our breakfast. She was a conscientious, good-tempered girl who at first wore her peasant dress, but soon discarded it for the usual finery.[4]

Frieda became a member of the Lutheran church on the corner of Pine and Lodge Streets. The Chars went there too. They all liked Dr. Magee, the minister. While Mother was ill and Jack at Union College, Hattie and I went there too. On Sunday mornings we went down to the basement and found Char ready to start. Char gave Hattie a quarter and me a dime for the plate, and he entered the items in a little note book. Then we went out the basement door and down Elk Street to the crossing in front of the Van Benthuysens.[5]

Academy Park was a wretchedly kept place at that time. When the land had first been levelled and the park laid out in 1833, the city built a handsome and expensive fence, set in stone like the fence around Capitol Park. Academy Park had iron gates that were locked by ten o'clock every night, and once Aunt Anna French and Mr. Orlando Meads almost got caught there for the night, which would have made a real scandal for Elk Street. The park had only one dim gas light in the center, and they did not see that the gate on Washington Avenue was already closed. Finally a policeman appeared and got them out, though I think they could have climbed out, as many of the iron bars of the fence were broken or missing. We were warned never to go there after dark, as there were "rubber men" who stole purses and cut off pigtails and frightened women. This meant that the men were shod in heavy rubber shoes and made no sound, but in the dimness they suddenly appeared.

We crossed from the park by the Old State House, where we had often gone to see the "Convict's Staircase," then down Pine Street where the weeds grew between the cobbles, and where good Mr. Meads lived at No. 4. We sat in a pew about five from the front, and on a line with us was the Martin Gorgas family, Mr. and Mrs. Gorgas and their daughters Juliet and Emilie. Martin Gorgas served in the family of Mr. and Mrs. George Evans for fifty years. He had married the French nurse. Martin had been coachman and then butler. They were friends of the Chars and just the same type of fine people.

Hattie and I liked the Lutheran church and the minister, Dr. Magee, who ran back and forth on the platform and waved his arms. The choir was over the platform so we could watch everything. Mr. Keene, who sang in it, had a row of gold teeth which shone when he sang. We knew that he would make the weekly round of our sixty clocks the next morning, and he liked to have us follow him. Dr. Magee came to call on Frieda and the Chars and was received in my father's old office in the front basement.

But calls that interested us far more were the ones he made on Miss Albina Bulkley at No. 9 Elk Street. This house was at the end of our garden, so we could watch him. His house was on the corner of Steuben and Lodge Streets behind his church, so he walked up Steuben Street to Elk Street, and Miss Albina was always ready to greet him at the door. We did not understand for a long time how she knew he was coming.

Jim Cooper, across the street, also wondered, and he finally saw that Dr. Magee began to tap his cane heavily, twice, on the sidewalk as he reached No. 6, then two more taps at No. 7, and a final one at No. 8. Jim tried it, with complete success. Miss Albina was at the door. Jim gravely took off his hat and walked on. . . .

Mother had some trouble about the fence that separated our garden from the Bulkleys. Our large willow tree had blown down in a storm, and the rears of the houses below us showed from the piazzas. Mother had a lattice built four feet inside our line and had vines started over it. Mr. Bulkley wrote a letter of protest. He said the lattice was too high, and that he felt it was both a fire and burglar menace. Mother wrote him that she did not think that he had any reason to fear trouble. He replied that the descendants of Lord Arthur de Bulkley did not know what the word "fear" meant. We did not see much of our noble neighbors, but we watched them with interest and drew lots as to which of us must be the victim who had to ring the bell and ask to find a tennis ball sent over the fence, usually by Dr. Battershall.

The Van Benthuysens lived at No. 8 Elk Street. Several had married before my time, but as the years went on, I became a friend of Miss Bessie, who lived there with her brother Frank. She sat on the little iron piazza on the front of the house in warm weather, and I sometimes joined her. We would watch all the doings in the park, and often May Cooper would join us, and then we knew all that we did not actually see, the inside lives of our neighbors. Miss Bessie had her nieces and nephews running in and out. Her brother, Mr. Charles H. Van Benthuysen, lived on La Fayette Street on the corner of Hawk Street, and his children were Fred, Boyd and Marian. Her brother

Arthur's children were Ethel and Edith Arthur, known always as Artie. She was an unusually beautiful child.

In my early years, before Dean Norton rented No. 6, Mr. and Mrs. Samuel Ransom lived there. Their oldest daughter was Nina, and she was very handsome. She wore a black court plaster spot which made her color look very vivid. Mr. Walter Chapin came to take her driving in a high "T-cart," and we used to watch her as she climbed up on the seat. She always wore flowers and Mr. Chapin wore a boutonniere as they dashed at a fast trot up the street. She and Mr. Chapin were married, and they lived on Washington Avenue in a house now torn down to make a playground for the Girl's Academy. . . . Irene, the youngest Ransom child, was a friend of Hattie's. She had a wonderful stove and made vinegar candy.

We had a fine toboggan slide in the garden. It was quite steep, and was built at one side of the tool shed. The sleds ran over the grass to the corner next to the brick wall of the Bulkleys' house. It was a great gathering place in the afternoons, and sometimes Hattie's friends took entire possession. But her friends and mine joined in resenting the grownups trying to coast. They took up so much space with their bustles, and they dug holes with their high heels in the smooth icy surface about which we were so careful.

In the January after the election of Governor Grover Cleveland to be President, the Hampden Robb children in the Townsend house next door and I decided that, as everyone else was giving some kind of a party for the President-elect, we would give one too. I still have one of the written invitations we sent to our relatives and friends. I wrote them, as the Robbs did not know how to write. They could only print and I was firm that would never do for an invitation to such a distinguished party.

We bought six small brooms and hung them over the slide, because in the campaign there had been banners with "New brooms sweep clean!" The audience stood in the Conservatory, and for the opening of our program we coasted down together on one toboggan, flying flags and singing,

> O' Noah, he built himself an Ark,
> One wide river to cross.

We proceeded through all kinds of fancy coasting, standing up on the bob with lighted candles. And at the end, Loulie Robb went down backwards on a coal shovel and fell over at the bottom. Governor Cleveland had us called into the Conservatory to shake our hands and thank us for his party. We were thrilled with pleasure.

The campaign of the previous fall is the first one that I remember. Whenever there was a large torchlight parade, we would sit on the Cornings' steps and fire off Roman candles while shouting ourselves hoarse. Smaller parades passed along Elk Street, and I was often waked up by the noise and lights, the torches flashing on the ceiling.

All the Democratic parades shouted,

> Blaine, Blaine, James G. Blaine,
> The continental liar from the State of Maine.

As the men marched they came down hard on their right foot. Then suddenly a Republican parade would appear from Hawk Street. One procession followed another, and they shouted,

> Ma, Ma, where's my Pa?
> Gone to the White House, Ha! Ha! Ha!

We had no idea what this meant. We carried large handkerchiefs, some red and some white, with pictures of Cleveland and Hendricks stamped on them. I had mine framed and gave them to the National Club at Washington.[6]

Governor Cleveland had appointed General Farnsworth his Adjutant General, and Elk Street credited Mrs. Farnsworth with really winning the 1884 election. She was interested in some families north of the city in the Lumber district, and she often walked over there, accompanied by her Irish setter. The local priest, who helped her with the various problems, greatly admired the dog, so Mrs. Farnsworth gave him a setter, and he was very grateful. About three weeks before the election, he told her that the north end would vote for Blaine. He said the Democratic city government had always made promises before election to give the north end paving of new streets, sewers, and lights, but once the election was over, nothing was done.[7]

Mrs. Farnsworth arranged to have the priest call on Governor Cleveland at the Capitol and tell him the situation. It must have been a satisfactory interview, as the priest went to work and his parishioners organized, had meetings and speakers and, finally, an enormous torchlight procession of several thousand men.

It is a matter of history that the vote of New York settled the election. At last, after three days of agonized waiting, when the news was one way one hour and the other way the next, the state was carried, but by only 1154 votes. Mrs. Farnsworth had probably mustered many more votes than that: which proves incontestably that it was energy from Elk Street, combined with the priest and the dogs, which won the election for Grover Cleveland.

But three days of uncertainty had been agonizing, as I look back. The day after the election, Aunt Mary Corning came into the library dressed in heavy mourning. . . . Tears ran down her face as she announced "Blaine has been elected. It is all settled, and we have lost again."

I cried too, and tied a black hair ribbon around my arm. I begged not to have to go to school the next day as the "Girls-for-Blaine" would jeer at me. I still had a black eye which I won in a fight with a big Blaine senior. Then suddenly Thursday afternoon the whole situation changed, and by Friday morning it was officially announced that Cleveland had won. . . .

Saturday evening there was a magnificent torchlight procession up big State Street. The National Guard marched with Uncle Amasa Parker in command. He rode "Tommy Dodd," who did not mind the noise. Strange to say, the Blaine Club joined in the celebration.

Senator Robb took Nelly and Loulie, and Jack took Hattie and me. We stood at the head of State Street at Capitol Park, and I felt sure that I never would see anything so wonderful again. From the top to the bottom of the hill, it was a blaze of light. The Burgess' Corp with its drum major, and the many bands all playing,

O' Noah, he built himself an Ark,
One wide river to cross

made it an unforgettable sight.

When the marchers came to Eagle Street, they narrowed into little State Street, and then they stopped to salute and cheer for Governor Cleveland, who stood on a small stone balcony outside his office in the Capitol. The cheering could be heard for blocks for the first Democratic President since the Civil War.

The night that Mother had a dinner for the President-elect, the Cornings gave him a reception afterwards at their house at 87 State Street. There was also dancing, and Hattie, who was almost eighteen and graduating at St. Agnes in June, was allowed to go. She wore a real evening dress, with an enormous bustle. This was a very exciting event. What added to my regret at having to go ignominiously to bed was hearing the next day in school from Harriet Corning that she and Parker had climbed out on top of the bow window over the front steps, and had blown beans at the guests until a policeman complained at being struck in the eye, and Edward Ryan hauled them in. It was hard luck to have missed all that. Hattie told me that they danced Lancers, Saratoga Lancers, waltzes, and polkas, and that she had not felt so very shy after all.

What was being shouted now in processions was:

Three cheers for Maria,
Three cheers for the kid,
I voted for Cleveland —
I'm damned glad that I did!

But we had no idea what this could mean.

It was during Cleveland's term as governor that the Niagara Park Bill came up before the Legislature. This was a subject of great interest, both at Grandfather's and at our house. Our neighbor, Senator Robb, was working for it, and I went over several times with the Robb children to sit in the Senate gallery and hear the debates. One day, returning from school, I stopped on the corner of Hawk Street by the Chapel. As I had read *The Argus* hastily before school and had seen that the bill would come up in the Senate for a vote at two o'clock that afternoon, I said to myself, "Why not go?"

I was dressed in a red blanket toboggan suit, cap, and mocassins, and had a satchel full of books, but I knew I would not get a seat if I ran home first. So I ran the other way, and was soon seated in the gallery, oblivious to luncheon or family. It was an absorbing scene as the roll was called, and I was happy to know, at the end, that the bill was passed at last. I knew various Senators by sight, as many of them had been at our house. In those days they generally took a house for the winter and brought their families, as did also many of the Judges. They did not come here for only three days a week, as they do now.

It was long after four when I began to feel hungry and ran home. To my great surprise, I was welcomed with shouts "Here she is!" . . . Hattie rushed sobbing down the stairs. She thought I had been kidnapped, like Charlie Ross [a Philadelphia boy who disappeared July 1, 1874 , never to be found]. Jack had been out in Spruce Street, and was on his way down to Canal Street by the Hawk Street stairs. Mother looked limp. They had had a bad scare. I said I thought they would be interested enough to come over to hear the vote.

I must have been younger than that when I first remember seeing Mr. Theodore Roosevelt. [Roosevelt was a member of the Assembly 1882–1884.] Mother and I were walking down Washington Avenue by Lord's corner, at Hawk Street, when a man ran out of the Capitol, his hat in one hand and his right arm waving, we did not know at what. He seemed very excited as he shook hands with Mother. He talked about a bill he was pushing and how he was going to herd the members. He dived off down the street very suddenly, and we went our way along Hawk Street.

"Who is that, Mama, and will he herd sheep?" I asked.

"No," said Mother. "He will try to herd men. He is here to reform the state."

I cannot remember a time when we were not familiar with the new Capitol, as it was known in my childhood. Mr. H. H. Richardson, the famous architect, often lunched with us. Our house was so near that it was easy to walk across the park. I remember, too, how enormously large he was.

We were taken to watch the two staircases being built at the east end, one named for Richardson and the other for his friend and fellow architect, Frederick Leopold Eidlitz. Not that Mother or Jack or Grandfather admired the staircases; they were the wonder of that era of monstrosities. The Governor's room, and the Court of Appeals' room, were more to their taste.

It was fun to go to the Assembly Chamber [of the new Capitol] and watch Mr. Hunt, high up on his scaffolding, painting his murals. He did not like to be disturbed, and we were warned not to talk, but he was not averse to disturbing others when things did not go his way. He shared the studio on La Fayette Street, just a short block away, with Mr. E. D. Palmer, the sculptor. Mr. Palmer would come in for a cup of tea and report the latest doings. I have copied from Mother's diary of 1878 the following:

> Mr. William Hunt said that, though he was a Bostonian, he was disgruntled with his people for not appreciating his talent, that Bostonians did nothing but cackle to him about his art, but he never had had a chance to show what he could do until he had this superb order from Albany. He came into Mr. Palmer's studio one night and said with great heat, "As I lay working on my scaffold this afternoon, so happy and in such a blissful state, who should pursue me and stand beside me on the scaffolding, but a Bostonian? Gad! The happiness and pluck all went out of me at such a sight. I was like a squeezed lemon, all gone. Gad! To be hunted down, even here by a Bostonian! It was too much! I could work no more. Gad! Damn Boston, and damn Bostonians!" [8]

Alas for those famous murals, each one costing $10,000. They began to chip almost immediately. Something must have been wrong with either the walls or the paints used. Soon after this came the scandal of the Assembly Chamber's vaulted ceiling, which was pulled down, and the present papier mache imitation of wood was substituted. The last view I had of the murals was many years ago, from a step ladder in a room or closet close by. We could see them faintly above the modern ceiling. . . .[9]

CHAPTER 5

S OMETIMES MY SISTER AND I behaved quite badly about guests. . . . [Among those we tormented were] Mr. and Mrs. William Waldorf Astor [who had] leased the old Austin house, with its lovely woodwork, over on South Hawk Street [when] Mr. Astor was in the State Senate.[1] Mother invited them to dinner, and as the ladies came upstairs to Mother's dressing room, I crawled under Mother's bed . . . where I could watch them prink [primp] in the long mirror set into the library door of her dressing room. I picked out my favorite dress, and heard the ladies wonder who else was coming, and who their partners would be. If they came near the bed, I would tickle an ankle. Then the guests assembled in the library, and when Char announced dinner, they marched downstairs two by two. [Hattie and I] then hung our bare legs through the bannisters, and those who were so lucky to see us waved.

Hattie played the piano quite well, and especially liked to play the Lohengrin march. The night of the Astor dinner, we went down to the music room so as to peek through the glass doors to the dining room. Mrs. Astor was very beautiful, and I wanted to see her, but she was at the further end of the table, on Jack's right. So I dared Hattie to play the Wedding March, and she immediately started off with a big crash.

But [we] did not get very far before Char dashed in with a horrified expression on his face. "I am required," he said, "by your mama, to ask you to go to bed at once."

But just then, Mr. Astor appeared. He said he was so glad to hear the March, as the next day was their wedding day. I think he must have interceded with Mother not to punish us. But when the next dinner came along, we had to stay in the nursery all evening. After the dinners were over, the men went up to the library to smoke and the ladies stayed in the drawing room, as we were taught to call it by the Chars.

The first house guests that I remember were Mr. and Mrs. John Walter,[2] with their two sons, a valet with black-and-white striped hair, and the inevitable maid that every English woman regarded as a necessity. Ralph Walter was my age. We fought all through the visit because he wanted me to give him my favorite wooden horse and cart. Missie Char tried to persuade me that it was only polite to a visitor to give it, but as they drove away to the station, I stood stubbornly on the front steps holding that horse and cart up to his envious gaze. . . .

At afternoon tea time we were always called in to the library to shake hands with the visitors and to try to extract some of Char's delicious thin bread and butter and any cakes. At Christmas and New Year time we could count on Olykoeks [fried dough balls filled with fruit].

English guests generally came in the fall by day boat from New York, so as to see the beauties of the Hudson. . . . Dean Stanley of Westminster Abbey brought over with him the Abbey organist, Sir George Grove, and his nice, little, fat Dr. Gerald Harper. They had been told a great deal about mosquitoes, so they hoped the "insects," as they called them, would feed on Dr. Harper and leave the thin, little Dean in peace.[3]

The party had stopped at West Point, and Dr. Harper had picked lovely red, yellow, and brown leaves, which he had pressed carefully. He told us he wanted to place them over the monument to Major André in Westminster Abbey. It was not so far from West Point that André had met his death, at Tappan. The leaves lasted for some years, as they were sealed under glass. We always went to see them when we were in London.

The Dean had overdone his traveling, and so, for his own good, Dr. Harper put him to bed for several days. On my own hook I wanted to see what he looked like in the wide, double bed in the blue room, and I was curious as to whether he wore a nightcap. I thought it would be nice to help him get well by calling on him. At first I could hardly see him, as the shades were down.

I had a boy doll, named Harold, who had an open mouth and teeth. I was very proud of him, and I laid him on the pillow beside the Dean, and said, "Please kiss him." The Dean opened one eye at me and said, "I would rather kiss you." I seized the doll and ran. . . .

We enjoyed hearing the questions asked by English guests who were on a voyage of discovery. What about your Indians — do you see much of them here? Is your government educating the blacks? What is your tax rate? How much do you pay for a ton of coal? Is your beef very expensive? How about your high wages? Do you have your gowns made by your maids?

I have seen, lately, in *The New York Times*, a quotation from an 1892 copy of Baedeker with advice to travelers going to the United States. "It is no longer necessary to carry weapons." . . .

❦   ❦   ❦

My brother had been living at Neuilly near Paris with Père Hyacinthe and his family, in order to learn the purest French, for which the Père was well known. It had been an interesting experience. The Père had been in the Carmelite Order and had lectured in several of the French universities, but he had been dropped from the Order.

He founded the Old Catholic Church in Switzerland, and later an independent church in Paris known as "Église Gallican." In England he had married an energetic lady named Emily Merriman, and they had a son named Paul Loyson. Loyson was the Père's family name.[4]

The Père came to this country twice, and the second time he came to stay with us and brought his wife. The Père was a modest, quiet, fine-looking man, who spoke very little English. His wife, Madame Loyson, made up for all this, and he seemed contented to have it so.

She shaved him every morning, and I was pleased when she asked me to stand by and hold a bowl of hot water. The razor was very sharp, and she was very quick, but every now and then, the Père would wince as she flourished it around his throat. She called him pet names, such as "Mon Bijou," "Cher To-To," and if he seemed impatient, "Monsieur Bébé." At the end of the performance, he said "Pax Vobiscum." He paid his respects to Governor Cleveland at the Capitol as the head of the State, and to Bishop Doane as the head of the Church. He and his church were in touch with the Old Catholics and Protestants.

❦   ❦   ❦

Our next door neighbours at No. 21 Elk Street were the Townsends. Dr. Howard Townsend had died before my time, but Mrs. Townsend and her sons, Howard and Rensselaer, and her youngest daughter Hattie Townsend, lived there. . . .

Mrs. Townsend had been Justine Van Rensselaer at the Manor House,[5] and her father was known in Albany as "the young Patroon" although his father had really been the last one. Mr. Van Rensselaer had bought No. 21 as a wedding present for Dr. and Mrs. Townsend. Mrs. Townsend was very nearsighted. I remember one day when I was walking down Elk Street holding Mother's hand, we met Mrs. Townsend. She said, "I am very blind, but I have the Begum's eye, and I can see how dirty the streets are." The Begum's eye was an old tradition in the Schuyler family. A Staats ancestor, who went to the East Indies as a doctor for one of the Dutch colonies, is supposed to have married a Begum, a Hindu princess, and brought her to Holland, and then to this country. The Begum's eye is a very bright, dark brown eye with a sparkle.

We were rather afraid of Howard Townsend, as he was very grand with us. Nevertheless, we had courage enough to stand behind the curtains of a nursery window and sing,

> There he goes — there he goes —
> All Dressed up in his Sunday clothes.
> Nobody knows — nobody knows —
> Whether he wears any underclothes.

He presented an imposing figure, particularly on Sunday morning when, with his mother on his arm, they started down Elk Street to cross to the park and go down to the Hudson Avenue Presbyterian Church. He wore a Prince Albert coat, a silk hat, and he carried a gold headed cane with a jaunty jerk. He did not like us to sing or whistle after him, and when he tried to walk faster or slower, we kept along also at his pace.

His younger brother, Rensselaer, was great fun, and he carried me about on his shoulder and was willing to run around the garden or up and down the street, playing horse. Both the Townsends were friends and playmates of my half-brother, and in the years before my father remarried, Mrs. Townsend had been more than kind to the lonely little boy next door.

Hattie Townsend was the youngest of the family. She was older than my sister, but she was lovely to us both. I cherished a silent but intense admiration for her, writing letters to her, scribbled on cards in the hall card bowl, and even inventing a telephone to her. She was a great friend of May Cooper and Kate Walsh, and they all came to the nursery to help us with paper doll books, and collecting advertisements and playing games with us. . . .

What we loved to do was to go to the closed Manor House on a Saturday morning, with Hattie Townsend and May and Kate and Hattie's little white Spitz dog, Prince. Mother always arranged to let us have the carriage on Saturdays if we wanted to go somewhere, and she always insisted that Missie Char or Frieda look after us. Missie Char loved to go to the Manor House as she was a friend of Jane McLeod, who lived in the lodge by the gate, at the head of Broadway. I was good-naturedly taken along, as the older girls knew Missie Char would look after me. . . .

Missie Char and Jane would sit on one of the deep window seats and whisper about the ghosts. I would hear and wonder about it. Jane would say, "There were several of the ladies in the upper hall this morning. They must have known the children were coming."

Then all of a sudden, the Spitz dog would face the stairs, his eyes would stand out, his hair bristle, and he would growl.

Jane would say, "They're coming down. I can hear the silk rustle." She seemed perfectly undisturbed.

Every morning she walked up from the Lodge and opened the house, pulled up the shades, let in the air, and swept and dusted. In the late afternoon she closed it up again. She did not seem at all afraid.

Hattie Townsend would stand against the wall which led from the main house into the wings, added in 1840, and stretching her arms as wide as she could, she could not reach the sides. . . . It was in the hall that I stayed with Missie Char and sad old Jane, who lamented the way the place was running down. The trees were still beautiful, and the gardens at the rear were in some kind of order, but Fink, the gardener, had gone to take charge of the new Washington Park. Just a few months before the Manor was pulled down, and part of it had to be dynamited, Mr. and Mrs. Eugene Van Rensselaer and Bessie and Steve came to stay for a month, for the last time.

It must have been difficult to live in the Manor at all, and it was very sad, but the effort to save it was not met with any response by Albany. Mrs. Nathaniel Thayer of Boston (Cornelia Van Rensselaer) had offered to give $10,000 if the City would raise another $10,000 to keep the Manor and make it a museum, either there or moved elsewhere. But, as nothing was done, it was sold and moved to Williamstown.

I have often been asked why 13 Elk Street was next door to 21 Elk Street. The two houses were built in 1845 by Henry G. Wheaton, a well-known Albany lawyer. Mr. Wheaton lived in No. 13 for several years, but he sold No. 15 to General John A. Dix. My father rented No. 15 from General Dix, but Father's first wife, Harriet Corning Pruyn, was an invalid. They decided to go to Europe for her health, so they sublet No. 15 to Governor Hamilton Fish. This house was the Executive Mansion during the two years of Governor Fish's administration. On the return of my father and his wife, Governor Fish did not want to move. His son, Hamilton Fish Jr., was born there.

My father bought No. 13 from Mr. Wheaton in 1851 for $16,500. His plan was to build a house in the vacant lots below, in what later became our garden. Plans were made for No. 11 Elk Street. I have seen the plans, and it would have been a hideous house. . . . Fortunately, these plans were never carried out. Instead large additions were made to No. 13 in 1858. The whole east side of the house was opened up, with windows and piazzas. In the rear they added the dining room, with large kitchens under it, and over the dining room, the fine library which was the center of our living.

I do not know in what year Mr. Daniel D. Barnard, at No. 25 Elk Street, had the city renumber the block, but whenever this was done, allowance was made to build four houses in our garden. They would have been numbered 11, 13, 15, and 17, making our house No. 19, and the one next door No. 21. My father and Mr. Barnard were good friends, but this change was too much. Father thought it was high handed, and he refused to change his number 13, which he liked. His paper, cards, front door, and trunks were all 13, so he kept it. The only concession he made was to have on his bank cheques in brackets [new number 19].[6]

General Dix sold No. 15 (or 21) to General John F. Rathbone, but they only lived there a short time. One of the children died suddenly, and Mrs. Rathbone did not want to stay there, so they bought 119 Washington Avenue. General Rathbone sold No. 15 (or 21) to Mr. Stephen Van Rensselaer for his daughter, Mrs. Howard Townsend.

To the regret of everyone, Mrs. Townsend and her family moved to New York about the year 1883. I think Albany was not a wide enough world for Howard. Mrs. Townsend let the house to her niece, Mrs. J. Hamden Robb, for two years while Mr. Robb was a State Senator from New York City. After that, it was let to the Dunbars of Cooperstown, and then to the Dean Sages, the winter Susan came out. It was finally sold to Mr. James T. Gardiner, about 1887 or 1888, and when the Gardiners moved to New York, it was sold to Mr. and Mrs. Dunkin Van Rensselaer Johnston. . . .

I have a very interesting old photograph of our library. In those days, a photograph of an interior took long time exposures, and it would be impossible for anyone to sit still long enough to be in a picture. So, the problem of the picture of all at tea was solved in a roundabout way. First the room was photographed, and I do not know how long the exposure took. Then each of us was photographed out on the piazza, sitting in the chair in which we would appear. Even out of doors, the exposures were not instantaneous. After that, we were each cut out of our picture and pasted on the picture of the room, and, when that was done, the picture was taken over again so as not to show the pasting.

It really is a very good picture. My father is sitting in a large mahogany and leather chair, one he had used in the State Senate in the old Capitol, near the glass door to the piazza. Mother is sitting at her tea table by the fireplace. My brother is standing with a cup of tea in his hand, while Hattie and I are at a small table where we used to have our regular evening meal while the grown-ups had their afternoon tea. . . .

The library was an interesting room. In the many memories I have of my mother, I think the one I most often remember is of her in the library at afternoon tea time. . . . There were several portraits: one of Mother done by Moscheles, which is now in the Institute; one of Father, by Elliott; and two large ones of Grandfather and Grandmother Parker, by Huntington.[7]

Under those portraits, on a table, was the Napoleon Camp service. It was very handsome, of silver gilt, with a green cloth cover that was lifted off by two handles. Pauline Borghese [a sister to Napoleon] had taken it from Corsica to Rome. She had then sold it to her uncle, Cardinal Fesch, and at his death in 1839, it was sold at auction. Tiffany bought the Camp service and sold it to my father. . . .[8]

The walls had bookcases on three sides. What we loved was the "pretend bookcase" that was really a door into Mother's dressing room. It was close to the tea table so that Mother could slip out if she heard someone coming up unexpectedly and did not want to be caught. No one would suspect that this was not a real bookcase. The only criticism was that the books should not have been all alike, but should have been varied as to height and color, and so have looked more like an ordinary bookcase. . . .

On the dressing room side, a door had a long mirror set in it. This mirror had originally been in a frame and hung on a wall. Once, when my father and his first wife were in Europe, the caretaker smelled gas. She stupidly took a lighted candle to investigate, and there was a terrific explosion. The back of the house was blown out. That was before 1858, when the additions were made. This mirror was blown out into Spruce Street and found with the frame smashed but the mirror itself untouched. My father thought this was so remarkable that he had it set into the door.

In the center of the library was a large desk. It was fun, when no one was looking, to run in there, pick up the feather pens and stick them over my ears, smear my face with ink, and run shouting through the house. Everyone was afraid to touch me for fear of getting the ink on them. . . .

Opening from the library on the north side was a small library, and from that opened the bow window where we had morning prayers. Hattie adopted the small library and had her favorite books there. It was a grand place for tête-à-tête, heart-to-heart confidences.

It had a fireplace with a deep-set window over it. The flue went up on one side. One morning Jack saw Owen stacking a pile of kindling wood in Hattie's retreat. He said he thought some logs of wood might make the fire last longer.

"Shure you're sayin' the truth, Mr. Johnny," said Owen, "but Miss Hattie just wants a show and a slow for a beau."

There was also another library upstairs, at the north end. It was a large room with a ceiling higher than the other ceilings. In that library was kept, under lock and key, my father's Literature of the Law Library, of about 2,500 volumes. Mother left this library to the State Library, with the understanding that, in the new Education Building being built at that time, there would be a special place made for this valuable collection. In the meantime the Commissioner of Education, Dr. Draper, asked to have the books in his section of the State Library in the Capitol. He said he wanted to have a chance to study the books. They were taken over there in June 1910, and were all burned in the Library fire of March 1911. If we had realized that one reason for having the new library in the Education Building was Dr. Draper's fear of fire, from wooden stacks, we would have placed the books in storage. . . .

Father's Literature of the Law Library had its own catalogue, and so did the china collection. This catalogue of china listed about 8,000 pieces, most of which were in the china room in shallow glass-fronted cases or hung on the walls. Owing to this collection, we were known as the "China Pruyns." The Robert H. Pruyns at 158 State Street were called the "Japanese Pruyns," as he had been appointed first Minister to Japan by President Lincoln and had brought home a valuable collection of ivories and lacquers.[9] There was also "Mrs. Missionary Pruyn," who did outstanding work among Japanese women and wrote a book called *Grandmamma's Letters From Japan*. She was Mrs. Samuel Pruyn and lived in the "Pruyn Homestead" on Pearl Street near Maiden Lane.

CHAPTER 6

I HAD THE GREATEST ADMIRATION for my sister Hattie, whose full name was Harriet Langdon Pruyn. . . . I remember when she heard that, if you saved one million cancelled postage stamps, you could buy a Chinese girl baby and save it from being killed. We took an old hat box and kept it in a nursery cupboard, and started, with great enthusiasm, to cut stamps from letters in the paper basket. I can see that box now, and the hopelessness of trying to count the stamps. Over and over we started to count them, as we were sure we had at least a half a million. We should have counted each hundred and put it in a separate envelope.

Anyway, we were later told that Hattie had been the victim of a foolish story, and that no Chinese babies could be bought for stamps. It was a blow, I blamed Hattie. I insisted it was the A.D.C. [a club of girls in the neighborhood, all Hattie's age] that had fooled her. I was at that moment in a rage with several of the members who had borrowed one of my dolls and lost its hat. I had also secretly determined that the Chinese baby should be kept in a lovely cradle that Grandmother had given me. Frieda built a fire, and we burned the stamps.

❦　　❦　　❦

I slept in the old walnut crib which had been used by all my father's children. When I got to be ten, other children came in to play and said, "Who sleeps in a crib?" I had to say that I did, and answer to the name of baby in school the next day. It was then I revolted. I really was too long for it, and I always claimed in later years that the reason I grew out instead of up was . . . that crib. So mother bought us the new brass beds. . . .

But in the many years before the brass beds, I used to climb out of the crib and into Hattie's bed. Sometimes it was still dark, and we played going traveling, under the bedclothes. The foot of the bed was called "Darkest Africa." Hattie invented a game called "Mrs. Come-tickle-me." She taught me "Pease porrige hot," "Cat's cradle," "Hickery, dickery dock," the divisions of the earth by land and sea, the colors of the rainbow, and the multiplication table.

Saturday and Sunday mornings we had more time for learning, to find the hymns in the Hymnal and the Psalms for the day. We both stood on the beds to read the quotations from Shakespeare on the wallpaper: "Hark, Hark, it is the lark who sings," "Nymph in thy orisons be all my sins remembered." The picture of Romeo, climbing up on the balcony to a waiting Juliet, was my favorite.

We had never-ending discussions about the days of the week on which we were born. She was a Friday girl and so should be "loving and giving," but she refused to give me a ribbon I wanted, which she did not use anymore, so that was out. I was a Tuesday girl and should be "full of grace," but she told me I was the clumsiest child she ever saw, and so we kept it up.

But the Sunday fish ball dispute was the hottest. Biddy made the most delicious codfish balls. They were beautifully browned and we ate them with very cold apple sauce. Hattie insisted that anything fried was very bad for any child under ten, and then she took all my crusts onto her plate and devoured them. She also took pie crusts if she could reach them, but although mother was not at breakfast, she was at the other meals, so I usually got the pie crusts.

Frieda liked to go shopping, and, as Missie Char did not enjoy it, we went in charge of Frieda when we had errands, and I always had them for my dolls. Washington Avenue from Hawk Street up to Swan was all shops, except for one house. Where Chancellor's Hall stands in all its modern glory was Lord's corner. It had first been Lord and Thornton. It was a red brick building painted cream color, and it had a crane in the Hawk Street gable for hauling up grain.

Mr. [Edmund J.] Lord and his daughter, Miss Emma, who kept the books, and the son, Eddy, were dwarfs. Mrs. Lord was large and quite normal height. We went regularly to Lord's to be weighed, and they kept our weights written up on the wall. The fire alarm for Elk Street was on that corner. It was a well known corner, and the horsecar conductors, and later the trolley conductors, shouted "Lord's corner." The Lords always gave us cookies or apples, and they had cats everywhere.

Shaw, the tailor, displayed the latest men's clothes in a large window, and above that was Miller's drug store. An Indian stood on a pedestal out in front of Miller's, a sign that cigars were for sale. Then came Mason's ice cream parlor, [which sold] delicious ice cream, even though it was said to be made with lard instead of cream. We bought it in paper boxes, tore off the flaps, and used them for spoons. Mason's was also famous for the candy called contrabands. He had a secret recipe and I read in the paper not long ago that the recipe had been kept in his wife's safe-deposit box. No other contrabands could equal Mason's. Mrs. Cook and her daughters lived in Dr. Sprague's old house in the center of the block. It was a little gem of a house with ironwork and woodwork. Later, Dr. Warren of the Boy's Academy lived there.

Bloomingdale's was a dark and dismal-looking dry goods store. It was under a brick hotel, with a yard behind it, where stage coaches started for Rensselaerville and other remote towns. Sometimes we went there to watch Anne Elizabeth Ryan start for Rensselaerville. She had been for years a favorite maid of ours at Grandmother's. When she came into town it was an event for her, and she came to see Mother. . . . We liked to watch her climb up on the rickety stage, and she usually claimed the seat by the driver. The horses started off with a crack of the whip and, turning under the arch into Washington Avenue, they vanished away.

Frieda liked best for us to go on further, to Reylander's, also a dry goods shop. Her great friend was Crissie Reylander who waited on us. Crissie also went to the Lutheran Church, so she and Frieda had a lot to discuss, and in German too, while we sat on high stools and waited. Then came Mrs. Blessing's little shop. She sold needles and thread and worsted and candy and comic valentines.

Nearer Swan Street was Miss Davidson's tiny millinery shop, and there we purchased our dolls' hats and bonnets. Sometimes a row of our doll carriages would be what is now called "parked" outside. We rivaled one another with these carriages. Their silk parasols could be tipped to shade the doll from too strong sunlight on a wax face. They were lined, too, to match the parasol, and the doll's cover also matched. We carried our dolls in, to be fitted for the latest styles, every fall and spring. Miss Davidson took the matter as seriously as we did and discussed the various shapes of their heads, and the colors of the eyes and hair. Above all, we each wanted our dolls' hats and bonnets to be different from any other dolls'.

In a doll's Saratoga trunk I have a large white straw hat trimmed with daisies, and it has a white ribbon to tie under the chin. This hat was worn with great success by my large doll, Anna. Aunt Cora Parker made her a full set of short clothes, with which she wore a gray felt hat decorated with a tiny feather, and a brown and white straw with three pompoms of red and brown. Hattie admitted these pompoms gave the hat great style.

For young dolls, as well as young children, the hats were worn with elastics under the chin. It was a certain mark of growing up to have the elastics worn at the back and under the long hair or pigtail. Many a little girl has been repudiated by older girls because she wore the elastic under her chin. It was hard luck to go to church in a new hat and then be greeted in the aisle with, "Hello baby," by a girl with her elastic under her hair.

In the lower story of an old brick house was Gomph's musical instrument store, and on the corner of Washington Avenue and Swan Street was another hotel, which was always changing names and owners. It had been an old-fashioned brick house. I think one of the Perry family had lived in it.

Against the Swan Street wall was the peanut stall of Johnny Eytal. He was a short, laughing little Italian, and in winter he wore a thick pea-jacket. He stomped up and down in the icy blasts, while his gas jet flared wildly under the peanut roaster. What good peanuts those were! Perhaps it was the taste of youth, [but] none have ever tasted so good. A five-cent bag in [one's] muff, or in a pocket of [one's] toboggan suit, kept frozen hands warm until [the peanuts] were eaten, one by one. No coasting or skating party was complete unless we stopped at Johnny's stand for peanuts first. He must have made quite a fortune.[1]

One winter his gas jet burned him very seriously, and he was taken to the City Hospital, then on the corner of Eagle and Howard Streets. Mother sent Chandler over to see what she could do for him, but Chandler returned quite dazzled to say that Johnny thanked her very much, and said that he needed nothing, and that when he recovered he would sell out his stand and return to Italy. He had a private room and his own nurse while in the hospital. We heard, later, that he had bought property near Naples and had settled down there with his family. . . .

The south side of Washington Avenue, from Swan Street to Capitol Cut, [a temporary construction roadway from Washington Avenue to State Street, between Hawk and Swan Streets] was all stores, except for one hotel which, I think, was called the Borthwick. Market teams made it their headquarters. On the corner of the Cut there was a saloon. This Cut went across to State Street past "The Cottage" on the corner of Congress Street. Congress Street had originally run from the old Capitol to Swan Street, but now only one short block was left. We were not encouraged to use the Cut.

The stone yard was on the lower side of the Cut, and there was a tall fence behind which were the sheds and the enormous stones that the poor horses had brought up from the waterfront. It was all very noisy. We could often hear the drills and hammering over in our garden when the wind was from the south. Bits of stone chips were apt to fly out, and Mr. Bleecker Banks almost lost the sight of one eye from a chip that became imbedded.

It was the north side of Washington Avenue that interested us. . . . The Education Building and Lafayette Park [now] cover the north side. Lord's corner, Reylander's, Miss Davidson's, Johnny Eytal, and all the other landmarks have vanished. A new generation has come up and the new order has certainly beautified the old city.[2]

Frieda's love affair turned out badly. She had fallen deeply in love with our young coachman and had taught him German. But after learning all he wanted, he switched over to learning shorthand, and also switched away from Frieda. She became very sad and looked badly and sighed all the time. We were told, by Missie Char, not to tease Frieda anymore.

Mother decided that the best thing for her was to start all over again in another city. Mother happened to hear of an excellent position in New York, and much to our grief Frieda left us. She lived in this place for over thirty years, but she never married. Her place in our home was taken by Mary Whalen of Greenbush. She was a very nice and capable woman, full of life and energy and humor. She lived with us for years until her mother died and she had to go home to keep house for her father and the younger children.

Missie Char always superintended the nursery in her quiet, but vigilant, way. She sat in a large chair by the table and had a basket of mending beside her. Her hair, parted in the middle and looped over her ears, her gold hooped earrings, the large brooch which held her linen collar which had been given to her by Char when they were married, her back bent over the endless mending of stockings and clothes torn by climbing trees and sheds, her gold-rimmed spectacles, her wedding ring, and her gray-blue seersucker dresses, all are part of the memories of nursery life.

Frieda had taught us to knit and crochet. We made endless reins with bells on them, and we made "clouds," which were to cover your head when you went out in the evening. Our relatives had to be grateful for our gifts of "clouds" and bed socks and fascinators [a crocheted head covering for women].

I loved dolls and had quite a collection of them. My photograph was taken with them. I also had a doll house with the outside made to look like bricks. Mr. Pratt, the carpenter, had made it, and he had also made, as a present, a doll's bed studded with brass nails. Frieda had made most of the furnishings for it, as she was very clever in covering cardboard with material, turning out chairs and dressing tables. I kept the dollhouse locked so that the A. D. C. would not meddle with it if I was out.[3] Those older girls had a way of taking things over and then leaving everything a mess.

I had also learned from Frieda how to make a rabbit's mouth. It is a difficult thing to learn and requires much skill. Missie Char disliked it and also my talent of making donkey's ears and kicking. Her gentle voice would murmur, "Anything but vulgarity, Bertie," or else when we both got on a high horse, she would shake her head and say, "Ladies never romp." It was no use to say we did not want to be ladies or that it was stupid to have to act like a lady.

When March came, Missie Char started on spring tonics and never was disturbed from this duty by any of our arguments. [We were given] large spoonfuls of "Extract of Dandelion" after dinner, or, if we liked it better, we could drink water that had stood in a "Quassia cup," the most bitter draught possible to imagine. . . .

On the wall near the clock "Dutchy" hung a walnut cabinet with . . . a door that was locked. In this [were] kept the usual remedies of that period . . . [including] Mutton tallow to rub on our chests for a cold. While this was being rubbed on, [we] sat in a large chair, enveloped in blankets, with our feet in a tub of very hot water with mustard in it. The open fire burned hot, and by the time the ten minutes was over, [we] felt parboiled but were rushed into bed with a stone jar of hot water at [our] feet. There were no rubber hot water bags, and sometimes the cork in the stone jar leaked, and we woke up in a cold puddle. On our chest was a red flannel square, tied around our neck and covered with more tallow.

In the little closet was camphor ice in a small cake, in a box; that was for chapped lips. Glycerine was for chapped hands, and there were several kinds of plasters. One plaster was French, and called "Papier Fayard." It had to be heated over the gas jet. I usually had some plaster on me somewhere, as we played rough games in the garden. But there were compensations. When we had colds, we were given horehound drops or lemon drops, and we chewed slippery elm bark. We liked all of these.

Missie Char had the usual old sayings. If we ate bread crusts, our hair would curl. Whistling girls and crowing hens always came to very bad ends.

To pierce the ears prevented eye trouble. Raisins gave fits. Dropping a key down a person's back stopped nose bleeding. Amber beads prevented croup. Tickling a baby on the soles of its feet made it an idiot. Worst of all for me, she said that the little cupcakes made by Biddy had a stone in their rounded tops.

Every December she quoted, "A green Christmas makes a full churchyard," and although I never remember a green Christmas, she was relieved when snow came. "You must never sigh," she would say, "it takes a drop of blood from your heart." When we had cut fingers or other wounds, if she could not find a black cobweb quickly, she would fill a bowl with hot water and pour it over wood ashes from the nursery fire, and in this we held the injured member. We had never heard of germs. A nickel-plated bowl with a handle was kept in mother's bathroom. When very hot water was needed for some special use, the bowl was fitted on a round metal holder and this was fitted on the gas jet. So, in a few minutes, the water was very hot.

Almost all bathtubs at that period had doors to shut them off. Mother's tub had large doors, and over each end of the tub were shelves for all kinds of bath needs. There was one good thing about those old metal tubs — they had sloping backs. By soaping them, we had a splendid slide and went splash into the tub of water, and [drops] scattered all over anyone trying to stop the fun. The water supply of the city was not forceful, and sometimes it was hard to get enough for a bath in the bathrooms upstairs.

In 1886 Mother decided to modernize her bathroom. It would be funny now for anyone to see what modernizing meant to [her generation]. Ridgway and Russ, under Van Vechten Hall on State Street, were the plumbers, and they installed the first porcelain bathtub in Albany for Mother. It was very heavy and deep and narrow, and it had to be hoisted up by a crane through one of the windows into the house, as it was too heavy to be lifted. The doors and much of the old woodwork, and the antiquated shower, were torn out, but the new tub had a wooden setting and was covered by wood, on the ends and sides. It was a wonderful improvement, and people wanted to see it, but many of them disapproved of the lack of doors for privacy. . . .

Jack Frost, who embroidered the nursery windows so beautifully in winter, lived in the tool shed in the garden [we were told]. So did that nuisance, Mrs. Manners, who was so particular about how to use knives, forks, and spoons, and fussed if anything was spilled on the table. The Sandman who would come in too early in the evening, he lived there too, but I never could find [any of these creatures] at home. I searched the place, but they hid behind old trunks and boxes and garden tools.

When we played robbers, we used the shed for the house that was robbed. Of course we all wanted to be robbers, and there was a great deal of time lost while we discussed it, but it was finally settled by the old way of "eeny, meeny, miny, mo," or by "One-two-three-four, Mary at the cottage door." No one could go into the house to hide, but there were the shed roofs and all kinds of places among the shrubs and down the hill to the fences.

Our dresses were torn, our hair ribbons gone, and we were a dirty-looking crowd as we stood on the rim of the Gooseman's fountain and washed ourselves in the spouts that came from the bills of the geese. Anyone lucky enough to have a handkerchief shared it with others, and then we would rush out of the garden gate and across the park to Mr. John de Peyster Townsend's on the corner of Eagle Street and Maiden Lane.

Mr. Townsend was the kindest man in the world, and he had the best syrups for soda water of any that I have ever tasted. They were all homemade. If someone came in for a soda and said they did not care what kind it was, Mr. Townsend would push the metal stopper that had over it the name, "Don't care." Just back of the marble counter and fountain, and against the wall, stood a set of small drawers, and in them were kept tickets. People were supposed to buy a lot at a time and then not bother to pay for each soda.

How proud I was if Mr. Townsend said, "Your brother bought a dollar's worth of tickets for you." Then I could treat the crowd, and that pleased them. If I had over 90 in conduct at school for a month, Jack would buy the tickets.

One day, Louis said he would give me a nickel if I drank three sodas. I took the offer and easily drank two sarsparillas, but it was a case of "Don't care" for the third, and I got it down, much to Louis' disappointment. The fact that I parted with it in the park soon after seemed to Louis to justify his not giving me the nickel after all. But I fought that decision and always have considered I was cheated out of the nickel.

Mr. Townsend's shop was a Mecca for us all. His assistant was Jim Beale. In the windows were the large jars filled with red and green liquid, the old advertisement of a drug store. The store was in a very central location and had a clear view up Washington Avenue. Mr. Townsend was a native of Elk Street, having been born at No. 2, the son of Mr. and Mrs. John F. Townsend.

Hattie and her fellow members in the A.D.C. petted me a little. Once or twice they even treated me to soda water, but when they found out that I had tickets, they wanted me to give them all to them. I held out, as they would not tell me what the initials A.D.C. stood for, and Mr. Townsend backed me up. I never forgot that. He said the tickets were mine to use as I liked. . . . Besides Hattie, other members of the A.D.C. were Irene Ransom from No. 6, Annie and Sarah Townsend from No. 3, Emma Olcott, Cora Weaver, Lily and Mamie Read, Fanny Ten Eyck, Susy Vanderpoel, Margaret Shortiss, Harriet McClure, and Daisy Pruyn.

The Club used me to try out roofs and sheds, and once I was hung in the middle from the overhang of the laundry lattice-way. My indignant cries brought out everyone, as the girls stood by helpless. A ladder was brought, and I was rescued.

The original stable of the house had been turned into a laundry, reached by a covered way from the main house. It also opened onto Spruce Street. There were all kinds of roofs, tin and wood and shingle. They all contributed to the destruction of the underclothes of the club members. Susy Vanderpoel climbed the iron rose arbor one day, and it fell down with her under it. That was the last straw for Mrs. Vanderpoel. She came to see Mother, and the ultimatum was no more shed climbing or else Susy would have to resign from the club.

At last I found out the meaning of the initials on the silver pins the girls wore. The club had been formed to act plays and not to climb sheds, so, as sheds were out, they returned to the plays as the "Albany Dramatic Club." I was quite amiable, for some time, about running errands when they started to rehearse in the playroom under the conservatory, where we had two large trunks of cast-off clothing in which to dress up. I do not remember the name of the play, but it was given at General and Mrs. Fred Townsend's at No. 3, and it was a Saturday night. I was allowed to go. I sat on the floor, right in front, and lost my heart to "Dora Fastone," a fascinating and flirtatious lady, wearing a charming bonnet and having golden curls. What a disappointment it was to find out that it was only Joel Rathbone dressed as a girl.

Joel lived at No. 5 with his father and mother, Mr. and Mrs. Clarence Rathbone. His older brother was Albert, called by us "Ally," and there were two sisters, Angelica and Ethel. Angelica had lovely, curly, auburn hair and long legs, so that she out-ran the boys in Academy Park. When Angelica fell on a slate stone step at our basement door and cut a wide gash on her cheek, she never cried. She went on playing. We called her "Birdie" Rathbone.

❦   ❦   ❦

There was quite a pond in the lower part of the park, and when it froze the children flocked to skate there. It was so shallow that parents did not have to worry. Others who skated there were Cora and George Weaver, the Whitneys from Lodge Street, Cuyler and Marcus Reynolds from Columbia Street, the Fred Townsend children, and most of the members of the A.D.C. My sister had real skates. They were wooden with clumsy leather straps and steel runners. I was anxious to go to the pond too, but slid around in red Turkish slippers that turned up in the front.

One afternoon, a boy hit me with a snow ball that had a sharp piece of ice in it. It struck my left eye lid and cut the left side with a deep gash. Frieda carried me home, yelling bloody murder, and we were followed by a string of children. She carried me through the basement and into the front room, which had been father's office. I was at once surrounded by family and household, and Char was sent running for the doctor. Missie Char first washed the cut with hot water, and then she went to the cellar and brought up the largest and blackest cobweb that she could find. She applied this on the deep gash "to stop the bleeding and start the healing." Dr. Cox and Char arrived breathless, having run uphill. I was told later that he feared I had lost the sight of the eye, but whether it was the hot water or the cobweb, I finally emerged with my sight intact, after wearing a bandage for six weeks.

CHAPTER 7

W E HAD ONE OF THE FIRST telephones [1878]. It was installed on a wall in Mother's room, beside the whistle to the kitchen and the metal disc with which you could call fire, doctor, police, or messenger. You used a pointer, and the bell buzzed. Frieda held me up to the telephone so that I could be the first one of the family to use it. The telephone man stood by and told me how to call the number I wanted.[1]

I said, "This is No. 14. Please give me No. 21." This was Marvin's telephone, also just installed. Tuy answered it. I said, "Hello Tuy, this is Bertie."

"Oh," came a glum voice, "it's just you then."

I said, "Did you think it was Cora Weaver?"

Bang went the telephone, and that was the end of my first talk.

We soon had another kind of phone in the little room between the nursery and Mother's room. It was also a wall telephone, with a large bell on top. Soon the first one was removed, as it was too confusing to have two kinds, and this second type was used for several years.

❧　❧　❧

Soon after the accident to my eye, we had a fire in the house. The front of the house was to be painted, and early one morning a painter began to burn off the old paint. A small piece of the lace curtain was caught under the glass door of the front drawing room window, and suddenly the painter saw flames in the room. My sister and I were dressing in the room overhead, and we saw smoke curling up by the front window. As I was nearly dressed, I ran into the hall, which was filled with smoke. Char was waving his arms and shouting, "Call the firemen! Quick! Quick!" The fire alarm was in my Mother's room, and she turned it at once.

The next thing I remember was that Jim Cooper was carrying me across the street, and Hattie was with us. He took us to his mother and sisters and ran back for help. The next we saw of him, he was pitching rugs out of the side window. I began to cry and say my mother was being burned up, but kind Mrs. Cooper held me at the window and showed me Mother out in the street, in a black tea gown. Pancakes with maple syrup were produced, and we were comforted.

The fire was kept to the one room, but the acids of the fire extinguisher did more damage than the fire. The room was shut off for weeks, and the house smelled of burned wood and plaster. I seem to have been quite a mimic, and for several years I was asked to tell how Char had shouted in the lower hall.

That same winter a photograph was taken of all the grandchildren at Notman's on Pearl Street. This was then no easy job. There were no instantaneous photographs. We had to stand still, with an iron clamp at each side of our heads.[2]

I am one in a group of three, Parker Corning in kilts, and Grace Marvin and I playing croquets. My head was turned so as not to show the bandage over my eye. Harriet Parker, a six-weeks-old baby, is lying on Louisa's lap. My sister holds a horse on which Harriet Corning is sitting. When it came to taking the two Parker boys and their St. Bernard dogs and cart, the picture had to be taken on the roof so as to shorten the process for the dogs. It is a funny group to look at now. In later years two more grandchildren were added to this array.

My sister was guilty of saying, "Darn it," while the picture was being taken. This was considered very bad, and when we went home, she had to wash her mouth with soap. She said, "Darn it," to that, but I did not tell on her.

When I was five, Aunt Cora Parker gave a "german" [a dance consisting of capriciously involved figures intermingled with waltzes] for her children at 323 State Street. I had no idea what this was, and I did not want to ask, but Hattie and I were allowed to go. This was a great concession, as we had gone nowhere on account of mourning for father. Hattie had, for several years, been a member of one of Mr. Hlaska's dancing classes in old Bleecker Hall down on Broadway. I had been down there in care of Missie Char, but I had never had lessons.

Aunt Cora had married my mother's brother, Amasa J. Parker Jr., and they had two boys and four girls. The oldest girl was Louisa, and because she was six weeks older than I, she always tried to put it all over me. So

Louisa was full of the preparations for the german. She and Grace had been members of Mr. Graves' dancing class, and even knew how to waltz, and as for the Lancers, Louisa said, "Only a child would not know how to dance that." Two or three times, several of us went up to be taught the Mother Goose Lancers by Aunt Cora. "Old King Cole" was for the back and forth figures, and the "Crooked Man" made the side steps, while "Mary, Mary Quite Contrary" was all hands round.

Louisa pushed me about and told me over and over that real dancers did not wear shoes [but] slippers, and [wore] dresses of tucked muslin and lace over pink silk slips. I had no slippers. A child my age was supposed to need high shoes for support, so I told Louisa that because she wore slippers her ankles had grown large. This was a body blow.

The great day came, and we were dressed, in the nursery, under the supervision of Mother, Missie Char, and Frieda. Hattie wore a white silk dress with a black hair bow and stockings, but she had slippers. It was her dancing school dress. I wore a French piqué with Hamburg flounces, white stockings, and buttoned black shoes. My hair was parted in the middle and curled with the long wooden stick by Frieda. I resented this torture, although I envied the girls with curls. Mine soon shook out.

I had a new doll named Grace, and Frieda had made for her what I so much wanted for myself, a pink silk slip with a scalloped flounce and a white overdress. She carried a fan and wore white kid slippers and white silk stockings, so she was really ready for the party. We drove up just at four, and as we went in the door, Louisa burst out at me in all her glory. "Baby brought her doll!" she shouted. "No one else brought a doll. You cannot dance with a doll." I followed Hattie upstairs, wishing both the doll and I had stayed home. I put the doll on the bed, and there she stayed through the afternoon.

The front room downstairs was arranged with the folding chairs against the walls. A drugget had been laid over the carpet. The favors were piled on two tables by the windows, and it looked like Christmas. [The chairs were grouped by twos, each pair] tied together by a ribbon, and Aunt Cora had a list of partners. Of course we all knew that Amasa 3rd would have Jane Kidd from the next house and Tuy Marvin would have Cornelia Battershall.

My fate was Learned Hand.[3] He wore a wide white linen collar, with a dark blue silk necktie. He had on Knickerbockers and silk stockings and patent leather pumps. He bowed in dancing school style, and we sat on two chairs next to the fireplace. He said, "Where is your doll?" Then he laughed.

Amasa 3rd led the german, and as the music started just then, I did not have to answer. As each four of couples went out, danced twice around the room, got their favors and gave them to others, I watched the bewildering scene with a sinking heart. Our turn came. We started out. We tangled up. Learned said, "You are walking all over my feet." Then, "I would rather dance with someone who knows how."

My blood was up at last. I had stood all that I could bear. I said, "We don't speak that way on Elk Street."

This fiasco of mine led Aunt Cora to beg mother to let me go to dancing school with her children. She stopped for me every week in Grandfather's carriage, and we drove down to the corner of Pearl and Steuben Streets where, on the top floor, in Murray Hall, Mr. Graves had his classes. We left our wraps and overshoes, usually the Aunt Libby's (that is, rubbers with long knitted tops) in a small room at the head of the stairs, and we went into the large room with iron supports down the center. There was an old square piano in one corner.

We stood up in a long line in front of Mr. Graves. He was tall and thin and had legs that seemed made of rubber. His daughter, Lily Graves, was a graceful dancer, and her father often had her dance in front of us to show us how to do it right. "One, two, and three," the first and second and third positions for the waltz, back and forth we went. . . .

We learned the plain and the Saratoga Lancers, which was longer and quite intricate, but both were necessary for our education. As a compliment to the invention of the telephone, Mr. Graves invented a dance called "The telephone." He would call out, "1 and 2 and 3 and 4 and 5 and 6 and 7 and 8; 1 and 2, 1 and 2 — 5 — 6 — 7 and 8." We also danced the "heel and toe polka," the boys hitting their heads very hard, and the plain polka, and the Schottische, as we grew more adept.[4] Then there was "Sally Waters a Sittin' in the Sun," in which you took hands facing your partner and slid forward and back, then three steps to the right and three to the left, then slid forward and back again. It was a rare day that, when we started to go home, we did not find our overshoes full of water. This was usually the work of the Miller twins or Hal and Sue Ransom or Johnny Douw. . . .

One of the excitements of Elk Street life was when the City Hall bell rang for a fire. There were volunteer firemen, and our neighbor at No. 4

Elk Street was one of them, Rufus King Townsend. . . . He would rush off while the bell was still ringing, clapping his helmet and heavy gloves as he ran. When the fire was out, the bell rang once. We carried fire cards with numbers on them and when we heard the bell ringing during church, it took all the frowns from parents to stop us from fishing out a card from our pocket.

. . . Number 4 had been built by Martin Van Buren during the years when he practiced law in Albany with his partner, Benjamin F. Butler, at 111 State Street. Both were members of the famous "Albany Regency," which controlled the Democrats for almost a generation. Mr. Van Buren did not live at No. 4, but afterwards his son, Smith Thompson Van Buren, lived there for a time. It was known as the "three-walled house." Old neighbors from Kinderhook came up to see Matty's three-walled house and were disappointed to find that it did not look different from the other houses. The astute Matty had used the wall of the house next door, so he only had to build three walls.

The house had fine woodwork and iron work. In my childhood it was owned and lived in by General and Mrs. Franklin Townsend. He was a brother of General Fred Townsend at No. 3, and of Dr. Howard Townsend at 21, and he was a cousin of Mr. Theodore Townsend at 39 Elk Street. Both General Frank and General Fred had been adjutant generals. One was a Democrat and the other a Republican.

Mrs. Frank Townsend had been Miss Anna King, a sister of Mr. Howard King, across Academy Park on Park Place, and of Mr. Rufus King at No. 2 Elk Street. Mrs. Townsend had red hair and quite a red temper, and she was much quoted. When Dean Norton of the Cathedral Chapel of All Saints rented No. 6 Elk Street, he had a doorplate with "The Deanery" on it. Mrs. Townsend felt that her Baptist beliefs in some way were outraged, so she named many of the other houses.

Beginning with her own, she called it "The Hellery." Mrs. Fred Townsend's was "The Bow-wow-ery" because of her little dogs. Mrs. James Kidd's at No. 7 was "The Waggery" as she also had dogs and Mrs. Kidd was a "Wag" herself. The Coopers' was "The Hennery," and also generally called "Cape Lookout." Our house, as reported by Jack, was "The Swellery." Miss Barnard's at No. 25 was "The Cattery" and the Hun houses were "The Pilleries," because of the three doctors. Bishop Doane at 29 Elk Street already had a doorplate with "Bishop's House" on it, but she called it "The Bishopry" and "The Popery." General Farnsworth's at No. 26 was known as "The Dudley Observatory."

The Paul Fenimore Cooper family at No. 10 Elk Street gave us unending interest. On the first warm day in spring, as we ran home from school, we could hear their voices as we crossed Hawk Street, and we knew the Coopers had moved out on their stoop. This was reached by a tall set of steps running sideways against that north wing of the Boy's Academy. From the street level there must have been about fifteen steps. The stoop itself held four wicker armchairs and two or three side chairs. Other Coopers sat on the steps.

There is a newspaper picture of this stoop taken in 1886. May Cooper and the dog Robin Adair are sitting on the steps, while Mrs. Cooper and Miss Sue are in chairs on the stoop. Miss Sue was the oldest, and then James Fenimore Cooper, then Miss Kate and our friend May. With such a vantage point, they swept the blocks. Nothing escaped them. We were sure they could see through the walls.

I admired Jim very much, and when he had typhoid and was very ill, I felt sad. We could talk across from the nursery window to May in her window on the west side, and once we had a string telephone with tin cans on the ends. We were sure we could hear just as well as with a real phone.

Mr. Paul Fenimore Cooper was a lawyer. He liked to walk around the streets at night with his hands behind his back. On Halloween we used to fill our mouths with water and run around the block. The first man you met, you would marry, [we believed]. But we gave it up because we always met only Mr. Cooper.

As we watched the doings in Elk Street from the nursery window, we often saw our rector of St. Peter's, Dr. Battershall, going in and out of the houses. Many of our neighbors were his parishioners. He walked very fast, and he ran up and down the steps. He never knew what time it was, and if he saw a light in a house late at night, he would suddenly run up the steps to make a call. Often the house was closed for the night, and sometimes an irate voice called down from an upper window to ask what was wanted.

The doctor lived in the rectory on the corner of Lodge Street and Maiden Lane. He had a son, Fletcher, and two daughters, Cornelia and Anna. His wife had died. Everyone was devoted to Dr. Battershall, and everyone understood his eccentricities and absent-mindedness.[5]

We sat in the fourth pew from the front on the left side of the main aisle at St. Peter's. Mother went in first, and I sat next to her so that she could keep an eye on me, and also so that I could lean against her during the sermon and take a nap. Hattie sat next to me, and Jack on the outside.

Dr. Battershall sat on the right side of the Chancel behind the Lectern.

The door into the vestry was on the opposite side. In the hymn before the sermon, the doctor seemed to watch the choir very closely. During the second verse, he would pull out his enormous handkerchief with his right hand and blow his nose violently. Then, with a rather puzzled air, he would try to return it to his pocket, but always unsuccessfully. Casting anxious looks at the vestry door towards the last words of the second verse, he half turned to get a better look. The third verse saw him, with a quick move, gather his surplice, dive out of his seat, and make for the door. Just as the "Amen" was finished, the doctor, with an abstracted air, would turn the corner of the stalls, and, sermon in hand, would hurriedly mount the four steps to the pulpit.

The old walnut pulpit had had a gilt Gothic light, and this had been transferred to the new pulpit, given by Miss Tibbits. The first thing the doctor did was to adjust the light so that it struck his manuscript right, and this took the time when we were settling back comfortably to listen. He then laid his glasses on the extreme edge on one side and his watch on the other. The enormous handkerchief hung down like a sheet. I never remember anything falling off. Looking at the congregation as if he was worried about something, he would suddenly give what Jack called his "Sermon smile," a smile of great sweetness like a guileless child, then, leaning forward far out over the pulpit, he would telescope back and read the text.

Sometimes I slipped down on a footstool with my head on mother's slippery silk lap. I could look at the high ceiling and the blackness up there in the deep shadows, with little splashes of color that came from the small windows in the clerestory. One splash moved slowly along the pillar behind the pulpit when the sun was out. I wondered if this shadowed roof was the "Cimmerian darkness" about which Dr. Battershall sometimes talked. I had no idea and never asked. . . .

In the old days the silver offertory plates had no lining, and it was fun to twist a quarter and make it twirl and fall with a clatter. The solemn members of the vestry sometimes smiled. Once when Jack and Hattie had protested to Mother not to give me a quarter to put in the plate, I came prepared. When the moment arrived, I produced a large pearl button twisted from Jack's underdrawers and hidden in my cuff. The following fall when we returned, the offertory plates had red velvet mats, and so the coin spinning ended. Jack timed the sermons, and behind us Chancellor Pierson rattled his keys, and Harry Pierson sighed and sighed.

One summer Dr. Battershall went to Europe and was expected to return by a certain Sunday in September. But when we came to church, there was a strange clergyman. Later he announced, "Your beloved rector will not be with you today. He is down at the bar and cannot get up." [6]

Mr. Harmon Pumpelly was a Warden when I first remember, and it was tempting to recite the jingle about his fall in the jelly when he passed the plate. [7] I liked to watch Mrs. Pumpelly in the third pew across the aisle. I was often told what a great belle and beauty she had been. According to legend, she had been courted by Martin Van Buren and her cousin, Harmanus Bleecker, but she had chosen plain Mr. Pumpelly, a widower with two daughters from Owego. . . .

[Another parishioner, Orlando Meads, had a garden with a very fine pear tree at his home on Pine Street.] One day Mr. Meads arranged a basket of pears for his friends the Pumpellys. But Mrs. Pumpelly, not caring for pears, sent the basket to the Doanes with her card. The Doanes were just leaving town, and not wishing to have the pears wasted, they sent them to Miss Sarah Barnard. She was afraid to eat pears, so she sent them over to the Kips. They were grateful to Mrs. Kidd at No. 7 Elk Street for many pleasant drives in her carriage, so they sent them to Mrs. Kidd, who was Mr. Pumpelly's daughter. She at once recognized the basket and pears, and sent them back to the Pumpellys with her card.

One Elk Street was built about 1795 by Dudley Walsh. Miss Catharine Walsh married Mr. Daniel Barnard and bought out the interest of the others in the house. Mr. Barnard was a widower with a daughter, Cora, who married Mr. Gilbert Wilson, an able businessman and a vestryman at St. Peter's. After their return from their wedding trip, [Mr. Wilson] acted strangely, and finally jumped out of a window. He was found in the early morning and carried into the basement, where he died a few days later. [8] His affairs were in good order, but it was just before the Civil War, and there were many troubles in the business world. [In fact,] St. Peter's was dubbed "The Church of the Holy Bankrupts," as there were so many failures among its members. . . .

After Mrs. Pumpelly died, No. 1 Elk Street was rented for many years, usually to someone in the State service. About 1896 Mrs. George Pratt, née Tibbits, and a cousin of Mrs. Pumpelly, returned to Albany with her daughter Bessie. We had been brought up on tales of Bessie. She was always a handful.

At this time she was married to her second husband, Count de Gasquet James.

A choice subject for Elk Street was where and how the count had found his title. He was from New Orleans, and many said it was an old French title. Others thought it was papal. The count did not appear much that winter, but Mrs. Pratt had a cozy time with Dr. Lewis Balch, and Bessie and her four children seemed happy too. . . .

After the death of the Count and Mrs. Pratt, Bessie married again, about 1910. Her third husband was Duke Heinrich zu Mecklenburg-Schwerin, who had been ousted from Germany for irregularities in the Army. He was about 28 and she was about 60 at the time of this ill-fated marriage, which did not last long. After a divorce, he married Mrs. Lily Oelric Martin of California. Bessie died many years ago. . . . [She] had been a romantic figure to us, but not to our parents. . . .

CHAPTER 8

WHEN SUNDAY SERVICES were over, we sometimes went down to call on old Mrs. Corning, but we generally drove home with Grandmother. Morrissey would be waiting by the corner of Lodge Street, and when he saw us, he would drive to one of the two wide slate stones that bridged the deep gutters. In fact, every house had one of these slates for carriages. The slabs must have been all of ten feet square.

State Street was paved with cobbles, possibly the same cobbles which had been laid under the sharp eyes of the "Yankee invader," Elkanah Watson, who was chased by the irate housewives with their brooms for making such a mess and letting dust into their houses. The crown of the street was very high, and a carriage might easily tip over into the gutter but for these flag stones. The crosswalk from St. Peter's corner to the other side of State Street had been named, when laid, "The Church and State Walk" because the State then owned the old building on the corner of Lodge Street, and the expense of laying the crosswalk had been shared by the State and St. Peter's. As the years went on, State Street was graded twice. It was this grading that left foundations weakened, as in the case of the second St. Peter's, when the walls cracked and the church was considered unsafe.

Big State Street was very interesting in those days, with the horsecars and the market on Wednesdays and Saturdays. Market wagons or sleighs lined up early in the morning on both sides of the horsecar tracks. The horses were generally faced toward the sidewalks, so that the cars would not frighten them. Many careful drivers unharnessed the horses and stalled them in one of the numerous stables around Washington Avenue, so that they could feed and rest after the long pull over bad roads. It was a quaint and unusual sight, and gave a foreign look to the city. Boxes and baskets of fruits and vegetables were piled in the carts and hung from the sides, and the farmers' families perched on the high uncomfortable seats. They went off shopping on Pearl Street or Washington Avenue.[1]

Old Joe Clark, with his one eye, had a provision store on the corner of State and Lodge Streets. He was a well known character. [He would stand for hours] bargaining with the farmers, carrying off boxes and crates of supplies to resell at large profits. Regularly every year Joe was arrested for selling game out of season, but just as regularly he swore they were curlew [for which] there was no closed season.

The upper blocks from Pearl to Eagle Streets had a few shops, but many private houses. There was much objection to the market, as it left litter of all kinds, and straw that the winds blew over onto the houses and sidewalks. So at last this relic, which had existed since the early days when beaver and other furs were traded for beads and cloth, was moved away to Hudson Avenue. It was the end of a picturesque but dirty custom.

The horsecars were small compared to the modern car, and the worn cotton-covered wooden seats ran the length of the car. The floor was covered with straw, and in the winter, a stove in the center of the car provided heat, but also singed the straw, causing it to give out a burned smell. The horses were sad-looking objects, as they strained to pull the cars up the hill. They started from Broadway with two horses. At Pearl Street, another team was waiting. While passengers got on, a man snapped a long hook onto an iron ring on the pole, thus attaching the second team. There was hardly a minute's delay.

The hauling of the granite blocks for the new Capitol was a sorry sight. The first stone had weighed three tons. The low, flat cars sometimes had a dozen horses straining to the worst pull from Pearl to Eagle Street. The driver stood on the front stone, whip in hand, touching up the horses he could reach and calling out what were supposed to be encouraging words. It was a brutal sight on a slippery day, or in the torrid heat of summer, and it seemed an almost hopeless task. What is done so easily now with gasoline or electric equipment was then as big an undertaking as the building of the Pyramids. The new Capitol was truly built at the sacrifice of animal flesh and blood.[2]

An old print of 1805 shows the house built by Mayor Philip Schuyler Van Rensselaer about 1790. He was the brother of the last Patroon. A generous and loyal citizen, he was a member of St. Peter's Church to which he gave the handsome offertory plates as well as the christening bowl. The old print of the house shows a fine Palladian window over the front door, but subsequent grading of the street changed the front, and it had to be underpinned with a basement and steep stone steps.

Mrs. Van Rensselaer died in 1855, and the house was sold to Mr. Erastus Corning, who lived across the street. He gave it to his son, Erastus Corning Jr. An office with a separate entrance was added at the basement level. It had quaint, wire window screens with pictures of woods and animals on them. When the house was pulled down in 1895 to make place for the Ten Eyck Hotel, the bricks had mellowed to a most lovely tone. Today they would be appreciated and eagerly sought after, but probably they were thrown in some dump.

In later years Erastus Corning Jr. married my mother's sister, as his second wife, so I was often at the house playing with her children, Parker, Harriet and Edwin Corning. It was a beautiful house, with a garden at the rear, and there we played croquet in the summer, and in the winter coasted on a toboggan slide. The garden had a high brick wall along Chapel Street side and down Maiden Lane. The brick stable was on the corner of Chapel Street. For many years Wheeler was in charge of the horses and carriages used by the family.

In the rear of the garden was a grotto with several water spouts cascading down over the stones from unexpected bronze mouths and spouts. Several carp swam about, and Aunt Mary would call the fish by name. . . . She always insisted the fish knew their names, and "Sammy Tilden," "Horatio Seymour," and a monster named "Roscoe Conkling" would splash around while she threw bread.[3]

When the front door was opened, guests were greeted by a most delicious smell of flowers. Gray, the Scottish gardener in charge of the greenhouses at the farm, delighted [in bringing up] his choicest blooms and potted plants for the house. Every room was filled with vases and china tubs of flowers. Sometimes, when giving a dinner, they had the table arranged so that a sunken zinc tank was in the center holding water. Around the edge were Farleyens ferns and lovely orchids, and small gold fish swam around tiny rocks and islands.

The house had deep window seats and wide windows. Over the doors, on the lower floor, were candle sockets so that, for special occasions, the house was well lighted. The library upstairs was on the corner of State and Chapel Streets, and the clock in the top of the Savings Bank across the street seemed very close. Uncle Erastus had a large desk at the window looking up State Street, and a pair of opera glasses lay ready to use when someone interesting appeared in the street. . . .

In the old attic, where we often played on rainy days, was kept an enormous English cheese. Once a year, with great ceremony, Uncle Erastus would carry a large bottle of brandy up there after Sunday dinner and pour it into a hole in the center of the cheese, making it very rich, and, it seemed to my childish eyes, rather mouldy and smelly. At the rear of the house there were large additions of rooms with bay windows. It was from one of them that Parker and Harriet shot at the gilded fish and pumpkin that was the historic weather vane on the steeple of the Second Presbyterian Church.[4]

When I went to play with the Cornings in the afternoon, we sometimes took out the two velocipedes, one a high red one, the other a low blue one. We pushed them to Joe Clark's corner and started even. The pedals turned around wildly, and we would sweep the wide curve into Chapel Street. . . . The velocipedes would slow up as we jolted by what we called George Ayres stable.

George was the typical-looking race-course veteran of that period, long and lean with a drooping mustache. This stable belonged to the Cornings and was the racing stable. George made a picturesque figure as he trotted out one or another of the high-steppers in his sulky. Almost every morning George came over to talk horse with Uncle Erastus in the cheerful library. He was always chewing hard and usually had a story to tell of winning some bet on the speedway or Western Avenue.[5]

The speedway was a prolongation of Washington Avenue, one of the few soft roads. In winter the races were held on Western Avenue. "We went 240 on the plank road," George would announce, "and we picked this up for our own use." I remember the names of the two horses, "Wilque" and "Harrietta." The stable itself was a narrow yellow brick structure, but it was interesting to us because tucked away up behind was a small cock fighting theater. Here a few well chosen sporting friends would quietly gather in the late evenings. Of course, gossip about it reached our ears, and we longed to be able to go and find out about it, but I, for one, never did.

This old Van Rensselaer house [the Corning home at the time H.P.H. was writing] was well shaded. There was, in fact, a double row of trees. After the first ones were planted, the sidewalk was doubled, and so another row was planted. The pedestrian slowly meandering up State Street was protected by the shade, and the street was made attractive even in the hottest weather. It is a very different corner now, with the blinding sun scorching down and all charm gone. It might be a street in any city anywhere instead of old Albany.

A bow window had been added over the front door of the Corning house, and although it was not in keeping with the architecture of the house, it was a wonderful place for seeing all that was going on from below Pearl Street to Eagle Street. The corner of State and Pearl Streets was famous as the site of the house where Philip Livingston, the Signer, had lived and where he had planted the elm tree. . . . [The Tweddle building stood on that corner when H.P.H. was a child.]

In the Tweddle building was Tweddle Hall. To reach the hall you had to climb two flights of stairs. There was always a strong smell of gas coming from the large chandelier. This was a wonderful, dazzling chandelier to my childish eyes, with its glass danglers. We went to the Tweddle Hall to see an amateur performance of the "Frog Opera." "O' Ma what can the matter be / boys throwing stones and trying to flatten me."[6] . . .

The Tweddle Hall was burned on a cold winter morning, and the Corning house escaped by a miracle. We stood in the snow regardless of school time, watching the vain attempts of the firemen to reach the flames, with totally inadequate water pressure and hose lines far too short. The firemen risked their lives as the walls fell about them. Edward Ryan, Wheeler, George Ayres, and many volunteers worked with the firemen to save the Corning house by keeping the roof soaked. . . . No trace survives to tell of the park, of Mayor Van Rensselaer, and his grandfather Philip Livingston, except a bronze plaque to Philip the Signer.

On the lower corner — the corner of State and South Pearl Streets — was the Staats house. Originally there were two houses. The upper house was the birth place of General Philip Schuyler and the winter residence of his aunt, Madame Schuyler of "The Flatts," the subject of Mrs. Grant's famous book, *An American Lady*. In iron letters the word "Anno" ran across the front of the Staats house, just under the eaves. Below the upper windows was the date 1667. The Schuylers' house was pulled down when the narrow lane which led to the pastures and had been laid out by the cows was widened and became the modern South Pearl Street.

It is sad that this Schuyler-Staats relic had to go. The Philip Schuylers would probably be surprised to know that Fort Crailo, the house in which they were married by Domine Frelinghuysen, which was owned by Mrs. Schuyler's father, has been restored. It is owned by the State of New York, as is also the house the Philip Schuylers built, "The Pastures." Their house at Saratoga will probably be included in the National Park at Saratoga Battlefield. [What H.P.H. predicts here has occurred.]

The fine old Stevenson house on State Street just above South Pearl Street was removed long before my day, as was the gable-ended house of Harmanus Wendell, the great fur trader. In that house his daughter Elizabeth was married to Jacob Bleecker. Their son was Harmanus Bleecker, whose bequest to Albany made first the Hall and then the library possible.

I remember the double brick house at 102 State Street very well. It was built in 1825 and bought in 1828 by Erastus Corning Sr., known as the "Old Gentleman." He had died before I was born, and it was to call on the "Old Lady" that we were taken after church on Sundays. Michael Rush would open the door, greet us warmly, and usher us into the front room on the right. I thought for years that Michael was called "Rush" because the old lady was always rushing him to do something.

I was very much afraid of old Mrs. Corning. She dressed in black and wore a white cap with long white streamers, which tossed about as she talked, and she talked very hard. She would motion my sister and me to sit on two little mahogany chairs in the back of the room, so that we had no chance to watch what was going on in State Street. She had one of those street looking-glasses, called "Busybody," so that you could know who was coming.

The fascinating lady who made use of this glass was the daughter-in-law, Mrs. Edwin Weld Corning. Her husband had died when quite young but she lived with her father and mother-in-law. She sat in the window with the looking-glass and kept track of her many admirers, deciding which one she cared to see. . . .

. . . Back of the house there was a little garden with an entrance to the stable which fronted on Howard Street. Some years later this stable was turned into the Fire Protection headquarters, and the firemen used to let us come in there and slide down the pole from the upper floor. The slide pole was then a new idea. For many years the old Corning house was the Albany Club, but now this has vanished and a modern Huyler's occupies the site.

Old Mrs. Corning used to drive in a "Clarence." . . . Hers was lined with dark red satin buttoned down, and it had swings at the side of each seat for [passengers] to hang [their] arm in. It held two on the back seat, and there was a small seat for a slim person opposite. A pair of very fine horses took the old lady for her daily drives, or down to the farm, where she had her own rooms on the ground floor, with the faithful Jane [her maid] in close attendance.

Near the corner of Lodge Street was the house where Mother first went to school. It was run by Mrs. Brinckerhoff. When Mother was ten, she threw her wet slate sponge at Aunt Kitty Gansevoort. When she went home, she carried a letter to her mother from Mrs. Brinckerhoff stating why "Anna had had to be disciplined." Grandfather thought Mother needed more discipline, so the next fall she was sent to the Female Academy. She graduated from there.

At 112 State Street was the comfortable old house of one of Albany's real characters, Colonel Walter Church, the grandson of General Philip Schuyler. His father, John Barker Church, had fought a duel with Aaron Burr; it was, in fact, Burr's first duel. Colonel Church had "The Begum's Eye," which was said to be an inheritance of the Schuylers from the Staats family.[7]

The Colonel was a noticeable figure wherever he went, walking or driving his pair in a wide double buggy. He swore picturesquely, and the black words slipped out so glibly that it took a moment to realize what he had said. His stories were as racy as his life. He had had many love affairs, but he never had married. His house was the last one here, as far as I know, where the table cloth was removed before dessert, leaving the lovely bare table with its candles and silver.

He bought many of the Anti-Rent farms, both on the east and west sides of the Hudson, from the Van Rensselaers. He often had troubles and always carried weapons when he drove out in the Helderberg country. He was the brave man who built the "Kushaqua" Hotel out at Altamont, but although it was attractive, and well placed, it was not a success. It was before the automobile age and was hard to reach by horse and carriage. . . .

      ❦   ❦   ❦

We were often taken to Geological Hall, on the upper corner of State and Lodge Streets. It was built in 1797 and called State Hall. It was used until the old Capitol was built.[8] There was a skeleton of an elk. Jack said it had roamed in our garden and so Elk Street got its name. I believed the story for many years. . . .

Mrs. John Tayler Cooper lived at 134 State Street. It was a fine old house, built in 1832, and had a portico supported by tall brown stone pillars. The mahogany doors and marble mantels were lovely. Mrs. Cooper was a beautiful old lady with white hair, and she went driving every afternoon. Her sleigh was especially picturesque, with its heavy fur robes, their long tails hanging off the back. . . .

Across State Street, at No. 113, lived Miss Cynthia and Miss Kate Dexter, and the doings at Mrs. Cooper's were a source of never-failing interest to Miss Cynthia in particular. It was said that she also kept glasses in order to see who went driving with them. Miss Cynthia wore soft pastel colors. In the afternoon, Mr. John Olcott was apt to drop in on his way home from the bank, a rather out-of-the-way route to Arbor Hill. . . .

State Street is one of the widest as well as most historic streets in the United States. St. Peter's Church is now the single thread that links it directly to the early history. All other links have vanished, and even St. Peter's is the third building and not on the same site as the little stone chapel built in 1715, at the base of the Fort, and called "Queen Anne's Chapel of the Onondawgus." . . .

As one stands on Pinxter Hill, now covered by the State Capitol, and looks down, a vivid imagination is not needed to recall the many outstanding events that have made the street famous. . . . [H.P.H. narrates stories of Albany's past. Included are events featuring Pieter Stuyvesant, Father Jogues, Peter Schuyler, and William Johnson. She comments on Albany's role in the various wars.]

My first remembrance of big State Street is that I was perched on my father's shoulder, and there were crowds all about us. I think it must have been a Fourth of July celebration, as it was hot weather and I wore a white dress. We stood at the foot of the elm tree walk up to the old Capitol. Bands played, and no doubt the Albany Burgesses Corp was part of the procession, having marched from their headquarters in old Bleecker Hall on Broadway.

In later years Major James C. Woodward was in command, and the drum-major was our envy as he juggled his baton. The heat of their monstrous, bearskin shakos must have been appalling. They wore red coats. In summer, they wore white trousers and in winter, blue ones. In the evenings the city had fireworks at the foot of State Street and all horse-drawn vehicles, including the horsecars, were forbidden from Eagle Street down. Families brought stepladders and sat on the steps, the smallest child on the top step. . . .

The history of Albany is largely written on State Street, the Yonkheer's Straat of the Dutch era, Prince Street of the British regime, and first Deer Street and then State Street in the last 175 years. Surely this street has an honored record.

CHAPTER 9

M
Y SISTER WAS THE OLDEST of the sixteen first cousins in our family. In that Victorian era she was supposed to set an example to us all, but this somehow did not work out just that way. Hattie was quite a tomboy with the three boy cousins who came right after her in age — Amasa J. Parker, 3rd, known as Amboy; his brother, Louis Parker; and Selden E. Marvin Jr., known as Tuy. I came along about in the middle of the sixteen, sandwiched by Louise Parker and Parker Corning.

Judge and Mrs. Parker, our grandparents, lived at 143 Washington Avenue, and they made their home a center for all of us.[1] . . . It was a great day when Grandmother, in her carriage, stopped at our house and invited us to luncheon. That meant that the eight oldest would be included, and that Mary Archer, the old cook, would make everything we liked.

Fortunately, we all agreed on this momentous question. First we had soup, then a large beefsteak, beautifully cooked, served with the delicious scalloped potatoes, as only Mary ever cooked them. There might be asparagus from the garden or new peas. There were always many dozens of hot biscuits, and at the last, ice cream and sponge cakes.

Amboy had beautiful manners, and he sat at Grandmother's right and escorted her in and out of the dining room. Grandfather undertook Tuy and Louis on each side of him, as they were apt to get into heated disputes. One day the dispute was about horseradish. Tuy said beefsteak needed horseradish to bring out the flavor. So Grandfather told William Tracy, the old butler, to bring out a jar of horseradish, and he helped Tuy to a large portion. We then waited for Tuy to put some on the steak, but he did not want to put on much, and Louis began to jibe him. In the end Grandfather had to bring peace and have the jar of horseradish removed. Tuy had been bluffing.

The boys and William were always at swords' points, as they stole everything they could lay their hands on from his closets in the pantry. He would not give up the keys. The boys tickled him until he gave them up in despair.

After luncheon, Grandmother took a short nap on the sofa in the third room, and Nelly, her maid, covered her with a knitted afghan and came out with her finger at her lip, hoping we would keep quiet. Grandfather took his forty winks in his large leather chair in his study.

Promptly at three the coachman Morrissey would drive to the door from the stable on Dove Street at the end of the garden. There were two carriages, but the one generally used was a "Democrat," with a place in front beside the coachman, and seats for four inside. The sides were of glass, [which] rattled, and the wheels had no rubber tires, so the combined noises as we bumped along made conversation hopeless.

Nelly would be waiting in the hall with Grandmother's many wraps. Even in summer she wore a heavy coat and a lace scarf and often an extra cape, if a breeze came up. Her black bonnet was tied with a bow under her chin, and she wore gloves. She carried a bag full of handkerchiefs, glasses, a bottle of something in case she felt faint, and a fan in the summer or a muff in winter. In fact, Grandfather sometimes became very impatient and would say, "Come, come, Hetty, the horses are being kept waiting." Then he gave her his arm, Nelly stood by the open door, and William hastened to open the carriage door.

Finally they were settled, and Morrissey said, "Get-up" to the horses, and they drove off up Washington Avenue to Lark Street, and then up State Street to the park. Morrissey drove around the park by the same route every day. He had made a map of the park many years earlier, and he kept it in a pocket of the carriage, though it seems impossible that he ever could forget the route.

They went in by the old entrance, as there was none then at what we called Knox Street and is now known as Northern Boulevard. They drove past the pedestal, on which the bust of good Dr. Armsby sits, and which was called the "Jack-in-the-box statue," and down around the lake, and up on ice cream hill where the ice cream was sold in the summer, and then past where the unfortunate deer were fenced in, then over to see the sad-looking Israelites watch Moses smiting the rock, and when the carriage reached a certain tree behind the swings, Grandfather [would] tap on the glass and say, "Now we will go home." Morrissey, looking completely surprised, would turn to the left and out by State Street, and down to Dove Street and across to Washington Avenue, and home.

We knew all this, and arranged our games to suit the drive. We generally played games according to the weather. If it was fine, we played in the garden, and often Nelly kept us enthralled when she told stories in the summer house at the end of the garden. She sang, too:

> O' where will the wedding supper be
> Ah hum?
> Down by yonder apple tree,

A slice of bread and a cup of tea
Ah hum.

In the house, we started Hare and Hounds the moment the carriage drove from the door, and Nelly played with us. She was the fleetest of us all.

One afternoon we decided to try something new, to dress Amboy in Grandmother's clothes and send him out to beg. Grandmother kept her gardening outfit near the side door, and Nelly produced a shade hat, spectacles, gloves, and a cloak, so Amboy was well disguised. He carried a basket. Hattie drilled him as to what he was to say.

We crowded to the door as he went down the steps and started for the next house above, where Mr. and Mrs. Bradford R. Wood lived. We watched from the window of Grandfather's study and saw him vanish into the doorway. In about five minutes, he emerged with a bundle and a book in his basket. As he came up the steps, we kept ourselves hidden for fear someone might suspect. Amasa displayed 25 cents, two bananas, and an old Albany directory. We were delighted and started him off to go to Mrs. Alfred B. Street's on the corner of Dove Street, when suddenly Morrissey appeared just turning the corner of Dove Street. It was too late.

Amasa was very quick, and when the carriage stopped, he was there to open the door and offer to help Grandmother. He walked beside her carrying his basket and telling his tale of troubles. Grandfather gave him several careful looks as they progressed toward the steps and we heard him say, "Very strange, very strange case. So you're a poor maiden lady all alone in the world with four children to support? That needs looking into."

His eyes twinkled, and we knew the game was up. All of us crowded out, much to Grandmother's bewilderment. She was going to give him something from a box she kept in her desk downstairs. As Nelly helped her with her wraps, Grandmother did not recognize the clothes Amasa was wearing, and only remarked, in her kindly way, that no doubt we had had a nice afternoon together, and she hoped none of us were tired.

Sometimes on Saturday morning Grandmother went shopping, and usually one of the aunts went along to help her. Several of us often went along too, and took turns sitting on the front seat next to Morrissey. In those uncomplicated days before motors or traffic rules, we did not have to bother as to which side of the street we stopped at. The only rule was to drive on the right of the streets; we could stop anywhere.

That was fortunate, as Grandmother did not get out of the carriage during her last years. One of the aunts would go into the store and have someone bring out the samples. Miss Taafe at the lace counter in Whitney's made Grandmother's caps. She would hastily pick out samples of tulle, lace, or ruches, and get into the carriage and have a long conference with Grandmother.

If we had any cash between us, we would vanish into Huyler's for one of the new ice cream sodas. Huyler had started a new era. The counters had marble tops, the candies were lifted by small tongs or scoops, the syrups were in large glass bottles with metal stoppers, and we were enchanted by the pretty baskets, with gay bows, and the lace mats and balls of tin foil. Huyler's had bright red window shades. It was on Pearl Street near Maiden Lane.

Next to it was the glass case with Dr. Woodbury's enormous foot, covered with various plasters. Next to Whitney's was Martineau's glove store. Miss Grady wet her fingers and fitted our gloves. You had to plant your elbow on a cushion while she coaxed on the always-too-tight gloves of those days. Mr. Martineau walked about the shop all day with his hands behind his back.

Both Whitney's and Myer's had cash boys, and the call of "cash here" brought boys scurrying to carry the bundle and return the change. Myer's first started the Lamson cash carrier by which the money and sales slip were placed in a wooden ball and hoisted onto a runway, which magically took the ball to the desk where it was emptied and then the correct change was returned. It was fascinating to watch this performance, as the ball always seemed to know which runway to take, and at which hole to drop down. But we found we never could take the dogs into those stores as they tried to chase the balls, although they were entirely out of reach. They barked and jumped with the excitement of dozens of balls rolling around all at once.

I remember when Grandmother bought the new stair and upper hall carpet. She made endless trips to Van Gaasbeek's carpet store on Pearl Street. Mr. Van Gaasbeek himself came out to the carriage bringing bales and rolls and samples out to show Grandmother, who sat surrounded with curtain and wallpaper samples. On the opposite seat was a mass of papers with notes of heights and widths of windows. Sometimes we stopped on lower big State Street at Mr. Johnny Crapo's, where beautiful linens and the Italian towels with long fringes were sold. Mr. Crapo always had something to show that was "superbly unique."

On Broadway Grandmother often stopped at Templeton's woodenware shop. He sold all kinds of baskets. Opposite Templeton's was Cotrell and Leonard's, where Grandmother's furs were repaired, and where she bought her new coats or capes. Holland Terrill sold things that Morrissey needed for the stable, and further along, opposite the Delavan House, was Reid's. This was one of a row of shabby-looking wooden buildings with two steps up from the sidewalk, where we bought worsted and knitting needles and new patterns for crochet work. Spelman's, at 532 Broadway, was a popular place to buy toys and fireworks for the glorious Fourth of July. . . .

After all this shopping, we knew our patience would be rewarded, and that our last stop would be at Mrs. Maidment's bakery on the corner of Pearl and Steuben Streets. Grandmother would say, "My darlings are getting tired, so you may tell Morrissey where to go." Morrissey knew as well as we did, and the minute the horses stopped, we would tumble out in a rush, and burst into the shop.

Mrs. Maidment was a dumpy little woman with a kindly smile for us, and she talked as if she had a hot potato in her mouth. She would lift up her hands and say, "God bless you my dears. I have been waiting for you, all Mrs. Parker's grandchildren. Now, what will you choose?"

There were large raisin buns, cream puffs, eclairs, sheets of fresh ginger bread, cookies, jumbles, doughnuts, and all kinds of pies. We knew we must not be too greedy, but it was hard to choose one thing out of so many. Generally there was a large order for Grandmother, and Mrs. Maidment would seriously consider which one of us could be trusted to carry out the fairy ginger bread without falling down and breaking it.

Mrs. Maidment owned the wooden forms for the old New Year's cakes. They were said to have been the ones owned by Sanders Lansing, who also made the old *dood koeks* for the funerals. The forms were heavy and clumsy and evidently hand-carved, but they were valuable. My brother tried to persuade Mrs. Maidment to let him buy them, on condition that she should use them during her life, but she would not agree. I have heard two or three different stories as to their fate.[2]

Grandmother gave away several baskets of cakes on Saturdays, and besides all she bought from the bakery, she superintended the cake-making after breakfast on Saturday mornings. Her own maid, first Nelly and then Johanna, actually mixed the cake dough and watched the baking and then laid the cakes out in the front basement room. The icing was laid on later. There was always gold and silver cake, made from her family recipes at Portsmouth, and there were crullers and the ginger cookies, especially for Grandfather. A basket of cakes and biscuits was ready for each family for Sunday.

It was a long table in the dining room every Sunday night at seven o'clock. If Grandfather had had his way, it would have been limited to a family party, but Grandmother was hospitable and welcomed the stranger within the gate, as well as lonely souls to whom the supper would give pleasure. Uncle Abe and Aunt Kitty Lansing were always counted as members of the family as they had grown up with the family.

After supper Uncle Tuy led Grandmother out on his arm, and they marched down the hall to the door of the middle room. She settled in her low chair near the fire with her daughters around her. Grandfather and the uncles gathered in the little writing room, where Grandfather had his books and desk and deep leather chair and a sofa.

We children played in the hall. It offered many kinds of amusements and was a fine place for leapfrog. Louis and I liked to square off as John L. Sullivan and Paddy Ryan, two popular prize fighters of that period, and the staircase made a wonderful gallery for the audience.

There was always a loud call for Louis to preach his sermon, and then Louis took to the staircase as a pulpit. It was always the same sermon, but was ever new to us. He began with his text, "Blessed is the man who sitteth on a tack, for he shall surely rise." Then he waxed eloquent about the unfair distribution of riches in an unjust world, and his peroration was made with waving of arms and a shout of "There is the dude with twenty pairs of trousers and the poor working girl with none."

Finally, one of the aunts would come out and say, "Come children, Grandfather is ready for the hymns." We would smooth our hair and rumpled dresses and follow rather reluctantly to the third room, where the piano, with an aunt ready to play the accompaniments, would be waiting. Grandmother [would be] seated on the sofa, and as soon as a hymn was chosen, one of us would [open the hymnal for her to the right place]. The boys liked the Moody and Sankey hymns, "Pull for the shore" and "Jewels, Precious Jewels" and "the Armour Bearer."

One evening Grandmother asked a guest to play and sing. She played in an unusual style, lifting her hands high up from the keyboard, and she sang in a very nasal voice. It was funny, and Grace Parker got under the piano and pinched the pianist's feet on the pedals. She gave a loud shriek and jumped up and said, "Mrs. Parker, one of your grandchildren has pinched me; she has very bad manners." But Grace had crawled out and vanished, and none of the rest of us could be guilty, as we had been in plain sight, singing like little angels.

Grandfather would come in at the end and say, "Now Mary, give us a real tune." Aunt Mary would crash into "Yankee Doodle" or the "My country 'tis of thee," played in two keys, and Grandfather would applaud. So the evening [would] end.

Grandmother frowned heavily on gossip. She liked news, real news of outside happenings. When Edna Lyell's book called *The Autobiography of a Slander* was published, she ordered twenty copies from Mr. Edwin Ellis's book store on Pearl Street. Aunt Kate saw them, and asked Grandmother what she was going to do with them. Grandmother said, "I am going to direct an envelope with my card in it to twenty people. Christmas is coming and Nelly will tie them up with paper and ribbon, and William Tracy will go out, on the box seat, with Morrissey and deliver them to twenty deserving friends, of whom my children will make four. I trust they, as well as their children, will read and learn the lesson."[3]

As I look back at the Sunday night suppers at Grandfather's, I think we were a very politically-minded family. Almost always some form of pending legislation or some sins of the opposite party would be the topic. We had only one black sheep in the fold, but we loved him nevertheless. He was General Marvin, known to us all as "Uncle Tuy." He had married my mother's youngest surviving sister, Katharine Langdon Parker.

Mother was devoted to him, but from her seat on Grandfather's right she would sigh and say, "He is such a fine man but he even swallowed Blaine." Grandmother would lean sympathetically over towards Uncle Tuy on her right, pat his hand and say, "He will see the light and vote for President Cleveland next time. He must realize the shoddy material used by his party ever since Lincoln died." Uncle Tuy would smile at her and keep on drinking the five cups of strong tea that he consumed every Sunday night.

Grandfather was a very handsome man, sitting quietly at the foot of the table and listening to the discussions. He had been twice the Democratic candidate for governor before the Civil War, and had been defeated by Governors Morgan and King. He had also been offered the post of Minister to Russia by President Buchanan, but he was away when the letter came, and Grandmother replied by telegram for him and declined. It was too far, and the children must be educated in the United States. I do not know what he said on his return. In his early years he had been a member of Congress, in the Jackson administration, and his letters, now in the Library of Congress, make interesting reading, particularly his account of the famous ball in the Russian Legation in Georgetown.

Grandfather was 80 years old on June 2nd, 1887, and Mother had a large dinner for him at which Bishop Doane read an original poem. Later there was a reception for about one hundred more friends. We younger children were allowed to come to the reception and to stay until ten o'clock, but as that covered the late supper, we were satisfied. The piazzas and garden were strung with Chinese paper lanterns, and Jack undertook, with success, the long and trying job of having the candles lighted.

It was a fine but hot evening and Fromo [H.P.H.'s dog] waded happily in the fountain with his ball, probably wondering about this invasion of his domain. There was an orchestra in the china room, so we could dance. Many old friends had come from out of town. There were no end of judges and retired judges, but I remember it as a happy evening.

In the house next above Grandfather's, at 149 Washington Avenue, lived the Bradford R. Wood family. Mr. Wood had once been our minister to Denmark. I do not remember him, but Mrs. Wood and her daughter, Miss Libby Wood, and Tom Wood are all vivid memories. It was a sad household. Miss Libby was melancholic, and every afternoon, just at four, she would emerge from the house, wrapped in a heavy gray shawl which almost covered her face too. She would walk around the block, neither speaking nor bowing to anyone. Her brother Tom, or "Tee Hee" as he was called, was another matter. He was a tall, large man who made terrible faces as he walked around and muttered to himself.

Once when we climbed the fence and slid down the terraces in the Woods' garden, Tom suddenly appeared on the piazza. We had thought he was in the Poughkeepsie Asylum,[4] or we would never have ventured over. We had been forbidden ever to go in there. So we were well caught, and Tom began to wave his arms at us and to call out, and worse still, he started to come down into the garden.

It was like a nightmare. We tried desperately to get to the fence, but we kept slipping back on the ice. It was the smooth side of the fence and difficult to climb over, and Tom was shouting nearer and nearer. Finally, Parker Corning stood against the fence, and we used his hands for steps and almost fell over, and just in time too. Tom looked over at us and scowled and ranted, but we were out of reach.

Once when Langdon was on the wood shed, Tom ran out with a long rake and threatened to rake him off. The trouble was that Tom blamed Grandfather for having him sent to Poughkeepsie, as Grandfather was one of the trustees there for many years. As a matter of fact it was the doctor who had had Tom sent there. However, we all came in for the blame in poor Tom's mind. Anyone in the next house was his enemy.

❦   ❦   ❦

Grandfather and Grandmother thought they could not live through a winter without having had the refreshing breezes and salt air of Fire Island [in summer]. Sometimes as many as twenty or more of our family would go with them, and often the Lansings joined us. Grandfather always made the reservations on the night boat "Drew," because of Captain Roe.

We were all admirers of the kindly captain, and on the mornings that the "Drew" arrived at Albany he would walk from the steamboat landing up big State Street, in his dark blue uniform with brass buttons and his visor cap. The boys from the Academy and High School would run to meet him before school opened and walk along with him a short way. He lived at 74 Swan Street, where the State [Office] building stands now. Captain Stephen Roe was our Admiral Nelson and Commodore Perry combined. . . .

Grandfather engaged the bridal suite on the "Drew" for Grandmother and her maid, and for several years he was persuaded by the boys to engage the "Texas" for them. This was the large cabin across the bow, named in honor of the largest state. This was the only one of the "states" left. The fashion of calling cabins for states instead of having numbers had passed by that time.[5]

When the evening for departure came, Morrissey would drive Grandfather and Grandmother and her maid down to the "People's Line" landing on what is now called the Plaza. Grandmother would be wrapped up as if she were starting on a mid-winter ocean voyage, instead of a boat trip on a sweltering night in July. We all would go in to see her suite. [We would] admire the light blue curtains edged with cotton lace, the bed spreads to match, and the gaudy white and gold china wash bowl. We then would leave our dolls on our own bunks and run around the decks, watching the river banks and dikes, and when we had safely passed the treacherous "Overslaugh," we knew the Captain would invite us up on the bridge. From there it was fascinating to watch the boat seeming almost to strike the banks, and then veer off just in time. After the bridge came an inspection of the huge paddlewheels, and then an inspection of the machinery from the windows that looked down on the walking beam. That was the chief object of our wonder.

My mother or an uncle or aunt would check up on us to be sure we behaved and did not give the kindly captain any trouble. It was the three boys who were apt to start something, but they were a little in awe of the captain, except when they were in the "Texas" behind a locked door. Sometimes they made a terrific noise playing rough games. Once a passenger complained to the captain, and he got one of the uncles to stop the uproar. After several trips Grandfather refused to reserve the "Texas" for the boys, and they were separated, much to their indignation. Mother would say to us, "You may stay up until after the bell tolls in memory of General Montgomery at Barrytown, but after that you must go to bed."[6]

It was all very exciting — the early arrival in New York, the breakfast served to the noise and confusion of having the trunks and freight rolled off, the Brevoort House carriage with Pat finding the porter to take Grandfather and Grandmother, my mother, and the maid to the 34th Street ferry. All the rest of us, the little girls carrying dolls dressed for traveling, would go with one of the uncles, who was in charge of taking us by horsecar to the ferry. Then followed the excitement of crossing to Long Island City and the bump against the wooden sides of the slip. [There we would find] the train in the wooden shed waiting to take us to Babylon. The arrival there [was also exciting as we raced to meet the other carriages and horsecars] to take [us] to the steamboat *Surf*. There [would be] cries of joy as we saw the boat and clambered up the gang way, to be greeted by the captain.

How we loved Fire Island. . . . We watched for the great lighthouse to appear first on our left, and then as we twitched and turned with the channel staked by tall poles or dead trees, the light would finally locate itself on our right, where it belonged. This settlement of the Surf Hotel and cottages run by Mr. D. S. S. Sammis was a favorite resort for Albanians, and quite a crowd would be on the long, wooden dock as we slowly came in and were roped to the piles.

The Frederick Townsends owned a cottage, and Annie and Sara and Freddy would be standing among the crowd to see the great event of the day. Mrs. Townsend's dogs were transferred from Elk Street for the summer, and they ran along the wooden walks yapping familiarly. Mrs. James Kidd and her dogs generally sat in the "refrigerator," which was an open place under part of the hotel where the breezes blew from both the bay and ocean. Nearly all the Albanians had rooms in a large cottage that was called the "Albany." Grandfather and Grandmother had rooms on the ground floor and a parlor with the only fireplace. In the old days they used to go to a hotel kept by the Domineys, further along on the island. That was before this larger settlement built by Mr. Sammis existed.

We deserted Fire Island for four years and went to Newport, quite a contrast. First we had a Cliff Cottage, No. 5, between the Weir Mitchells' at No. 4 and Miss Rhinelander's at No. 6. The meals were brought down from the Cliff Cottage Hotel, and Mother thought this would mean a great rest for her from housekeeping.[7]

But it was neither comfortable nor satisfactory, so she rented "Cliff Lawn" from the Winthrop Chandler estate. It was a lovely location and a large and airy house. The view of the ocean rolling in on Easton's beach was very fine. We bathed at this beach, close by, and all our friends bathed there too, as the present Bailey's beach was far off, and no one bathed there but the few people living around there.

Hattie rode to the hunts, and we both went to dancing classes at the Casino, taught by a Mr. Marini of Boston. I was also a member of a prisoner's base club. We wore whistles on a ribbon around our necks, and we met at the houses of the members, and we provided cookies and lemonade.

One of the highlights of those summers was the Golden Wedding of Grandfather and Grandmother at our house, with their four surviving children and thirteen of their grandchildren present. Admiral and Mrs. Taylor, who had been at their wedding at St. John's Church in Portsmouth, New Hampshire, on August 27, 1834, also attended.

A second highlight was the wedding of Emily Meredith Read to Mr. Francis Aquila Stout of New York, at which I was a bridesmaid. General and Mrs. Meredith Read rented the McCarthy Little house for several summers, and the wedding was there on Everett Place at noon on August 21, 1884, with Bishop Potter officiating.

Mrs. Read had been Miss Delphine Pumpelly of No. 1 Elk Street, and General Read had been consul general in Paris and minister to Greece. They had four children. The eldest was Major Harmon Pumpelly Read who lived with his aunt, Mrs. Kidd, at 7 Elk Street. Miss Emily was the next, then Meredith Jr., and lastly my friend Marie Read, who was just my age. We bathed and played together almost every day.

I was wild with excitement at being a bridesmaid. The two grownup bridesmaids were Miss Harriet Gammell of Providence and a cousin, Miss

Emily Stevens, of New York. Marie and I were to walk together in front of the others. Mrs. Read bought the dresses and shoes for us in New York, and my excitement had a dash of cold water thrown at it when I saw the shoes. Marie was larger than I was, and my shoes were as large as hers. They were hideous, high, white leather with glass buttons. The dresses were white cotton lace; Marie's had blue ribbons and mine had pink.

The bride was twenty-two, and the bachelor bridegroom was fifty-eight. He had a long beard and was as large and stout as his name. But it was all wonderful; every moment was a thrill. The groom gave us brooches with our initials on them, in blue satin boxes. We each also had a cake, and I found a lovely ring in mine. A large tent was added to the house, in the rear over a garden, and the "collation," as Marie called it, was served there.

Many stories were told about the celebrities invited to the wedding. It was said that a week before the wedding, the butler brought to General Read the cards of two visiting European princes who had come to call. General Read had looked at them carefully but told the butler to say to the visitors that, as they had not brought any introductions from his friend the king of Greece, he could not receive them. I have the invitation to the wedding and a newspaper article and other remembrances of a big day in my childhood.

One of the summers in Newport, Hattie and I had our portrait painted together by Miss Sara Freeborne.[8] It was a most terrible nuisance to us, and I am sure we were not cooperative. The painting was done in a large attic which had a northern light, and Miss Freeborne came at nine every morning. The idea was that it was a good time in our lives to have us done together, before I grew larger and older. The portrait was to fit over the mantel piece in the library at Albany, so the top was rounded to match the setting. Hattie stands with her right arm around my shoulder. She is dressed in a dress she never owned at all, and I am in a white dress with a green hair ribbon. I never had worn a green ribbon.

Miss Freeborne got so provoked with me that she sat up one night and painted me into a white horse and put Hattie in a riding habit with her arm around the horse instead of me. I was delighted but Mother did not like it at all, so Miss Freeborne and I had to arrange a truce and I was painted in again. She said we had noses that were hard to paint, so she laid us out by turn on a mattress, on a hot night, and took plaster casts of the noses, and almost smothered us. I laughed and split my cast. I have the portrait at Mattapoisett, and after all these years it does not seem so bad.

Another high moment was when General Winfield Scott Hancock came to call on Mother and she was out. Grace Marvin and I were playing around, and the General came over to us and asked our names and then kissed both of us. He was a tall and handsome man. He had run for President on the Democratic ticket in 1880 against Garfield, who had won. We ran to tell Mother when she drove home because there had been a great deal of fuss in Newport about the General's visit, and we had seen part of a parade in his honor. Mother said that Hancock and Garfield had first met at a dinner given by my father in Washington when he was in Congress.

During the summers in Newport we had had various guests such as Caroline Duer, who was very charming and gay, Katy Patterson from Washington and her fiancé, Pierre La Montagne, and the Lord Chief Justice of England and his son, Gilbert Coleridge. Lord and Lady Exmouth came on their wedding trip. She was a handsome young woman, and he was a funny, ill-tempered, little man. She was anxious to go to California, but because she wanted to go, he would not.

One day at luncheon he offered to compromise. "Edie," he said, "this is what I'll do. I'll take you to San Francisco, but never as far as California."

Everyone kept quiet. Then Edie said, "That's quite right, whatever you say." . . .

Mother was often a guest at the "Town and Country Club," a literary group that met at the house of Mrs. Julia Ward Howe near Portsmouth. Mother took me to hear Mrs. Howe preach at the Channing Memorial Church on a Sunday afternoon. Mrs. Howe was rather short and wore a bonnet. Of course she was very famous, not only as the author of the "Battle Hymn of the Republic," but for her advanced ideas.

Several years later she came to Albany on her way west, arriving on a nine o'clock train in the evening. She came unexpectedly and happened to meet Mother in the station here, just leaving for New York. Uncle Tuy Marvin was seeing Mother off, and he brought Mrs. Howe up to the house, where Hattie and I were finishing our favorite supper of hot chocolate, hot biscuits, chicken hash, and pancakes. Uncle Tuy, with a twinkle in his eye, marched her into the dining room and said he had to go home, but would return in time to take Mrs. Howe to the train. Mrs. Howe was very nice. She made it all very easy for us, and we managed to give her a more grownup dinner after a while, thanks to Biddy.

Mrs. Howe said she would like to see the collection of china and everything else. Although we had been brought up with the china, we really knew nothing about it, and after several bad guesses on Hattie's part, the butler came to the rescue, as he had asked Mother questions about various pieces. Hattie also gravely informed Mrs. Howe that our father's portrait was painted by Stuart, and Mrs. Howe's eyes twinkled and she said, "No doubt from life." Hattie eagerly assented, and then she said the portrait of Washington was by Elliott, and that was that.

Many years later when I married and went to live in Boston, Mrs. Howe recalled this visit with keen amusement. In April 1904 we went to a one-act drama given at Fenway Court, Boston, in honor of Mrs. John L. Gardner's birthday. I sat next to Mrs. Howe. She said, "My child how much you look like your father. In 1850, I was at St. Peter's in Rome at a service, and I tried to draw your father's head as he sat in front of me. But he saw what I was trying to do and he smiled and turned away." . . .

CHAPTER 10

O NE OF THOSE SUMMERS [1881] my brother returned from a trip to Europe and, having stopped off in Albany, reported the news that Elk Street was to be lighted with electricity and paved with Belgian blocks. This was news indeed. The gas lamps were to remain for the present, as the authorities felt that the experiment of electricity might not be a success. Hattie and I regretted the passing of the old cobbles. The crooked kerb stones made wonderful deep gutters for sailing ships down in the spring when the snows melted. But the street had looked like the bed of a brook, with cobbles washed out in great masses [leaving] bad holes for horses to sprain ankles and for carriages to break springs.[1]

When we returned in September, in time for school, the street was half finished. The new lights were blinking and sizzling and often going out entirely. Often when we were going to sleep [we] heard Mother trying the new telephone to complain about the new lights to the new company. We also regretted the passing of the old lamplighter, but we had some compensation in watching the man who came around every morning to climb up the iron spokes of the pole, insert a new carbon, and throw the old one down on the street. It became a rage to collect these sticks. I cannot now imagine why, as they were good for nothing.

At this time my brother was at Union College, but he came home for weekends. After the Sunday night supper at Grandfather's and a call at the Doanes' on the way home, he would take a train to Schenectady. He lived in the house of the Professer of belles lettres and Mrs. Lamoureaux, on Nott Terrace. When he was a little boy, Jack had gone to Miss Gaylord's school at Catskill with his two friends and neighbors Bayard and Howard Van Rensselaer.[2] After that he went to St. John's School at Sing Sing, and from there to Union College, where he graduated in 1881.

We were taken up to his commencement. We went up in the train, and we were dressed in white and carried little white shawls. I dropped my shawl on the railroad track at the Schenectady station, and so it had a band of soot that distressed me greatly. . . .

Two other boys from Elk Street also went to Union at that time, Harry Pierson at 32 and Dick Meneely at 30. These three boys had a certain whistle to call one another. Jack would whistle as he walked up to the Law School on State Street, on part of the land now covered by the State Office building. Harry and Dick would rush to their windows, and then they would arrange some plan for meeting that sounded wonderfully grown-up to me. When either of them whistled at our house, I ran to the window, and as soon as I learned the whistle, I answered it. It was fun when Hattie and I walked up to St. Agnes in the morning, to run ahead, whistle, and run [leaving] Hattie alone, with the boys at their open windows asking her what she wanted them to do. This was too much for Hattie, and I was forbidden to whistle anymore unless Jack was with me. . . .

Mr. and Mrs. Erastus Corning Jr. lived at 22 Elk Street. He was always known as "Tip" Corning. His grandfather had been lame, and [as a] little boy [Erastus] used to call him "Tippy," so the grandfather called him "Tip." He was quite deaf, from having scarlet fever when he was a boy. He married Grace Schenck, the daughter of Rev. Dr. and Mrs. Schenck of Brooklyn, and Hattie wrote a poem for that wedding too.

Cousin Tip had canary birds, and we used to watch his experiments. He wanted them to grow red feathers at moulting time, so he fed them a mixture of egg yolks and red pepper. There were a few signs of red in the new feathers. Their children were Erastus 3rd and little Gertrude, who died when she was nine. After a long illness, Cousin Tip died at the farm. . . .

My father and mother had always given a dinner for the various governors and their wives. They found it difficult [in one case, however.] After [this particular governor and his wife] had accepted, and others had been invited to meet them, they sent a note about 6 P.M. to say they were unable to come. . . . After several dinner invitations had been treated in this way, people gave up inviting them. It was only at the end of his term that the governor and his wife suddenly reformed and went around a bit.

My mother kept up this custom of giving dinners, and I well remember how the table was pulled out in the morning, the long cloth was laid, and the creases were ironed out. Mother had a small jewelry safe in the little room between her bedroom and the nursery, and in it she kept the keys to the large safe in the pantry. From the outside this looked as if it was just a closet, as the door was like all other doors. It had a steel lining, [however,] and it opened with a large key. When that door was open, it showed a steel door, and this had an intricate lock.

I learned the mysteries of that lock some years later, when Mother was ill and trusted me with the secret. There was no dial. A long key was inserted in one hole, and then by turning it, a bit was unscrewed, and the bit left in. Then another key turned the bit, and if all went well, the steel door opened, after a long hasp had been pulled down.

Inside, the safe was as tall as the ceiling. You could sit down on a metal case of silver, and I very often did that after I had come down to the pantry surreptitiously during a dinner party. Having helped myself to the various platters as they were brought out, I would hide in the safe, so that no one could complain that I was in the way. This safe was only opened when there were more than ten people for a dinner. There were two small safes, also in the pantry, where enough silver was kept to serve at least ten people.

Mother used to allow Hattie and me to arrange the place cards on the table and also to place the little bouquets or baskets of flowers at the place of each lady and the boutonnieres for the men. Once I tried to mix the cards, just for fun, and have people sit in the wrong seats, but Hattie caught me in time, and after that I was carefully watched. There were about six glasses at each place, and rows of knives and forks, as there were ten or twelve courses. Roman punch was served in glasses with gilt spoons in the middle of the feast. The punch was supposed to refresh and cool the overfed guest, and get him ready for the game course served with salad and currant jelly.

Mother liked to have a dinner over in an hour and a half, but this was then considered very short, and people complained that they had been hurried. It was the common sense of the Prince of Wales, later King Edward VII, that set the fashion for dinners of one hour or less, not more. The hours of dinner changed from seven to 7:30 or 8 during my time.

Madeira was served to older men who knew and cared. Albany madeira was always famous, and was imported in, and often named for, the old sailing ships. Mr. Dudley Walsh had a well known madeira, "The Wanderer." We used to have a few bottles.

My father had a special closet for the safe keeping of wines. It was not against any outer wall of the house, as it might be too hot or too cold. It was, in short, an inside closet. . . . Mother kept the key in her little safe and I liked to go with her, as she carried her glass-shaded candle because the closet had no light.

There was old sherry bought at the sale of Joseph Bonaparte's effects at Bordentown, N. J. and other sherry bought at Xeres in Spain by a relative.

The word sherry was a corruption of Xeres, just as [the word] port came from Oporto. Some of the bottles of madeira were labelled "Harriet" for the ship and "Farquhar and Bininger" for importers. There were a few choice bottles of 1776 used for very special occasions, and others labelled "Chief Justice Marshall." This was used for Grandfather's 80th birthday. There was also "Alpha brandy." There must have been several hundred bottles in all. I still have a few of them after all these years. [The wine] used to be recorked every three years, a long job. Herbert McGinness at the Fort Orange Club used to do it for us.

At a dinner of sixteen people given to meet Governor and Mrs. Hoffman[3] on December 21st, 1872, the following appalling menu was served.

Julien soup
Oysters
Chicken patties
Baked salmon
Sweet breads and peas
Terrapin, asparagus
Quail and partridges and salad
Roman punch
Roast turkey and chestnut sauce
Filet of beef with potato croquettes and cranberries
Ices — two kinds — napolitaine and flower
Dessert

We used the rose water bowl, . . . a beautiful ewer and basin of silver gilt, with the arms of the duke of Sussex in the center. The old custom was to place it in front of the hostess, and before dessert was served and the plates put on the table, the hostess poured the little pitcher full of rose water into the basin, dipped the corner of her napkin into it, and wiped her fingers. She then pushed it along to the man on her right, who was supposed to [copy] what she did and push it along to his right, and so on around the table.

It was not often used, and when it was, it was a nine-days'-wonder to be talked about. I remember in later years a dinner for Governor and Mrs. Flower[4]. The governor evidently did not quite understand about it, in spite of being on Mother's right, [because] when the basin was pushed in front of him, he joyously [dipped] both hands in it and announced that it smelled "real sweet."

Sometimes Russian dessert was served in the china room, which opened off the dining room and had in fact been the dining room in the original house. Mrs. George Evans [in a little book, *Reflections*, printed privately] tells of going with Mr. Evans to a dinner at our house [at which] the guests went from the dining room to the smaller room where dessert, fruit, and after-dinner wines were served. . . .

One Lent, Hattie got up a series of weekly evening meetings at our house, in the library. Different people read papers. Hattie was deeply interested in astronomy and in the condition of the Dudley Observatory, then placed so badly, with the New York Central's four tracks shaking the instruments.

Professor Boss was at the head and nobly holding on, and one evening he gave a talk on his special work and the need for a new building. People began to be interested in the almost forgotten observatory, and not long after, the present one [no longer standing] was built on city land. . . . Miss Boyd always took a class to the observatory every year, and I well remember how Dr. Boss showed me the spots on the sun on the white lining of my hat. . . .

CHAPTER 11

OUR RULES FOR SUNDAY ALWAYS seem to me to have been inconsistent, as we were allowed to do some things but not others. We had the usual Sunday dinner at 1:30. Besides soup, we generally had roast beef with several vegetables and Biddy's famous vanilla ice cream. . . .

When asked for the recipe, Biddy was always willing to give it, but she did not know how to read or write. When you tried to write it as she gave it, you were up against a problem. She would start, "I pour in the cream, and a handful of sugar, and probably beaten eggs."

"Yes, but Biddy, how much of each?"

"Oh, enough to make it come out right."

The ice cream freezer stood on the brown stone steps at the kitchen door. This door opened onto a large enclosed area with stone flagging. The kitchen maid was the one who turned the freezer, but if for any reason we did not go to church, our one wish was to help make ice cream. The stick was what we wanted, that delicious stick covered with the delicious mixture — each had a lick in turns.

After Sunday dinner we went to the nursery, where we recited to Mother parts of the Catechism, the Commandments, and a hymn. Mother had given each of us a Bible on our tenth birthday. On the flyleaf of mine is written, in her distinctive writing, "Be Thou her Ruler and Guide; that she may so pass through things temporal that finally she lose not the things which are eternal."

We were allowed to paint texts on cardboard, and these usually were bestowed on our long-suffering grandmother, in the evening. We could not play any games. We could not skate or coast, no matter what a perfect day it might be, but we could go for walks.

Jack loved to walk, and he often took me. He had long legs and walked so fast that I often had to run to keep up. Sometimes we walked all around the park, but I never would admit that I was tired, as I felt so pleased to go with him. On the way home he usually had a call to make on some older woman, perhaps a dinner call. Then some cake was found for me, while a silver tray with glasses of sherry or old madeira refreshed him and his hostess. . . .

Sunday ended for Mother and Jack with high tea at Grandfather's at seven o'clock. Then Hattie was included and I was only asked in case there was danger of thirteen, as Grandmother was superstitious. How I longed to hear the new telephone ring during the afternoon and to hear the voice of Grandmother's maid ask if I could come to make the fourteenth. Dear Grandmother! I am sure she often did this just to please me. Sometimes after we arrived for supper, there would still be thirteen, and so a little table for two would be set up near Grandmother. How we fought to sit there! We could reach over when Grandmother was talking to her left hand neighbor and borrow the silver cow full of rich cream.

Grandfather kept two cows, which grazed in a large pasture where Sheridan Park has now been filled in. There was a pond, probably from a spring, at the bottom of the pasture, with several large trees to shade it, and at noontime in warm weather the cows rested from their labors and chewed their cuds. Elk Street [did not] continue above Dove Street, and the lower part of the stable at that corner opened onto the pasture. The cows had a large airy barn under the horse stalls.

For several years we had cows too. They lived under the stable on Spruce Street and reached their quarters by a side alley next to the stable. As they had a sparse grazing place in the rear, because of the steep hillside, they used to join Grandfather's cows every morning. They ambled up Spruce Street to Hawk Street. There was no viaduct then, but a very steep hill. Then they continued their way up Elk Street to the pasture. This was a long way, and someone had to escort them back and forth, so it was given up.

Our milk was bought from a milkman, who drove to our door in the early morning and rang the bell at the basement door. The kitchen maid came out with two large white china pitchers, and they were filled from the metal containers in the back of the milkman's cart. These pitchers in turn were placed in the ice box, which was filled with square cakes of ice from the river.

The ice man drove around in his big, lumbering, two-horse ice wagon, loaded to the top with ice. One man drove, and the other man stood on a step at the rear, holding an ice pick. When he had the cakes ready, he took two pairs of ice tongs and, lifting a cake in each one, threw them on the sidewalk. He did a neat job, but he often seemed to pick out the dirtiest spot on the sidewalk. As I remember, we had six cakes of ice every other day. After a time our man would come out with his ice tongs and carry in two cakes at a time, in the garden gate and through the kitchen into the refrigerator room under the pantry.[1]

There were two large ice boxes, and two cakes went into each. One box had a heavy lid, and the other had two doors. The ice was placed in the top of each. The last two cakes went up, in the dumb waiter, to the pantry refrigerator, where the butler kept fruits and butter and cream for use in our dining room. But often our man did not get about bringing in the cakes of ice for some time, and so the ice had a fine chance to be covered with dust, be spit upon by tobacco users, or enjoyed by the dogs. The cakes were always washed off with the hose first, but even so it was scarcely sanitary, according to modern standards.

All our drinking water had to be boiled. It was poured into a filter, where it went through charcoal, and then it was drawn off into pitchers. There was a great deal of typhoid in Albany. It was particularly devastating to strangers, who did not understand the wretched conditions. Our boiled and filtered water was carried in carafes to each bathroom, to be used for brushing teeth. Mother always warned guests to be careful.[2]

I have an interesting list of the wages paid to our servants in my childhood. Even such a valuable pair as the Chandlers received only $60.00 a month and their laundry, while our good cook Bridget received $20.00. Our excellent laundress, Mary O'Mara, who claimed descent from Lord Beresford de Waterford, was paid $15.00. We lived in the days of starched white underskirts and drawers with Hamburg flounces, pillow slips with fluted edgings, and my brother's starched white shirts, seven a week.

Mary was always contented and happy, except when we plagued her. She sang by the hour, in a loud cracked voice,

'Tis me shadow on the wall Molly dear, Molly dear
Shure 'tis not me self at all, Molly dear.

Mary and Biddy and two other maids had their bedrooms over the laundry. There was a bathroom and a large stove in the upper hall, for heat.

We loved to talk to Mary and sometimes she let us use her fluting iron, of which she was very proud. "Shure and I never likes to see folk buried. I starts wid the procession from St. Mary's,[3] and whin they get to Pat Rouin's, I gets out and takes a horsecar home." We thought for a long time that this was a saloon, but finally Hattie asked her where Pat Rouin's was. "Shure 'tis thim as lives in the big house and calls themselves Pat Rouins — 'tis the old Manor House ye call it."

It was in the laundry that we gave out the Christmas presents at three o'clock on Christmas Eve to the children who lived on Spruce Street. We had talked with them, and Hattie kept a list of their names and what they wanted. During December we had spent hours settling the presents we had bought at Morrison's toy store on South Pearl Street, or in the new glories of Whitney's basement, with its sizzling electric lights.

Hattie had fifty cents a week and I had twenty-five cents, if I was in bed by seven thirty every night. We had saved our allowances for months, and kept the money in metal safes. Mother added $5.00 for the large cornucopias from McElveney's to go with each present. Hattie was the one who started this custom, and we kept it up until the Christmas before I married, that is, just fifty years ago.

There were about twenty-five children, and long before the hour they would begin to gather around the laundry door. There were Hogans, Leonards, Hannavans, and Murrays. There was also old Mrs. Coleman, who lived to some tremendous age. She watched us from her house across the street and was called by Mary "That ould divil." She lived on one side of our stable, and good old Mrs. Hanley lived on the other side.

Christie Murray was lame. He drove an ash cart and wanted books. He had a pretty sister, Tessie Murray. Jerry Hogan would write us a letter with his list of wants, and he signed it, "From your loving little friend Jerry."

One of Mrs. Leonard's little girls was named for me, the whole Dutch name too, but she was called Bertha. She is now a grandmother several times over. I felt very much pleased this last Christmas, 1947, to be invited to six o'clock Christmas dinner by the youngest child of Mrs. Leonard. She has been married for some years and has a dear little girl named Marguerite. She invited others of the old party, with four coming down from Schenectady. We had a wonderful evening talking over the old days, but few of us are left to tell the tale now, after fifty years.

Mullon was our coachman for some years. He and his wife and six children lived over the stable. I admired Maggie Mullon very much. She was several years older than I was, but every chance I had I slipped out of the rear garden gate and across to the stable to see her.

One day when I returned from school, I was told by Mary Whalen that there were guests for luncheon and I was speedily dressed in a new gray French linen dress just sent up from Mme. Felice in New York. It had a tucked guimp with lace edgings. I was told to return to the nursery directly when luncheon was over and put on a play dress. But when mother and the guests had gone to the conservatory for their coffee, I was left to my own devices, and the new dress was forgotten.

I went down the steps from the dining room piazza to the garden, and was soon playing with a cat. Then the steps to the back gate looked tempting, and I was soon in the stable calling Maggie to join me. We played in the carriages, patted the horses, and then my roving eye noticed the manure slide was open. It was where the manure was shoveled out into a pile back of the stable, and on investigation, I saw that the pile was a very high one. I loved coasting, and felt very sorry when the sliding board was taken down in the garden for the summer. This was a tempting pile. Why not slide in summer as well as winter?

No sooner said than done. I slid down beautifully almost to the lower fence. I did hear a loud protesting voice from Mrs. Mullon, in an upper window. When I called Maggie to join me, Mrs. Mullon shouted to her not to do it. Nevertheless, I continued up and down. It was a wonderful discovery. It was a real slide, and that was what I wanted.

Then Mary was heard calling frantically for me. She was horrified when she saw me. She took me gingerly by the lace-trimmed collar and ran me across to the garden, where a hose was playing on the grass. She stood me right under the nozzle. It was delicious. I had always wanted to try this. One by one, and at arms length, she took off everything and threw all of them on the grass. From there they went to the laundry to be boiled and soaked.

I was then enveloped in a sheet and taken up to the bathroom and given three baths — one after the other, hair and all. But even so, the smell stuck to me. For several days Jack and Hattie objected to my eating at the dining room table with them, so I had my meals out on the piazza. Mother wrote to Miss Boyd that for excellent reasons she was obliged to keep me at home for several days.

It was about this time that we had a visit from Matthew Arnold, the famous British writer, who had come over to give lectures. He was to give one at old Martin Hall on South Pearl Street. The hall was considered a firetrap, and it was a stormy night, so he did not have a good audience. Char was sent to call us to the library at tea time, to meet the famous visitor.

Mr. Arnold gave us a limp handshake, asked us if we went to any school, and then forgot us, while he talked with Mother and Dr. Battershall about the English windows at St. Peter's. He had been down there that afternoon to see them and the Queen Anne Silver. He is quoted as saying the Burne-Jones window was the most beautiful he had seen. . . .

Sometimes an English visitor wanted to see the Shakers at Niskayuna. It was one of the rare occasions when the horses were used on a Sunday. We knew the Shakers very well. Lydia was the Spiritual Mother and Mary the Temporal Mother. After their marketing was finished, at the market in the center of big State Street, they would come to see us. Their wagon looked like a "Black Maria," and the brother who drove was reminded sharply by Lydia not to allow the younger sisters to leave the wagon, or even look out at the possible worldliness of Elk Street.[4] Of course the Fenimore Coopers knew when the Shakers came. One or another of the family were always on the watch at Cape Lookout, and May would run over to hear what they had to say. Lydia was round and rosy and very blunt in her remarks. She would say to May, "I never read any of your family's writings. Too long-winded for me."

Sometimes on a cold winter morning Lydia and Mary would find us still at breakfast, particularly if anyone had been out late the night before. They would come in and sit by the table, and Mother would give them tea. Lydia would carefully extract her teeth and lay them safely on the table. Then they would both be very glad of a meal, as they would have started early over the rough roads of those days. "Be this your dinner, Annie?" Lydia would say to Mother, with a twinkle in her eye. She had known Mother since she was a child, but seemed unable to remember that her name was Anna.

We had regular visitors on Elk Street, like John Mahar, the banana man; his wife Mary worked for the Walsh's on South Hawk Street. Then we had Jane Summers with her soft voice and kindly manner, who went the rounds to shampoo hair and to pass on all the gossip. She went to Troy for one day a week, so we had all the Troy news as well. Miss Delia Guardinier, with her long double breasted cloak and floating blue veil, was another regular visitor on Saturdays. She carried a large basket with a white cover carefully drawn over it, and in the basket were dozens of the most delicious cookies I ever ate, and in the winter the wonderful *olykoeks*, dear to the hearts of all of us. Miss Guardinier was hailed with joy by all of us playing in the snow. But she never gave us any of the cookies. She delivered the orders, and after that it was for us to get them the best way we could.[5]

❧   ❧   ❧

Gilmore, the swill man, was a great problem in Elk Street. He beat his black horse most brutally. His wagon had loose planks for the bottom and big cracks between them, so the street was a trail of litter whenever he came, usually not more than twice a week. It seemed as if he always chose the time that guests were arriving from the station. Everyone complained, and Cousin Grace Corning would lean far out of a front window to plead with him about his horse.

Finally the end came. One hot June day, in front of our house, the horse began to kick. He kicked so fast and vigorously that Gilmore could not get near enough to reach him with his whip. Then the whip broke and Gilmore stood there helpless with the handle in his hand. When the horse finished, there was nothing left of the cart but the four rickety wheels and a pile of planks and barrels. The street was a disgusting mess. All had to close their windows. Hoses were run out from all the houses. A policeman led off the happy horse, and Gilmore vanished from the Elk Street scene.

❧   ❧   ❧

For years we had a regular Saturday morning organ grinder. His tunes were "Wait 'til the clouds roll by, Jenny," "Darling I am growing old," "The wear'n of the green," and "Every night at the end of the street, I whistle and wait for Katy." He was very friendly and had a monkey who climbed up to the balcony for cookies. . . .

❧   ❧   ❧

You had to be up very early to see [Mr. Rufus King of 2 Elk Street] hurry down his steps and vanish down Steuben Street. He went to the station every morning to see who went to New York on the 7:05 train. Angel Booth stood at the gate, punched the tickets, and gave greetings and advice to all, from the governor down.[6] Angel had a squint, or was cross-eyed, and he had flowing whiskers and rosy cheeks. Mr. King always stood by him, leaning against the iron bars of the gate. You could see the [two men] whispering confidently about why so-and-so was going to New York so soon again.

"Now let me think," Angel would say, "he went down last Tuesday and this is Friday. When did he return in between? I wonder what he is up to."

"Going to the city?" he would remark to passers-by, and shake his whiskers. "Don't stay down there. New York's Satan's own dwelling place, but we're all good here."

After Mr. King had seen what he wanted to see, he would go to the restaurant and have his morning coffee. The coffee, as well as everything else, was excellent there. By 7:30, Mr. King could be seen returning by Steuben Street and vanishing into his house. We thought he went to bed again.

CHAPTER 12

WHEN A GIRL HAD TO BE EXPELLED from St. Agnes,[1] it was an occasion to be remembered all one's life. The whole school, except the kindergarten, would be gathered in the school room. After everyone was seated, the big doors would be closed. Mother Helen would stand on one side, Sister Eliza on the other. The bishop and Miss Boyd would walk down the center aisle together to the desk.[2]

A frigid silence [would fill] the room. We would all stand up, and I am sure everyone shook in her shoes. I did, though I had never been guilty of carrying a note from a boarder to a choir boy. That was the usual offense. The bishop always looked white and sad, and he gave us a little talk that reduced us to tears before he ended, and we inwardly vowed to lead better lives, for a few uplifting minutes anyway.

He would begin by telling us how deeply he and the trustees and teachers felt about what to him was a tragedy. He would continue by saying how much each one of us meant to him, and to the morale of the school, and all it stood for. It was unfair to the other scholars, who appreciated the opportunities offered by the school, to have such a girl remain among them. A spirit of insubordination must be dealt with by home influences, and, it was hoped, would be eventually overcome, or a spirit permanently unruly would be the inevitable outcome.

One of the cases was of a curly-headed, auburn-haired girl whom I greatly admired. She was gay and nice to the little girls, but she had been caught writing notes to a choir boy whose name was Willy. He asked her to meet him at the foot of the schoolroom fire escape, on the terrace. She reached the last step, where a dark figure was waiting, and said, "Oh, Willy! Willy! I am here at last!" Willy proved to be the bishop himself. I do not vouch for the truth of this tale, but it was whispered around the school halls.

The lower panes of the dormitory windows overlooking Elk Street were heavily painted with white paint, so that the girls could not look out on possibly dangerous passers-by. The boarders were exercised in what we called "Snakes." Every morning before school, and after school hours, they were walked out, two by two. At least one teacher followed. She had on each side a girl who might need an active eye. In those days this promenade, with the additional time that they could walk on the terrace or covered piazza, was considered enough out-of-doors exercise. In later years they had a nice toboggan slide, and two tennis courts were developed on the gravel of the terrace.

When I was about fourteen, the gymnasium was built. This was a great asset to the school. It proved without question that we were up-to-date. Miss Cushman, a trained teacher, came to take charge. She wore a brown gymnasium suit with very baggy trousers that looked almost like a full skirt. But it was disturbing to Miss Boyd that she did not wear a skirt too.

Miss Cushman was adamant on this point, and she pleaded that our dark blue gym suits might be made without skirts over the full trousers, but it was no use; we had full skirts. Parents were allowed to sit in the gallery and watch us perform, but no brothers were admitted.

My sister was in a German play at St. Agnes. She and Leila Herbert took the parts of two students. They wore long dressing gowns or wrappers, with a cord tied around the waist. . . . A wide piece of gray lining cotton was stretched across the front of the stage, to hide the legs entirely. I often wonder what the good ladies of that time would say now.

Before we scattered for the holidays, Miss Boyd would give us a short talk from the schoolroom desk. "Children, remember that no lady crosses her knees. She may cross her ankles, but never her limbs." Or this, "Children on your journeys to your homes for the holidays, if you need information, ask only of someone in uniform." Dear Miss Boyd naturally thought of the conductor or ticket puncher, while our thoughts were of a possible gold-braid officer, or at least an Academy boy. When the discovery was made that two southern boarders used powder on their faces, it was incredible. But when it was found that these same girls had gone to Chapel with unnaturally red cheeks, and that they used a red rose from a hat for their rouge, this was news indeed.

Miss Boyd drilled us every morning before school from her Bible Outlines, compiled expressly for the use of the school. I am fortunate enough to have kept one of these little gray paper-covered books, and I often consult it for much needed information. We learned the jaw-breaking names of the "Kings of Israel and Judah," the "Camping places of the Children of Israel," and the "Companions of St. Paul on his missionary journeys." We loved these latter because most of the names had an "S" in them, and we could hiss them. On Friday we had the Catechism. While still very young, we surmounted the intricacies of "Our duty towards our neighbor," and "What desirest thou of God?" and the Lord's Prayer.

Sometimes Miss Boyd would unexpectedly vary the exercises and give us a spelling and general information lesson. I am grateful indeed for having had instilled into me the correct spelling of such words as separate, judgment, prejudice, and privilege. Other odd bits of information were the origins of such phrases as "A Roland for an Oliver" and "Robbing Peter to pay Paul," and that the word "News" was made up from the first letters of North, East, West, and South. Then there was the origin of why men took off their hats, which I have now forgotten, and why dogs turn round and round before lying down. [We also learned about] "the seven Wonders of the World," how to tell when Easter falls, and the meaning of "née" and "via." This last was most important. Once an old girl wrote a letter to Bishop Doane and signed it, "Mary Jones via Smith." This was terrible, and we could not be sufficiently warned against making such a mistake.

One morning Miss Boyd gave us a talk about various forms of baptism, and she described immersion. This made a great impression on Mary King. Mary was a stalwart child of about twelve at this time. She went home, resolved to try immersion, and she picked out little Walter Gavit, who was about five years old, for candidate.

He was a handsome little boy and was playing in Academy park when Mary cajoled him to her house at 2 Elk Street. She locked the bathroom door and drew a deep bath, undressed Walter, and popped him in the tub. Mr. and Mrs. King were not at home, but [her brother] Rufie heard the uproar from Walter as Mary ducked him three times according to Miss Boyd's description of immersion.

Finally, so the ever-busy Elk Street grapevine told, Rufie got his Uncle Howard King to come over from Park Place. He made Mary open the door, and Walter was rescued. Luckily, nothing happened to Walter beyond fright and indignation. Mary released him and solaced his feelings with some cake. Now she understood about immersion.

At five o'clock every afternoon the St. Agnes boarders marched to Evensong. In the early years they marched to the Chapel by the brick cloister, then down into the wooden cloister, and up more steps into the Chapel. When the Cathedral was built, they marched across Elk Street and up a long flight of covered shallow steps leading to the side door, and then filed into the choir stall. It was a lovely service, [with the girls as] the choir. Usually the bishop was there, and when service was over, he stood by the choir door and shook hands and bade goodnight to each little girl, always remembering every name. We went very often to this service, particularly in Lent.

The Pruyn home at 13 Elk Street.

The Pruyn family in 1875: J.V.L., John V.L., Huybertie, Hattie, and Anna P. Pruyn. This is the last group photo before the death of J.V.L.

Composite photo of the family at tea in library. This was prepared after death of J.V.L.; his image was inserted from the earlier photo.

The nursery at 13 Elk Street, with wallpaper depicting scenes from Shakespeare and a border from "Under the Window" by Kate Greenaway.

The dining room. Portraits are of Mayor David Davidse Schuyler, Hibertje Lansing Pruyn and George Washington (by Rembrandt Peale). The glass doors open onto the piazza.

Mrs. Pruyn's dressing room. The mirrored door leads to the library.

*The library. The full bookcase conceals the door
leading to Mrs. Pruyn's dressing room.*

Huybertie and Hattie with their nurse Freida, in 1877.

*Thirteen first cousins in 1878. L. to r.: Huybertie, Grace Marvin, Selden E. Marvin Jr. (Tuy),
Parker Corning, Hattie, Harriet Weed Corning, Amasa Parker 3rd (Amboy), Grace Parker,
Anna Parker, Langdon P. Marvin, Louisa Parker (holding Harriet),
and Lewis Rathbone Parker.*

*Huybertie's maternal grandparents, Harriet Langdon Roberts
and Amasa J. Parker, Jr.*

Huybertie, age 10, with some of her dolls.

Some maternal aunts and cousins at the Corning farm, about 1884. Back row: Huybertie, Louise Parker, Harriet Parker, Edmund Marvin (almost hidden), Erastus Corning IV. Front row: Grace Parker, Harriet Corning, Langdon Marvin, Anna Parker, Catherine P. Marvin (Aunt Kate), Mary P. Corning (Aunt Mary), Hattie.

Bishop Doane.

Catherine Gansevoort Lansing, Huybertie's "Aunt Kitty."

Hattie (with reins) and friend at entrance to 13 Elk Street.

Elk Street looking west, about 1883–84.

Huybertie and Fromo in garden at Elk Street, about 1887.

*The Parker family. L. to r. seated: Lewis, Harriet, Anna, Amasa Jr.
L. to r. standing: Grace, Amasa Sr., Louise.*

My sister graduated in the Class of '85. . . . Mother had planned, when the graduation was over, to take us to Europe for educational purposes. That had an awful sound to me. . . . We were to sail at the end of August, after taking Grandfather and Grandmother to Fire Island and then settling them safely at home. But our well-laid plans went astray.

My brother Jack became engaged to a very charming girl, the daughter of a clergyman. He had met her at North East Harbour, where she was spending the summer with her parents and sister. It was a case of love at first sight with him. He had first seen her when he was ringing the bell for Sunday service at Bishop Doane's chapel of St. Mary's-by-the-Sea. There had been romantic canoeing and the usual simple picnics and buckboard rides and no doubt many hours of sitting on the rocks. The engagement was announced, and the wedding was planned for October 7th. . . . Our sailing was postponed.

For me this was a real respite. I thought that leaving Albany and my Elk Street world was a tragic waste of time. But also, the excitement of having Jack engaged was wonderful. He had written me a note all to myself, telling me of his engagement, and of how much I would love a new sister. I have the letter now. He was my godfather — always interested in my welfare, [always urging] me on to do better in school.

At this time he was twenty-seven, and his fiancée was twenty-two. Hattie was to be a bridesmaid. She had been to New York City to fit the dress at Guerin's. It was of cream lace. The bridesmaids were to wear fetching little bonnets of the lace with dark brown velvet ribbons tied in a bow at one side of the chin. I was to wear a dark red china silk with cream embroidery, made for the golden wedding of our grandparents, celebrated in Newport the previous summer. I went around singing,

Before you're married, 'tis nothing but love,
'Tis O' my honey — you sweet turtle dove.
After you're married, 'tis quite a different thing,
'Tis go to work you hussy — you good-for-nothing thing.

Exactly one week before the wedding, when I returned from school at one thirty, I found the family half through luncheon. As I slipped into my seat, I asked why they were early, but no one seemed disposed to reply. Then Jack said he was going to catch a train to New York. I made some remark about his being in a hurry to see his girl again.

Then the butler brought in the mail. He laid a letter by Jack's plate. I could see it had the picture of a hotel on it. He quietly opened it, and after a minute, read it aloud. It was from his fiancée, and it told him that she had been married, and that they were to sail on the *Werra* that afternoon. She said she was very sorry to cause him so much trouble and disappointment, but it was better to know in time. She did not give the name of her husband.

For a long time there was dead silence, then a sob from Hattie, who ran out of the room. As long as I live, I will associate a chocolate layer cake with that scene, [for the butler chose that moment to carry] in a large one and put it down in front of Jack.

Our cook, Bridget, in despair of our coming departure, had taken consolation in making all our favorite dishes, and I had asked for a large chocolate cake. As Jack took up the knife, he said to me, "I know you want an extra large slice." I broke down with a sob and fled to the piazza, where he followed me with the cake. We were all absolutely collapsed by this blow.

I later found out that Jack was going to New York [because that] morning . . . a package for him had come by express. In it was the engagement ring and also a ring that had belonged to his mother. Later a telegram had come to Mother saying stop all wedding preparations. It was from [the bride-to-be's mother]. The next morning came news that the girl's sister, who had been ill, had a serious case of typhoid fever.

Jack decided to go at once to see what he could do to help them all. He was able to have the wedding presents returned to the donors. Then, after another week the sister died. . . . Jack was a bearer at the funeral. In the meantime, the eloped couple arrived at Bremen, where they received a cable of the girl's sister's death, so they returned at once.

It took some days to understand just what had happened about the wedding. [Jack's fiancée had gone] to New York to fit her dress for the last time. She had met her cousin who was to be a bridesmaid. In some way — whether by accident or design — [a] young man who had been in love with the bride-to-be had appeared on the scene and evidently renewed his suit. He had urged her to let him return home with her and break the engagement properly from her parents' house. But she had said it must be marriage at once, or she would keep her promise to marry my brother. The cousin joined with the suitor in urging her not to elope, but nothing could persuade her.

So, [a] man was found at a Club [to serve as witness], and the four then drove to Bishop Potter's house and [the couple] asked him to marry them. He asked their names and, recognizing the name of the girl, inquired if she was a daughter of his old friend. She declined to answer, and he declined to marry them.

Finally, they crossed to Jersey City and were married by the rector of St. Mark's Church. They had just time to reach the *Werra*, but no time to buy any clothes. Years later, Mother met some people who were on the *Werra* and they said the passengers collected articles of clothing for the couple. The marriage turned out to be a very happy one, and they had several children.

The morning after the news came I did not want to go to school, as I dreaded being asked questions about this terrific sensation. In those days the art of newspaper pictures was not developed, but in this case a New York paper had published a very crude picture of a girl flying to the open arms of one man, and my brother standing aside, out in the cold.

So when I reluctantly walked slowly to school, alone, I saw what I dreaded, a group of girls waiting at the gate. One of the older ones called out, "Here she is! Do hurry and tell us about it before the bell rings!" I was frigidly polite but firm. I felt too deeply for Jack to discuss anything, and I ran in and got to my desk. After school I ran straight home.

All my spare time I sat with Jack in his rooms on the top floor. They had been done over especially for him after he returned from college. He did not want to see anyone and was in a very nervous state. . . .

PART TWO

COMING OF AGE

1885 ❦ 1892

CHAPTER 13

I T WAS FINALLY PLANNED that Jack should spend several months
in Colorado Springs, where he had been before . . . and that we would
sail at last on the *Etruria* of the Cunard line, the last of October [1885].
I questioned Jack about winter conditions in Europe, as he had been over
several times, and whether there would be coasting anywhere — I must have
coasting somehow. Did they have pancakes and soda water and doughnuts,
peanuts and Huyler's candies?

I wept over leaving the cats, the garden, and every piece of furniture. I
carried a book filled with a leaf from each tree and bush in the garden, and
pressed flowers. I also took several of my favorite little cooking sauce pans
used on my gas stove and a flag to hang over my bed.

It was on a Friday that we left. In those days it was considered necessary
for some family member to see [others] off on the perilous voyage. This
time it was Aunt Kate Marvin, although she did not like to travel on a
Friday. Family, friends, and neighbors saw us off from the house and station.
I carried my large doll Anna, and wept floods of tears.

Half way down the river we stopped. The train had run over and killed
a [man]. Aunt Kate implored Mother to give up the trip, saying that this
accident on top of Friday meant disaster. But we continued on our way and
sailed early the next morning with the tide.

It was a terrific voyage, and often Hattie and I were sure Aunt Kate was
right, that nothing could save us. The ship was very wide in the center, and
her rolling was so bad that all the steamer trunks and furniture slid back
and forth. Hattie was very ill for days. The food was horrible and although
it was a new ship, it was full of bugs and rats. We had electric lights, which
were a great improvement over the oil lamps of our former trip,[1] and there
were soapstone bathtubs. Our stateroom had a leak somewhere, and our
carpet was sopping wet. No doubt that accounted for Hattie's developing
a bad cold.

We arrived at Queenstown [now Dun Laoghaire] on a perfect fall day,
and were landed on a tender. We went to Dublin at once and had to stay
several days for Hattie to recover. Then we went to Parsonstown to stay at
Birr Castle with Lord and Lady Rosse. He and his father before him were
astronomers and had an enormous reflecting telescope on the grounds.[2]

The daughter was Lady Muriel Parsons, a bit younger than I was and very pretty. She had a French governess, and I was taken into their schoolroom life, with dolls and toys and English schoolroom food, all very simple and wholesome. I took keen pleasure in boasting of our Saturday morning pancakes, when we had time to eat all we could hold. My record was twenty-seven. I [also] boasted about the soda water fountain and all the joys of life in Albany.

With regret we left there, and as Hattie's cold was no better, we gave up the visit to "Kilderry," where Lord and Lady Brabazon lived. Instead, we crossed to London and Dr. Harper. Hattie was anxious to have us settle in a small city in Germany, where she could have singing lessons and could perfect her German. . . .

We crossed to Paris, and the comforts of the Hotel Bristol and glorious weather. Even I was carried away by the beauty of Paris and its fascinating gas lighted streets, as seen from our windows. In the end we got no further. Mother found that the Protestant pastor of the Église de L'Étoile and Madame Bersier took four girls into their family, and that there were two vacancies. So instead of German for the winter, it turned out to be French. Madame Bersier had someone ready to fill our needs, and soon a young governess, Marie Berton, was in charge of me. Hattie was settled at the Bersiers' on the Boulevard Pereire, with Sally Tibbits of Troy to fill the last vacancy.

The Hampden Robbs, who had spent two winters at 21 Elk Street, arrived in Paris, bringing Kate Walsh with them. They had a governess too, and between us all, our governesses did not have beds of roses. We played horse on top of the Arc de Triomphe and refused to wear gloves in the streets. We hated the "jeune fille," and "comme il faut," and walking, not running, in the streets. But all the same we had a wonderful winter, and as Mr. John Thayer of Boston, who was Mrs. Robb's brother, was also in Paris and drove a coach and four, we took long drives to historic sights like Versailles and St. Germain. Hattie had singing lessons from a pupil of Mme. Marchesi and violin lessons too. But the letters from home with all the news were the exciting events of each week.[3]

In the spring we took a trip to the Italian lakes, and in May we crossed over to London where Mother had rented Lady Rayleigh's house in Onslow Gardens. The house was one of a row built in the style prevalent in Kensington. Behind the house was a large garden, well kept, and a morning room back of the dining room opened right onto the garden. It was there that I had my lessons with another French governess, Mlle. Durchamp. She was young also, and I soon found she liked to take long walks, or ride one of the omnibuses drawn by three horses abreast.

The omnibuses were plastered all over with advertisements of "Pears Soap," or "Epps Cocoa — Grateful and Comforting," or "It comes with a boon and a blessing to men / the Hawk and the Owl and the Waverly Pen." The bus would leave us at some interesting point, and then we would often walk for miles, finding lanes and by-ways and old churches. I used to boast that I could find my way anywhere from the City out to South Kensington.

Mother had Lady Rayleigh's servants and her landau with the old coachman, Day, wearing the cockade of a baron on his hat. A rather melancholy lad named Frank assisted the butler and rode on the box with Day, so we called him Night. The landau was an enormous and clumsy carriage, and rolled sedately along the streets behind two fat horses. In the afternoon I often went along, and sat backwards, facing Mother and Hattie, who were dressed for calls and teas, with long tan gloves and gay parasols.

Hattie was now very much grown up, and soon after our arrival in London, she was presented at Court by Mother. The rule was then that if a mother had been previously presented, and it was in the same reign, she could present her daughter. Mother had been presented in 1872. Mother and Hattie had had their dresses [with] trains three yards long on the floor, made by Worth of Paris. Mother's was purple velvet for the train and the puffed sleeves, and the front was of heavy lilac ribbed silk with some pansies at one side of the waist. Hattie's dress was all white tulle, with clusters of maiden hair on the skirt panels. The train was of heavy ribbed silk, and of course both wore the traditional tulle veil with the three feathers.[4]

Jack had joined us after a long stay in Berlin, and he and I went out in the crowds of the Mall to watch the procession. The Courts then were in the daytime, and it was a lovely May day. The particular star of the occasion among the royalty was Princess May of Teck. She was the daughter of the popular Princess Mary of Cambridge, and we had the good luck to see them both in a royal coach, and to hear the hearty cheers of the crowd. Princess May later married her cousin, the son of the Prince and Princess of Wales. The son succeeded his father as George V, and his wife survived him as the dowager Queen Mary.

Some of the ladies, in their big C-spring barouches, seemed almost grotesque in their vivid velvets and satins and family jewels, and endless necklaces, chains and bracelets. I could quite credit the stories that much of the jewelry had been rented for the day. The London crowds considered

it their right to climb on the carriage steps and remark on what they saw.
After church on Sundays the world walked in Hyde Park, the "Prayer
Book Parade" it was called. Crowds rented the little green chairs and waited
to see the gay world, and particularly the beauties of the era. In the late
afternoons the turnouts were beautiful — the fine horses, the carriages with
crests on the doors, the cockades of the coachmen's and footmen's hats
proclaiming to what part of the peerage they belonged, and the lovely ladies
gracefully twirling lace parasols with jeweled handles. Often the Princess of
Wales drove by, smiling and gracious. The three daughters dressed alike were
plain by contrast.

The previous winter in Albany, Mother and the Cornings had had their
portraits painted by Felix Moscheles. He and his pretty German wife had
stayed with us, and he had used the upper library with its northern light
for his studio. The Moscheles were now in London, living in a charming
cottage in the center of Cadogan Square. This cottage and another close to
it had originally been built for gardeners, but they had been remodeled and
made over into picturesque little houses.

They knew all the actors of that time, and while I waited in the carriage,
or better still, played all afternoon with Charles Dickens's grandchildren
who lived in the next cottage, I often saw Ellen Terry. She was usually dressed
in some stage costume, having taken part in a matinee or a rehearsal and
not wanting to dress again for the evening. Henry Irving usually accompanied
Miss Terry, and one afternoon we crowded around him as he came in a
scarlet costume with the tail and horns of a devil. Perhaps he had been
acting in "Faust." Toole was another actor.[5]

Henry James came one afternoon with another man and a woman, and
there were several of the pre-Raphaelite artists pointed out to me. Usually
there was music, either piano or singing and perhaps violin too, as the
Moscheles were very much in the world of art. It was nice to sit on the
grass those summer afternoons and watch the world and listen to the music.

Mrs. Moscheles was interested in the Children's Hospital at Chelsea,
where a new wing was to be dedicated by the Prince and Princess of Wales.
It was arranged that I should be one of the children who presented a purse
containing five gold pounds. I found out that I would have to walk up on
the stage, and while presenting the purse (which was made of red satin with

silver fringes and the Prince's feathers and coat-of-arms stamped on it), I should have to make a curtsy to each of them, and then to their daughters.

I got what Mother called one of my "Yankee Doodle fits" and decided I would never bow to royalty. Every argument was brought to bear on me. Mother feared I would embarrass Mrs. Moscheles and thought the plan had better be given up. I was supposed to wear a new dress that I did not like, from Swears and Wells. I had set my heart on wearing a favorite dress with animals in white on a blue background. It was made in New York, but was now much too short and outgrown.

So we arrived at a compromise. I would bow to the royalty as I would to anyone of any nationality, and I would wear my old dress. In the end I did just what the other children did, and made bob curtsies, and I had a close look at the Princess of Wales. She wore a wonderfully made wig, and though the Court was supposed to be in mourning for a German royalty, she wore a lovely openwork, tan straw bonnet with a small black feather.

We often drove out to Dover House at Roehampton, particularly on Sunday afternoon. It was Mr. J. S. Morgan's place, and he had lovely gardens and espaliered fruit trees. He often stopped at our house and left baskets of fruits and flowers, as he drove into the city every morning to go to his office at 22 Old Broad Street. He usually had several grandchildren with him, and we all played games while the grownups talked and had tea.[6]

Mr. Morgan invited Mother and Hattie to drive in his coach to Derby day. I went with Mademoiselle to see them start from Mr. Morgan's town house at Prince's Gate. On the front seat was old Dr. Oliver Wendell Holmes. It was just fifty years since he had last been at Derby day, and Mother said he had a great ovation. Someone in the crowd shouted, "Did you come in your one hoss shay?"

The American Minister at that time was Mr. E. J. Phelps of Vermont. They lived on Lowndes Square, and when Mother and Hattie went to their day "at home," I sat in the carriage reading and watching the American visitors. At a dinner there Mother's partner was Mr. Robert Browning, the poet. She thought him heavy.

London in the season, even for a homesick child, was something to be remembered. Those days are gone forever. They must have been full of leisure and charm, hansom cabs and four wheelers, and void of telephones and bathtubs. For me London presented an everlasting panorama of history in the making. I absorbed the past history from reading books of Bulwer Lytton, Miss Yonge, and Scott, and verified it by visits to the places of which they wrote.

We left London in July for a visit to Lord and Lady Exmouth at their place "Canonteign" near Exeter. They had visited us in Newport while on their wedding trip, and now they had a daughter a year old. My outstanding recollection of the visit is of a morning when I went down early before breakfast. The mail was handed to Lord Exmouth. He sorted it carefully and said he would read his wife's letters and see if they were interesting.

He said, "By George! Edie's sister has accepted that fool of a Lionel!" With that, he threw the whole packet of letters in the fire. When Lady Exmouth appeared, he told her and said, "Your sister is another fool. I have no idea who wrote the other letters."

We took a trip to Torquay, and a long two-days' drive through Holne Chase, then to Bath and wonderful Wells and back to London. In August we went to Scotland. We drove a great deal in funny, old carriages, but it was the only way to see the scenery and to reach some of the places. In later years, when I first met ex-President Taft, he said, "I remember you, though you do not remember me. Mrs. Taft and I were on the same boat with you and your Mother and sister, going to the Island of Skye." He said, "I was so impressed by your Mother, and her bearing and carriage, that I found out your names and where you came from. You were absorbed in feeding the gulls."

We returned to London for last shopping and then went for a visit at Lady Camperdown's at Weston House, Shipston-on-Stour. There I fell in love. It was with a Russian poodle named Fromo, belonging to Lord Abercromby, who had married Lady Camperdown's daughter. Mother had promised me a dog when Hattie came out, and now I decided it must be a poodle.

When we returned to London, we had the use of Lady Abercromby's carriage every afternoon. As she was a lady-in-waiting to the queen, she had certain privileges. One was to be allowed to drive through Constitution Arch and have the carriages saluted. I wanted to do this every day, much to the disgust of the fat coachman.

He tried to sell us an ancient and wheezy King Charles spaniel for an enormous price, but in the end we found in the animal department at Whiteley's a litter of Russian poodles ten weeks old. One of them looked at me. . . . He had pleading eyes, huge paws, and a coat of tangled curls. I held out my hands, and he licked them. I lifted him out, and then and there I said, "This is my Fromo." And he was, for fifteen happy years.

Our return trip, again on the *Etruria*, with an overcrowded cabin of passengers, was even worse than the trip to Europe the previous year. Dogs were under the care of the butcher, and Fromo was very ill. My bunk was even harder and more uncomfortable than before. After two nights I pulled the bed to pieces, and found a large wooden box right under my pillow. Mother had bought a silver alms basin or offertory plate for St. Peter's, to be given as a memorial. Owing to a delay on the engraving, it had not arrived at the hotel in time to be packed, so Mother told Marie to be careful of it. She had been so careful that this large, hard wooden box had been hidden in my bunk.

The joy of "home-at-last" overcame the troubles of the voyage, and [I was happy to know that] soon we would be in the land of pancakes, doughnuts, soda water and Huyler's candy. With Fromo howling in his basket, we reached the Forty-Second Street depot and took an afternoon train for Albany. The bliss of it! The river, the Palisades, Storm King, Poughkeepsie, and cream puffs, and Hudson, and then the first glimpses of the Corning farm lights across the river, the Convent high up on its hill, the house in Greenbush where Mary Whalen's family lived, the turn onto the bridge, and there in the station stood Grandfather and Tuy Marvin and the Lansings. It was just too wonderful for words. . . .

Fromo was left with the Chars at 13 Elk Street, and we went to stay with Grandfather. What a welcome from Grandmother, who had forgotten all our sins of the past, [and] served supper with all the different kinds of food we had written her to have for us. William Tracy, grumbling as usual, remarked next morning, after I had consumed sixteen pancakes with syrup, "Furrin parts ain't cured you."

CHAPTER 14

THAT WINTER [1887] AT ST. AGNES I sat with Bessie Oliver. She and her younger sister, Cora, were new girls. Bessie was an earnest scholar. If she stood high in her school reports, her father paid board at the Pierson's stable for her fox terrier, Fetch. We sat together for several years, though I was a low-mark scholar.

We were really devoted friends, but we seldom agreed on anything. She was a Republican and I a Democrat. She was High Church and I Low. We even fought tooth and nail over whether St. Bernard dogs in the Alps had long or short hair. . . .

The winter centered about Hattie. From Paris and London she had brought home lovely new clothes, and all of them had large bustles and long and elaborate skirts. Sometimes she called me in to help her, as evening dresses had waists that had to be laced up the back, and when Marie was busy with Mother or guests, I was useful. Everything she wore and said and did was wonderful, and I spent much time hanging over the stairs, watching callers and keeping count of how many times a week the same men called.

After interrupting Hattie one afternoon at tea time when she had a "heavy beau" and I felt it my duty to do some chaperoning as Mother was out, I was kept away from the library unless Mother was there. I felt I had seen the height of romance when I burst into the conservatory one afternoon and found a young man on his knees before Hattie. Evidently he was offering his heart and hand. I rushed off shouting, "Come quick and see what's happening!" That man scowled at me for years.

It has always seemed to me that our celebration of Christmas was really the feast of St. Nicholas [December 6], combined with the originally sacred celebration of Christ's birth. The Dutch held the good Santa Claas in great reverence. . . . All of us in ancient Fort Orange knew for a fact that if you go out after sundown on St. Nicholas Eve and cut white lilac slips, they will flower by Christmas. They must be put in a vase of water and kept very warm. The old coal ranges had a shelf, and this was a good place for the slips, as the hot coals gave off heat all night. Every Christmas morning on our library table stood an old Russian silver vase of lovely, white lilacs. The leaves were small and very light green, and the blooms were fragile, but there they were — white lilacs at Christmas.

I do not know where the tradition of Santa Claas' wife comes in. The settlers from the Netherlands brought her over, or she originated over here. Her name was Molly Grietje, and she played a great part before the St. Nicholas day arrived. It was she who decided what children deserved the coveted presents.

Bishop Henry Yates Satterlee, the first bishop of Washington, D. C., was brought up in Albany at his Grandfather Yates's home in the old Kane-Yates house at 102 State Street. When I was a small child, he came to visit us, and he wrote out for us this children's hymn to Santa Claas.[1]

> Santa Claas goed heilig man,
> Treknwe beste tabbaert an,
> Reiz da me'e naar Amsterdam,
> Van Amsterdam naar Spanje,
> Die Appelin van Oranje,
> Die Appelin van Grenaten,
> Die rollen door die Straaten.
> Santa Claas myn goed friend,
> Ik het u allen tyd gedient.
> Will u my im vat gaven,
> Ik zal dienen all mijn leven.

He did not vouch for the accuracy of his spelling, as his so-called "Bible Dutch" had become blurred in the passing years.

As outside influences crept in here, English customs overcame Dutch customs. The German settlers brought over the idea of the Christmas tree, and finally our modern Christmas festival evolved — a trinity of three customs in one.

Our own Christmas celebration began in earnest when school closed about December 20. We had lists of presents we wanted to buy, and we took our lists to Morrison's toy shop on South Pearl Street, and the Whitney's basement. We spent, with the greatest care, our copper penny and two-cent pieces, the tiny three-cent pieces, and the five- and ten-cent pieces. The combinations of these coins helped our arithmetic, as many articles cost seven cents.

Christmas Eve was a rush of white papers and red ribbons. There were yells of joy when the door bell rang and mysterious packages were carried up to Mother's locked closet upstairs. While this was going on, John Murname would arrive in a delivery sleigh and, grinning from ear to ear, would carry in a large Christmas tree. He [would] set it in the window of the front drawing room, and the delicious smell of spruce would pervade the house. We were not supposed to see it again until the great moment arrived on Christmas night.

After we had given out the presents to the Spruce Street children, we rushed back to the nursery to finish tying up our presents for everyone else. At six o'clock, when darkness had settled down, we started in the sleigh to deliver presents like Santa Claas. We had large baskets piled with presents, painstakingly tied in white paper and ribbons and the names illegibly written outside. Sometimes, with the dim street lights and dimmer sleigh lamps, it was difficult to read the names and pick out the right present at the right house.

We called out "Merry Christmas" over and over at each house, and sometimes the horses were frightened and cavorted in the cold air. Heads appeared behind window wreaths, and hands waved at us. Then off again in the gloom of the ill-lighted streets, the sleigh bells jingling, the snow crunching under the runners, and the heavy bear rugs tucked in snugly around us.

Every Christmas Eve the choir boys of the Cathedral of All Saints came to Bishop's House, 29 Elk Street, and sang a carol outside. Then Bishop Doane would come out on the stoop and say, "Merry Christmas, boys. Come in and welcome." They would file into the hall and on into the middle room, shaking hands with Bishop and Mrs. Doane on their way to the piano.

For many years the organist was Mr. J. Albert Jeffrey, with his long hair. He played the accompaniments, and the choir sang the old, familiar carols, like "Good King Wenceslas." The bishop sang solo several verses, beginning "Hither page and stand by me." The page for many years was Decatur Griffin, who had a lovely voice. . . .

After we had sung "Holy Night," "Noël," and a carol written by the bishop, we trooped into the dining room to help give the boys their supper. Young Griffin, with his angelic voice, was a bottomless pit and should have been a giant. In the bay window stood the tree with books and candy stacked about it. The bishop had a wonderful memory for names and could greet each boy as he gave him his present.

The Cathedral clergy and Chapter and their families, whoever was left at St. Agnes over the holidays, the Sisters of the Holy Child Jesus, and a few friends gathered at the Doanes' every Christmas Eve. . . . Bishop's House presented a cheerful and comfortable air, with many lighted candles besides the gas lights. The house was built in 1812, and the old part had good mantels and woodwork. Sprigs of greens and holly hung over every picture, and there was a larger decoration over the painting of the bishop and his brother Monsignor Doane when they were little boys. After singing "Gloria in Excelsis," everyone wished everyone else a "Merry Christmas!" and we filed out into the snow of Elk Street, on our various ways home.

There were one another's stockings to be filled, and Mother's presents, safely hidden from her, to be arranged in the library. We felt sorry for her that her presents were mostly books and flowers, but now I have reached that age too, and I am glad to be remembered at all. After that we went to bed, tired but happy.

When we were supposed to be asleep, Mother, carrying her glass-shaded candlestick, would come into the nursery and begin to arrange our presents on the large table, Hattie's at one end and mine at the other. There was a long mirror in the bedroom door, and we could see in that the size and shape of the packages. . . .

It seemed no time before Hattie pulled me awake, as she had the stockings in bed with her. Both rooms were a mass of papers, ribbons, string, and boxes by the time Mother came in to wish us "Merry Christmas!" It was hard to have to waste time on baths and dressing. Breakfast was eaten piecemeal, and then we ran to the kitchen and laundry with presents, and then dressed for church. After that we went to wish Grandfather and Grandmother a Merry Christmas and thank them for the ten dollars that they gave to every grandchild for Christmas and birthdays, for us to put in the savings bank. Then came presents to their old servants who suffered nobly from our pranks all the year round.

In the afternoon, we had time to gloat over our presents, to coast in the garden, and then to dress for the grand event — the tree. Not only all of our family, but many near relations came to the tree. Among the latter were General and Mrs. Robert Lenox Banks and Lenox, Jr. and little Mary. We knew that Lenox, Jr. was not interested in going anywhere unless he had a chance to see pretty Julia Cushman, so he looked bored. The Tip Cornings with Ratty and little Gertrude, the William Lansings with Willie and Susy, Miss Anna French, May Cooper, and Miss Nelly Rathbone also came to our tree celebration, as well as the Doanes and Battershalls and all those at the school, and "strangers within the gate" at that season always attended.

One of the aunts accompanied the carols, and our first effort was "We Three Kings." We sang the first verse together, then each of the three oldest boys sang a solo for the next three verses, all of us joining in the chorus.

Our favorite carol was one written by George William Warren, formerly organist at St. Peter's. The cover [on the carol book] made one feel cool on the hottest day, as it had frosted bells strung across it. The last verse was "To young and old, to sad and gay, a very merry greeting on a Christmas day." "The First Noël," "Venite Adoremus" and "Stille Nacht" were other favorites.

Near the end our eyes turned longingly towards the large folding doors, and we became impatient for the great moment when two uncles would pull them open. What a glorious sight it was! A Christ Child hovered over the top, and the manger, with the wise men and shepherds and animals around the little cradle, stood at the foot of the tree. On the branches were icicles, stars, tinsel, and snow, all white, green, and silver.

The tables of fancy bonbonnieres were for the grownups, and each had a number on it. One of the uncles called off the numbers, and the one holding the same number came forward amid clappings and applause to claim the present, while jokes and appropriate remarks were made — no one escaped the jibes. Then the children had their presents. As we grew older, the Santa Claas was given up and one of the uncles took charge.

After this came supper. A long table in the china room was set for the children, and a Santa Claas in a sleigh, driving reindeer, was the center piece. The sleigh was piled with small candy boxes. Tables for four in the dining room were for the grownups. Of course we were ravenously hungry after the most exciting day in the year, and we fell quickly on the good things spread in abundance before our greedy eyes.

Having eaten to a standstill and stolen extras from the grownups' serving table, we started games and dancing. The little children played "Hunt the Slipper," "Button, Button, Who's Got the Button," "Hide the Handkerchief," and other games. One uncle whirled people out to dance and deposited each one breathless on the side lines.

Another uncle started "Do you know the muffin man who lives in Drury Lane?" It was Uncle Tuy Marvin, and he would rush at shy or diffident guests. No one could resist him as he joyously cut shines and sang the words all out of tune. Bishop Doane, Dean Robbins and his sister, Miss Emily, and others who had sought the seclusion of the library were gathered into the crowd, protesting, but it was no use. The devil was in Uncle Tuy that night, and they all had to be tumbled downstairs to join the dance. At the end came the Virginia reel, and another uncle cut pigeon wings and capers, the rest of us turning and twisting our partners. Mrs. Doane kept time with her right foot, which was usually reserved for the approved lines of the Bishop's sermons. She tapped vigorously until it seemed as if her diamond shoe buckle must fly off.

There always was a beautiful bunch of mistletoe hung by a red ribbon over the large door. We bent our best efforts to maneuver Dr. Battershall to stand under it in his absent-minded way while talking to some spinster. Someone would call out, "See Dr. Battershall under the mistletoe! What happens next?" The doctor would break out into one of his delightful chuckles, and his horrified companion would back off.

We were all tired after it was over. Coats and wraps were pulled out of the hall closets, and the worn-out grownups would vigorously pull the children into them with an utter disregard for curls or flounces. Elk Street was full of sleighs with merry bells, driving up and down to keep the horses warm. The frosty air and crunching snow are all part of the happy associations of happy days. Weary but joyous children clutched presents, candy, tree decorations, all hanging over the sides of the sleighs, as they piled in and covered up. It was a great day. . . .

An old-fashioned New Year's day in Albany was cheerful, though fatiguing for hostess and household. By eleven A.M. the dining room was open, and it continued open and very busy until about ten P.M. For several years Mother did not receive on account of mourning or absence. If not receiving, a little basket with a slit for cards was tied to the doorbell by a black ribbon.

An extra man was stationed in the hall as doorkeeper, and messenger boys, newsboys with calendars, postmen, policemen, and many others rang the bell and said, "May God bless everyone in the house and a Happy New Year to all!" Over and over we would hear this and the man at the door would hand each one a paper bag containing four of the large *nieuwjahrskoeks*, stamped with flowers, figures, or the State seal, and filled with caraway seeds. In a dish were a pile of dimes, and a dime accompanied every bag.

Tea and coffee were served all day, and during the luncheon and dinner hours tureens of oyster stew were brought up, with chicken croquettes and salads. In a silver basket were the *olykoeken*, and they were continually replenished, as they were by far the most popular of all the New Year goodies. We used the Lansing recipe. Aunt Kitty Lansing used the Gansevoort recipe. There were several other families with their own particular recipe, and these were a subject of grave discussion as to which was the best. We also had the Dutch crullers. They had to be folded by a skilled hand and fluted by an old cutter. Regent's punch, in a ten-gallon East India punch bowl and ladled by a punch ladle which had belonged to General Gansevoort, was on a side table, and very popular. In the late afternoon some madeira was served to appreciative older men.

Ladies did not make calls. They stayed at home to receive guests. In came the men, laughing and talking in the clear air. Sleigh bells jingled and plumes dangled from the horses' ears. By five, the rooms were crowded, and each man was telling how many calls he had to his credit. They were always ready for another glass to keep out the cold and give strength for more.

All our uncles and other male relatives came in during the long day. Two to three hundred callers were an average. Sleighs full of men dashed around from house to house. It was etiquette for them to call on the governor and his lady at the Executive Mansion,[2] on the wives of the State officials, on the wife of their spiritual pastor, and after that, on their friends the ladies, God bless them. My grandfather and one of the uncles went the rounds together, and even managed a few calls in Troy. They never stopped short of one hundred, and the last call was at our house in the late evening.

If [New Year's Day] was not an Inauguration Day, the governor usually called, with members of his glittering staff. The adjutant general, with his staff, and the mayor, accompanied by several companions, generally made the rounds. Bishop Doane in the English Bishop's get-up, gaiters on his legs and shoestring hat in hand, was certain to be a caller.

Then there was Dr. Battershall, rector of St. Peter's, and his son Fletcher; Dr. Reese of St. Paul's Church; the Roman Catholic Bishop, McNierney, with a chaplain. The Chancellor, if he lived in Albany; judges of the Court of Appeals; Dr. Dewey of the State Library (who introduced the card catalogue system, as well as simplified spelling); Professor Boss of the Dudley Observatory, and Mr. Dudley Olcott, as well as Canon Fulcher making his one call of the year all paid their respects. Mr. Richard Varick De Witt and Mr. Charles H. Van Benthuysen with his son Fred; Harmon Pumpelly Read, who was a record-breaker caller; Mr. Frank Pruyn; Mr. Dexter Reynolds and Cuyler called every year. Many younger men came too, like Harry Peckham, the Walsh boys, particularly Townsend Walsh and his friend, introduced as Mr. Robinson, though they were both about twelve years old, and the Cox boys. The first caller was always Professor Hailes. He made a short greeting and passed on to the dining room, and it was fun to watch him settle down to a regular meal.

It is hard to say when this good old custom faded out. It lasted longer in Albany than anywhere else. Perhaps it is the development of country clubs and outdoor sports that has undermined this old-time tradition.

The Pumpellys at One Elk Street dispensed the famous Bleecker punch. One year, at the end of the afternoon, Mr. Pumpelly went upstairs to rest. He met Ellen, the old housekeeper, in the hall.

"Ellen," he said, "I think we have had a very successful afternoon, don't you?"

"Yes sir," said Ellen. "It was a grand afternoon. Shure I met Mr. Fenimore Cooper in the third floor hall, and he says to me, 'Ellen where be I?' Yes sir, 'twas a grand afternoon."

CHAPTER 15

THE RIDGEFIELD TOBOGGAN SLIDE had been built the previous winter [1886] while we were away. It was a great sight, particularly in the evenings, with the oil flares burning every six feet on either side of the chutes. All ages wore the Canadian blanket suits, with toques, and on their feet heavy stockings with ankle turn-over socks to match the coat, and warm comfortable mocassins. About a hundred feet from the bottom of the slide was a bridge for spectators, across the four chutes. They could stand there and watch the loaded toboggans speed under them.[1]

It was our good friend Harry Pierson who gave me my first slide on his toboggan. There was a man for each of the two chutes. That is, one man sent off the toboggans on two chutes. He was the "sender." The toboggan was carefully placed on a platform, and everyone climbed on board, being sure to tuck in their skirts and feet. The one who was to steer was at the back, and when he said, "ready," the sender pulled a lever. We were tipped down the slide and went rushing at a terrific speed to the bottom, under the bridge, and as far as we could go into the fields. The toboggan that went the farthest carried the lantern to show the line.

My brother had a wonderful toboggan made of papier maché with steel runners, and often carried the lantern. When he was away, he allowed me to use his toboggan, and though it was very heavy to pull up the slide, I did not mind as long as I could coast.

We children liked to go there in the afternoon, but we had to take some grownup with us, which was a nuisance. Charlie Weaver was in charge of Ridgefield, and my generation owes him a debt of gratitude for his never-failing good-natured help and his warnings of trouble for us if we did not behave.

Many young married people and Hattie and her friends had a snowshoe club called the "Tanglefoots." They went out in the evenings, usually starting from some house on the park. They would walk all over the park and out on the Log Cabin road, now called New Scotland Avenue. They would end the evening by going to some house for supper, and dancing in their mocassins. These parties were called "Galumphs."

We children organized the "Tanglefoot Jrs.," and in the afternoons we marched around the park and slid down the hills by pressing the tails of the snowshoes hard, which lifted the front part so we could slide. On Saturday mornings we had what we called a "Field Day" on the mall in front of the Olivers' house at 42 Willett Street. I have a photograph taken by General Oliver. There are twelve of us with our ten dogs. All our dogs went with us as a matter of course.

We liked coasting on Elk Street, Columbia and Steuben Streets. It was so convenient for many of us who lived around there. Steuben Street was eliminated for sliding for several years, as the trolley ran up from the station for the accommodation of people arriving on trains. The trolley turned left into Eagle Street and joined the Washington Avenue line above City Hall. But it was not used enough to pay, and so, to the relief of our neighborhood, it was abolished.

We generally had a large crowd out. We had short bobs as well as sleds, but the new flexible flyer was the popular sled. The runners did not get so rusty as the old ones. The two Hun families were stand-bys — Lydia and Katharine and Johnny in one family and Ellen and Mary and Tom in the other family. Susan and Elsie were too young to join us at that time. Edmund Marvin and Ledyard Cogswell Jr. would come down from State Street, Joe Gavit and Fred and Boyd Van Benthuysen came from La Fayette Street. The Jones, who came to live in Chancellor Pierson's house at 32 Elk Street; Meredith Read, with his gold-headed cane, his pumps and his dogs; the Gray boys, and many more made the street gay.

It was against the law to cross trolley tracks, but as we coasted down Columbia Street, we could see the trolley lights reflected in the plate glass windows of the Kenmore Hotel on one side and Mrs. Maidment's bakery on the other, so we went flying across Pearl Street and often down to Broadway. We had a sympathetic friend in Willy Coogan, a policeman on that beat. He kept us out of trouble with policemen who were not so sympathetic. Towards the end of the evening we would take Willy to Mr. Townsend's and give him some sort of treat. He even winked at our coasting on big State Street, as he knew the salt on the trolley tracks at Pearl Street, placed there by unsympathetic authorities, must stop us. Harry and De Witt Walsh and Bob Olcott were older boys who joined us when they were not playing whist in the evenings. . . .

❦   ❦   ❦

Of course the great event of her coming out winter was [Hattie's] ball. It was a cotillion, and she led with General Oliver and Harry Pierson. Bleecker Hall was a shabby old place, the headquarters of the famous Albany Burgess's Corps. On the wall was a faded painting of the Corps, done about fifty years previously. Smilex covered this picture and hung over all the walls. The favors had been bought at the Maison Bail in Paris, and I was breathless with excitement as they were unpacked from the trunk. . . . Of course I got in everyone's way though I was there on the excuse that I could help.[2]

The house was full of guests — boys and girls, Hattie's friends from out of town. Mother sent a sleighload of us down about eight-thirty, various cousins of my age and two great-aunts staying at Grandfather's. It was a fine winter night with deep snow. In fact, the sleigh almost tipped over in the drifts at the corner of Broadway and Steuben Street.

We had to wait there a long time to let the "Bobbing Parade" pass. It was a long procession, and each bob was decorated and had paper lanterns hung from the poles. Each bob club pulled its bob. It was a pretty sight. They were on their way to supper somewhere, [probably to end in prizes] and prize-giving for the best decoration, for the fastest, et cetera, and probably a booby prize for the slowest.

So we reached the hall later than was planned, and our time was cut short, as the sleigh had to return for the use of the guests. We broke loose out of the crowded sleigh and ran up the curved staircase to the ball room, which looked like a fairyland. We sighed with envy and wondered if we would ever have such a ball. But we did see the favors all hung up, the many bouquets, and the band tuning up. As we reluctantly went downstairs, we met first guests arriving on the dot of time. They were our opposite neighbors at 20 Elk Street, Mr. and Mrs. Leonard Kip and their niece, Katy Johnston, with her two brothers, Russell and Dunkin Johnston.

I believe Mother and Hattie created quite a sensation by holding bouquets, and so not having to shake hands with the guests, but just bowing instead. Jack was determined to keep any description of the dresses and favors and supper out of the papers. He gave out a simple statement that there had been a ball, by whom it was given, and where. He heard later that there was great disappointment, as many had sent in descriptions of their ball dresses and jewelry.

                ❧   ❧   ❧

In those halcyon days we almost always had about one hundred days of sleighing. The city looked and sounded gay, as every vehicle was on runners and all had sleigh bells. After the first real snowstorm, it was fun to hear Mother say at luncheon that the carriages had been sent down to Long and Silsby for storage and repairs and the horses had gone to be sharp shod. The next day the sleighs would be sent from storage to the stable, and we could have a ride.[3]

Mother's sleigh was a landau, lined with plum-colored cloth, and the bear rugs had a lining of the same cloth and a scalloped edging. That sleigh held four inside, and it could be open or shut according to wind and weather. The coachman sat high up in front, and the footman sat beside him. There is a very good photograph of mother sleighing in the park.

Hattie had a Russian sleigh. It was painted a dark blue and had white plumes on either side of the dashboard and white fur ruffs around the back of the horse. Two could sit in it, with a footman in the rumble. Jack had a cutter and a horse named "Moses."

The turnouts on Western Avenue every afternoon were quite a sight. It was wide enough for four columns of sleighs. Spectators of the cutter racing[4] drove out on the right hand side next to the kerb and returned on the other side. In the center of the street were the racers. Neck and neck they tore along, with the spectators cheering, and along the kerbs crowds were mildly betting.

Alta McDonald was a nationally known racer. . . . Donald McCredie always had a fast horse, and he generally packed in with him Ike Lansing, known as "The Last of the Albany Dutchmen." Mr. Lansing was as stout as Mr. McCredie was lean, so they made a noticeable pair. Oscar Hascy was another inveterate racer, and often he and George Ayres, from the Corning stable, ran about even, George, with his black cigar and drooping mustache, shouting his favourite slogan, "240 on the Plank Road!" (although Western Avenue had been paved with granite blocks). They had track horses and drove low, single cutters.

Dr. Cox, in his gray cape coat, with his gray whiskers flying, would find time to run his pacer, "Olympus," at least once between visits to his patients. One or another would take a sudden spurt as they flew by the Christian Brothers School. E. D. Palmer, the sculptor, with his picturesque white beard, drove his mare "Nelly Gray," and loved to win a race. Harry Sweny always had a fast horse. Uncle Amasa Parker, wearing his seal skin cap and collar, rushed along with "Railey" or "Pericles," and usually a daughter clinging on with both hands.

Into all this excitement, Uncle Abe and Kitty Lansing would trot at a completely leisurely gait. They too had a cutter, but "Joe Lansing" was no race horse. He had an almost fatal habit of veering suddenly to the left, just as racers rushed by. The Lansings did not seem to mind the irate drivers calling them names. They jogged along placidly.

The Cornings usually drove among the spectators in a two seater. From Elk Street came Mrs. James Kidd with her dogs, and Mrs. Pumpelly, driving decorously back and forth, was a little annoyed by the bits of hard snow thrown out by the racers. The Bleecker Banks of 327 State Street came by in their dashing double sleigh. Chancellor Pierson from 32 Elk Street sometimes drove a pair, and then again, a single horse. Later, Judge and Mrs. John Clinton Gray from 6 Elk Street, who always had the very latest in turnout, added real glamor to the procession. The return races ended at the junction of Western Avenue and State Street, and often there were violent interchanges between the horse owners.

Nothing was more exhilarating than a fine winter afternoon and a sleigh and horse with furs and bells. Western Avenue and the adjoining streets were not then so closely built up, and the views of the Helderbergs and the blue tips of the Catskills, with the sun setting behind them, made an unforgettable picture. . . . [5]

There was a group of us who were very fond of skating. The park lake had been popular for a long time, but finally it was so cut up that we went to the canal before the snow came, or up to Little's Pond at Menands, or on the river, which was best of all.[6] The early skates were clumsy contraptions, with steel runners on wood, and leather straps, which were always breaking off at the buckles. But we had American club skates, of nickel, which fastened on the side with a key. How those keys were lost and borrowed! It was hard to keep one.

These skates had to be carefully fitted on to shoes with soles thick enough for the clamps to be secure. They also had to have a hole in the heel, or otherwise they were apt to fall off and perhaps throw you. We had fancy skating bags, a source of great rivalry — Hattie's was dark blue, with her initials done in black velvet, elaborately stitched on with colored cross-stitch. Mine was dark red, and both were lined with chamois and had tape so that they could hang from our shoulders.

Saratoga had a fine toboggan slide on Mount McGregor. It was quite the rage to take a party up on a late afternoon train, have dinner at a club, and spend the evening on the picturesque slide in the woods. Mother took a party up one Saturday, and I begged to go, but I was the only youngster. On the train going up, everyone was reading an evening paper. I think it was the *Express*, in which, on Saturday nights, the "Estelle" letters were published. As far as I know, the writer was never discovered.[7] The real names of people were thinly disguised. There was a description of a tea given by Mr. and Mrs. "Savings Banks" when Miss "Leather-stocking" poured tea. This referred to Mr. and Mrs. Bleecker Banks and Miss Susan De Lancey Fenimore Cooper. "Pretty Kate Waltz" was Kate Walsh. Hattie was furious because it gave a description of a tea at our house and said the guests gathered in the conservatory to watch the two little daughters of the house and their little friends slide down their sliding board in the garden. A footman stood at the top to see them start safely, while another stood at the bottom to guard the little dears from any accident. The evening we went to Saratoga the items seemed to be particularly amusing to the party.

The older young people indulged in sleigh rides to Sloans, where they had supper and dancing. Sloans was an old-fashioned tavern about eight miles out on the Great Western Turnpike.[8] Large open sleighs, with straw on the bottom, holding about twenty people each on side seats . . . carried gay parties over the snow-covered plank road, by moonlight if possible, while banjos or guitars accompanied the singing.

One winter there was an ice palace in the park, on the hill near the old Taylor place. Tennis courts cover those grounds. The palace had flags of all nations flying from the ice battlements, and inside real lights glimmered on the large cakes of river ice. A band played every evening.

But the real palace of my dreams was the old Lake House.[9] It had a large round covered bandstand with open sides. In summer there were concerts up there, and great crowds, in carriages or row boats, gathered in the afternoons to enjoy the noise. If you could persuade some kindly older relative or friend to row one of those clumsy boats and take you under that wonderfully beautiful bridge, it was real pleasure. Even crowding around the little stove on a cold winter afternoon, trying to fasten on skates with numb fingers, did not lessen the glamor.

I have given to the Institute my last blanket toboggan suit with the long double mittens, the cap with a tassel, and the mocassins with the red turn-over ankle socks. On the left sleeve are sewn the Ridgefield badges for several years. We were very proud of the badges, and each of us tried to outdo the other by having the most. The blanket suits were ordered at a small shop, kept by S. Ed Miller, on Maiden Lane, under the Hun building. Most of his stock was imported from Canada. The early toboggans were of birch bark, but they proved to be too frail, so the light wooden ones, with their gay turkey red cushions, came into use.

Tobogganing became an expensive sport at Ridgefield. It cost $100 to pave the four chutes with heavy blocks of ice. One winter brought a succession of thaws, which ran the club into debt. The slide was a very tall one, and it was made of wood, which needed constant repairs and finally became unsafe. Also, the slide was in the way of the games which were played most of the year. So to our deep and lasting regret the slide was pulled down. When the Country Club was started several years later, a slide was made down a side hill which ran out on the lake. It was maintained at a small cost, but it never had the glamor and the fascinating rattle of the icy chutes.

For indoor exercise there was a tennis court on Jay Street in a ramshackle old building presided over by a patient caretaker named Wilson. On Saturday mornings Hattie and her boy cousins used to play there and end the games by chasing Wilson around. When this was over, they adjourned to Grandmother's, and in the pantry a doting grandmother provided a dozen cream puffs or eclairs. That was all consumed right before our eyes, and we younger ones never had a crumb.

On Lark Street, down in the gully, there was a wooden building — an old fire trap — where all kinds of things happened. The December of the year that Hattie came out, there was a "Kermesse" there for some charity. (Hattie was at a flower booth, dressed to resemble a violet.)

For several winters the building was a roller skating rink, presided over by Mr. Hickey, who was a marvelous skater. He wore a fur cap in cold weather and a derby over one ear at other seasons. He twisted and turned, went backwards, took side steps, whirled on his toes, and never fell on his nose, as we did if we tried to imitate him.[10] He would sweep up some lucky girl, seize her hands crosswise, and off they would go to the tune of Fritz's

"Sweet Violets — they're sweeter than all the roses," or "Sweet dreamland faces passing to and fro," or our favorite, "See-saw, see-saw, now go up and down; See-saw, See-saw, and now we're off for London town." . . . This old wooden building had to be used for occasions like a concert by Myron Whitney or Mme. Albani when the theatres would not hold the crowd.

❦   ❦   ❦

When Barnum's Circus came in early June, we sat on Aunt Kitty Lansing's steps or peered through the iron fence at Grandfather's, waving flags and eating peanuts, in anticipation of the procession, which was slowly marching down Central Avenue, on its way from Schenectady. It was when the calliope reached Townsend Park that we first began to hear it, but we were forbidden to go outside the gate. Jumbo was the hero of many processions, and we felt his loss deeply when he was struck and killed at a railroad crossing while trying to save a young elephant from being hit by a train.

In the afternoon Uncle Amasa Parker would marshal about twenty of us to "The Greatest Show on Earth," then held on the Troy road in Watervliet. When we arrived at the grounds, he would line us up two and two, the smaller ones close to him. Then he [spent] heavily on peanuts and popcorn. We liked the pink lemonade too, but it was frowned on as a possibly poisonous concoction.

It was a marvelous afternoon of never-to-be forgotten joys. The clown sang:

> Where was Moses when the light went out?
> Where was he and what was he about?
> Now my little man, tell me if you can,
> Where was Moses when the light went out?

We shouted, "In the dark — he was in the dark!" This made the clown roll over and over, laughing, cackling, and turning somersaults. He would stand on his hands and feet and shout back, "Ha! Ha! Moses was in bed! Ha! Ha!" Visits to side shows, with the snake charmer, the fat lady, midgets, and tattoo men, and the man who swallowed knives, ended our day of joy.

Our favorite book at that time was *Toby Tyler or Ten Weeks With a Circus*. The boys put on circus shows in the pasture, now buried deep under Sheridan Park. We girls might be asked to help them if they needed us. Grandfather's horses were let out in the pasture, while Morrissey milked

the cows, and the boys would catch them and try bareback riding. Even
our dogs, wearing paper ruffles, were included in the parade. We imagined
ourselves as circus queens as we jumped through paper hoops.

> Ask your mother for fifty cents,
> To see the elephant jump the fence.
> He jumps so high that he touches the sky
> And he won't be back 'til the fourth of July.

When the coasting season on Elk Street was over, our group or gang of
coasters did not altogether break up. There was Valentine's Day, which came
while the coasting was still going on. We left comics on the doorsteps of
the houses, and rang the bell and ran. Everyone was remembered. The comics
were very large, and sold for two for a cent at Mrs. Blessing's or at Mason's.
Our neighbor at No. 23, Mr. John McHarg, liked to coast with us, so we
left a sporty valentine for him.

Then there was April Fool's Day, a day and night of terror on Elk Street.
During the day we tied old purses, stuffed with paper, to a black thread, or
better still to a hair from a horse's tail. The purse was placed in a strategic
place, and the end of the thread or hair was held by someone who was
hidden. It was wonderful to see how many [tried to] pick up the purse.
What fun it was to shout "April Fool!" Or we might glue a nickel onto the
sidewalk and watch out the window as passers-by tried to pick it up.

But best of all was the trick whistle from Hattie's trick box. It was wooden
and quite long, with a small bowl half-way down. The trick was to fill this
bowl with flour. You could whistle all you wanted, with no trouble, if you
pressed the spring on the end of the whistle, but if it was not pressed, then
flour blew up through pin holes all over your face.

One year Grace and I were wandering around on April first to see what
we could do, when the bishop and his dog came down the street. He stopped
to speak to us, "What a clear, fine whistle you have."

Grace said, "Bishop it would be splendid for calling your dog. Please try
it."

The bishop good-naturedly took it and blew. Immediately he was covered
with flour, and we danced with joy and shouted "April Fool!" The bishop,
good sport that he was, laughed, and then we felt perhaps we were the fools
after all and helped brush him off.

In the evenings, we divided the block up. Each person had the care of two door bells. The bell was pulled out as far as it would go and was tied to a string, which in turn was tied around a tree. The consequence was that each house dweller was out on the steps trying to find the string and stop the noise, while we hid behind doors, yard fences, and trees.

A very successful April Fool was to call up a drug store, not too far away, and order an emergency dose of castor oil sent at once to Miss Barnard, dear little Miss Condit, or old Mr. Meads on Pine Street. Sometimes we were lucky enough to have several drug stores running on this errand at once.

Huyler introduced delicious-looking candies with little wooden centers or hard rubber centers. These were useful at recess at school, to give to the always hungry boarders. When the trolleys first came in, we said "eeney, meeny, miny, mo." The one who was "it" at the end had to go to Lord's corner and stop a trolley, put a foot on the step and tie the lace of his boot, thank the amazed conductor, call, "April Fool!" and leave.

Some of us had a mania for blacking up. It was quite an art to put the burned cork on evenly, and even more so to take it off with cold cream. One evening when Mother was away, Julia Walsh came to supper, and we blacked up. Marie was supposed to keep an eye on me after school hours. She made violent protests in her excited French way. She waved her arms and kept saying, "Oh! What would my former employer, Madame la Duchesse de Maille, say to my having charge of Apaches — 'les peaux rouges' — here in this wild city?"

Julia was dressed as an old lady and wore spectacles. I wore Jack's clothes and had a banjo strung around my neck with a yellow ribbon. We ran into the congregation of one of the churches, and Julia rattled a small bank for money, and I sang, "Clarence McFadden, he wanted me to waltz, but his feet were not made in that way."

People stopped and seemed to like the show, so we went to Miss Bernard's. She and Miss Walsh were at church but expected home soon, so we waited. In a few minutes the doorbell rang. Julia said, "You pose with the banjo, and I'll open the door." There stood a policeman! Julia slammed it. The policeman rang and rang. We finally persuaded the maid to go down to the basement door and find out what he wanted. The policeman told her that we were masquerading and collecting money and that he had followed us and would stay there. He sat on the steps, and when Miss Barnard and Miss Walsh returned, there sat a policeman on their "innocent" steps. In the meantime we had escaped by the back yard to Spruce Street and were safely in our house, plastering ourselves with cold cream. Another evening Harriet Parker and I wandered about, but no policeman bothered us.

Mrs. Edward Hun had a dance one evening for either Lydia or Katharine. It was a bud [debutante] party, so of course I had not been invited. But I thought it would be nice to go, so I went home from coasting and blacked for a low-neck dress. This was quite a job, but long black gloves of Mother's covered the lower arms, so only the upper part had to be blacked. It took so long that when I burst in, the party was at supper. What an uproar it was when I kissed Mrs. Hun on both cheeks. Everyone fled as I started to kiss all around. I danced a Highland fling and departed — much to the relief of the party.

One fall Amasa Parker Jr. and others got up a horse show at Ridgefield. It was on two afternoons in October, and there was an elaborate programme, paid for by advertisements. At the foot of every page was a "Note" — "The soundness of a horse does not count in any class." When there were some protests about this, Amasa replied, "If soundness is required, there could be no show." Eddy Reed entered his bay horse as a "Gentleman's Riding Horse," a "Trotter," a "Park Hack," and finally as a "Jumper." The talented steed received rounds of applause for his varied performances, but never won a prize. . . .

It was the fashion then to have a knot of artificial flowers attached just below the horse's ears. Usually there was a strap to hold them in place. The straps were made in England and sold at harness shops like Mark Cross in New York. Most people chose red flowers, such as three or four small poppies with leaves. The red geranium was popular, and so were blue cornflowers. Lilies of the valley were used for festive occasions like weddings.

I drove my spider phaeton with a pair of horses that became temperamental under the strain of the crowds and the clapping and refused to keep in step. I also rode "King," but he was so nervous that I could hardly control him. For this show my flowers were red daisies with black centers, and a boutonniere for myself, which was very swagger.

Dr. Battershall was fond of riding, and he liked a white horse that he hired from Person's stable on Maiden Lane, just below the jail. One day the doctor heard the boy who was holding the horse saying, "Whoa Emma!" He naturally thought that the horse was named "Emma," as he did not know that was a popular song at the time. In the park, when the doctor tried to stop the horse in order to speak to Mrs. Kidd and her dogs, he shouted lustily, "Whoa Emma!" as the horse shot by the carriage.

Eddy Reed (Edward Townsend Reed) often rode with us. He rode over from little State Street and joined us on Elk Street. Another rider who often joined us was Colonel Harry C. Cushman who lived further up on State Street. We met in the park. Eddy Reed considered himself quite a sport, and he often had his riding horse harnessed to a "cut-under" and drove his mother in the afternoons. His mother sat in the rear seat, and they would drive over Eagle Street to Elk and stop at No. 8 to pick up Bessie Van Benthuysen.

The Reeds lived at 156 State Street and Mrs. Reed, Marianna Townsend, was a character. The Reeds belonged to the Second Presbyterian Church on Chapel Street, that beautiful example of Philip Hooker's architecture, where the pews had doors. When the service was over, Mrs. Reed would usher her family out and then lock the door of the pew and take the key in her pocket, so no one — not even the cleaner — could enter the pew.

Mrs. Reed's brother, who did not live in Albany, died one spring. A friend, seeing her across the street, started over to offer condolences, but to her astonishment Mrs. Reed was wearing her usual brilliant colors. She explained that she had already bought her spring and summer clothes and decided that she would not don her mourning clothes until the fall.

The Reeds kept a parrot in a room back of their dining room. One night they had a dinner party, and Mrs. Reed said to Eddy, "Please ask the blessing." As he started, the parrot said, "Oh! Whew! Whew! Whew!" . . .

One summer when the Reeds were away and Eddy was alone there, he heard the City Hall bell ring the fire alarm. He ran downstairs and into the street in his night clothes. The wind blew the front door shut. There he was, and no one in the house to let him in. Fortunately, someone in an adjoining house rescued him. . . .

Usually the snow began to melt by the middle of March, although I remember one spring when we coasted out on the hills on the third of April.

Our garden would be wet, and coasting would end. Then we played on Elk
Street, and we ran small bits of wood for boats down the Elk Street gutters.
Sometimes we were guilty of damming the gutters and flooding the sidewalks
and having the fun of seeing people get very cross. After the gutter-boat
season was over, we had skip ropes, return balls, hoops, and roller skates,
and endless games of hopscotch.

In the spring of the year that Hattie came out — always a wonder year
to me — the papers came out with the story that the city was going to have
dogs licensed, and, worse than that, they were going to enforce a rule that
dogs must wear muzzles during the summer months. We were all dog lovers,
and these plans aroused our indignation.

We decided that something must be done about it, and one Sunday afternoon we gathered at the Parkers and started to write a petition. My uncle
helped us, and the petition started with this sentence, "Dear Mr. Mayor.
We love our dogs, and we strongly protest the cruelty of muzzling. We
embark on this petition, and we cling to it with dogged tenacity." We were
very pleased with the puns.

Mother offered to escort us to the City Hall the next morning to present
the petition to Mayor John Boyd Thacher. There were four Parkers, three
Olivers, two Sards, and myself. Each of us had a dog. All of the dogs had
been washed and combed and wore ribbons. Though we had them on leashes,
they nipped and growled at one another all the way across Academy Park.[11]

We were met by the mayor's secretary and escorted into the mayor's room.
He stood up and bowed ceremoniously. We presented the petition, tied up
with blue ribbon. The dogs, in the meantime, were restless and succeeded
in tangling their leashes, and two started a fight.

The mayor had a vase of flowers on his desk. He gave each of us a flower.
I still have mine, pressed in an envelope and marked with the date. He
promised to give the petition grave consideration, which pleased us very
much. Then he bowed us out.

We were thrilled to have the *Journal* publish the story with the petition
and all our names, and we were not at all surprised when the mayor and
Common Council announced the plan was given up. Of course we knew
we had done it. There was no doubt in our minds but that our petition
made them see the error in their plan. That night of our triumph Fromo

broke into the refrigerator room and ate all the sweet breads that were to be one of the courses at a dinner party.

On July 4th, Fromo was a year old. Though he was born in England, his birthday was on Independence Day, so [I insisted] that made him an American. My conclusion was questioned by my cousins and friends, and this led to heated discussions as to his nationality. Whenever there was a quarrel [amongst the dogs], they alluded to the "British dog" having started it.

Fromo sent out invitations to his dog friends to come to our garden at four o'clock on July 4th. The heat was terrific, and the dogs all jumped into the fountain, which Fromo regarded as his special lake. The dogs were of all kinds. Most of them wore ribbons on their collars, but the dogs pulled the ribbons off each other, and in a few minutes ribbons were dragging, and the fountain had become a muddy pool. The goldfish had taken refuge under the iron pedestal on which the old man with the spouting ducks stood. We tried to play croquet and other games, but the dogs really were the center of attention. Fromo was the recipient of various presents.

Supper was served in the dining room piazza, and the ice cream had a dog made of white icing on it. (To this day I have that icing dog. It is in a china box at Mattapoisett, together with a dove from the golden wedding cake of my grandparents.) The dogs were naturally anxious to share the ice cream and cake, and they crowded up the steps from the garden, dripping wet and quarrelling as usual.

Just as we were about to carry the cake to the garden to share it, there was a terrific thunderclap. We had not noticed the blackening sky, and now the deluge fell. The lightning was frightening to us, and to the dogs terrifying. Fleet Sage had to be put in the cellar. Fromo vanished, and it was several hours before I found him cowering under my bed. Hendrick Hudson and his crew had been playing ninepins in the Catskills that day. But in spite of it all, we had had a wonderful afternoon. I made a winter blanket for Fromo out of an American flag so there could be no doubt as to his nationality.

CHAPTER 16

A FTER SOME WEEKS AT FIRE ISLAND, the summer [of 1887] was spent in making several visits, and in the fall we went to Washington for the winter. My laments were loud and long, but Mother thought it would be nice for Hattie to have a winter there. Hattie was a native of Washington, having been born there when my father was in Congress. At that time they lived in a house on H Street. This time Mother rented a house for the winter on the corner of 16th and K Streets. . . . It was quite new, and in the over-decorated style of the 1880s.

Needless to say, Fromo accompanied us and had a most exciting life. He was continually being stolen by the squatters in the small wooden shanties that then disfigured the vicinity of Scott Circle. Offers of a reward usually brought him home promptly. I went to school at Mrs. Flint's on 1734 I Street, where seventeen girls were crowded into a small parlor and dining room, with the old pantry turned into a coat room.

As for Hattie, she enjoyed every minute of the winter. . . . The Leiters gave their famous Leap Year party, and it was the winter that the delegates came from England about the fisheries question. Mr. Joseph Chamberlain was a familiar figure, and his courtship of Miss Mary Endicott of Salem, daughter of the Secretary of War, was the great news.[1]

As I ran to school every morning, I was apt to have a smile and handwave from Mr. William C. Whitney, Secretary of the Navy, who lived across the street from Mrs. Flint's school, in the old Frelinghuysen house. Whenever I caught sight of lovely Mrs. Cleveland walking with her poodle Hector, I stood watching her. Once our poodles met on the corner of K Street and had a fight. I was a poor scholar, always telling the people at school how I hated Washington, and how wonderful Albany was. Mrs. Flint raged because I was often late in the morning, on the excuse that Fromo had run away and had to be caught.

Hattie had a devoted admirer who was much older than she was — much too old, I protested. I disliked him intensely. . . . Hiding his silk hat and pouring water on him when he rang the bell had no effect on his attentions. One afternoon he stayed very late, and Mother invited him to stay on to dinner. He accepted, of course, but said he must return home first, as he expected an important letter, but he would return. When he did return, he had hurriedly dressed in his evening clothes, so hurriedly, in fact, that one side of his dress shirt stuck out in a big bulge. As I sat across the table from him, I had ample opportunity to take it all in. Mother asked me to say grace. I was so completely fascinated with the shirt that I began to say the Lord's Prayer by mistake. Mother called me by name sharply, and I said, "Just look at that bilge." Needless to say, I was sent to my room, but I soon finished my dinner very comfortably in the pantry.

In March, Grandfather and Grandmother came down from Albany for a visit. Grandmother was quite an invalid and never went out anywhere. But she liked guests at home, and as a great concession, President and Mrs. Cleveland came to a seven o'clock dinner one night. I was told to be sure not to speak of it to anyone. I was allowed to come to dinner.

Just before their arrival, the smilax twined over the hideous chandelier in the dining room caught fire. It was soon extinguished, but the table was a mass of smudges. Everything had to be taken off. I was stationed in a front window to give notice when the White House carriage arrived, so that Christian, the Swiss butler, and his wife Fanny could be on hand to open the door and take the wraps. It was really wonderful the way things were cleaned up and the table reset, with only a few minutes delay.

In those days the White House invitations were delivered by a man on horseback. When we heard the clattering of hoofs, it was exciting to see which house was to be honored. The horse was fastened to the hitching post, then in front of every house, and the man delivered the invitation at the door. Often some of the children playing in the street would produce a lump of sugar for the waiting horse.

Aunt Mary Corning and Parker came down to stay with us, and Aunt Mary went to a diplomatic dinner at the White House. Besides Mr. Chamberlain, the other special lions were the first Korean delegation to be sent to Washington. The Koreans wore tall hats and beautiful silks and were an interesting sight in the streets. The night of the dinner Parker and I went to the White House too, and Colonel Daniel Lamont, who was the President's private secretary at that time, took us upstairs where the procession was forming.[2] I quite well remember Mrs. Richard Townsend's pink tulle dress with large dead blackbirds hung on the skirt, and an extra large one on one shoulder.

Parker and I were put in the charge of a house detective, and we stood where we could see the procession come downstairs. The President, with Miss Bayard on his arm, led the way, and Mrs. Cleveland, all in white, followed on Secretary Bayard's arm. . . . [3]

❦   ❦   ❦

We came home again in May, and Hattie had a house party of Washington friends in early June. Grandmother was unable to leave Albany that summer, and to my joy, we spent most of the summer at home. The garden, tennis and croquet, and my gas stove in the playroom for parties for Fromo, kept me busy, together with a great deal of reading. Jack had given me a set of the Waverley novels, and at four every afternoon I retired to the bathroom, drew the tub almost to the top, sank down in it, and read there, cool and comfortable. Mother raged one afternoon to find that Fromo was in the tub with me, and the water a muddy pool. He was hot just as much as I was.

After tea and lemonade on the piazza, we usually took a drive. Often we drove out of town to make a call on the Genets across the river, the Netts at Normanvale, the Sages at Menands, or the Harrises at Loudonville. If we went to the Genets, they would give us tea from the cups and saucers of Royal Sevres, ordered by Mr. Genet's aunt, Mme. de Campan, lady-in-waiting to Queen Marie Antoinette. Mr. George Clinton Genet, though half-American, looked like a typical Frenchman. It was wonderful to realize that he was the son of Citizen Genet, and that his aunt had read to the daughters of Louis XV.[4]

The Genets lived at Cantonment Farm, which had been a barracks in the War of 1812. In the winter they lived in New York. They took their historic possessions with them or placed them in storage. In the end they gave many of them to the Albany Institute. Mr. and Mrs. Genet drove around in a low Victoria. I have a newspaper picture of them in their carriage on State Street.

Sometimes we drove up to the Olcotts at Crow Nest, where the view was so beautiful. Bob did dairy farming. If we were very energetic, we took the ferry to Bath at North Ferry Street and drove to the Burdens at South Troy.[5] In summer Mrs. Proudfit was usually there, and their places were beautifully kept.

While over there we drove to Forbes's Manor, which was really Beverwyck, built by William P. Van Rensselaer in the 1840s. It must have been a wonderfully beautiful place when well kept. The grounds were second to none on the whole river, but in my childhood the caretaker hung her wash in the front hall. The Forbes had left so hurriedly that personal things, as well as furniture and musical instruments, had been left behind. It seemed to me like an enchanted palace with a curse left on it.[6]

All the roads around Albany were bad. Most of them were plank on one side, to help the farmers driving in with their heavy loads. The other half was mud to the hubs in the winter and dust in the summer! The planks were full of holes where people had pulled a board up to help pry a wagon out of a mire. In theory, the toll system was supposed to care for the repairs as well as provide dividends to the stockholders, but it never did.

To go across the river on the quite new bridge for carriages and foot passengers, which took the place of the south ferry, you paid a toll. Then you made the best of it over the cobbles of Greenbush streets to the Columbia pike, down a steep hill with a rickety wooden bridge over the tracks and advertisements everywhere for "Kicapoo Ointment," "Carter's Little Liver Pills," and "Smith's Cough Drops." In the fall we took a lovely drive by turning to the right and taking the road high up above the river, known as the Ridge Drive. On a fine afternoon the Catskills seemed very close, and a distant tip was said to be the Donderberg.

The road was not much more than a cart path, and the drive from our house and back took about two and a half hours. We returned to the Columbia pike by the old red brick East Greenbush Reformed Church, where the Genet family was buried in the rear churchyard. Citizen Genet, born to all the pomp and luxury of the Court of Versailles, found his final rest in far-off Greenbush, in this little country cemetery. His two wives and several children are buried there with him.

There was a toll gate at the junction of the roads going north, at Shaker Road, Loudonville Road, and the Van Rensselaer Boulevard. On the latter road, Fritz Emmett, the actor, had built an extraordinary place called Fritz's Villa.[7] He was grateful to Albany for being appreciative of his "Fritz" plays, so he decided to build out there. . . . Fritz Villa had a high iron fence, a pond with a gondola, and a mill beside it. There was also a small waterfall. The grounds were full of iron dogs and deer, and the house was long and low and covered with cupolas, towers, gables, and everything else possible. We had crossed the ocean with Mrs. Emmett and her son, Joe, and our seats on the deck were next to one another. She was a quiet, sweet woman. I was consumed with curiosity to see what was inside the fence, and I longed to ride in the gondola. We often went to the cemetery, so I had the chance to look in.

Finally, Mother took me with her to make a call. She gave me the cards, so that I could ring the bell and ask for Mrs. Emmett, but all I saw inside was a statue of a colored boy holding a card tray. Mrs. Emmett was not at home. She never returned the call, so I never had a chance to ride in the gondola.

When Mr. Cleveland became President, he was succeeded [as governor] by Lieutenant Governor David B. Hill of Elmira, a bachelor. He lived in the Executive Mansion with his cat "Veto" and later with Harry Pearse, a student at the Medical College in whom Governor Hill was much interested. . . .

Governor Hill was the Calvin Coolidge of his day, silent and observant. Rumors were thick and fast that he was to marry the beautiful Miss Hotchkiss of Elmira. She and her mother came to stay at the Mansion, and he gave a large dance for her. Everyone was sure the engagement was to be announced then, but nothing happened. Finally, the Governor bought the Fritz Emmett place and made it his home [renaming it Wolfert's Roost]. He was a United States Senator, and he practiced law in Albany. . . .

During the reign of King David B. Hill, as he was called, the Executive Mansion was done over under the supervision of Mr. Isaac Perry, the superintendent of the Capitol. It was an era of bad architecture, and the Mansion bears witness to this day of the mutilation a nice, plain house can endure. One room that was badly needed, however, was a large reception room. This was added at the north end of the house, but it had only one door into the hall, where two were needed for the easy circulation of crowds.[8]

Governor Hill asked Mother to come over to advise him about having a wooden floor or a carpet. There had evidently been great discussion on this momentous subject. Mother strongly advised a wood floor, with two or three large rugs that could be taken up for dancing, but he decided on the carpet. Several years later the Mortons discarded the carpet and had a wooden floor laid.

Governor Hill went quite regularly to St. Peter's, and sat in the governor's pew, the second from the front on the left of the main aisle. This pew had been reserved for governors for many years. I remember Governor Cornell and his family used it too. My brother Jack was on the staff of Governor Hill. He had one of the gold-ornamented uniforms and became at once another colonel. Dr. Harry Pearse usually went to church with Governor Hill. Dr. Pearse lived at the Mansion for some time.

At the cemetery our lot was on Beminden Drive. It was a peaceful and lovely spot, with Norway spruces as a screen. But the spruces died, and new ones did not thrive. At Grandfather's cemetery lot we could go down to the pretty "Noontide Walk" in the ravine, by a brook with wooden bridges crossing it. It was always cool, even at noontide, hence its name.[9]

We all loved to go to the Sages at "Hillside" on Menands road. They were most kind and hospitable. Often Mrs. Sage would stop at our house in her carriage, called a "Democrat," and carry us off, or else arrange for us to come for a meal or over night. On Sunday nights they had supper at small tables set up in the dining room and living room. All ages were there, as the five Sage children all had their own friends.[10]

In the fall Sarah and Betty and I often made fires in flower pots and roasted potatoes or apples. We went up to the grove behind the house, and sometimes in the evening they had a campfire there, but usually that was for the friends of Susan and Henry. Several times they had a gypsy queen who told fortunes. Mrs. Sage had an interesting Shakespeare garden. It had all the flowers mentioned by Shakespeare. Many of them had been difficult to find, as they have other names now.

Mr. Sage added a fireproof room for his valuable collection of Shakespeare and Izaak Walton books and folios. There were always interesting guests like Mark Twain and others of the Hartford group, as the Sages had lived in Hartford. They spent several winters on Elk Street, and Sarah went to St. Agnes before she went to Farmington. She used to run home at recess to see how the dogs were doing without her, and I have been known to [have played] hookey with her. . . .

South of the city the Prentices lived at Mount Hope. There were two lions on the pillars at the gateway, and inside the gate was a stone vault that frightened me badly. The road up to the house was narrow and winding, but when you reached the house, the view was lovely. . . . The land fell off quite steeply, and across the road below they owned the meadows down to the river. The West Shore Railroad was built on an embankment and ruined the shore property all along the river. . . .

Before we reached the Prentice place, we came to Cherry Hill on South Pearl Street. The old house, built in 1767, stands so high and so far back, with trees protecting it, that the house is forgotten. It was built by Philip Van Rensselaer of the Claverack branch of the family. . . .

We often called on Miss Mary Cagger at the Convent of the Sacred Heart. She lived there the last years of her life. The Convent had originally been the summer place of Mr. Joel Rathbone. Kenwood was Rensselaer Mills, but on a visit to Scotland, Mr. Rathbone admired a village called Kenwood, so the name was changed. . . .

To reach the Corning farm we passed through a toll gate and always sang, "You must not pay the toll gate because it is a sin." Then we crossed the Normanskill on an iron bridge, where there was a sign that warned, "There will be a fine for a horse going faster than a trot." Then came the long hill, "Ta-wassa-Gunshee," then down the other side. All this has been eliminated by the road on the river level. . . . [Mrs. Hamlin here describes houses along the drive south of the city.]

One of the things we most liked when we were children was to be allowed to spend Saturdays at the Corning farm, called "Ta-Wassa-gunshee," meaning the "Lookout Hill." The farm lay at the mouth of the Normanskill, which the Indians called "Tawasentha." The Place of Departed Spirits, a burial hill, lay opposite the lookout. Around 1618, the Dutch had made a treaty there with the Indians, which was never broken.[11] The Mohawks used the hill as a real lookout on the river. There were Indians with whom they were always at war, particularly over the ownership of the islands in the river. Later Captain Kidd was supposed to have hidden treasure in this hill, and the Dutch called it "Kidder Hooghten."[12]

Dr. Cox's son, Jimmy Cox, was not very strong as he grew up. He went to the farm to live with the farmer and Mrs. Vanderbilt and to do outdoor work. Jimmy, like his father, loved a joke. He produced some old coins and other junk, and people got the idea that he had discovered Captain Kidd's treasure. There was a great run on the hill. People armed with shovels drove to the foot of the hill, tied their teams, and went to work. Of course this all got into the papers, and finally Jimmy had to own up to the hoax.

When we went down to the Corning's farm for the day, we usually carried our luncheon. There were always five or six of us piled into the carriage, with Missie Char or Frieda in charge. There was so much to do that it was hard to choose what to do first. Mr. Gray was apt to be in the potting shed, and he would send someone to show us the wonderful orchids. He was afraid we might touch or even pick one. Just before Easter they were a wonderful sight, and all were picked and carried with the greatest care, to decorate the old Chapel for Easter. . . . [Mrs. Hamlin here describes outings at the Cornings' farm.]

At Thanksgiving, we often had the family feast at the farm. Often there was snow and we could go down in the sleighs, which were much more fun than the carriages. One year Louis Parker had some terrapin which his cousin in Savannah sent. They were in a box, but unfortunately it had no string tied around it. Louis was driving. The carriage swerved on the car tracks, the box fell out, and the terrapin vanished in the dark. We all got out in our evening dresses and slippers and tried to find them, but only one was caught. . . .

I have run ahead of the winter that Hattie came out. I know that it was a very gay winter, that she received many bouquets for all occasions, and that she had many callers. At tea time there were always callers, but they were usually girls and older women making dinner calls. The young men called in the evenings. They were properly dressed, either in full dress suits or a Prince Albert coat. I am quite sure that the "Tuxedos," as dinner jackets were then called, were not introduced until several years later. If an older man were present, he would offer a cigar to the guest, but the guest did not produce a cigarette case, pass it around, snap a patent lighter and start chain smoking.

In the serious affair of the visiting cards, there were accepted rules. They had their language. Someone writes of them as being "dog-eared," and that is a good description. Turning down the upper right corner meant that you had called in person. The upper left corner turned down meant that your cards had been left [by another, in a perfunctory way]. Where the whole end of the card was turned back, it meant condolence if turned back at one end, and congratulations if turned back at the other.

Endless books on etiquette were published, several by Mrs. John Sherwood, who seems to have been the Emily Post of her day. She discussed chaperoning and the difficulties in arranging for a girl to go to a ball, unless a parent accompanied her and stayed up all night. Chaperoning was strict, and my mother would sit in her leather armchair in the library, sometimes glancing at the clock over the mantel with glazed eyes. A young caller would do his best to be entertaining, but often stayed much too long and needed to be helped out.

Mother became quite skillful at this. She would ask the caller if he had seen some picture, or some interesting antique, and then would offer to show it to him. Having once [been gotten] out of his chair, he never had a chance to sit down again. It was often the only way to help him leave, to have the house closed for the night.

Mother finally had an even better method. There was a gas chandelier over the large desk in the library. It was difficult to light, so the latest invention was attached to two of its jets. It was an electric lighter that lighted the light in the upper hall and lower hall, in case of burglars. But the lighter in the library made a frightful noise, a kind of long screech. When this suddenly sounded, any young man jumped to his feet. In fact, everyone did. Mother always looked innocent, if she came in later, and disclaimed any intention of ousting anyone or giving a visitor a nerve shock.

CHAPTER 17

O NE OF OUR FREQUENT afternoon callers was Aunt Kitty Lansing. I [would] always desert my lessons for the next day, and slip into the library, where she and Mother would be having tea. Aunt Kitty always had unusual experiences. She never did anything like anyone else. She was not really our aunt, but she was just like one, and had always been Mother's close friend. In fact, she came to Mother to discuss all her troubles. She had been one of Mother's four bridesmaids, and she was related to us through my father's family.

Uncle Abe Lansing was also a cousin, related through several families. [He and Aunt Kitty] lived at 115 Washington Avenue, in the house built by Aunt Kitty's father, the second General Gansevoort. It was a fine solid old house with good woodwork and mantel pieces and full of interesting furniture, china, and portraits.

Aunt Kitty waged a continual war with her next door neighbor at 119 Washington Avenue, General John F. Rathbone, John the Baptist, as she called him. Her complaints were many, but the particular one was that the smoke from his greenhouse chimneys ruined her fruits. She thought he should build the chimneys up eighteen inches higher, and then the smoke would roll off above the fruits. His pear tree had a limb that hung over her fence. One night she had her man, Gottlieb, cut the limb off, and she picked off the pears and chuckled.

Yet when she and Uncle Abe returned one fall from a trip to England, she brought a silver candlestick especially for the General and Mrs. Rathbone, "to bury the hatchet," as she put it. I went with her when she carried in the package and left it at the door with her love. The truce did not last long. Soon after, she renewed the war over the chimney.

❦   ❦   ❦

I loved to go with Aunt Kitty on her expeditions. She and Uncle Abe had decided to do over the house and to add rooms at the top for servants. I was about ten at this time, and much interested in her plans. The contracts were signed and the work begun, but no one would stay long, as Aunt Kitty was always changing her mind about the plans. Masons, carpenters, plumbers, and all the rest, came and went. Uncle Abe could not stop her. He was a busy lawyer and not at home to keep track of her doings. He only knew that the repairs did not progress.

One Ash Wednesday after church, Aunt Kitty asked me to go down to Pearl Street with her for an errand. I was delighted and trotted along beside her. She told me that Uncle Abe was impatient to get back into the house, and she thought she could induce the original workmen to return and carry out the plans if she gave each of them a watch.

We went to Mr. Bob Williams, the jeweler on Pearl Street near the Elm Tree corner. Mr. Williams himself came forward to wait on Aunt Kitty, and he showed her various watches suitable for men. Aunt Kitty finally picked out a regular turnip watch and said she would like to have twenty-one of them as soon as possible.

I have never seen a more astonished look on any face. Like everyone else, Mr. Williams knew that Aunt Kitty was "unexpected" in her ways, but he was evidently bursting with curiosity to know what she was going to do with all these watches. Aunt Kitty did not choose to explain anything to him. He told her that it would be several days before he could get the watches, as they were made in Connecticut, but when they came he would send them up at once.

Aunt Kitty thanked him for his help and then started to walk up big State Street. As we ambled along, Aunt Kitty told a long story about a piece of thin white material that she had bought two years before and laid aside for her shroud. A few days before she had happened to open the parcel and had found, to her astonishment, that it had turned a light blue. She did not know what had happened to make this change, but it was no longer of any use for a shroud. So she had given it to a friend, who had a daughter being married, to use for a wedding dress.

We stopped at Townsend's on Eagle Street for her to treat me to a soda water, and she and Mr. Townsend conversed about the state of the streets and why the city did not keep them cleaner. Then she started me across the park on my way home, and she vanished by Washington Avenue. A few days later, she came in at tea to report to Mother that the men were delighted with the watches and had returned to work, that she would not bother them any more to make changes, and that in a month she and Uncle Abe could return to the house.

❦   ❦   ❦

Aunt Kitty and Uncle Abe had a maid named Louisa. At least that was the name Uncle Abe gave her. Her name was Kate, but as he often called Aunt Kitty "Kate," it would be confusing, and he liked the name of Louisa. She seemed to accept it. Louisa was very small and thin, almost to emaciation. Over and over she tried to leave when things got too mixed up. Twice her trunk was actually packed, but kindly Uncle Abe, realizing the situation, managed to pacify her, and at last she became a real part of the household.

Aunt Kitty was the granddaughter of General Peter Gansevoort, who had held Fort Stanwix, in the Mohawk Valley, against the British forces in the summer of 1777. He had therefore contributed heavily to the defeat of Burgoyne at Saratoga. Aunt Kitty was justly proud of her grandfather and often told us of his great height and his strength, manifested by the fact that he had a row of double teeth.

In 1886 Albany celebrated the bicentennial of its charter as a city. A committee of two was appointed to wait on Aunt Kitty and ask her to lend the portrait of her grandfather by Stuart and the Gansevoort tankard, in which Aunt Kitty had been placed when born (she was a very small baby), as well as any other relics she would loan for the exhibit collection in the Boy's Academy.[1] These two men, Mr. Harry Ten Eyck and Mr. Henry Garfield, were reluctant to face Aunt Kitty, fearing that they might not receive a cordial reception. But when they asked her for these exhibits, she was very pleased and said she would be delighted to loan them all.

When the time came, the committee went personally to her house in a Harris hack and transported everything to the Academy with the greatest care. The next day was the opening for the exhibitors themselves, and Aunt Kitty and Uncle Abe arrived promptly to see the show. One of the committee came forward to greet them and proudly presented a catalogue. "The portrait is hung in the front room and in the best light," said the member. "If you will turn to No. 33, you will find the name."

Aunt Kitty, all smiles, turned to No. 33. The smiles vanished. Two red spots appeared on her cheeks. With a trembling finger she pointed to No. 33. Alas! Alas! It read, "An old Dutch mug."

Uncle Abe managed to calm her enough so that she did not carry home the portrait, as she at first threatened. The committee was overcome. The numbers had been mixed, and the General should have been No. 38 [and the tankard No. 33].

❦   ❦   ❦

Every May, Aunt Kitty invited the children of her friends to a lilac and lily party in her garden. The lilac bushes were very tall and stood along the fence that separated her property from the Rathbones'. I have never seen such bushes. They were really small trees. Her man Gottlieb and the smiling John Murnane [would stand] on tall ladders, and we would pick up the flowers as they fell and stack them along the path. Later, after we had carried off all we could hold, Aunt Kitty had Gottlieb carry great bunches out to the street, where any passer-by could take all he wanted. I have watched the pleasure with which weary clerks from the Capitol took home a large bunch and friends with no gardens helped themselves generously. We gathered bunches of lilies of the valley, and we ate ice cream and cake on the enclosed piazza at the end of the afternoon. Uncle Abe was always there and enjoyed helping us pick the flowers. In his buttonhole he wore a large "Johnny-Jump-Up" from the flower bed in the center of the garden.

In one corner, under Uncle Abe's study window, grew the pink "Fraxinella," and not far off the clumps of lemon lilies. Every June, when both were in bloom, Louisa would stop at our house on one of her rare days off and leave a bunch for Mother. The message would be, "Mrs. Lansing, she sends her love and hopes Mrs. Pruyn will enjoy the flowers from her garden." I have a photograph of Mother on the piazza, and on the table by her side is a vase of "Fraxinella" and lemon lilies.

By the west parlor, in the front garden, was a thorn apple tree, and every boy in the neighborhood seemed to know when the little apples were ripe. They would swarm up the tree after dark and strip it, unless someone was on guard. Even if the heavy wooden gates were closed and locked, the boys climbed over them. When Aunt Kitty managed to harvest the apples, she made delicious thorn apple jelly. In June we were invited to supper on the piazza and to eat white strawberries, which were a great delicacy.

Aunt Kitty's first cousin was Herman Melville, and from time to time he came to visit her. I remember him quite well. He was a large man with a beard. Mother told me once, when we had seen him there, that he had written a great book called *Moby Dick*, but it was almost forgotten. Yet she was sure that in time it would be placed among the most famous books produced in the United States.[2]

The Lansings often drove to Lansingburgh in the buggy sedately drawn

by the faithful Joe Lansing. We would see them start off on the long drive
and knew they were going to enjoy an ancestral evening with Mr. and Mrs.
Augustus Peebles and Miss Van Schoonhoven and her brother. On other
days or evenings the Peebles and Van Schoonhovens would come down on
the Troy local and take a horse car up to Washington Avenue.[3]

When Aunt Kitty did have guests for dinner, it was always well done and
the food was delicious and served on lovely old china that had belonged in
either the Gansevoort or Lansing family. Both families had been among the
thirteen who ordered china when Captain Stewart Dean sailed in the sloop
Experiment to China — the first to sail from Albany on such an expedition.
The voyage was a complete success, and the china he brought back is
cherished in Albany families.[4]

Aunt Kitty's father had left an excellent wine cellar of madeira, old sherry
and port, and also French wines. Uncle Abe kept the key and he and his
cronies of the Owl Club liked to sip it in his study before the fire. . . .

Strangers were a bit upset when dinner began, as Aunt Kitty and Uncle Abe
bowed their heads and said the silent grace often used in Dutch households.

The Lansings sent out invitations around this time to a reception for
Governor Nelson Miles, who was coming to Albany for some special occasion.[5] Aunt Kitty's brother, Henry Gansevoort, had served with him in the
Civil War, from the effects of which Henry had died. For some unknown
reason Aunt Kitty ordered the hot food from Sinisbaugh's in Troy, and the
ices and cakes from McElveney's in Albany. The day of the reception there
was a great snow storm. The cold food arrived on time, but nothing was
heard of the food that had to be reheated before serving. The telephone was
not at all satisfactory then, and anyway Aunt Kitty had ordered hers taken
out because she thought the service so poor. Finally, in some way, about ten
that night, when all the guests had arrived, word came through that the
wagon, or sleigh, sent from Troy had broken down in the drifts at the
cemetery, and so there was no hot food for General Miles.

Trolleys were introduced about 1890. It seemed like magic to watch them
climb up State Street hill with the overhead prong sticking up like a witch's

broomstick. But Aunt Kitty Lansing started a war on the AlbanyRailway that lasted all her life. She complained that they went at such a pace as they passed her house that plaster was shaken from her ceilings and her old portraits were so shaken that they hung askew. She predicted that they would not last long, and the city would make the company return to horsecars.[6]

She fought them, but she used them. She got even with the company by refusing to pay any fare. If a conductor held out the new-fangled kind of slot machine in which the nickel was inserted, Aunt Kitty simply shook her head and said, "No, I never pay a fare. The company owes me money for the damage they do to my house. I have a right to free rides." If he insisted on arguing, she wrote down his name and number and reported him. There was no use in any discussion, and after a while they passed her. They accepted the situation, and so did the officials of the company.

There was a street crossing in the center of the block on Washington Avenue that was very convenient for Aunt Kitty, and for several years the trolley stopped there. But later this stop was abandoned, and stops were only made at corners. She did not know this, and for some time she would wave, but the cars would pass on. When she found out about this new order, she soon settled the question by standing in the center of the track. The motor man would clang his bell furiously, but she would not move. So in order to avoid killing her, he had to stop. Then she climbed on board, refused any suggestion of paying, and was on her way. John Murnane, the gardner, remarked, with his usual grin, "Miss Lansing, she do have different ways from most." And John was certainly right.

CHAPTER 18

THE PRESIDENTIAL CAMPAIGN came in the fall of 1888. Cleveland and Thurman were the Democratic ticket, and Benjamin Harrison and Levi P. Morton ran on the Republican ticket. In October we had guests, Victoria and Amalia West. Their father was the British Minister in Washington. It was said that the Foreign Office told Sir Lionel that he could have either the post at Washington or Constantinople. They were the only two countries that would receive him, owing to his marriage, or lack of marriage, in Spain.[1]

He was a seasoned diplomat, but he made a very stupid blunder. He received a letter from a man named Murchison (which turned out to be an assumed name), who lived in California, asking advice as to his vote in the coming election. This man had been born an Englishman, but was now a naturalized United States citizen. The letter should not have been answered, but, unfortunately . . . Sir Lionel did reply. The gist of the answer was that, although he could not discuss the politics of any country to which he might be accredited, he thought that Mr. Cleveland would be the best for any English interests. The letter was published at once and caused a great sensation, much to the surprise of Sir Lionel. He made the situation worse by a tactless interview, published in the *New York Tribune*.

The two West sisters had been with us for about two days and were to stay on for several days more. The plan for one of the afternoons was that two carriage-loads of us were to drive to the Mohawk River, via Loudonville, where two more carriage-loads from the Sages in Menands would join us. We would cross by one ferry, drive down the other shore to another ferry, and home by early evening. These ferries then were open flat boats, pulled across the river by heavy wires overhead. I was told to be sure not to dawdle after school, as we must start promptly.

[When I returned home,] I was surprised to find the guests about to leave. . . . Victoria had received a rather enigmatic telegram from her father to return to Washington at once. The *New York World* arrived in the noon mail. It had headlines about the Murchison affair and the letter published in full. Mother sent out for other papers, and so Victoria had the news. She hurried to pack, saying, "If I had only been there, Papa would never have answered that letter. Oh! Papa, Papa!" she moaned over and over, as everyone tried to help her with her innumerable bags, trunks, shawl strap, and umbrella holder.

After the girls had started for New York, the evening papers published the cable sent to the Foreign Office by Secretary of State Bayard, to the effect that the usefulness of Sir Lionel was at an end. Lord Salisbury, however, refused to recall him, and he was dismissed. Great excitement was stirred up by the Republican campaign speakers. "No North, no South, no Sackville West!" was shouted all over the country. Undoubtedly the Irish vote defeated Cleveland, although he received a popular majority.

I had admired Victoria very much. She was about twenty-three when all this happened. She had been brought from the convent where she had been educated, to preside at the legation. She was only eighteen. Her father had been minister for some time before she and her two younger sisters joined him. She was clever and beautiful, with wonderful blue eyes and black hair. A conundrum went the rounds, "To what country should Sir Lionel now be accredited?" Answer, "West-phalia."

❦   ❦   ❦

An outstanding event in November of 1888 was the dedication of All Saints Cathedral.[2] As it was not nearly finished, it could not be consecrated. I can remember four years earlier leaning out of a side window of the school to watch the bishop and a long procession march up from the chapel to consecrate the land on which the cathedral was to be built. This service took place in the yard of a brick house next to Armstrong's stable, opposite the school. On the site of the cathedral was an old barn. It was covered with advertisements, and was very dilapidated looking. . . . The cornerstone . . . had been laid on a warm day in June of 1884, with Governor Cleveland among those present. And now came the dedication, and we had as guests Bishop Gilbert of Minnesota, Bishop Ethelbert Talbot of Wyoming, the Lord Bishop of Nassau, and Brother Churton.

We had all been at the last service in the old chapel the previous Sunday, when Bishop Williams of Connecticut, the presiding bishop, had preached. The chapel was full of memories for St. Agnes girls. In Lent there had always been a noon service of fifteen minutes, and the girls from the school would come in by the wooden cloister. That cloister was carefully constructed so that there were no windows on the Elk Street side for the choir boys to look through. I remember the tramp, tramp, tramp of feet as the procession of girls marched on the wooden floor and up the steps into the chapel, where they filed into seats in the choir. Now that was all over, and bishops and clergy and laity had come from long distances for this great occasion.

Jack and Hattie and I decided that we would like to see the procession start from the chapel and march up Elk Street. We stood on the corner of Swan Street and had a fine view of an impressive procession. When Bishop Doane reached the center door of the cathedral, he knocked on it with his crozier. It was opened by the chapter.

After this we squeezed into the cathedral and stood in the rear. The building was absolutely jammed with people. The members of the chapter took up the offertory, and so much was given — or perhaps because there were so many to give — the plates overflowed, and money began to drop on the floor. As they picked it up, the good chapter members had to put the money in their pockets. It seemed strange that anyone should misunderstand this, but we actually heard whisperings [of impropriety].

Rev. Wilford L. Robbins was at that time the dean of the cathedral. He was greatly admired by ladies, old and young, and was visibly annoyed — not flattered — by finding notes of praise mysteriously placed on his desk. After Sunday service one of his admirers would stand in wait for him behind a pillar, and as he came down the south aisle, out she would pop! She would raise her hand, and shaking her finger at him, would invariably say, "Now Mr. Dean, I have a bone to pick with you!" They would leave the cathedral together, leaving the neighbors to draw their own conclusions.

The verger was Bingham. Benevolent and white-bearded, he was all that a verger should be. Once he was showing a stranger around the cathedral and was asked, "Do you have Matins?"

"No," was Bingham's gloomy reply. "We have linoleums. Can't you smell them?"

It had been expected that the Hamersley Memorial Reredos would have been installed, as had been promised to Bishop Doane by Mrs. Hamersley, née Price of Troy. But when the time came for the reredos to be ordered, Mrs. Hamersley was no longer interested. She had married the Duke of Marlborough.[3] I believe a copy of her letter offering to give the reredos is in the cornerstone. The land for the cathedral was a gift from Mr. Erastus Corning in memory of his parents, and a pillar commemorates the gift.

In 1885 and 1886 the Women's [Diocesan] League was formed to raise money for the cathedral. Each member had a cardboard mite box shaped like a cathedral. We pledged to drop ten cents down the tower every week.

Even Fromo had his mite box and was listed in the annual report.

There was a league fair every December, the idea being that people would buy their Christmas presents there. The fair began on a Monday evening and lasted until Saturday. It was a nightmare for all of us. We were supposed to go to it every day after school, to fill in anywhere, to run errands, and to take the place of tired workers who wanted a rest.

Aunt Mary Corning was the president of the league, and no one ever worked harder for a cause than she did. The first fair was in the Corning house at 87 State Street. Then Mrs. Roessle had it at the old Delavan Hotel. After that it was usually in a vacant shop. There was one under the Kenmore that was very popular.

Lunch used to be served at small tables. In those days there were no electrical contrivances, and gas was used when possible. Smelly oil stoves were installed at the far end of the shop, and soups were reheated there. Curtains were hung up for a partition. We could smell McElveney's delicious chicken croquettes as soon as the front door was opened. Donations of salad were welcome, and jellies or ice cream were the climax. There were no thermos bottles, so reheated coffee was carried down in covered cans.

Mrs. Oliver was usually in charge of the luncheon. Capable, energetic and cheerful, she had a hard-working committee to help her. Usually, her sister, Mrs. Bowditch, Miss Estelle Van Vechten, Mrs. Tip Corning and Mrs. Bayard Livingston helped, and there were many more. In the late afternoon choir boys appeared to carry home bundles, but on Saturday the fair kept open until ten o'clock, and everyone was worn out.

Mrs. Doane, in her zeal to help, had been known to go to New York and to send up all kinds of things on commission, to the despair of the committee. One year it was brass andirons, desk sets, ash trays, etc. — all very ugly. No one wanted them. If at the end of the week somewhere near a thousand dollars had been made, usually some kind-hearted man — interested in the cause but canny enough to shun the fair — would step into the breach and make it a full thousand. Everyone would be relieved to have it over.

The bishop always came every day to encourage the good work. Everyone felt his charm and his great appeal. He knew what each one had done to help the cause so close to his heart, and his presence served to revive the tired workers.

But the league sale was only one of the efforts made during the year for the various enterprises the bishop had started. There was a wonderful fair in the schoolroom at St. Agnes during vacation one winter for the benefit of the Child's Hospital. The doll table was the center of attraction. Aunt Cora Parker had dressed twenty-five dolls. The bride and groom and bridesmaids were the special lure for the children. I was Mother Goose in another show, one year at Easter, when I was about thirteen.

Hattie was in a play called "The Spirit of '76, or The Coming Woman." We thought it quite a joke, but since then everything has come true. Aunt Anna French was an astonishingly masculine Mrs. Badger, and Mrs. Marcus Hun as Miss Wolverine Griffin. Mrs. R. S. Oliver was Mrs. Judge Wigfall, and Hattie was the daughter, Miss Victorine Wigfall. She sang:

> Come into the garden, George.
> Don't sit there all night and groan.
> Come into the garden, George,
> For I'm smoking here alone.

This was considered by many as going rather far. In fact, it was not "comme il faut," and we hoped no one would tell Grandmother.

Two other plays, "Betsy Baker" and "One Too Many for Him," had Susy Vanderpoel in them, and she was very clever. Mrs. Hun and the Olivers and Bowditches were really not amateurs. They had had great experience. Their cousin Guy Baker, who never bothered to learn his lines, ignored his cues, and once brought in his dog unexpectedly, was always a success.

In the spring of 1889 the plays for one of the causes were at our house. There were two evening performances and one matinee. The stage was in the front drawing room. The front hall was used for one exit and the conservatory for the other. Everyone came in by the basement. The audience sat in the music room and the dining room.

"A Morning Call" had two parts, taken by Hattie and Guy Baker. "The Widow's Husband, or a State Secret" had five parts, taken by Mrs. James T. Gardiner, Miss Nelly Rathbone, General Oliver, and Mr. and Mrs. Roessle. "A Cure at Baden" had three parts, taken by Miss Jessie Danforth, Miss Gardiner and Mr. Lundberg, a Swede with a fine voice. He lived here for several years. "Freezing a Mother-in-Law," with five parts, taken by Mr. Joe Paige, General Oliver, Mr. George Hilton, Madeline Palmer, and Mrs. Hun, was wonderful. We all laughed till we cried at Mrs. Hun. No one who saw that play could ever forget it. . . .

One winter "Mrs. Jarley's Wax Works" was given at Jermain Hall.

Mrs. Jarley was played by Aunt Anna French, who could always be counted
on to do a grand job. I was a "Prima Donna," and I was gorgeously attired
in pink, with paste jewels. I warbled:

O' Susan quit your foolin
O' give your heart to me
I'll give you back your twenty-five cents,
And, then I'll let you be.

I was supposed to run down gradually to a low squeak, and a "John"
was to wind me up and set me going again. But I burst out laughing
instead, and Mrs. Jarley reprimanded me severely and had me rolled off the
stage.

The most horrible, and entirely unsuccessful, performance was at the
Kenmore one spring. It was called "A Russian Fete" — nobody knew why.
It was arranged by Miss Emily Robbins, the energetic sister of the dean of
the cathedral. It lasted two awful afternoons and evenings, from three to
ten o'clock. There were a few so-called Russian articles for sale, and tea
with lemon (thought of as being strictly Russian and cheaper than cream).
The principal performance, on which Miss Emily counted for profit, was
the play done by five actors who stood behind a tall screen covered with
white cotton. Holes were cut in the screen for heads to be poked through,
and fantastic bodies, grotesquely small, were painted below the slits. I have
no idea who painted those bodies, but they were awful enough to suit the
most exacting expectations.

As women's suffrage was one of the burning questions of the day, a play
was written [set in the year] 1996. Suffrage had long been legal for women
and each of the states was an independent nation. The Bishop outlined the
play, and Selden Marvin put in the lighter touches. Aunt Anna French was
Mrs. Bullyall. Ellen Hun was Miss Violet Voteoften, and I was Rose Repeater.
Selden was General Dotham Brown, and Louis Parker was Colonel Killem-
dead, an Irish-American war correspondent. The name of the play was "The
Coming Woman and the Going Man." Everything went wrong, and we had
to keep the audience waiting, much to the indignation of old Dr. Hun in
the front row, who rapped his cane on the floor impatiently and kept calling
for the players.

The really well-done charity performances were "Pinafore" and "Patience"
and "Iolanthe" at the Leland Opera House. . . .

These plays represented long hours of hard work from busy people, and
they were always most successful. I have an excellent photograph of General

Oliver as the Lord Chancellor, and I cherish some of the programs of the various efforts for charity. No one can forget the delighted encores of the audience when the name of our local fire chief was substituted for that of the First Department chief in London, the famous Captain Shaw, who was reknowned for both fires and flirtations.

> O' Chief McQuade, type of true love kept under,
> Could thy brigade
> With cold cascade
> Quench my great love? I wonder.

During the Christmas holidays the winter I was fifteen, Judge and Mrs. Hand gave a dancing party for Learned Hand at their house at 298 State Street. I did not want to go. I did not like parties or having to wear a party dress, and I did my best to get out of it, though all the other girls were very excited about the party.

We danced in the front and middle rooms, and the Judge and Mrs. Learned sat at the side and seemed to enjoy it. Miss Grace had undertaken to run it for them, and she worked very hard. . . . Miss Mabel Learned was there in her wheel chair, and we took turns sitting with her. In fact, I liked that better than having to dance "girl," as I was used to dancing "boy" at school. I suppose Learned asked me to dance, in spite of my failure long before, but I do not remember that either.

The trouble was that we all were told that we must make a "party" call. We gathered one afternoon at Amsdell's corner grocery, across the street from the Learneds'. There we had an animated discussion as to how we would manage the call so as to please our mothers. I had calling cards which had been given to me by Jack for a Christmas present. I had brought only one card with me. So we borrowed a pencil at the store desk, and all the others wrote their names on my card — there were eleven of us.

Then we decided that one of us must take the card over. Which would it be? Another discussion followed, and we settled it by the old method of "eenie, meenie, miny, mo."

The lot fell to me, the most diffident of the crowd. I grasped the card with a "do or die" look and rang the Learneds' door bell. When the bell was answered by a maid, I thrust the card into her hand and said, "Please tell Mrs. Learned we are sorry she is not at home."

Then I ran down the steps, deaf to the maid, who said, "She is at home!"
I joined the others, and with this duty done, we rushed off to coast again.

We went quite often to the matinees on Saturday afternoons when the
weather was bad. The first play I ever saw was "Uncle Tom's Cabin." Little
Eva seemed to be as beautiful as an angel, and when she died and was
carried up on a golden cloud with pink rays, I wept noisily. It was of no
use for Frieda to assure me, all the way up State Street, that Eva was not
really dead but would soon have her supper just as I would. That made it
even worse. I felt terribly cheated.

Tom Carl was very popular. I think he was the hero of the "Chimes of
Normandy." He was a real matinee idol of that era. Fanny Ten Eyck had
actually shaken hands with him, and her brother Harry knew him. Fanny
was a member of the A.D.C. and the envy of all of them. "Lotta" was very
popular. Fritz Emmett had a great run with his "Fritz" plays, "Sweet Violet,
they're sweeter than all the roses," "Come O' Zilla dear, I've plucked them
and brought them to you," and "Come my darling, come to your papa —
sunshine of my heart!"

When the English Rosina Vokes Company came to town, it was sure to
have a warm welcome. "The Dress Rehearsal" was one of the funniest plays
I have ever seen, and "The Circus," when all the Vokes family were on the
stage at once [was] a real side-splitting farce. In later years Ada Rehan won
all hearts, and her rendering of Katharine in the "Taming of the Shrew"
was famous. John Hare in "A Pair of Spectacles" was the star of the Palmer's
Madison Square Troupe. The performance in Albany was for the benefit of
the Women's League at All Saints.

I remember also some play at the Leland where a crowd of us sat in a
box. In the play there was supposed to be a fire, and they used a real hose.
By mistake, they turned it into our box and soaked us — but it was funny.
Sometimes "Hermann" came with a trick show, which was a joy to Hattie,
who had a real talent for doing tricks.

When there was to be an enormous audience, as when Madame Albani
[who had started her career in Albany at St. Joseph's Church] returned, the
only available place was the skating rink on Lark Street, a poor barn of a
place. She always sang "Home Sweet Home" with the greatest feeling.[4]

CHAPTER 19

O NE DAY IN FEBRUARY — I am not sure which year — Mother told me at luncheon that guests were coming at four o'clock and that she wanted me to help entertain a boy and take him coasting in the garden. It sounded boring to me. I asked his name. "His name is Franklin Delano Roosevelt," said my Mother. "He is named for his great-uncle, Mr. Franklin Delano, who was the kind old gentleman who showed you and Harriet the Swiss music box when we spent the weekend at Steen Valetje. Now I trust you to be polite and helpful." She added pointedly, "He is sure to have very good manners."

I asked indifferently how old he was. Mother thought he must be about nine. She had seen him in New York. He was tall, and looked much older.[1] I was not enthusiastic. I had had other plans for the afternoon, and I grumbled that he would probably break my new sled. Later I saw Erastus Corning III making snowballs across the street in front of his house at 22 Elk Street.

"Ratty," I called, "there's a boy with a long name coming here this afternoon. Mother says I must take him coasting. You can come along too, if you like." This was a condescending invitation on my part, as Ratty was much younger than I was. I had a secret plan to turn the innocent guest over to the tender mercies of Ratty as soon as I saw a chance to dump him.

Ratty climbed over the snow piles and said in his deep voice, "I can settle him for you. I can trip him up so he won't know what happened, and then wash his face. He's probably just a New York sissy."

I agreed that was just what he would be. Just then our sleigh rounded the corner of the Steuben Street hill. The horses broke into a trot, and the sleigh bells rang gaily as they drove up to our house and stopped so that the stone step on the curb would be in front of the sleigh door. It was an open sleigh. Bear rugs were thrown over the seats and over the knees of the three guests, Mr. and Mrs. James Roosevelt and their son, from Hyde Park.

Ratty and I stood there with our sleds. I am sure we did not look any too cordial. I hope the guests may have thought us shy — a merciful way to cover discrepancies in manners. I was a big, strapping girl in my red blanket coat and red knitted cap with a tassel, and mittens made by the Shakers at Niskayuna.

Almost before Owen, the footman, could jump off the box to open the sleigh door, the tall boy on the back seat jumped out. Coming over to us, he said, "May I go coasting with you?" He took us completely by surprise. We forgot our inhospitable plans, pushed open the garden gate, and ran to the toboggan slide.

Our guest was no sissy. He soon showed us that he knew more about all kinds of coasting than we did, and he turned hand springs down the slide. We had a wonderful afternoon with sleds, the toboggan, and my brother's bobsled.

We were finally summoned in to tea in the library, and the boring necessity of shaking hands all around. The grownups were having a dinner party at eight, so the boy and I had supper in the pantry, which, we agreed, was much nicer. We were good friends by this time in spite of the difference in age. He was old for his age, and I was young for mine. I was about fifteen. He told me how he loved the winters in the country, about skating and ice-boating on the river, and that he was going to Groton and Harvard.

I suggested that we hurry and get out by the playroom door to the garden before I was caught to do my lessons. It was a lovely evening, and the slide in fine condition. . . .

The City Hall bell boomed once for nine o'clock. Franklin said he was supposed to be in bed, that his mother would be sure to go upstairs after dinner and would find that he was not there. I said I was supposed to be in bed about this time. I got fifty cents a week, if I was prompt.

"They all talk about alike," I added. "My sister will be after me for my lessons, but we cannot go in now. The dinner party is over, and they are going into the conservatory. We must get the ice cream!"

We went down the outside cellar stairs and through the blackness of the cellar, with only the glow from the furnace to give faint light and to make the shadows look blacker. I had no idea that the boy was frightened when I told him to wait by the inside stairs, while I went to loot the ice cream. In my moccasins no one could hear me. Luck was with me too. The silver platter of ice cream was on the dumb waiter, which had been sent down from the pantry. More luck, there was also a plate of cakes.

I rushed back with them, almost falling downstairs in the hurry and darkness. We carried our loot out to the garden, and, sitting on our sleds, we took turns eating from the serving cutter. As we sat there we could see the dinner party in the conservatory, sipping old madeira. The shades on the garden side were not pulled down at night.

Leaving the remains of the ice cream and cake for Fromo, who was eagerly waiting, we hastened to the garden gate to fire snow balls at the ankles of the hapless congregation returning by Elk Street from evening service at a nearby church. In the distance we heard Bridget, the cook, calling wildly, "What have they done wid me platter? Is it coasting they are on it? Shure that poor boy will be sick wid the goings on! No, it's the dog is eating off silver — God help us all!"

Soon we heard Mr. James Roosevelt calling Franklin from the dining room piazza. There was nothing we could do about that but go in and receive their mild scoldings about the lateness of the hour.

I had to go to school by nine the next morning. When I returned at luncheon time, the Roosevelts had gone to Boston.

In April [1889] came the centennial celebration of George Washington's inauguration as President of the United States. As it came during the Easter vacation, I went along with Mother and Hattie. We stayed at the Brunswick Hotel on Fifth Avenue at Madison Square, as the old Brevoort was so far downtown. Two of our horses, Tommy Dodd and Lanark, were taken down on the night boat, to be used in the parade. . . . Governor David B. Hill would use Tommy, and someone else in his group was to ride Lanark.

Mother and Hattie went to the Richard Hunt's on Washington Square to see the parade from their stand, built over their front yard. Jack and I went to the Misses Rhinelanders on the corner of the Square and Fifth Avenue. We had the best view because we saw the parade turn the corner into Fifth Avenue. Then we saw that Governor Hill could not keep his seat on my Tommy Dodd, the easiest and most intelligent horse in the world. The governor had protested having to ride, but they thought with a horse like Tommy he could manage it. So he slipped off, while Tommy, who seemed to understand the trouble, was led off along Eighth Street. The governor slipped into one of the carriages and leaned back with evident relief.

President Harrison had arrived, as Washington had, in a barge from Elizabeth, New Jersey. In the procession were the governors of the thirteen original states, with their troops. It was a fine sight on a fine day and well worth remembering.

In the evening Mother and Hattie sat in the Hunts' box, and I went with the Robbs. The Metropolitan Opera House was a gorgeous sight. It had a false floor, so the square dances could be seen by all. Those who took part were all descendants of the original dancers of 1789. Mrs. Levi P. Morton was one of them. Her husband was at that time the Vice-President. Mrs. Morton was one of the most striking dancers. She had an enormous pompadour. There were also historical tableaux, but I do not seem to have preserved any programs; I only have a ticket.

We also saw the review of the ships in the harbor. We were with a group of friends, and it was very rough and windy. As our large boat approached each of the visiting fleet, our band played the appropriate national anthem. The [Russian] flagship, the *Dimitri Donskoi*, was particularly impressive. . . . They had a very large band which played superbly. We sing the words, "Rise crowned with glory," to their national air.

I had two new dresses for this trip. They were made by Maggie Murphy in Greenbush. I was deaf to any appeal to wear a bustle, even though I had so greatly admired Emily Read, who wore so large a bustle that her little dog Mignon rode around on it. My day dress was of medium-weight light-green camel's hair, trimmed with yards and yards of darker green ribbon in three rows on the skirt. The ribbon also trimmed the waist and the high-boned collar and deep cuffs. I had a green straw hat to go with it, trimmed with ribbons and a feather. I felt very grown up, as the skirt touched the tops of my shoes. Jack had been rather discouraged over my lack of interest in clothes, so I was pleased when he looked approvingly at me in the hall of the Brunswick.

For the evening I had a white silk with light Roman stripes. The white chiffon vest and collar had ruffles at the neck and sleeves. I was really quite pretty. What a relief it was, however, to go home and return to the joys of Elk Street. How I pitied people who had to live in New York City!

One of Hattie's devoted admirers was Verplanck Colvin, who for years was engaged in surveying the Adirondacks. Jack had once camped out with him, and it was he who first brought Mr. Colvin to the house. He was quite a handsome man, but very silent, and when he came, he stayed for hours.

However, he was eloquent about a panther of enormous size that he had shot. The panther's skin was then on exhibition at the State Hall on Eagle Street. He insisted that the panther had been so obliging as to wait quietly while he photographed him, and that the animal also gave him time to make notes for a poem. Jack said the poem began, "Oh! Panther thou!" We never saw the poem, but we did go to see the skin. Mr. Colvin was always called "The Panther" after that.

Mr. Colvin lived with his mother in an interesting old house with grounds on Western Avenue. He followed Hattie, and he wrote her an acrostic that was quite clever in which he insisted she had vanished down the Hawk Street stairs to avoid him. I once poured water over him from the nursery bedroom balcony as he was leaving, and I hoped he would not come again, but it did no good. Nor did it help to sew up the sleeves and pockets of his overcoat or to put things in his hat so that, when he went to put it on, they fell about him in a shower. Nothing would keep the "Panther" away.

He frightened Hattie by coming into the library late one afternoon carrying a large gun. He told her he wanted to show her how he killed the panther. She called Mother, who, unfortunately, was in her room. Hattie said, "Mother, I want Mr. Colvin to show you how he killed the panther." Then she fled.

Mother never let him sit down. Finally, when Christian arrived to carry away the tea tray, Mother managed to get Mr. Colvin to leave too. Aunt Kitty Lansing insisted he was not crazy or unsafe to have around, but for some time Christian held him off at the door, and we were spared.

Aunt Kitty had had a new dress that Easter. It seems that Uncle Abe, who liked pretty clothes, asked her to pay more attention to them. She came in one afternoon in February and said she was going to buy some black silk at Whitney's and take it to New York. Mrs. Peebles knew of a very good dressmaker there, who would make something suitable that would please Uncle Abe.

The next we heard of the dress was on a Sunday after church at St. Peter's. Aunt Kitty was very indignant. She had bought the silk on Friday, and it had not been sent. They planned to go to New York on the 2:40 train, and she had an appointment with the dressmaker for eleven the next morning. As her number on Washington Avenue was 115, she thought that the silk must have been sent to another number with a five in it.

I was delighted to go with her, and we went to No. 5 Washington Avenue just above Park Place. It was a saloon called "The Blimmer," and the barkeeper assured us that "There was no ladies there to wear black silk."

So we proceeded to No. 15, which was the Bayard Van Rensselaers, but no one there had seen a bundle from Whitney's. No. 55 came next. Mrs. Cook and her daughters lived there, but their indignant cook was quick-tempered and seemed to think that we had designs on robbing the house. We went on and finally ended at 155, but Mrs. Manning knew nothing of the silk.

Nothing daunted — it was almost one o'clock by this time — Aunt Kitty determined to get to the root of the matter, and we went down to Lodge Street, where the Whitneys lived. We routed out kind Mr. Willy Whitney, who took us down to the store, and there was the bundle, tied and addressed, but not delivered. Aunt Kitty grasped it eagerly and, thanking Mr. Whitney, we walked over to State Street and caught a horsecar.

It turned out later that the reason the bundle had not been sent was that the previous year Aunt Kitty had tried to return a long piece of crepe which she had bought some months before but had not used and did not want. Of course the store refused to take it back, so Aunt Kitty had written a letter to tell them to take her name off their list, as she never would go there any more. She often went there anyway and bought what she wanted, but she had not charged anything until she bought the silk. She must have completely forgotten that she had requested to have her name dropped. The bundle had not been delivered because she was not on the charge list. . . .

Mr. Frank Rogers, the organist at St. Peter's, was in New York with Rev. Miller, and they went into one of the large churches at which there was a funeral with the full choir. To their surprise they saw Aunt Kitty in a pew in front of them. She seemed quite overcome with grief, and they thought the funeral must be for some relative. However, when the service was over, she turned and saw them and said, "Now can you tell me whose funeral this is?"

❧   ❧   ❧

Just after Commencement at St. Agnes, in early June, came the announcement of the engagement of our charming French teacher, Marguerite Carron, to Major Harmon Pumpelly Read. It was no surprise, since he had been calling on her very often in the evening. Indeed, I counted seventeen of his calling cards in a dish on the table in her room, and I hung them all over a little tree she had in a pot. Also, she had gone to Sunday supper at Auntie Kidd's for many weeks, and all her cronies who gathered there, both at supper and later, knew the little Major was dead in love.

When he told Auntie Kidd of his engagement, she wagged her head and said, "How will you support her?"

"The Lord will provide," answered the Major.

"This is the first time I have ever been called the Lord," replied Auntie Kidd.

Major Read had first seen Marguerite Carron as she walked up big State Street one afternoon when he was calling on Aunt Mary Corning. She wore a very becoming bonnet. She was then about twenty-two, and her younger sister Louise was with her. Harmon said to my aunt, "Who is that beautiful girl bowing to you?" It was love at first sight. They were married in August and lived for many years at 236 State Street, the house in which his father and mother had started housekeeping, and in which, I think, Harmon had been born.

Major Read had been very ill at one time, and as he recovered, Mrs. Kidd would invite two girls at a time to come to see him in the afternoon — strictly chaperoned of course. Rumor, by the grape vine in Elk Street, stated that the Major was propped up in bed, with gay pillows and gayer counterpane, and wore a gorgeous brocade bed gown. It was said also that the Major's hat and cane lay beside him on a chair, and that the chair had been given by General Washington to George Read of Delaware, a signer of the Declaration of Independence.

In later years, Meredith Read, who had quite an artistic talent, painted a large genealogical chart of the Read family. It started with Chaos, and after a while it reached down to Adam, and then through the ages down to the present generation. It was all a serious matter. In still later years Harmon Read published a large and expensive book called *Rossiana: The History of the Descendants of the Earl of Ross*. Mother bought a copy. It lay on the library table and all Elk Street came in to see it, but they did not buy it. It was full of illustrations. . . .

Mrs. Kidd's Sunday nights were quite unique. She sat in a large arm chair, with her little dogs in her lap. If they were restless or yappy, she poked them into a large bag. . . . She was a real wit, and her sayings were widely quoted. She never was malicious or hurt anyone's feelings. She was kindly in her own way, and generous in her hospitality, particularly to her relatives. . . .

Grandmother Parker had been taken very ill in May [1889]. She had not been well all winter and drove out less and less. On her birthday in March we had all been marshalled into the big hall. Then we walked in one by one and gave her a rose as she sat on the sofa in Grandfather's study. She seemed bright and called us each by name. She said that when the weather got warm she would be well and would be ready to tell us stories again on the piazza.

We loved her stories, particularly [those about] her father, Edmund Roberts, in the Persian Gulf. He was sailing to Muscat to deliver to the Sultan the Senate's ratification of the Treaty of Amity and Commerce that he had negotiated on a previous voyage. During the administration of President Jackson, Mr. Roberts had been sent out with two ships, the *Peacock*, in which he lived, and the *Boxer*, which contained all kinds of presents. It was impossible to come to any terms in the East of that day without gifts. There were animals and machinery — particularly agricultural — china, tools, and more.

Mr. Roberts had succeeded in making treaties with Siam and Muscat, but his negotiation with Cochin China took many weeks. The Minister of State raised the question of the right of Mr. Roberts, because of his low rank, even to communicate with him. Mr. Roberts was about to explain to the minister that no one in the United States had any titles of nobility when he realized in time that this would be hopeless. [The minister and his associates] would not understand, and the weeks of waiting and haggling would go for nothing. Mr. Roberts decided to humor them and said that he would give them a few of his titles, but he was a modest man and preferred not to use them himself.

The principal deputy prepared his Chinese pencil and a half sheet of paper. Mr. Roberts quietly told him that it would require a whole sheet. That was the first of their surprises. He dictated, "Edmund Roberts, a special envoy from the United States and a citizen of Portsmouth in the State of New Hampshire." Then he proceeded to add all the counties of the state. The paper was filled, and it had taken much time to spell the names. There were many counties remaining.

It had been his intention to proceed with the names of the towns, mountains, lakes, and rivers, always choosing Indian names if he could. But the ship was rolling, the scribe complained of a headache, and they all bowed to the ground. There were no more objections on the score of rank. They declared he had more titles than the Emperor.

I especially remember one warm afternoon when we had a funeral for the Marvin's canary at the far end of the garden. Langdon Marvin always acted as clergyman, as he had a solemn air even as a small boy. Langdon was robed in one of Grandmother's nightgowns, which [had been] pulled off the clothes line and was not quite dry. It was much too large and long, but with a red hair ribbon for a stole, he looked quite impressive. Of course William Tracey, the old butler who was always after us, broke in, but the boys ran off with a pelting of rotten fruits.

After that was over, we waited until Grandmother came out to the piazza from her nap in the third room. She found Tuy and Amasa, Jr. sitting glumly in two chairs. Grandfather had caught them climbing the Gansel Bergamot pear tree and had ordered them to sit with folded hands for ten minutes. In the meantime the two youngest Parkers, Emma and Harriet, had come out to the garden in charge of Mammy and Edmund. Marvin had come with a maid. So when Grandmother came out in her fresh cap and lace scarf, put on by her maid, she had an audience of twelve grandchildren — ranging in age from about two to twelve — waiting to listen to her stories. . . .

The boys always wanted the pirate story which happened after the *Peacock* had struck a reef off an island north of Arabia Felix on September 21, 1835. Mr. Roberts and six of the crew manned the twenty foot long second cutter and started on a four hundred mile sail up the Persian Gulf to ask the help of the Sultan. They were out one hundred and one hours, chased by pirates and endangered by storms. When they reached Muscat, every honor was paid them. Troops were dispatched, and the perilous condition of the *Peacock* was reported to the governor of Zoar. The pirates were caught and killed, and the *Peacock* was floated and sailed up to meet [our greatgrandfather and his crew].

Then came the part that sounded like the Arabian Nights. Mr. Roberts was lodged in a palace, banquets were given, presents were exchanged, and the treaties were ratified. The sultan gave Mr. Roberts a very valuable ring as a token of his esteem. Unfortunately, the ring was stolen many years later from Great Aunt Caroline Parker.

Mr. Roberts had instructions to proceed to Japan to try to make a treaty to open their ports to the commerce of the United States, but fate intervened. At Macao his ship's crew developed cases of Asiatic cholera, and he himself became a victim. He died at the house of an American, William Wetmore, and is buried in Macao.

It was usually about five when these story parties broke up and Morrissey could be seen coming up the garden path with his two pails of milk from the two cows who lived under the stable and went to pasture where Sheridan Park is now.

But there were [to be] no more Portsmouth stories. Grandmother grew steadily weaker and died on June 27th. The funeral was at St. Peter's Church on the 29th, after a service at the house.

I will always remember Grandfather's last look at her, as she lay there so peacefully in her white cap, with the usual white about her neck. I should not have watched him, but I am sure he was quite oblivious of us all and did not realize that the service was over and people were leaving. He stood and stood by her and mechanically brushed off a fly from her forehead. His expression showed that the fifty-five years of their married life were passing before him, picture after picture. The first meeting with "the pretty girl in a poke bonnet," [the births and deaths of] their four children who had gone before, on and on — every phase was reflected on his handsome old face.

Many came from far away to pay tribute to her for her long and fine life of service to everyone with whom she had come in contact. Several of her sisters and nieces, her cousin Walter Langdon and his nephew Nicholson Kane of Hyde Park, Mr. John Langdon Erving of New York, and Dr. Davenport attended the funeral. Her four oldest grandsons were the bearers, and Bishop Doane, Dr. Battershall, and eight other clergymen conducted the services at St. Peter's and the cemetery.

Grandmother had been a wonderful grandmother. While she thought her geese were swans, she was also aware of our many faults. I had been a bit of a black sheep in her fold, but she told me she had hopes for my future. She was very pleased that I had been confirmed at St. Peter's on Palm Sunday. Unable to be at the service, she had sent me a prayer book with a verse quoted in it and my name on the cover. Grandmother believed in Kingsley's poem, "Be good, sweet maid, and let who will be clever," but the boys thought it funny.

After Grandmother died, Mother had a great deal to do arranging her possessions. So I was the one who drove with Grandfather every afternoon at three o'clock in the sizzling heat. He and Morrissey went through the same familiar formula as to the length of the ride and the tour of the park, so I knew just how much time I would have the rest of the day.

Later on we all went with Grandfather to North East Harbour to stay at the Cornings in their new house "Stoneacres." Hattie had had a blue straw hat the previous summer that I greatly admired, and she gave it to me.

I liked it so much that after Grandmother died, I spent one whole morning blacking it with six coats of French shoe black, while I sat on the hot, tin roof of the conservatory. . . . After the last coat, the hat looked jet black, and Marie trimmed it with a black silk bow.

Our first Sunday at North East Harbour was very foggy. Harriet Corning and I sat with the volunteer choir, and just before the sermon, we noticed a terrible smell. Then someone behind us leaned over and said that black streaks were running down my neck and dress. I felt the hat and it was a squash! We fled out of the church. My hat was a ruin from the dampness.

CHAPTER 20

MOST OF THE SUMMER [of 1889] was spent in Albany, much to my joy. The garden, Fromo, the gas stove, and games in the garden were just what I liked best. While Mother, Hattie, and Grandfather went to Sharon Springs for the baths, I went for a visit at Bread Loaf Inn, Vermont, where the six Parkers were spending the summer under the care of their Grandmother Strong. We had an hilarious time and did many things that we ought not to have done.

On my return I found that Mother was planning to go to Europe for the winter and that Grandfather's sister, Aunt Caroline Palmer, would spend the winter with him. This was a terrible blow to me. I hated the idea of leaving Albany again, but Mother said Louise [Parker] was going too. That made it better, but Louise did not want to go either.

In the meantime we had two visits from two English friends, Lady Shrewsbury and Lady Selkirk, and of course their maids too. Lady Selkirk was on her way to Winnipeg for the celebration of the settlement which her husband and his father had founded. Selkirk Range was named for them.[1]

Lady Shrewsbury had been a noted beauty, but now she wore a hideous black wig, rouged badly, and had deep black circles under her eyes. She wore black gloves of the kind then called Biarritz gloves. They were of rather heavy kid glace. They pulled on without buttons. She wore them all the time, even when eating her meals.

Lady Selkirk was entirely different. She had most lovely violet eyes and dressed attractively. She had been very much younger than her husband. They only spent one night, as they had to be in Winnipeg by a certain day.

On their return trip in September they came again and stayed for several days. I tried without success to find out whether Lady Shrewsbury slept in her gloves. She promised Mother to find her a house with servants by the end of January, in the Mayfair or Belgravia section of London. Mother had a small dinner for them, but as she was in mourning it was a quiet visit, with several single beaux for the worldly, painted Countess.

We also had a visit from Lord and Lady Meath. She had given up the "Ministering Children's League," and had another line, "The Girls Friendly." It was just as strenuous, and the patient and bearded Lord Meath was just as devoted to her new cause as he had been to the old one.

It was decided that we would sail on the new White Star twin-screw steamer *Teutonic*, quite the finest modern passenger steamer then afloat. We left Albany on the 2:30 train, which that day was very late. This prolonged the agony of our departure, as over forty people came down to see us off. Among them was the Panther, who almost boarded the train. I was in tears, and so was Louise. Jack had given me a Kodak for Christmas. It was the newest type and on the way down I became interested in trying to take pictures, but they had to be time exposures.

The ship looked enormous. It had masts with sails to balance it, and it had a covered deck, lighted by electricity, so we could sit out comfortably in almost all weathers. More people came to see us off and to see the marvelous new ship. Once again Elk Street and Fromo and all the joys were left behind, as we ploughed into a heavy sea and much fog.

After landing in Liverpool, we went up to London, but then, as the fogs were very heavy, we went via Paris to Rome. During our entire stay there the weather was lovely, and we found friends and took long drives and saw most of the sights. On the return we stopped on the Riviera to see Aunt Sarah Boreel at Nice, and Mr. and Mrs. Franklin Delano at their Villa Giraso at Monte Carlo, and Mr. J. S. Morgan at his Villa Henriette, also there. It was only a few weeks later that Mr. Morgan was killed in a carriage accident. In Paris we were fitted out with new riding habits at Redferns and purchased new clothes. In between we did much sight-seeing, particularly for Louise's benefit.

Then we went back to London, where Lady Shrewsbury — the painted Countess — had found us a house at 88 Eaton Square. It was a lovely old house facing the square, which was really an oblong. Each house had a key to a gate, which was opposite our door; our key hung in the hall. The house belonged to Mrs. Meynell Ingraham, and it had been the Speaker's house when the Houses of Parliament were burned.

There was a housekeeper cook, with two scullery maids to help her. One of them had to carry up all the dishes from the kitchen to the pantry, as there was no dumbwaiter; in fact, there were no modern improvements at all. The kitchen arrangements were primitive, but the cook seemed perfectly happy with a dim gas jet, her heavy copper utensils, and a spit for the meat and game. I have never tasted such tender, delicious meat. One of the scullery maids basted it tirelessly, and I loved to watch the old-fashioned spit.

Fanny was the head housemaid and had charge, with two undermaids, of the bedrooms and all the other rooms on the three floors. Fanny was very stiff, and she wore starched clothes that fairly rattled. Mother had engaged the butler she had had at Lady Rayleigh's house, as she found him unemployed. He had a footman to help him, and there was also a little "Buttons," who seemed to fit in everywhere. Marie, our own maid for many years, was also there.

This may sound like a large household, but it was a large house. Also, service in England was reduced to very minute lines, and woe to any servant who did not keep inside the regulations! If you told the butler you needed more coals for the fire, he would bow and say, "Very good Madam. I will send the proper servant to supply it." So it was easier to do it yourself, but that was not according to the rule either.

One of the reasons Mother took the house was that it had a furnace, and she wrote ahead to be sure it was lighted before we came, as the last of January in London is very raw. She found that it only heated the halls, and was so thoroughly out of order that the furnace man reported it unsafe, so it was put out. Fanny, the housemaid, had already complained of the heat. She and the other maids found it "Quite unbearable, Madam."

There was no telephone, ice was scarce, and it took several hours every day to clean and fill the oil lamps. But there was a bathtub that was quite a curiosity, standing on a platform up two steps. On the main floor under the stairs, which were quite impressive, there was a door that opened into a large gloomy bedroom in an ell. Behind this room was the bathroom, where there were enormous taps but only a trickle of water. We never used it, but it must have been quite a historical tub, perhaps one of the earliest installed in London. The tub itself was of metal and was surrounded by elaborate woodwork.

On the left of the front door was a delightful living room, with three windows looking out on the front. The furniture was covered by pretty chintz, and the chairs were comfortable. There were two desks, which Mother and Hattie used, and a large open fire. The dining room opened from this room as well as from the hall, and was quite large.

There were two large drawing rooms upstairs. One was across the front, with three large windows opening onto a covered piazza looking over the square. The front room had two fireplaces, and the walls were covered with a soft green brocade. The rear room walls had pale yellow brocade, and in that room hung a lovely Sir Joshua Reynolds painting of a little girl. The lighting was done by large sconces on the walls and chandeliers holding candles. It took eighty candles to light the rooms, but it was a soft and becoming light for all ages.

On the same floor, and over the "bathtub suite," there was a very pretty little sitting room. Behind it there was a bedroom, which Fanny kept locked, because it was kept for Mrs. Meynell Ingraham's possessions. The little sitting room was used by Louise and me, and we had our lessons there.

On the floor above were the bedrooms. Louise and I had two on the front, opening into each other. They had a fine view over the square and contained many photographs, evidently family pictures, many of which were signed.

One of them over my fireplace interested me very much. It was of a boy of about ten. He had a sailor suit on, and the picture was signed in a childish hand, "Edward Frederick Lindley Wood." The head was a fine one, and his forehead showed great intelligence. When Fanny came in every morning to superintend her undermaid, Rose, who pulled back the curtains and carried in cans of water for the funny-hat tub, I noticed that she always looked at the photograph quite reverently, and sometimes murmured, "My little gentleman."

But to get Fanny to talk was a problem. It was "Yes Miss" or "No Miss" or "Is the water quite right Miss?" It was several weeks before she melted enough to be a little more human, and then she talked quite fluently, and seemed only too willing to tell us about "Little Master."

Mrs. Meynell Ingraham's brother was Lord Halifax, and two of his sons had died young. Another was very ill, and this last little boy in the photograph was delicate, and had a withered arm. Fanny wondered how he would ever be strong enough to go to school and college. Later we heard that the [third son, the one who had been ill] died soon after we left London.

Louise and I soon settled down to regular lessons. We had a French teacher two mornings a week, and we took walks with her. The other days we had a German teacher, who was a very fine teacher and took no nonsense from us. We also had Latin lessons, so as to keep up with our class at St. Agnes, and we had piano lessons from Mr. Lichterstein, a Dane who was recommended by Mrs. Moscheles.

When the weather was fine, we rode with Mr. Ferguson, usually in Rotten Row. [One governess or the other] took us to the galleries and exhibitions and to the afternoon concerts. Life was quite strenuous, with so much education and sightseeing thrown in. Hattie was hard at work with her singing lessons from Mr. William Shakespeare, known as the "Guinea Pig" because he charged a guinea a lesson. Mother and Hattie went out to dinners and had dinners at home too.

One Friday Hattie went to spend the weekend at Bowden Park with Sir John and Lady Gladstone, who were old friends. It poured all Sunday. Mother had a heavy cold, and so we did not go to church. We had written letters, studied lessons, and practiced on the piano. In fact, we had been good all day and were as restless as colts. Mother was taking a nap and would not be down until five o'clock tea, so we fell from grace.

The three windows of the living room were on a level with the sidewalk, set back by an iron fence and steps into the entrance area. The congregation from St. Peter's, Eaton Square, were leaving from the afternoon service. Why not collect a crowd just for fun?

No sooner said than done! We each took a window and knelt down so that only our faces showed. Then we pressed them hard against the glass so our noses were flat and so were our lips and tongues. We must have been horrible.

We succeeded beyond our wildest dreams. A crowd collected at once. One old dame shook her umbrella at us. She shouted we were devils and called on the others to kneel and pray. Younger people laughed.

An older man hesitated, looked the house over carefully, and rang the bell to report us. The door into the hall was open so we heard Gough open the front door. The man said in a loud voice, "His this han hidiet hasylum?"

Gough replied, "What do you mean?"

The man said, "Go look at the window."

We ducked behind the desks, so there was no one to be seen. Gough went out muttering about "crazy folks." He fired some choice Billingsgate at the man and closed the door.

We went to work again and made even worse faces. The complaining man settled himself against a tree, evidently waiting for a "bobby," but rain began to fall in torrents, and no "bobby" appeared. Darkness fell. We slipped back to the fire and were diligently reading when Mother appeared.

One evening when Mother gave a large dinner, Louise and I sat on the stairs, where we had a fine view of the guests assembling in the drawing rooms and then marching down to the dining room. We were supposed to study or read an improving book and be in bed by 9:30. But this particular night, Richard, the footman, came and whispered to us that Gough was drunk. Although he was in the dining room, he could hardly stand up, and he could not pass anything. At first this seemed unbelievable, as Gough had always seemed so respectable.

We discussed what we could do and felt very important. After dinner he would be supposed to carry the coffee upstairs. We hit on a remarkable plan. Gough would try to get Richard or the other man to do it for him, so we made them hide. When Gough found he would have to do it, we hung over the stairs in a thrill of excitement.

He had a large silver tray with eighteen cups and saucers, a tall coffee pot, and sugar and cream. It swayed from side to side, narrowly missing crashing over the stair rail. Richard was grinning in the hall, and the other man was peering anxiously from a door. Gough just managed to make it, and he got around the room safely. I am afraid we were disappointed. Our idea was to have Mother see Gough. We did not realize that a disaster would have been embarrassing. We hoped that perhaps some coffee might fall on the "Painted Countess," who was a guest.

We waited until the guests left and then broke the news to Mother. She was frightened and feared he might set the house on fire, but he had gone to bed. Next day Mother asked Gough for the keys to the wine cellar or cupboard, and she took him with her. There was hardly anything left of the stock she had bought from Fortnum and Mason a short time before.

On questioning Marie, Mother's maid, we found that Gough had been drinking heavily ever since we came. As he sat at the head of the upper servants' table and said grace, then refused to eat anything, they had almost starved. It was not etiquette to eat anything refused by the butler, so the dishes went away untasted. He gave thanks at the end of the meal, whether they had eaten anything or not.

Mother felt badly that she had not been told, but Marie said they had all realized that it was not for long, so they had not complained. Fortunately, our own Christian and Fanny returned from a visit to Switzerland, so we went on with no trouble. Louise and I for some reason felt very proud, as if we had unearthed a Guy Fawkes plot.

Louise and I were allowed to walk alone in the square, but otherwise we had to be chaperoned everywhere, as no girls ever drove alone in a hansom cab. When we wanted a cab, the footman blew a whistle, one blast for a four wheeler, known as a "Growler," and two blasts for a hansom. We never had to wait long.

Mother invited Rosalie Bard to return with us, as she had not been in America since she was a baby. Her father was John Bard, formerly of Annandale at Barrytown-on-Hudson, and my father's closest friend. We called him "Uncle John." He and his first wife had given the land for St. Stephen's College at Barrytown, and my father had long been a trustee. Mr. Bard had remarried in England, so Rosalie was free to return to America.

Mother became anxious about Grandfather and summer plans, so she took passage again on the *Teutonic*, sailing from Liverpool on May 14th [1890]. Lady Playfair, an old friend, asked Mother also to chaperone Lady Griselda Oglivy and Eva Einloch, who were going out to join their married sisters in Estes Park, in which Lord Airlie had great interests.[2] Griselda's mother, Lady Airlie, brought her to call, and butter would not melt in her mouth. Lady Airlie was an imposing lady in a very full flowing black dress, an imposing bonnet and veil, and a heavy black coat. Griselda never spoke that day while Mother and Lady Airlie discussed plans, so we decided she was no fun.

When it came to leaving, we were very sorry. London was looking lovely, with flower boxes on window sills, and the park was green, and trees were out. We had to spend the night at Liverpool, and Lady Airlie, with the two girls, met us there. We boarded the tug to take us out to the ship. It was very crowded, and an older man dropped dead against Fanny. She was very superstitious and excitable, and she started to cry. She said we had started on the 13th, and something was sure to happen.

Lady Airlie inspected the cabin and went all around the ship and found out how near Griselda's cabin was to ours. Then she said a tearful farewell and went off on the tug, and Griselda waved until she was out of sight. Then a complete change came over her. She began to run around the deck shouting, "I feel the free air of America!" Mother decided that she had quite a job on her hands.

We landed in Queenstown [near Dublin] and took a drive in a jaunting car, and Mother was disappointed that she could not buy a copy of the *London Times*. Griselda proceeded to have quite an affair with a nice elderly Mr. Greenough, and he fell completely for her. Louise and I could hardly wait to get home. We said over and over how slowly the days passed. I remember the kindly old stewardess who kept shaking her head and saying, "Young ladies, never wish the time away. 'Tis bad luck."

We entered New York Harbor on a radiant day and the custom's boat brought Mr. John Corning. He asked for Mother and speedily put the whole party through all the bothersome formalities, then he vanished. Suddenly in the gangway I ran into Jack, Aunt Mary Corning, and Uncle Tuy. Aunt Mary was in deep mourning. I was so glad to see them but they asked me to take them to Mother's cabin. Aunt Mary went in and closed the door.

Then Jack told me that Grandfather had died very suddenly on the afternoon of the 13th, the day we left London. A notice of it had been in the *Times* that we were unable to buy at Queenstown, so Mother had been spared the knowledge for the long trip. Fanny began to weep noisily and said it was because we started the trip on the 13th and the man had died.

At the station at Albany and at our house were various members of the family, but Mother had adored Grandfather and was completely crushed. I went down and sat with Fromo, who had been bathed and combed. He was very glad to see me, and I was joyful to see him. It had all turned out so differently from our happy plannings. "Angel" Booth had looked so sadly at our party as we passed through the gate, and he had made none of his usual wisecracks.

CHAPTER 21

THE GREAT EXCITEMENT IN ALBANY during our absence had been the opening of the Hawk Street viaduct at the head of our block of Elk Street.[1] It was a wonderful improvement and a popular walk. I returned to school, took examinations with my class, and I made the momentous decision to try to graduate. At first the teachers were inclined to take this with a grain of humor, but with Hattie's help and her talks with Miss Boyd, it was finally arranged that I should go to Miss Edith Brown for special tutoring.

In early July we went to Bar Harbor, where Mother took the Lyon place, "Edenfield," on the bay side. Through the assistance of Dr. and Mrs. Samuel Eliot, Ezra Thayer was highly recommended as a tutor for me. He was twenty-three and in the Harvard Law School; everyone said he was very learned.[2] He was understanding and saw me plow through the rest of Virgil, Horace, parts of Tasso, and algebra. In the meantime Louise was tutoring at home under Miss Brown, as she too was determined to graduate. Perhaps our trip had produced some ambition at last.

In the fall we passed innumerable examinations and entered the Class of '91, a class of twenty-two girls, most of whom had been there for many years. This firm purpose of mine rather anchored Mother in Albany for the winter, and we settled down, except for making some changes in the house, particularly cutting a new window in the music room, so that it looked out on the garden.

But the real sensation came with the news that Judge John Clinton Gray of the Court of Appeals had leased No. 6 Elk Street for a term of years. He was a widower with five children, but they had never come with him — they lived in New York. Judge Gray also lived at the Kenmore. He was a great horseback rider. Judge Danforth of Rochester and his handsome daughter, Miss Jessie, also lived at the Kenmore and also rode in the morning. People rather suspected that Judge Gray had centered his affections on Miss Jessie, and as they passed up Elk Street, we could see that she wore a bunch of violets pinned on her tight-fitting black riding habit.

But during the past summer the announcement [had been made] in the papers that Judge Gray had been married at Newport to Mrs. Henry Turnbull of Paris and Newport. Mrs. Turnbull had given a dinner party which included her clergyman. When dinner was over, Mrs. Turnbull and the Judge were married; the dinner guests became the wedding guests.

Mrs. Gray had been Miss Grace Townsend of New York. She had married a Mr. Smith and had a son. Both her husband and her son died. Then she married Henry Turnbull in Paris and had a second son. Later she was divorced from him and returned to live in Newport [where she met and married Judge Gray].

Elk Street was tremendously excited by such an event. From the nursery window I watched the arrival of piles of trunks, furniture, a fox terrier, and finally the family and numerous servants. By the grapevine it became known that the oldest of the Gray children was Pauline, and that she was seventeen. Next came Harry and Clinton, and last Edith and Albert. The Turnbull boy was about nine, and soon his name was changed to Austen Gray, so there were six children there.

The next Sunday afternoon about 4:30, the door bell rang, and I heard the voice of Julia Walsh calling me. Her voice fairly fluttered with excitement. I ran to the stairs and she said, "Put your coat on quickly and come and see the new Mrs. Gray, sitting in her front window reading. She is smoking, too." This last bit of information was in a whisper so that Christian would not be corrupted by such gossip.

Julia guided me across the street. "For," she said, "if we walked on her side, she might think we were staring, and anyway, you can see her better from the park side." So we passed along slowly, and there, sure enough, she was sitting right against the long window, a New York paper in one hand and a cigarette in the other. She was wearing a lovely pink chiffon and lace tea gown trimmed with fur and low in the neck. "That's to show her pearl necklace," said Julia. "And, she is going to stay at home on Sunday afternoons and have tea too, because she says it is the only day the men are rested and can talk."

Our previous excitements had been Mrs. Snively's flirtation with handsome Mr. Jimmy MacNaughton and her marriage later to someone else, in California, and the troubled careers of Peyton and Kitty Van Buren Miller. The Millers had settled happily for a time in a house with a new brick front at 313 State Street, but their ship had not sailed smoothly, as they were frank to admit to anyone. Peyton had moved to the Kenmore, where he saw a great deal of Judge Gray. So as Julia and I walked and talked up and down by the park, we were not surprised to see Peyton coming across to call on Mrs. Gray.

"That's quite a new kind of window picture for old Albany," said he, cocking his eye toward No. 6. "I wonder how some people will take it when they see me going in there. They will probably remark, 'Birds of a feather flock together'," and bowing in Peytonese style, he left us.

We walked by the house once more and then retired to our conservatory to watch the later happenings. Soon two of the other judges came up by Steuben Street to vanish into the Gray vestibule. A door slammed above us, and General and Mrs. Farnsworth, from No. 26, walked down towards No. 6. Miss Annie McClellan, escorted by her devoted admirer, Rev. Russell Woodman, came across the park, soon followed by Judge and Mrs. Wallace from little State Street. Just before it became too dark to see, Dr. Battershall, evening service over, sprinted along and also vanished into No. 6. Julia said, very seriously as she was leaving, "Do you think Mrs. Doane and your mother and cousin Sarah Barnard will ever call?"

It was indeed a new era for Elk Street, but it turned out to be a very successful one, and Mrs. Gray did a lot of stirring up. She was very direct and never minced words about what she had to say or do. Everything she wore and did was well "turned out." Her carriages and sleighs were the very latest.

They took the old Pierson pew at St. Peter's, just back of ours, and she sang every verse of every hymn with fervor. Her voice made up in strength what it lacked in sympathy. Mrs. Gray marshalled the family in exactly on time every Sunday. She sat in the corner with Edith next to her and Pauline, the oldest, and the boys squeezed in. Judge Gray came in last and sat at the end of the pew.

We could distinctly hear Mrs. Gray's whispers, such as, "Edith, ask your father for the cough drops." This request would be relayed along until it reached the Judge, who would reach down into his pocket and fish out the box, which then would be rattled along to Mrs. Gray. Sometimes the whispered comments on the sermon would make people in nearby pews smile or frown. "Dr. Battershall never wrote out that sermon. He wanders from the text." Or, "The doctor returned too late last night from New York, so we must suffer from a poor, old sermon." She was frank with Dr. Battershall, but he took her criticisms good-naturedly.

At No. 5 lived Colonel and Mrs. Sweny and their son Harry. Soon after the Grays came, Colonel Sweny was very ill, and tanbark was spread all over the street to deaden the noise of the traffic. This tanbark annoyed Mrs. Gray, as it crumbled and made dirt to be tramped into her house. Hearing that Colonel Sweny was better, she wrote a courteous note to Mrs. Sweny to say how glad she was to hear of his improvement and that she hoped the tanbark could now be removed. To this Mrs. Sweny replied that she was happy to say that her husband was improved, but that she had never had but one husband, and she was taking good care of him, so the tanbark could not be removed. . . .

❦   ❦   ❦

Mother was in New York a great deal that fall [1890], as Aunt Mary had to have an operation. She went to a private hospital in the city, where Mother stayed also. As I look back on that dismal hospital, in a very cold brownstone house on a side street near the elevated road, I wonder how anyone lived through anything. The conditions would never be accepted nowadays, but at that time it was considered one of the best, and my aunt was fortunate to get into it. I was supposed to be busy at school, and Hattie was supposed to keep house and keep a strict eye on me. But when a beau called on her in the evening and stayed after ten, then I felt responsible.

One evening "Dutchy" struck ten, and an ardent admirer stayed on. So I felt it necessary to get out of bed and do something about it. First I set an alarm clock to go off in five minutes and placed it outside the library door. Then I woke up Fromo and tied a sign around his collar and wrote on it, "First call for breakfast." Fromo could be counted on, and he did just what I told him. He ran down the hall to the library and right up to the caller. At that moment the clock went off with a crashing noise. I was in bed again and appeared to be asleep when Hattie came rushing in to blow me up, but I did not mind, as the caller left and the house could be closed.

One of the constant callers now was William G. Rice. He came often and stayed late. He and my sister always seemed to walk home from church together, so Elk Street tongues began to wag. Mother returned for two or three days on business, and William was to come to dinner. It was after five when Mother arrived, and she brought with her two love birds in a cage for me. Hattie had ordered dinner, but I went down to the kitchen, and after much diplomatic work and many promises about Fromo's future behavior, I persuaded Biddy to change the menu.

So we had: soup with rice, rice croquettes with sauce, boiled rice with the meat course, fried rice with the game course, and rice pudding for dessert. Mother was completely mystified and kept saying, "What a queer dinner. Why all this rice? Which of you ordered such a dinner?" Hattie got redder and redder. William was perfectly serene, but he must have realized what a nice time I was having at the table.

❦   ❦   ❦

That September when I returned from the summer at Bar Harbor, I stayed at the Parkers, who had moved into Grandfather's old house. Mother was chaperoning a riding party through the Berkshires. Christian, the Swiss butler, telephoned me that Mrs. Doane had telegraphed from Boston that she would arrive at seven, and he implied that I should return to receive her. Then Christian said he supposed that the telegram was from Mrs. Doane, as he knew the bishop was in the northern part of the diocese. The telegram was signed "D. L. Doane," and Christian knew those were not her initials. He did not know that the Doanes all signed their telegrams like that, and that the "D. L." stood for "Dear Love."

It was very provoking for me, as Grace and I had well laid plans for the evening, but I went home very nobly. The carriage went to the station and I was on the steps to welcome her, and Fanny was on hand to help her unpack. After I had settled down to my lessons again, I heard a cry of distress and a call over the stairs for me to come up. Mrs. Doane and Fanny were gazing spellbound at the contents of her bag, spread on the bed. There was a pair of pajamas, a shaving outfit, a pipe, a shady-looking tooth brush, a pair of worn bed slippers, and a large program from Koster and Bialls, with a picture of Cissy Loftus high-kicking. Mrs. Doane said the porter had taken her bag and handed her this one when she left the car. She had not noticed any difference, and she was sure it was almost identical with hers.

After much telephoning and the dispatch of Owen to the station to return the bag, we had a very late dinner. The story grew as the dinner was served, and by the time we reached fruit, the tale had grown to a mix-up of four bags. Mrs. Doane's bag was not recovered for several months. It was finally located in Troy.

School began again in early January for the long term. Two of the class, Mary Drury and Daisy Brown, wrote a very clever play called "A Chip Off the Old Block" or "The Mummies' Marriage." It was given several times on the stage in the gymnasium. Enough money was raised to buy, and have lettered, the cornerstone for Graduates' Hall, which was to be laid on Commencement Day. We had several parties, and the rigid regulations were lifted a bit for our last year. . . .

That year Miss Boyd drilled us very thoroughly on art history. She was rather floored when one of the girls, when asked the styles of Greek architecture, replied instantly, "Doric, Ionic, and Platonic." [She taught us] the difference between an ambulatory and an aisle, a triforium and a clerestory, an apse and a transept. [We also learned] that the cathedral was ten feet shorter than the choir of St. Paul's in London.

Miss Boyd took the class to New York one Friday night in May. About twelve of us went down on the night boat. We went around New York in horsecars on a very hot day. We had to describe all the architecture, especially St. Patrick's Cathedral. The boat was old and dirty, and to Miss Boyd's horror, she discovered we were singing,

> The butterfly's wings are gauze,
> The firefly's wings are flame.
> The bedbug has no wings at all,
> But he gets there just the same.

[Mrs. Hamlin here narrates an adventure of Lady Griselda Ogilvy.]

For several years the younger set had wanted to start a country club. This sounds easy nowadays when every small city has such a club, but it was an almost unknown institution in 1889 and 1890. The roads were bad. There were toll gates on every road, and only those [who drove carriages or rode] could use such a club. Skating could be enjoyed on the park lake, the canal, the river, or on Little's Pond; why another skating place?

It was hard to argue against all this, but some brave spirits undertook to start a club, and one of them was my sister Harriet L. Pruyn. Others were Mr. Robert Pruyn, Mr. Sard, Miss Grace Learned, Mr. Frank Saxe, Mr. Edward Bowditch, and the two Van Rensselaers, Bayard and Howard. They met with the endless discouragements that are always the lot of the pioneer.

One great bone of contention was the site. The sand plains seemed the logical place. There was a romance about them. In those days, many people had never heard there were any sand plains, or they had forgotten the unusual long stretch so close to the city. [These plains] had once been the bottom of the lake covering Albany and reaching back to Schenectady, [with] the Helderbergs [as] their western limit.[3] They had been a hunting ground for the Six Nations, and arrowheads were often found there, relics of the buffalo-hunting days. In the spring the Shadblow, [which] bloomed at the time of the shad run in the river [were beautiful]. In the fall the area was carpeted with goldenrod, Michaelmas daisies, and waving sumac.[4]

We had always loved the sand plains for these reasons. The old New York Central track was plainly visible, and we could ride along the top of it. There were a few squatters and truck farmers, but you could ride fairly straight for miles without meeting a soul. We usually entered the narrow dirt trail from the continuation of Washington Avenue beyond Manning Boulevard. The Boulevard had been recently laid out, named for Mayor James H. Manning, and with rare foresight, planted with trees. . . .

Hattie Banks Green led the opposition group that wanted to locate on the New Scotland Road because it was a better road and the old Pierson farm was for sale. But there was no pond there, and we had to have a skating pond. The land was hilly and the views were lovely, but it did not seem practical.

So at last it was voted to start the Club in the old tavern on the old Schenectady Road. For a small sum this was rented, with several acres of land, and everyone went to work to make it more attractive. A murder had been committed in the cellar of the old tavern, and the presence of a ghost gave it a romantic feature. A small piazza was added on one side. Chairs, tables, and a stove were contributed, as well as china, glass, and small rugs. I have a small Kodak picture of the first tea. It sounds simple and primitive, but this was a long step forward.

It is wonderful that the club survived the many inconveniences; perhaps we did not then look at them as such, but we do now. Teas were given every Saturday, and members took turns in providing the food. . . .

On the first Thanksgiving after the opening of the club, there was to be a fox hunt, a real one. Dr. Lewis Balch, the M. F. H., . . . a handsome and interesting man, and a good doctor, [was adamant that a tradition of excellence be established]. He was of English descent; his father had been an English canon of the Montreal Cathedral. He knew all about hunting.

Ten hounds were borrowed from the Dutchess County pack and were promised to arrive in crates by express the day before the hunt.

As Hattie and I rode out, . . . we wondered if we could bear to see the fox caught. I decided that I would gallop to the club as fast as I could to avoid the sight. It was a bitter cold day, and snow began to fall as we assembled at 2:30 sharp. There were more than fifty people on horseback, and many more were arriving in all sorts of vehicles, as the hunt had been widely advertised in the "Social Notes" of the paper.

As we approached, Dr. Balch was riding up and around, furiously calling to this and that one and swearing roundly at Dr. Walter Foote Robinson. Dr. Robinson could not control a large black horse that cavorted into the other horses and crossed their bows, much to their indignation. A boy stood on the side, holding four small hounds on one leash. They looked tired and spiritless and shivered in the blast.

It soon transpired that Dr. Balch's ire was aroused because six other hounds were still in the express office. By some mistake four had arrived first, and the other six had come on a late train. The Express Company, which was closed for the holiday, had shut them up in the office on Broadway the previous night, and everyone in authority had gone home to celebrate. Hence, no dogs.

Finally, we started. The four dogs were unleashed. There was a trail, but two of the dogs preferred to chase a rabbit and vanished early in the run. Another dog sat down and began to scratch himself with great satisfaction. The fourth ran after the heels of Dr. Balch's horse, up hill and down hill, keeping just out of reach of the doctor's whip and yapping like any street cur.

We tore on, the snow blowing in our faces. Finally, we reached an opening in the woods, about half a mile from where we had started an hour earlier. There was the same little boy, but this time he had a box on the ground at his feet. We came to a breathless standstill. The M. F. H. gave a whistle. The box opened, and we could see a long nose and bright eyes. We waited with our hearts in our mouths, and I forgot to run off.

The one hound sat comfortably lolling his tongue. The fox thrust out his head, gave a leap, and flouted his tail at the dog, who did not seem in the least interested. They looked at one another. Then the fox returned to the box. No doubt he was cold. The boy closed the box and started to walk off, swinging it by a strap. The hunt was over. . . .

🦊   🦊   🦊

The next year I wrote in my diary, "The Thanksgiving Hunt was unusual, like most of the others, as Dr. Walter Foote Robinson fell off his horse, and we all chased the horse, who was a fast runner. That was the Hunt."

After about two years in the tavern, the club purchased the old William Cooper place called "Wellhurst" (it was later owned by Mr. Paul Cushman). The lovely Cathedral Woods were part of it. Bonds were sold at $100 each and were taken up fairly quickly. With the move into the new Club, stages were run during the skating season, once in the afternoon and once in the evening, from the end of the car line on Madison Avenue. They were better than nothing but slow and cold, and if you missed the one trolley that met the stage, you had your ride in vain, unless you walked, [which I did several times].

The little pond at the club was gradually enlarged, and in winter there was a campfire in the ravine so that it was very picturesque at night. In the afternoon we had hockey teams and played Snap-the-Whip. The tennis courts were very poor the first years, but they were gradually improved as funds came in. I think golf started about 1896. At first it was made great fun of, and the few who took it up were called "British Lions." It was considered a game for the idle rich. If anyone had predicted municipal links, they would have been accused of misuse of the taxpayers' money.

More land was bought, and Marcus Reynolds, fresh from the study of Touraine architecture, in 1896 and 1897, remodeled the old house and designed the front door and fireplace. These alterations were handsome in their way, but they did not fit the house style. The caretaker, Van Bissikumer, kept hens, and we used to buy eggs from him and scramble them in a chafing dish and make coffee in a can held over the flame. After building a fire in the room on the right of the Touraine front door, we would settle down and sing and tell ghost stories until the chaperone rebelled.

I remember one night when about twenty-five of us met at our house to go out skating at the club in a big sleigh. At the last moment the chaperone telephoned that she could not come. Consternation! What would we do? Some of the party, like May Cooper, were well over thirty, but none were married. We telephoned several women. None could come. The sleigh waited. Half past eight struck.

Then De Witt Walsh appeared with Mr. George Douglas Miller in tow.

Kind Mr. Miller had been half asleep in his smoking jacket and felt slippers, but De Witt persuaded him to come to the rescue; so off we went — having appeased all parents. . . .

I went through the terrific agony of writing a class poem for the class supper and then the valedictory for Commencement. At last the great day arrived. June 11, 1891, was a perfect day. I was dressed in a white organdy dress with lace insertions and an organdy hat with ostrich tips as I walked up Elk Street for the last time as a lamb of St. Agnes.

We assembled in the library. It was a wonderful feeling to be so important at last after years of being underdogs. The bishop in his gorgeousness came out of No. 12. We fell in behind him, grasping our bouquets of the Class Flower, daisies. I had the unhappy valedictory tied with yellow and white ribbons. Miss Boyd, in her stiff gray and white silk, and standing by her, Miss Gavit, in black, looked worried as we passed them in the lower hall. Possibly they were worried over forgotten details. The younger classes craned their necks from the doors on the landings. In fact, it was a great day, and one that I had never counted on as a remote possibility for me.

In the hot schoolroom Dr. Jeffrey at one piano and Pauline Rathbone at the other were playing the March. The crowds, flowers, and ushers — it was all unreal and wonderful, and I felt happy. We sat on the stage with the clergy, trustees, and chapter, and the bishop had a word for every one at the right moment. How dull my valedictory sounded! All the strong touches had been cut out by Canon Gray. It was flat, and I knew it.

We filed over to the cathedral. Ours was the third class to graduate there. Hattie's graduation had been in the old chapel. The bishop used our class motto, "Omnes Virtutes Amore," for the text of his address. Then he gave out the diplomas.

It was a tremendous moment in my life to return to my seat grasping the precious sheepskin. The signers were "Wiliam Croswell Doane, S.T.D., L.L.D., Bishop of Albany and President of the Board," "Thomas B. Fulcher, Secretary of the Board of Trustees of the Corning Foundation for Christian Work in the Diocese of Albany," and "Ellen W. Boyd, Head of St. Agnes School." There were the seals of the diocese, of the founder, and of the bishop, and in the lower left-hand corner, on a wide blue ribbon, was the white seal of St. Agnes herself. It was quite a joke to read, "We do by these presents give and grant unto you, of whose soundness of learning and faithfulness of living, we have good proof, this testimonial of our approbation and confidence; in token that you have by diligent study completed the prescribed course of study in our school of St. Agnes."

The bishop always gave a special benediction. It was very beautiful, and his voice rang out clearly through the cathedral. There was a moment of silence, and then the organ started "Ancient of Days." The words were written by the bishop, and the music by Dr. Jeffrey, for Albany's Bicentennial in 1886. We filed out of the north transept, the music ringing to the roof, and took our stand by the cornerstone of the Hall. "Filiae eorum compositae" — "Her daughters shall be as the polished corners of the Temple."

No ice cream or cake or strawberries ever tasted so good as those we had at Commencement. The reception, the charming bishop, Canon Fulcher, Dean Robbins looking very stiff, the parents from in town, the parents from out of town, the relief the examinations were over, the regrets this was the end, all mixed feelings with "Ancient of Days" ringing an undertone — these are the indelible memories. The many good-byes said, I walked home carrying my flowers, "The Last Word" squashed in among them.[5] I felt flat and wondered what could come next. It seemed to me that all the excitements of life were over. . . .

CHAPTER 22

OTHER WAS RATHER UNCERTAIN just what to do next about me. She felt, and it was quite true, that I needed further education. I was very young for my age and had no wish to come out. All I wanted was to live in Albany and do whatever turned up there. The Cornings were in the west and decided to spend the summer, so Mother took their place, "Stoneacres," at North East Harbour. I was delighted. If I had to leave Albany, I liked North East best.

But Hattie felt very sad. The Sunday before we left, she and William Rice walked up from church and stood by the stoop for all Elk Street to watch with interest. They were oblivious of time. Luncheon hour had arrived. Still they talked.

Mother had some torpedoes she kept to frighten the cats who prowled and howled in the garden. She gave me one, and I went out on the little balcony in front of the nursery and dropped it on the steps. It went off with a loud report, and the windows were crowded with excited neighbors. As it did no good, I tried a second one. But the pair always asserted later that they had not heard either of them. . . .

❧　　❧　　❧

We returned to Albany in September [1891], and then the question what to do about me was seriously debated by the family. Mother thought a boarding school that she knew about in England would be the best training. I had been to dances that summer, both at North East and Bar Harbor, but I was shy. I danced with vigor and was used to dancing "man" in school. While all my cousins seemed to know what to do and how to do it, I was much happier at home. I had no self-reliance. It would have been very good for me to have been thrown among strangers and on my own.

But matters had a way of settling themselves. As the fall advanced, nothing was done about me, but it became evident that Hattie was very happy. Colonel William G. Rice was a daily visitor, and it seemed as if he stayed for hours. It was easy to put two and two together. Then one day invitations were left at the house for Sarah Townsend's wedding to Guy Lansing at St. Peter's, and one invitation was directed to the "Misses Pruyn." I thought that was wonderful and decided I wanted to go. As I look back, this invitation seems a milestone. It pointed to the fact that people knew I was eighteen and rated an invitation. . . .

The next excitement was that the Paul Fenimore Coopers [invited me to] a tea for Miss Bosse, of Quebec, who was engaged to Jim Cooper's law partner, Mr. James Tracey. . . . To my astonishment, [soon] I had a real beau. The boys at North East had been very nice and polite, but I did not expect any of them to like me enough to give me what was called a "rush." Others had rushes, and that was to be expected, but not me. Perhaps I had what is known as an inferiority complex, but I was happy about [my solitude] and thought the others very funny.

The "beau" was very nice, and we often coasted and skated. He was about twenty-seven, and I thought that very old. He had come from out of town and had brought a letter of introduction from some friend of Mother's. He was English and had come over with Hope Brooke, son of the rajah of Sarawak, who also came to visit us for a few days. My beau decided to stay in the United States and went into banking. He was sent here to represent some British interests, but it is all so long ago that I have forgotten what they were.

It seemed to me to be a tremendous joke that anyone in his senses should court me. I laughed so hard at him that I became hysterical, and he became very angry. He said he had waited almost two years for me to be eighteen and finish school, and now he was afraid someone else would get ahead of him, which made me laugh more. He said he was returning to England in the spring and wanted me to go with him. I would have had a winter here to go about it. I said that settled it. Albany was where I meant to live and die, and nothing would induce me to live anywhere else.

He wanted to talk to Mother, but finally I persuaded him it was just no use. He was going west on a business trip for several months and wanted to carry with him the assurance that I would think it over carefully. I was so glad when he left. I hid in the coal cellar all one lovely afternoon, as he had written me a note on crested paper to say he would call to say goodbye. Christian would not think of finding me in the coal bin. When I appeared at six o'clock, he had been and gone.

He kept writing me for a while, then stopped. The next I heard from him was that he had met a girl, the image of me, somewhere in California. As I was hard-hearted, he had asked her to marry him. So he [wished me well and hoped] I would not regret my unwise decision. Later he inherited a very nice title from an uncle. I never saw him again. I think it did me good as it proved that I was not such a pill. I actually had had a beau, and it helped my morale.

The next step was having visiting cards engraved. "Mrs. Pruyn, Miss Pruyn, Miss Huybertie Lansing Pruyn" — how funny they all looked. Hattie was very mad when I said it was a waste to put her name on the cards, when, if we waited, I would be Miss Pruyn.

After that, Mrs. Dean Sage at "Hillside" drove to our house and left a note for me asking me to luncheon and adding that the guests would be invited to meet me. My first party all to myself! Mother said she must do something about my clothes. I have never felt so important as when Mrs. Sage led me to the place at her right, but I was so overcome that I was tongue-tied. Nobody had told me I would have to leave first. It was only the arrival of carriages to take us to the station that finally started us.

Mother and I went to New York, and it may interest a later generation to know what we bought. The dresses came from Kate Reilly, whose shop was in a brownstone front on Fifth Avenue. First there was the coming-out ball dress of white chiffon over white satin, with the puff sleeves of the period. From the left shoulder to the right side of the belt there was a white velvet ribbon about three inches wide. It had a knot on the shoulder. On the left shoulder there was a bunch of white heather, and some more heather on the skirt, which was long with a slight train — enough to make a modern dancer wild. At Slater's on Broadway we bought plain white satin slippers with seed pearl bows.

Then there was a simple yellow chiffon dance dress and yellow satin slippers with gold and gauze rosettes. A dinner dress was what is now called a "period dress." It was of soft white chiffon with a tiny stripe, and it was made in Empire style, then much in vogue. It was high-waisted, with a sash of white velvet with gold embroidery and fringe, and it was worn over a fitted slip of soft white taffeta with a gold edge. The slippers were of gold leather.

An afternoon tea dress was especially pretty. It was very high-necked, with a boned collar. The material was Sicilian. It was pink and had a silver belt and collar and an edge of mink fur around the bottom of the skirt. The yoke was of heavy guipure lace.

The winter suit was of dark red Bedford cord made in a Russian style. All were separate waists and skirts, except the Empire one. . . .

After all that was settled, our troubles began. It was an old custom to take a girl to call on every friend in the city. One was not properly introduced unless this was done. Mother had taken Hattie on this round, and there was no escape for us. [My cousin] Louise [who was also to come out], would groan when I telephoned her to be ready at 3:15, and we would stop for her and start another block of visits.

It was slow work. The old custom was for one member of the family to stay at home every afternoon to receive callers. Our only hope was that when there was only one woman in a family, she might be out. We usually used the landau, a very heavy carriage, which had two men on the box. One took the cards to the doors, and we would watch like cats to see how the cards were taken by whomever answered the bell and whether the door was held open for us or closed.

Sometimes we seemed to be let in at most inconvenient times and had to wait for the hostess to dress. Sometimes it sounded as if she were taking a bath. Once a very green maid said to us as we came in, "She's been having a shampoo but I guess it's dry by now."

We were always asked, "How do you like coming out?" and we had to try to smile sweetly and answer, "Very much." We arranged before the call which of us, Louise or I, would answer the inevitable question. Sometimes sherry or madeira and biscuits were hurriedly produced. We admired Mother's stoical attitude and amiability, as she sat chatting about the weather.

Elk Street had to be done on Saturdays. Columbia Street, Lodge Street, Lafayette Street, and Park Place were done on foot. Broadway had many people living there, like the Harrises, Talcotts, Chases, Treadwells, Miss Vosburg, and the Clinton Ten Eycks. Big State Street was also a partly residential street.

By December 15th we had come out as far as Lark Street. After that we were so busy that it was hard to get a free afternoon, but we finally did finish the whole city, even Mrs. Andrew J. Colvin, the Panther's mother, out on Western Avenue. We visited Professor Hall's family in Beaver Park and friends down River Road and Menands and spent two afternoons in Troy.

A call that really interested me was on old Mrs. George William Clinton. She had been Laura Canfield Spencer, the daughter of John C. Spencer, who had been Secretary of War and Secretary of the Treasury. . . . She had been married in 1832, so she must have been about eighty-two or eighty-three at this time. . . .

Mrs. Clinton told us this interesting anecdote. She said she went to a small school very near their house. It was so near that she was allowed to go and come alone. One day after school she played with some of the children and then started for home, but somehow she got twisted about and did not know the way. She began to cry, and a nice kind older man came to her and asked her name. He said he knew just where she lived. He took her hand and they walked along together. As they neared the Spencers' house, she saw her mother anxiously watching from the window, as she was late.

The kind man rang the bell, and the door opened, but no one could be seen. He bowed and went down the steps, and she ran to an irate mother, who told her she had disgraced the family. She had walked through the street holding the hand of Aaron Burr.

❦   ❦   ❦

On December 14 the family had a meeting at Harmanus Bleecker Hall to decide on the date and arrangements for the coming-out Ball. Mother and Aunt Kate Marvin were to give the ball together because Grace was to come out too. It was all wonderful, and we lived in a whirl — a well-chaperoned whirl. Mother gave a dinner for the brides and grooms of the previous year, and on December 23, a dinner for the eight "buds."

Hattie thought it would be a good idea to invite older men so that we would at least know them. It was a funny mix-up, and no doubt the men were badly bored. Later a lot of boys came in for dancing. The table was lovely, with Georgian silver and American Beauty roses.

Mother felt she ought to take me to New York, not only for shopping but to a Patriarch's ball at Delmonico's on the corner of Fifth Avenue and 29th Street. Mr. Nicholson Kane sent me an enormous bouquet of heavily wired flowers from either Thorley or Klunder. Good Mr. Kane was a second cousin and about thirty-five years old. He wore side whiskers and was most kind. A card with the flowers said, "With Mr. Nicholson Kane's compliments, and his hope that he can have the pleasure, for which he will ask this evening, of taking Miss Pruyn in to supper." I wonder now what a young girl of eighteen would say to such an escort.

Two other massive bouquets arrived, and Isabeau came to do Mother's hair. Mother hoped I would let her do mine, but I was firm. It was bad enough to go to such a ball. I repudiated the idea of having a Psyche knot, then the rage, with a ribbon tied around it, a bow on the side and hair

waved back from the forehead. My hair had never been waved. Why should
I have it done for a New York ball? Isabeau sighed as she looked at my
plain hair, parted in the middle and in a plain low knot.

To add to my troubles, I was to wear my white coming-out dress —
"wasted on New York," I remarked tragically — when I wanted it absolutely
new for Albany. Mother wore black lace and her little tiara and diamond
necklace, and we set forth for Delmonico's. Mother looked very handsome
and did not seem at all worried or frightened, as I was.

We arrived about eleven, and I would have given all I possessed to have
been safely at home with Fromo instead of with Mr. Kane. A shy fit overcame
me, to such an extent that I felt as if I must escape from the overpowering
smell of the mass of flowers banked on the stairway. Mrs. William E. Rogers
and Nelly were waiting for us in the dressing room. They were old friends,
but Nelly had been out a year and never was shy, and she was entirely
up-to-date with a Psyche knot. Kind Mr. Kane had produced another man
and they waited for us at the ballroom door. So we were properly escorted
in to shake hands with Mrs. William Astor, who was receiving. She was
resplendent in gorgeous brocade, with ropes and chains of diamonds, and
her heavy tiara made her look even more imposing.

Mr. Kane saw that Mother was seated on the side lines between two old
friends. Then he marched me slowly around the ballroom, while I staggered
along with the three heavy bouquets and a large fan. Old Mr. Peter Marie
had a group around him, probably trying to find out what beauty he was
to have painted for his miniature collection. He bowed as Mr. Kane introduced him to me, "My cousin, Miss Pruyn of Albany, a debutante." I could
feel that I was far from measuring up to the standards necessary for inclusion
in his collection. I was too out-of-date to have any chance. A lancers struck
up, and poor Mr. Kane immediately bowed and led me out, although I was
sure it must be a terrible bore for him. We did a stately step that would
have done credit to the eighteenth century.

When this was safely over, we resumed our promenade and came to Mr.
Ward McAllister, then in the height of his reign over the famous "400."
There was a group around him too, and they seemed to be jollying him to
make him do something. My faithful diary states that on my return to
Albany, I wrote, "He is a F – O – O – L. We would not tolerate him here.
I enjoyed it all as a sort of show circus, but I would not care to go again."

❦   ❦   ❦

We had the Christmas tree, after two years of absence and mourning, and the Spruce Street children's party too. The holidays were wildly gay, as all the boys came home from school and college. Dinners had become much less formal and shorter, and there were no longer the elaborate bouquets, boutonnieres, or expensive place cards. Roman punch had been dropped, except in old-fashioned houses, and there were many fewer wine glasses. Also, the enormous centerpieces, which kept you from knowing who sat across the table, were reduced to a reasonable height. . . .

In early December there had been a meeting of mothers of buds at our house to arrange for the assemblies to be given in the new wing of the Kenmore Hotel on Columbia Street. The Kenmore had a side entrance, so we did not have to use the main entrance on Pearl Street, with its leather chairs filled with smokers and loungers. It seemed to me that it was much finer than anything provided by Delmonico's. The only trouble was that the dining room was also the ballroom. No dancing could start until the last diner had finished, and then it took time to clear away the tables and chairs. The real touch that turned the room into a ballroom was when a glass vase was produced and perched on the mantelpiece. It had sprays of imitation greens to look festive. They were always the same ones. Neither time nor dust touched their splendor.

There was a weekly paper called *Capital Chips*, and in my scrap book I find a few choice clippings from it. The description of the "buds" differs so widely each time one is mentioned that there must have been different reporters. . . . A description . . . gives an idea of the style of the paper.

Although Tuesday night was all that was horrible in the line of weather outside, the large dining room at the Kenmore presented a captivating array of feminine loveliness. There was little attempt at decoration. The mantel at the end of the room was ornamented with green vines, and a large bower of palms and ferns screened Parlatti's orchestra from view and made a pretty background for the dancing. The first to enter the room was Mr. Edward T. Reed, bearing upon his arm a pretty, graceful girl in fluffy, white satin and long lover's loops of white satin ribbon floating from her shoulder, looking as placid, amiable and lovely as though the

pouring, raving, crushing rain had not beaten upon the windows
of her sleigh on her way to the hall.

We insisted this lovely creature was Louise but she indignantly denied enter-
ing any room in such a way.

I have the invitation, filled in by Mrs. Doane, inviting me to dinner at
Bishop's House on December 30, at 7:30. The dinner was in honor of Grace
and Louise and me. As the daughter of the oldest member of the former
generation, though the youngest of the three, I was taken into dinner by the
bishop. There were sixteen of us, all young and green and rather shy.

Pauline Gray had stopped for me, and we walked up to the bishop's
house together. She was in a panic, and, once inside the house, she stood
behind the door and insisted she must go home. She never could face the
drawing room full of people. The bishop, seeing that something was wrong,
came out in the hall, and with his wonderful tact, tucked Pauline's arm in
his and devoted himself to her, showing her several portraits until dinner
was announced. She was quite restored. The bishop told some of his best
stories and soon put us at our ease. The Doanes never gave a sign of being
bored. . . .

❦   ❦   ❦

Our coming-out ball on January 6th [1892] gave *Capital Chips* a chance
to wax eloquent. We had several guests: Nelly Rogers from Garrison, Sallie
Livingston from New York, and Miss Lucy Trowbridge of New Haven. We
dined with Mr. and Mrs. James T. Gardiner at 21 Elk Street and arrived at
Harmanus Bleecker Hall by 9:30.

When the Hall was built, it had a deep setback, and there was a circular
driveway in by the wall of the Girls' Academy. There was a wide porte-
cochere, so three carriages could be under the shelter at the same time. . . .
The grass was well kept, and the Hall looked simple and dignified in its
early days.

The false floor was laid for the first time for our ball. The galleries were
used by older people who did not dance, and the boxes were wonderful for
a nice flirtation. They were in use all the time! Mother had had red felt laid
in the halls and corridors to give warmth. Many Christmas trees were used
to bank the corners, and the rear of the stage was a mass of smilax and
laurel, with bunches of poinsettias.

Eyres had charge of the decorations, and Parlatti and his orchestra played

The Parker girls: Louisa, Grace, Anna, and Harriet.

St. Agnes School, on the north side of Elk Street, above Hawk.

St. Agnes graduates in procession to the Cathedral on Commencement Day.

Wistful pledge of seventeen-year-olds Nelly Robb and Bertie Pruyn to meet in five years — if they are living.

Picnic at Altamont, 1889 or 1890. Mrs. Pruyn is second from right; Huybertie is in center, chin in hand; Hattie is in black hat with feather; her suitor, William Gorham Rice, is at far left.

Friends relaxing in Adirondacks at Camp Santanoni, 1893.

Huybertie dressed for presentation to Queen Victoria, 1895.

Anna P. Pruyn in her sleigh in Washington Park.

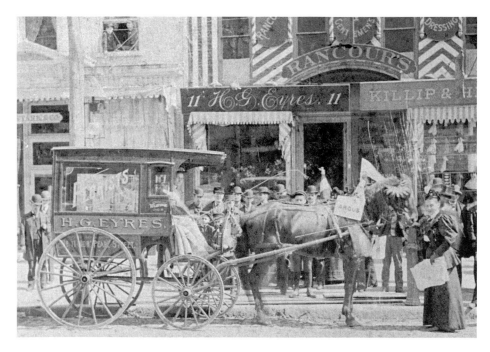

Huybertie (at horse's head) and Bessie Oliver (with reins) prepare to deliver the women's edition of The Argus, *1895, for the benefit of St. Margaret's.*

Huybertie (top step, middle, with black hat) and friends in "informal camping clothes" at Camp Santanoni, 1898.

Charles S. Hamlin in 1897.

Huybertie in her bridal array.

Huybertie and Charles with their attendants on June 4, 1898.

The wedding reception in the garden at 13 Elk Street.

Fanciful wedding photo by Huybertie's good friend,
the photographer Emma Farnsworth.

Huybertie's half-brother, John V. L. Pruyn, about 1902.

Huybertie's daughter, Anna, age 3, 1903.

*Huybertie with her two Annas — her daughter and her mother —
on the dining room piazza of 13 Elk Street, shortly
before her mother's death in 1909.*

Huybertie and Anna, 1917.

from the stage, which was only a little higher than the false floor. Supper was served at eleven by McElveney's. It was at small tables. There was a fruit punch, but no champagne or other wines.

Mother stood first in line. She wore black velvet and diamonds. Aunt Kate Marvin stood next to her, wearing black silk and net and Grandmother's old-fashioned seed-pearl necklace. At the end of the line stood Grace, Louise, and I, dressed alike except that our artificial flowers were different. We each carried a bouquet, and the rest were piled on tables behind us.

At last we were released from the receiving line and allowed to join the dancers. The favors were from the Maison Bail on the Rue de Rivoli in Paris. There were more than one hundred couples, and Amasa Parker Jr. led the cotillion dancing with each of us in turn. We had partners too. Grace sat with her partner at one end of the row and Louise at the other, while I had the center place.

To quote *Capital Chips*,

> The most magnificent ball of the season — the one looked forward to so longingly — is a happy dream of the past, and three charming girls have made their debut in society and been admitted into the inner circle of its balls and whirl of pleasure. Harmanus Bleecker Hall was turned into a floral bower on Tuesday night. The Cotillion was led by Amasa Parker Jr. assisted alternately by the three debutantes. The favors, imported from Paris, were extremely handsome. For the first figure there were golden girdles for the ladies and tennis racquets of oak and silver with a silver ball attached to its meshes for the men. In the second, there were automatic dancing figures which sprang forth from flower pieces, and the daintiest and most Parisienne of all were the feather flowers. For the ladies, the favors were in the form of a golden handled fan, and for the men, exquisite boutonnieres. For the general dancing, the ladies were presented with a pure white lily and the men with a white rose.

I do not recall any pure white lily, and some of the other things sound a bit fanciful. . . .

As we stood in the lobby waiting for the sleighs, I thought the portrait of Harmanus Bleecker wore a pleased smile. He must have realized how much pleasure his bequest for the benefit of Albany had given to the generations that followed him. My father's and grandfather's portraits too, as successive trustees of the Bleecker fund, were hung near Mr. Bleecker's portrait, and all were decorated with garlands of greens. . . .

It was snowing: a soft steady fall came down on top of the old snow, which had made a firm foundation for the sleighing we had enjoyed for a month. The green wooden pump outside the Hall on the curb of Washington Avenue held out a snowy arm. Everything was quiet and very, very still. We were quiet too, and far too sleepy to talk, but blissfully happy over the wonderful evening.

As I look over the faded and brittle newspaper clippings, it is fascinating to picture the scene. *Capital Chips* describes the dresses worn by many of the guests. Governor and Mrs. Roswell P. Flower of Watertown sat in a box, and the paper states,

> Mrs. Flower wore a handsome gown of red satin and a necklace of rubies to match. Mrs. Bleecker Banks was superb in pink brocade trimmed with white point lace caught with bunches of pink ostrich feathers. . . . Mrs. Doane wore black velvet, and Mrs. Bayard Van Rensselaer wore pink crepe with pale green brocade. Mrs. Charles L. Pruyn wore pink silk with embroidered chiffon, and Mrs. Harry Cushman looked charming in pale pink silk with bands of sable. Mrs. John E. McElroy's commanding beauty was enhanced by the superb gown of gray brocade and the diamond ornaments she wore. Miss Vanderpoel was particularly lovely in white, cut on long lines. The Pruyn Ball is a glorious dream of all past, what more is there to live for.

᯼   ᯼   ᯼

My brother gave a dinner for me at Delmonico's in New York. Mother sat at the foot of the table. To everyone's amusement, Jack escorted me in with great formality and placed me on his right. Mr. Amory Carhart was on my other side. There were twenty at the dinner.

The round table was beautifully decorated with yellow roses. Jack had written to ask me what I was to wear, and the yellow dress seemed appropriate, so roses were to match. He liked the yellow roses but disapproved of the high-heeled slippers [I wore]. Mother had lent me her little string of pearls for the winter, so I felt very set up.

Jack had taken no end of trouble about the guests, the food, and the flowers, and it went off beautifully. Although my pointed slippers pinched badly, I tried to be philosophical. . . . There was a ball to which we all went afterwards, and I was much less shy and stiff than [I had been] the previous month at the first dreaded experience.

Mother had sent out cards for three "Thé Dansants" on Saturdays in January. They seemed to cause a nine-days' wonder. Dancing teas were unknown, although in my childhood I had had "Kettledrums," which were the same thing with another name. People I met made discreet inquiries as to just how one was expected to dress. In day or evening clothes? And how about hats? Parlatti played for us in the china room, so the music was clear for dancing.

The last dance was a cotillion, but it was hot work. The clothes were cumbersome. We wore long heavy skirts, usually patent leather Oxford shoes for afternoon, and cotton stockings that seemed thick and warm. Silk stockings cost four or five dollars a pair and were saved for evening. The hats were enormous affairs with long hat pins sticking out at the sides, a real danger to a partner's eyes.

Parlatti had a special waltz that was dreamy, and it made quite a hit, until the chaperone decided it was really a disreputable song. A verse ran,

> Thine arm around my waist, dear love,
> Thy hands are clasped in mine,
> Thy head upon my shoulder, love,
> As through the waltz we twine.

Aunt Kitty and Uncle Abe Lansing had dined with us one night in December and had told us that they wanted to have a reception for Grace, Louise, and me, about the middle of January. This was very kind of them. Aunt Kitty said they were going to New York and wanted to order the invitations at Tiffany's. She said the reception was to be from nine to twelve o'clock and that Parlatti would play for the dancing, in the east parlor. But a week before the party, no invitations had been received by us or anyone else. People were used to Aunt Kitty's ways and would probably go to the party anyway, as the papers had announced it several times.

Mother suggested that I go up there one snowy morning and find out what was going on. I pulled the heavy old bell, and Louise opened the door and immediately groaned about the weather. She said Aunt Kitty was very busy about the "invites," and she opened the door of the east parlor.

There sat Aunt Kitty, spectacles on the end of her nose, and Tiffany boxes piled around her. She seemed glad to see me and said I was the very one she needed, as Gottlieb was so slow, and she never would get the invitations out on time. It would be too bad if they reached people after the party, but it would not be her fault.

Just then Gottlieb appeared. He was a stocky little German who was supposed to look after the furnace and sidewalk [in winter] and the garden in summer, and to bring Joe Lansing and the buggy from the Evans's stable, where their horse was kept. Gottlieb liked to wear a bright red cravat and an enormous gold watch chain across his vest.

Aunt Kitty said, "Gottlieb, did you find Mrs. Robertson?"

"Yes," said Gottlieb, "I found her all right. There was crepe on the door, but I rang the bell, and the maid said, 'Mrs. Robertson did live there only she just died!' But," he concluded, "I left the invitation just the same, for I knew she would like to be remembered."

Aunt Kitty looked thoughtfully at him and said, "I wonder how your Uncle Abe will feel about that." I wondered just which part Uncle Abe was supposed to wonder about.

Aunt Kitty handed Gottlieb two more invitations and said, "These had better go next."

Gottlieb looked at them and said, "But Mrs. Lansing, these are both in the same block as Mrs. Robertson's. I could have left them all at once and saved time."

"Yes," said Aunt Kitty, "that is true, so you could, and saved that strength of yours too, if I had had them ready. Probably tomorrow I may have two more for just the same block, but you are so slow I never will get them finished."

Gottlieb departed, but not to deliver the notes. I heard his German accent in the kitchen just before I left. I suggested sending the rest of the invitations by mail, but that, Aunt Kitty said, was turning a pleasure party into a business party, and, anyway, nobody trusted the mails now in this administration.

I suggested messenger boys, but she got quite excited at such an idea. She said that only last year two people had given parties and sent the invitations by messengers who had been too lazy to deliver them. Mrs. Townsend's cards had been found by the street overflow drain on the corner of Elk and Hawk Streets, when the snow melted. No, Gottlieb must do them all.

I then suggested we direct all the Elk Street invitations at once, and I would leave them on the way home. Aunt Kitty seemed to like that idea, and after working for an hour, we accomplished those anyway. She begged me to return after luncheon. "I cannot ask you to stay here, as I scarcely keep anything in the house because Gottlieb carries it all home. His pockets bulge when he leaves by the side door."

When I returned after luncheon, Aunt Kitty's eyes were glistening with excitement. "I have directed an invitation for General and Mrs. Rathbone next door," she said. "And I am going to ask their son Jack and his wife too. I have never called on her, but she looks pretty. Gottlieb is to take them in, and we will watch from my bedroom window and see what happens."

"What could happen?" said I. "What is strange about Gottlieb leaving two invitations at the Rathbones?"

"You wait and see!" said Aunt Kitty, darkly. "You never know what people like that will do. He may be kicked all the way down the steps, but do not warn him, for he might refuse to go."

Gottlieb was summoned again and told about the Rathbones' invitations. Then we mounted to the upstairs window to watch. It was exciting, and I wondered if Gottlieb's legs would be broken or his head cracked. He walked out the side gate, arrayed in his red cravat and gold chain. He walked up to the Rathbones' gate, walked up the tiled path, then up the steps and rang.

I held my breath to see if General Rathbone had been watching from his library window and whether he had a gun or stick to chase him off. Gottlieb moved forward, disappeared from view, then turned about, and came down the steps, empty-handed. He soon vanished from sight by the side gate. It was very flat. We both felt as if we had been cheated as we went downstairs to discuss and haggle over a few more invitations.

Every little while Aunt Kitty would say in a voice of satisfaction, "Well, your Uncle Abe will be glad I did that, though I think now he ought to invite Colonel Walter Church, but he won't."

This last allusion was about an altercation between Uncle Abe and Colonel Church at the club several years previously. Uncle Abe was usually the mildest of men, but once in a while his Dutch got up, and evidently the old colonel had been unusually provoking. So Uncle Abe reached for an ink pot and pasted the colonel on his head.

When the great evening came, Mother sent me up in the sleigh at eight o'clock, to be on hand and help, if possible, as Aunt Kitty would probably be in a raving, distracted state by that time. Mr. and Mrs. Bleecker Banks had invited all three of us to dinner that night, but Mother said I must decline, as the party was a great effort for the Lansings, and I must be prompt. As I came into the hall of the old house, it already smelled heavily of chicken croquettes, and Aunt Kitty and Uncle Abe were having a serious discussion about the band.

"The band," said Uncle Abe, "belongs in the east parlor by the piano. That is where you said the young people were to dance."

"Yes," said Aunt Kitty, "but that will come later, when there is a crowd. At the beginning the band must play in the kitchen, so that we will only hear soft strains in the distance."

Louisa meekly offered the suggestion that this would crowd the kitchen badly and would make it difficult for McElveney's cooks and waiters, and perhaps they could play in the laundry.

Aunt Kitty promptly vetoed this. Pointing to her bosom, she said seriously, "Louisa, you know I locked the laundry, and I have the key here. If I open it, the caterers will join the musicians, and they will go in there and drink champagne and afterwards take baths in the tubs to clear their heads. No, the band must group around the dumb waiter in the kitchen, and so the sounds will be soft and mellow. I will not have Parlatti bathing in my tubs. Later they can come up and drown out all the talking."

So it was settled, and Aunt Kitty vanished up to her room to take out the curl papers that were a concession to the importance of this occasion and to finish her dressing, which had been proceeding at intervals for two hours or more. While Uncle Abe and I were admiring the Gansevoort tankard, the lovely china, and the nougat candies with our initials on them, the door bell rang. Aunt Kitty appeared on the stairs, hooking her dress all crooked down the front, and we flew to our places. We stood in the west parlor between the window and the mantelpiece under some palms. Aunt Kitty came first. I came next, and Uncle Abe, tall and distinguished-looking, stood next to the mantel.

He was just telling us about his wedding in that room in 1873, when the first guests were ushered in, the whole household from next door, General and Mrs. Rathbone, and Mr. and Mrs. Jack Rathbone. They tried to look very solemn, but there was a twinkle in their eyes. For the evening the hatchet was being buried again, and an armistice was declared over the fence. The next arrivals were Mrs. Andrew J. Colvin and her son Verplanck, the "Panther." I could see the Rathbone party slip on their wraps in the hall. Having done their duty nobly, they felt free to return to their fireside and to wonder how long the truce would last.

Then people arrived thick and fast. The Peebles and Van Schoonhovens, from Lansingburgh, had come down by train and dined at the Delavan so as to be on time. Aunt Kitty's cousin, Miss Melville, from Pittsfield was staying in the house, but nevertheless she swept in with grand entree as if she were a stranger. The Leonard Gansevoort Ten Eycks assured us they had only received their invitations the previous day, but had set all else aside to come.

Miss Sue and Miss Anna Lansing came together. Miss Anna was Uncle Abe's sister. She was not pretty, and in her high-neck black dress with a narrow white ruche showing around her collar, she looked ready for church. "I call her Ann-tique," said Aunt Kitty, who was usually at daggers drawn with her sister-in-law over china or silver possessions. Miss Sue was quite different, and though her dress was black, it was softened by a great deal of white, and her smile and manner were very cordial. . . .

Aunt Kitty kept up a constant flow of remarks about people's hair, clothes, tempers, and other peculiarities. . . . The line now moved very slowly, for Baron Fernow, the learned Pole who had a special position at the State Library, leaned heavily on his stick as he limped along, and he held back the others.

"Here comes Mary Benedict," said Aunt Kitty, in a voice so loud that I trembled for fear someone would hear. "She once bathed in the Dead Sea, and it made her that color. And here comes my Lord from England, like Henry the VIII and his wives," as the bishop and his household approached. Mrs. Doane was resplendent . . . with her sister Miss Condit a step or two behind her, and Mrs. Gardiner and Florence [bringing up] the rear. . . .

The De Witts from 202 Lancaster Street came too, tall and delicate Miss Sally, little Miss Kitty, and their good brother, Mr. Richard Varick De Witt. Miss Kitty confided in a whisper that they understood about the invitations. They were so late. In spite of the trouble about a portrait, which Aunt Kitty disputed, they had decided to come.

"And now behold the Lord of the Manor of Livingston," [quipped Aunt Kitty] as Mr. and Mrs. Bayard Livingston appeared. Then in quick succession there arrived Mr. and Mrs. Jacob Ten Eyck and their neighbor Miss Anna Vandenburg, the Schuylers from "The Flatts" at Watervliet, Miss Kate Van Rensselaer from "Vlie House" in Greenbush, and her niece Katy Van Rensselaer, the Philip Ten Eycks and the Cuyler Ten Eycks, the Augustus Pruyns and Francis Saltus Pruyns, the Robert C. and Charles Lansing Pruyns, Mrs. Charles B. Lansing with Miss Abby, the Townsend Lansings and the

Guy Lansings, and Mr. I. D. F. Lansing, known as the last of the Albany Dutchmen. There were the Vosburgs from Broadway and the descendants of many more who had preceded the Yankee invasion.

Grace and Louise appeared from the Bankses' dinner party and joined our line. The rooms became so crowded that Mr. Dudley Olcott and Judge Rufus Peckham, members of the Owl Club, speedily vanished into Uncle Abe's sanctum, where they could refresh themselves in peace. Uncle Abe had wandered off, but now he returned with a disturbed look on his face and whispered to Aunt Kitty.

"Kate, supper is ready, and the band in the kitchen is completely drowned out. Which will you have come first?"

"Both," said Aunt Kitty quickly. "Put them both on the dumb waiter, and some can dance and some can eat, for they cannot do both at once."

With an absent-minded smile, she greeted Dr. Battershall, who remarked that "The rooms felt like a summer day," by which he meant to imply that the heat was almost beyond bearing.

Parlatti, the band master, now made his way up, looking cross and black. He explained that the east parlor was so crowded that he could not get in with the men and instruments, and what should he do?

"Sit on the stairs," was the instant reply. "The guests will have to pass by as best they can to leave their wraps."

Finally, the hapless band wedged its way to the piano, and before the evening ended we were able to dance on a small patch in the center of the red and white carpet in the east parlor.

This famous party was in January 1892. Aunt Kitty wore a lilac silk dress made by Worth in Paris in 1879. It had been worn at intervals in the meantime, and now it had pieces inserted in the sleeves to bring them into fashion. I wonder if anyone anywhere has parties like this one given by Uncle Abe and Aunt Kitty Lansing for our coming-out.

The Cornings' contribution to our debut was an oyster roast at "Ta-wassa-gunshee." There were three long sleighs with straw on the bottom. One came to our house, and I have the list, written by Aunt Mary, of the fourteen who were to meet there.

Amasa Parker Jr. had charge of that load, which started at 6:45 o'clock. Those who went with him were: Amasa Jr., Louis and Louise Parker,

Henry and Sarah Sage, Florence Gardiner from [the] bishop's house, Robert and Douglas Olcott, Miss McElroy and her brother, Nelly Arthur, Pauline Gray, Dr. Howard Van Rensselaer, Pauline Rathbone, and Clark Durant. The other sleighs started from the Marvins, with Aunt Kate in charge of one and Uncle Tuy of the other.

We sang all the way as the sleighs joggled along South Pearl Street and out into the open country. . . . The front door was opened wide by Edward Ryan, showing the house glowing with lamps and candles and open fires. Uncle Erastus and Aunt Mary gave us the warmest of welcomes while we discarded our heavy blanket coats and proceeded noisily into the kitchen. There the men were being tied into gingham aprons and set to work, with long handled shovels, at the kitchen and laundry ranges and stoves, to roast the oysters. Long tables on trestles stood in the kitchen, and on them were plates piled high with white bread and brown bread, farm butter, saucers of drawn butter, pitchers of farm cider, layer cakes, doughnuts, and pies — apple, pumpkin, and mince.

The girls sat at the tables and started calling to the men to hurry with the oysters. We tried to eat as many as quickly as possible so as to make the men work very hard and run back and forth at our commands. Pointed remarks were in order for those who were slow or burned the oysters.

We forgot that all this exercise whetted their appetites. So when our turn came to don the aprons, the men kept up an uproar of orders and accused us in turn of being slow. It seemed to us as if they consumed barrels of them. So we were hot and tired when we all sat down peacefully together to eat the cakes and pies.

Then came more fun. We trooped into the dining room of the house, which was entirely cleared except for the platform in front of the French glass door. There, seated in sublime dignity, was the famous "Professor" Van Buren, the banjo teacher and talented actor of Albany. He had an assistant with him to alternate in case he got tired.

They played the old favorite Negro airs, and we sang as we waltzed to modern music, the polka, and barn dance that were popular then. How we sang the new song of "The Bowery — the Bowery."

The cake walk, which was the real business of the evening, was treated with great ceremony by the Professor. His platform must have been built especially for him, as he was a large man, and as we danced, he stood against the wall and swayed and stamped in his effort to swing the music to the right time.

Each couple went around the room separately, twice, in the manner they thought approached nearest to their idea of the cake walk. The rest of us stood against the wall, slapping and laughing at their interpretations. I "walked" that night with De Witt Walsh in a dignified and haughty demeanor with not a smile for the cheering that greeted us. We had practiced out in the hall.

Charley Pinkerton and Nelly Arthur won the cake, with most remarkable and intricate steps. Uncle Erastus presented the cake to them, with a speech that more than hinted at their engagement. The cake had been standing on a side table. It was surmounted by two colored dolls, and the winners had to go around once more, carrying the cake, while the Professor almost broke his arm to make the banjo give out noise enough to be heard over the cheering.

There were about fifty of us to enjoy that evening. As we returned about midnight, we sang the jolly tunes of the Virginia Reel which had finished the party. It had merged into "Good night ladies," as a hint that all good things must end. As our particular sleigh load jingled up Elk Street, we were shouting at the top of our lungs in every key, "T'was from Aunt Dinah's quilting party, I was seein' Nelly home."

Hattie's engagement to William G. Rice was announced on January 13th [1892]. *Capital Chips* observed:

Cupid has been rather reckless with his darts this season if all reports are true. Dame Rumour whispers that Miss Pruyn is engaged to Colonel Rice.

Then later:

The marriage of Miss Harriet Langdon Pruyn to Colonel Rice, at St. Peter's Church, on February 8th, will be one of the fashionable events of the winter. Those of the younger set, who were reluctant to credit the rumor that their set was to lose its most enthusiastic leader, were convinced by the superb solitaire which blazes on her third finger. The stone is of unusual size and brilliancy, looking almost too heavy for the fair hand it guards.

. . . The presents began to come thick and fast. All the books were moved out of the nursery bookcase, and small presents were placed on the shelves. The table and extra trestle tables were filled, and the room looked like a shop.

I gave much thought to my present and finally decided on a white linen tea cloth, on which Miss Goodwin made designs for me. In one corner were bunches of prunes for Pruyn. In another corner were sprays of what was supposed to be rice. There were Dutch tulips and New England Mayflowers in the other corner. My embroidery was never of the best, and the heavy purple of the prunes screamed across at the vivid yellow of the tulips. It was the worst-looking production imaginable, and no wonder people asked about it.

On a lovely winter day, February 8, 1892, with heavy snow on the ground and sleigh bells ringing gaily, Hattie and William were married at noon at St. Peter's Church by Bishop Doane and Dr. Battershall. Dean Robbins and Dr. Fairbairn, the Warden of St. Stephen's College at Annandale, were in the chancel. I was maid of honor. There were eight ushers, four cousins of Hattie's and four of William's. Instead of the *Lohengrin March*, the choir sang a hymn, written by Bishop Doane for his daughter's wedding. Jack, very nervous, took Hattie up the aisle, and Mother gave her away, standing in the chancel by the rail.

Capital Chips says:

> The bride, who is a handsome and stately brunette, wore a classically simple gown of heaviest white corded silk, made without ornamentation. She was completely enveloped by the clinging folds of the long bridal veil. Her bouquet was of lilies of the valley and white violets, with maiden hair fern, tied with many loops of white ribbon.
>
> The Maid of Honor's gown was of white silk trimmed with chiffon and pink roses. Her short tulle veil was fastened to her coiffure by rosebuds and a handsome diamond bow knot. She carried a large bunch of long stemmed Bon Silene roses and ferns.

As a matter of fact, my dress was trimmed with rows of narrow gold braid. The yoke was stiff with it [as were] the long cuffs. I should have worn a large hat. I do not know who originated the idea of a wreath of roses. They were real roses, and the effect was messy. The wreath was probably crooked, too, on account of my cowlick.

The *Times Union* reported:

> Hail wedded love. The only bliss of Paradise that has survived the fall. All the world loves a lover, and when a love match is made, there is always a group of acquaintances to manifest interest in the union of hearts and hands. Colonel Rice has certainly followed the advice of the Rev. Worthy who, when asked

for counsel in regard to matrimony, said, 'Take the daughter of a good mother.'

The bride and groom stood in the conservatory under a large bell of lilies. Mother and I stood in the front room, and an aisle was made into the conservatory by white ribbon. The crowd was terrific. Our neighbor Mr. Theodore Townsend lost his silk hat. The bride and groom sailed on the *Umbria* the following Saturday, and one week later, February 17th, Mother and I sailed on the *Teutonic*.

CHAPTER 23

OTHER WAS WORN OUT and stayed in her berth almost the entire voyage. The doctor had warned Mother that fall, after an illness at North East Harbour, that she was overdoing and should take more exercise. In those days, none of the older women leaned back in the carriage as they went driving. They sat bolt upright, so there was no relaxation. Mother, like Grandmother, never seemed to us to get any real rest from a drive.

The doctor suggested that Mother should take Del Sarte lessons at home as a good way to use muscles and dispose of surplus fat. Mother was not enthusiastic, but finally agreed to try exercises if I would take them with her. A very attractive girl was engaged to come two mornings a week, and we had our lessons in Mother's dressing room.

The Del Sarte system was all the rage. The idea was complete relaxation, or "devitalization." You melted into a chair; you did not just sit down. You floated around and eliminated jerks, and your arm had to become entirely limp as you shook hands — no warm clasps any more.

Mother was amused and did not make any too much of the effort. When it came to posing as the flying Mercury in her gray Mother Hubbard dressing gown, it was too much for me. I did learn one thing quite well. That was to faint gracefully on the floor without breaking any bones.

So the rest on the ship was a godsend to Mother. I had a delightful voyage after the first rough day out. I sat at Captain Irving's table, next to Mrs. William Astor, who was kindness itself. Miss Helen Dunham of New York and Mr. Eugene Winthrop of Paris joined us. An extraordinary Mr. Cavendish Bentinck, who took himself very seriously and carried his family guest book around with him, was also at the Captain's table. He took a whole afternoon to impress me with his wonderful autograph collection. . . .[1]

We reached London by five in the afternoon of the day after landing in Liverpool and drove to 88 Eaton Square, which Mother had leased again. We found the bride and groom having tea. Old Lady Camperdown was with them, wearing her usual enormous bonnet with plumes. The Rices had even hired a hand organ to come at six and play the popular song "Mary and John." I was anxious to find Fanny, the stiff housemaid in her starched petticoats, and ask about the "Little Master." Fanny was quite glad to see me and told me, with her imitation of a smile, that the boy was doing well at school and seemed much stronger.

Griselda Ogilvy soon appeared and gave us the latest description of her many relatives. [The portraits] were amusing but not flattering. Her uncle, Lord Stanley of Alderley, had married a Moslem when he was ambassador to Turkey, and he had become converted to Islam. When he died, he had to be buried standing up, and as he was a tall, large man, this presented difficulties, on which Griselda dwelt with keen relish.

Another uncle was Monsignor Stanley. She called him "My uncle the pig," and I found out why when I sat by him at dinner on Shrove Tuesday night. He failed to respond to my efforts at conversation except by grunts. He had come to eat. I asked him if he would begin a fast tomorrow, but he only grunted.

Finally, I took to the alphabet. I said, "Do you like apples?" He shook his head and continued his repast. Then, "Have you ever eaten beaten biscuits?" Again a grunt.

Finally, with the letter "F," I tried, "Have you been to the Fiji Islands?"

He seemed transported with joy. "How did you hear that I spent a year there?" and he was off until dinner ended.

Lady Airlie and Griselda were in their house in Lowndes Square, and we dined there a few nights later. I had the pleasure of sitting by James Barrie, the Scotsman who had written *The Window in Thrums* and lately had published his *Little Minister.*[2] He was a quiet man and did not like being a lion. Lady Dorothy Neville was another guest and also a character for many years in the London world. Almost every book of that era brings in some anecdote about her. Her clothes were very extraordinary, but I got the idea that she wanted people to notice her. . . .

Our old friends next door, Sir George Warrender and his daughters, were glad to see us again. He said the noise we heard through the wall was his trunk elevator. Mrs. Meynell Ingraham had complained of it, so he had complained of her coffee grinder. One morning about eleven Sir George came in to ask me to go with him to the Guild Hall exhibition. We sat talking in the morning room, but our Victorian second man went up to tell Mother, in a respectful but worried tone, that I was alone with Sir George, and "— ahem, Madam, the door is closed."

Lady Airlie gave us a whole morning for my education. She came for me in her coupe and took me to the National Gallery to show me her favorite paintings. She was quite an artist herself and had several pictures on exhibition. I returned to luncheon with her and Griselda. As I left, she gave me a lovely black velvet bag with a silver top; engraved on it is "Bertie Pruyn from Blanche Airlie."

Our Minister to England was Mr. Robert Lincoln, son of President Lincoln. They were just receiving again, as they had lost their only son, Abraham, called Jack. There were two daughters, one of whom was married at this time. . . .

I am sure it would be very tiresome to enumerate the friends, old and new, and the parties to which we went. It was a delightful experience in a world that has vanished, probably for good, but certainly for my lifetime. I retain memories of London in the season, of window boxes and green parks, of beautiful carriages with beautiful ladies twirling fancy parasols. Flowers were everywhere, sold in the streets in picturesque little hand carts. Driving in Hyde Park in the late afternoon would make an attractive movie, particularly if the Princess of Wales were added, and the Prince, too, riding in Rotten Row, wearing his Homburg hat with a cigar between his teeth.

Those were the days of well known beauties who allowed their photos to be sold in shops. Emma Eames was singing at Covent Garden with immense success.[3] . . . She and her husband, Julian Storey, dined at the Lincolns. I sat next but one to her, with Larz Anderson between us. She was very striking and shocked the diners a bit — I think perhaps on purpose.

At the first ball to which we went, I became quite dizzy dancing the waltz. "Reversing" was considered "Not the thing at all." That bogey of the nineties. We went round and round in one spot while our trains tripped up other dancers. In my diary I write, "They are just introducing the 'Kentucky Jubilee' and they do it so queerly."

This dance was at the house of Lord Stanley of Alderly, who had succeeded his Moslem brother. Their daughter Margaret was also a "bud." The house was very crowded because all the mothers had to be invited too. They sat in rows around the wall and yawned. . . .

At a dinner at our house I had as partner a nice elderly man whose name escapes me. It was a rather dull dinner for me. My partner did his best. Near the end he said, "All American young ladies have some talent, what is yours?"

I assured him, truthfully, that I had none.

He persisted, "No doubt you are modest. You paint or draw, sing or play."
By this time we had reached the drawing room, and I suddenly remembered
the Del Sarte — I could faint. So I dropped on the floor, full length as
gracefully as I could do it. There were exclamations of alarm from all sides.
I was lucky not to have had a cup of coffee poured over me.

As it was, everyone called for water. "Poor girl, she has been out too
much."

Mother knew perfectly well that I never had even felt faint in my life,
and she assured the others that it was just a trick I had learned lately. My
partner stood by, and as I was helped up, I said to him, "Now you know
what my talent is. I can faint. Did you ever know any other girl who could
faint?" . . .

🍎　🍎　🍎

Mother was still hopeful [that I could develop some musical talent], so
I started singing lessons with the "Guinea pig," Mr. William Shakespeare.
A pupil of his, Mrs. Bartholomew, helped me practice and also taught me
accompaniments. I dutifully had a lesson twice a week, and I sang more or less
vigorously, "Orpheus With His Lute," "Ave Maria," and the ballad of the
"North Country Maid." But other things were much more interesting to me.

One Sunday we lunched with Mr. Boughton, the artist, who had lived
as a boy in Albany and had made drawings all over the hat boxes in his
brother's shop. Mr. Henry James, who also had roots in Albany, was another
guest. He was a most complete Englishman of that period.

Larz Anderson invited me to a dinner at the Amphictryon Club on Alber-
marle Street, and as General and Mrs. Anderson and Elsie were there, it
was considered quite "the thing"- for me to go. Marie accompanied me to
the door and saw me safely inside and returned for me at 10:30. Larz had
painted an appropriate name card for each guest. Mine was Eaton Square
— the iron fence, trees, and a lamp post, with me sitting on a bench reading.
This was almost wholly an American dinner, and the other guests were Mr.
and Mrs. William Waldorf Astor, who had just rented Lansdowne House,
Mr. Robert Lincoln, Mrs. Mahlon Sands and her daughter, Willie Chanler,
and a German secretary. I sat on Larz's right and later Mrs. Anderson and
Mrs. Astor tried to smoke cigars on a bet, but they did not get very far.

Mother and Larz and I went to Ascot, where we had seats in the Royal
enclosure. The Gold Cup races were thrilling. We lunched at the Bachelor's

Club, and I sat close to Princess Henry of Pless, a radiant beauty, who was all dressed in white. I have never forgotten her. It was with deep regret that I read that the Nazis had imprisoned her in her own castle because her son was fighting on the British side in the last war. A later report said she had died after many tortures.

On May 16th [1892], Mother and I were presented. This was her third time. Our dresses were made by Kate Reilly on Dover Street. She had a branch in New York. Mother's dress was gray satin embroidered with tiny jet beads around gray chiffon tulips. It had a black velvet train, and it was a handsome and becoming dress.

Mine, of course, was white — chiffon over silk, with a wreath of white tulips and green leaves garlanded around the skirt, and one tulip at the square neck. The train was of white corded silk, with a ruching around the edge. The stiff little white veils and three feathers were the same as nowadays, but the trains were three yards on the floor and enormously heavy. Mother carried a bouquet of orchids and I a shower bouquet of white tulips.

We commenced to dress by 12:30, and then had luncheon, and by 2:00 had our photograph taken at Thompson's. The procession along the Mall was very funny, with people peering in the carriage windows and even climbing on the steps. One who looked in at us remarked, "Yous aint so bad. Yous oughter see the frozen faces ahead of yous!" Sometimes there were waits of fifteen minutes, but it was fun seeing the various escorts pass and the costumes of the Beefeaters. . . .

We met Mrs. Stanley and Margaret and Lady Wright, and we kept together so they could point out many celebrities. What might have been a great sight, as it is now at night, was a badly managed jam of tightly wedged people, trying to scramble through the gates placed at the doors of rooms through which [they] had to pass. No one looks well in evening dress by daylight. Everyone's veils were pulled crooked, and their feathers were tipped to one side. Many women looked cross and catty. [However] the string band of the Cold Stream Guards played the national anthem stunningly.

In some way Mother and I got separated. She had the card with both our names on it. So when I came to the last bars, it was lucky for me that Mr. Alex Yorke, in imposing court clothes, recognized me and let me through.

Lady Abercromby had had me come to her house several times for lessons in making the correct curtseys. The deepest was to the Queen, and a bit less deep to the others — in this case there were six. I passed along well to the Princess of Wales and the Duchess of Connaught, but then came the Dukes of Cambridge and Connaught and Edinburgh. They had their backs turned and were looking out of a window onto the gardens.

I quickly decided I would not bow to backs. I turned about, and a page threw my train over my aching arm as I walked out into a gallery to find Mother. But an English lady, who looked like a picture in *Punch*, rushed up to me.

She said, "You're an American! I know that most favored nation! You should be made to return and bow to their Royal Highnesses! Lady So-and-So forgot one last year, and she was made to return. I think it is shocking of you!"

I am afraid that I was rather fresh. I said that in America we were not used to having men turn their backs on us, that their Royal Highnesses should have better manners, and I left her.

We enjoyed watching the sweeping curtseys of those who came after us. The Queen did not stay long. She got dizzy with the swaying and bowing crowds. The Princess of Wales, looking very beautiful in lilac velvet with gorgeous jewels, took her place.

By 5:30 we drove home and found many people waiting for what we called a "train tea." Several others were in their court dress. About forty people came; among them Lady Rosse and Muriel, May van Alen from Newport, Mrs. Harriet Lane Johnston, the Andersons and Playfairs and Warrenders and de Billes. My diary ends, "We were dead beat and my left arm is paralyzed from the heavy train. I am glad the shindig is over."

❦   ❦   ❦

. . . I remember so well the really very handsome Archdeacon of London, Sinclair by name. He was very proud of his legs, and he used some very strong perfume. He grew confidential at a dinner and told me he was descended from Charlemagne, Alfred the Great, St. Louis of France, and St. Margaret of Scotland. I said I thought he had done well to choose the best of the lot, but he did not like that and said if I doubted it, he could prove it. After that he never saw me. Instead he looked through me in an un-Christian-like manner.

I was allowed to walk alone in Eaton Square, and in warm weather I often read there in the late afternoon. No one dined before 8:00 or 8:30. One day I saw a friend of ours, a well-known young man, a cousin of the Stanleys. I'll call him Johnny, although he is dead now, so it does not make any difference really. He was dressed in the correct clothes of the period, a

Prince Albert coat and striped trousers, a silk hat, lavender gloves, and a gold-headed cane. He was on the other side of the square from where I sat and should have walked around to the gate if he wanted to speak to me. But he decided to climb the iron fence. He caught his coat on the iron points and hung there. His hat fell into the dusty bushes, his cane clattered on the gravel, and his gloves split up the middle. I could not help laughing as I ran to his assistance.

But a man on the sidewalk tore the rest of the coat to the collar and set him free. He looked very furious as I handed him the hat and cane. He began to try to tell me that he had come on purpose to ask me . . . and then he ended and said, "Good bye," and walked off.

His sister told me he came home in a hansom and tried to get in without their seeing him, but she caught him and said, "I know where you have been — to see that American girl in Eaton Square, and she gave you the sack." I never saw him again. . . .

The night of the Foreign Office's reception on the Queen's birthday, I drove to Colonel North's soon after ten to meet Mother and go to the reception together. Lord Salisbury was Prime Minister; he was the real heavy John Bull type so dear to *Punch*. It was an amusing evening, as we met many friends in the crowded rooms. Outside the streets were a show of great magnificence, with transparencies and everything that gas illumination could produce.

I was very sorry when it came time to leave Eaton Square. The spring had passed quickly and delightfully. We said good-byes to many kind friends who had given us interesting opportunities to see unusual places. We had [for example] often been to the House of Lords with kind Lord Camperdown and had tea on the terrace, an informal way that was fascinating.

The last song Mr. Shakespeare gave me was "Wake Not But Hear Me Love," and I argued with him to the last that love must be awake in order to hear. Someone remarked that Mr. Shakespeare had said that he could not teach me anymore.

Our last day was a Sunday, and we lunched with Mr. and Mrs. Astor at

Lansdowne House. Mrs. Astor said they did not intend to stay in England, and Mr. Astor told my mother that it was threats [to their children of kidnappers that had] sent them [to seek] refuge in England. The next morning [we left] for good, and I said farewell to the "Little Master," little dreaming how and when we would meet in years to come.

We went down to Knole at Sevenoaks, Kent, to visit Victoria West, now married to her first cousin, who was heir to the title. Victoria was always fascinating, and she had a little girl, named for her but called Vita.

A more beautiful or interesting place it would be impossible to imagine. Our rooms looked into a large court. Mother's was called Archbishop Cranmer's room, and mine opened from it as a large dressing room. It had been cut from the thickness of the stone wall. Victoria took us all over the house in the afternoon. How she loved that house and its history! Yet she had collected postage stamps and papered a small room upstairs in patterns, a tiring and hardly worthwhile undertaking, when she had such really price-less and wonderful things all about her.

Part of the house was over eight-hundred years old, and much of it was Elizabethan. There were eight courts, fifty-two staircases, and seven hundred windows. It had four-and-a-half acres of roof and two miles of bell wire. The wages of the staff amounted to over $30,000. The cloisters had been glassed in and made a fine sheltered place to walk or sit.

Lord Sackville was as dull and silent as ever. He was hard put to run the place, as his brother had left his personal property to the Maids of Honor of the Queen, but I believe that [bequest] was decided in his behalf later on.

We returned to London to start at once for the continent — first we went to Brussels and a real sightseeing round, then to Antwerp, where we walked on Pruynen Straat and found the tomb, in the floor of the Cathedral, of Anna van Pruynen, (d. 1682). We went to Bruges and Ghent and heard "Roland," the big bell in the Carillon. Finally we arrived, via many places, at The Hague, where we stayed at the "Oude Doelen."

Madame Boreel-Langdon was most kind and hospitable. We called her "Aunt Sarah," though she was a cousin. We were there almost every day for a meal or to go for a sightseeing drive in her carriage. The daughter-in-law, Mme. Boreel, née d'Yvoy, who married Alfred Boreel, was as charming as ever. We drove with her to see her sister Baroness van Heeckeren, who was also very lovely.

One of Mother's special reasons for going to Holland was to see the two sons of Mrs. Harmanus Bleecker, who had married her cousin Mr. Coster.

They came from Arnhem to see us. Our stay was made even more interesting by hearing, while there, of the nomination again of Grover Cleveland. This meant more to me than I could realize then. It really slanted the rest of my life.

Our goal was Carlsbad and a cure for Mother. We went there by degrees, up the Rhine and to Nuremberg, and from there to the Villa Teresa, belonging to the Konig's Villa. Mother went under the care of Dr. Kraus, who made a schedule for her.

The next morning she began to drink glasses of Schlossbrunnen water, with a walk between drinks. Mother was not a good patient. She was not interested, and she did what she had to do in a half-hearted way. She was to eat spinach, which she hated, and as she was hungry, she broke training all the time.

She started vapor baths and massage, so I was left rather to my own devices, and I found many friends. I played a lot of tennis with Mr. Alan Marquand of Princeton and Graf von Hohenstein, governor of Bohemia. Mrs. Warder and Ellen, from Washington, were also there, and Prince Dulip Singh, a very fat boy, also joined our walks and games. I really enjoyed the weeks there and had a lot of fun.

Then Mother was supposed to take the after-cure at Regatz, but we departed for Bayreuth instead. Mother told the distracted doctor that she would take the after-cure on the way home on the ship. We had a grand send-off at the station, with many bouquets.

At Bayreuth we lodged at the house of Herr Krocker, who was a high official in the town and took us all about. . . . I was devoured by fleas, but no one seemed to mind the pests. At 3:30 we went to "Parsifal" in the heat and crowd. Between the first and second acts, there was a half-hour for tea, and one hour between the second and third acts for dinner.

We met many of our Carlsbad cronies, and strange Mr. Alexander Yorke turned up carrying a huge sun umbrella, so he looked like an Eastern potentate. Herr Krocker was a director of the Wagner theatre, and Mr. Yorke went with us to see it. Frau Cosima Wagner was conducting a rehearsal of the "Meistersinger." She conducted with skill and knowledge and a bad temper. Mme. Ternina lived in our house, and as the windows were open, we heard her practicing. It was really lovely. . . .

We went sightseeing in Munich and then to Partenkirchen to see the Olivers. Mother had promised me this treat, and I did enjoy it. We found Bessie and Cora and Joe Choate on the platform. It was wonderful to gossip about home. We sat up most of the night.

From there we drove along the Iser, through the Bavarian Highlands with glorious views, and then we followed the River Inn into Innsbruck, a most interesting and beautiful place.

Mother decided, after all, to take her after-cure at the Insel Hotel on Lake Konstanz. But she did not really melt much, as we took long and beautiful drives. We were in Baden, but Switzerland, Wurtemberg, Bavaria, and Austria were around us, and we had to pass custom houses all the time. We returned by Basle to Paris, where we stayed at the charming Bristol and did a lot of shopping.

Then we crossed to London and stayed at the Albemarle Hotel on Piccadilly. We found many people in town and went one afternoon with Lord Camperdown to the House of Lords to see the Lord Chancellor, Lord Halsbury, come in for the last time. We heard Lord Salisbury's speech, resigning his office, and Lord Kimberly's reply. The Duke of Edinburgh was also sworn in. . . .

We sailed for home on the *Teutonic* on August 24th and sat with Captain Irving, as did also Lord and Lady Playfair. There were a great many people we knew, and we had a wonderful voyage and lots of fun. When we reached Quarantine, early one morning, we found to our amazement that cholera had broken out in Europe since our sailing, and that it was being seriously debated as to whether we would be allowed to land. It was rumored that we would be kept twenty-one days down at Quarantine, and this was indeed hard luck. There had been one suspicious case of illness on the voyage, a little Alexander girl from San Francisco, and we waited in suspense while the doctors consulted. We filed along the lower deck, stuck out our tongues for the doctors, and told where we had been for ten days before sailing.

We sat and stood around in the heat all that long day, listening to rumors and surmises. At last, in the late afternoon, we headed up the bay, and so we knew we were to be released. We were met at the customs by Mr. Corning, who was always kind in hurrying us through. We had over fifty pieces of baggage, which were soon piled into a Barney Biglin cart. We climbed into the Biglin cart and made for the Holland House.

We were very lucky. We were the last ship let in. All the others had to stay twenty-one days, and Governor Flower bought, from his own pocket, the old Surf Hotel on Fire Island as a place for the passengers to stay. Later the Legislature repaid him. Dr. and Mrs. Henry Hun were also on the ship and at Holland House. They were returning from their wedding trip.

We took an early train the next morning. How lovely everything looked!

There was the old porter at the station to welcome us and carry the bags. Then came the tunnels, the East River, High Bridge, and Spuyten Duyvil. We sped up the glorious Hudson, past West Point and Storm King. There was a stop at Poughkeepsie for cream puffs, and then the first glimpse of the Capitol, Greenbush with all its frowsy hordings, then slowly over the bridge, and home at last.

Several of the family were there to greet us. Angel Booth smiled in the brick archway. The carriage with the dear old horses climbed the slope up the hill and made the jog to the right from Steuben Street. There was Elk Street, the house and garden, and the bride and groom were on the steps holding Fromo, resplendent in a huge yellow bow, but with an eye on a cat across the street. Oh! How blissful to be home again.

PART THREE

COURTSHIP AND
MARRIAGE

1892 ❦ 1898

CHAPTER 24

THOSE WERE THE DAYS of the "Yale-Harvard" football games at Springfield. There were usually several special trainloads of enthusiastic crowds, all carrying the flags of their favorite college. On a fine day it was a great sight, and we met our summer friends coming from all points. There were no stadiums in those days, and we sat on the usual wooden trestles, but we did not mind.

On the way home there was always fun with those who had bet on the wrong college. My two uncles, Mr. Corning and General Marvin, were like boys. The former was for Yale and the latter for Harvard. The one who was beaten had to treat the other one to dinner on the diner, including champagne, and then he was cheered or jeered into a speech giving the reasons why his college was defeated. One of the Yale songs was,

> Hold the ball McClung is coming,
> Barber signals still;
> Heffelfinger's in the center,
> Win we must and will! . . .

❦   ❦   ❦

The bride and groom, Hattie and William Rice, were living in Mrs. Field's house on Thurlow Terrace, where on December 30th, William G. Rice, Jr., was born. I felt very proud of being an aunt. . . .

❦   ❦   ❦

One of the outstanding events of the winter [of 1892-93] was the house party given for Bessie Oliver by her cousin Guy Baker, at "Hawkwood" at Ballston Spa. It was for over the New Year, and the chaperones were Mr. and Mrs. Bowditch and Mr. and Mrs. Billy Green. The trouble was that Guy had invited more guests than he had rooms. Even the cook was ousted from her room. . . . [She] had to sit up all night in a chair. Jane Kidd, Bessie and Cora Oliver, and I had a room together. There was a wide old-fashioned bed and a sofa, and the fourth had to be contented with chairs and pillows by the fireplace.

Hattie Green called loudly for a steam bath, but there was only a trickle of hot water in the one bathroom. The rest of us kept warm by clearing the pond for skating. Guy was making an honest penny by boarding Erie Canal mules, and we went to see them in his barn. Mrs. Bowditch had had experience, so she had brought a large cooked ham which, with loaves of bread and butter, milk, and pancakes, made our dinner. There was someone to play the piano in the evening, and we danced to keep warm. The Smith boys, May Potter and Walter, and Julia Wood from Hoosic, joined us for an hilarious evening.

❦   ❦   ❦

Governor and Mrs. Flower were kind and hospitable. Mrs. Flower had the traditional days "at home," and I was asked by her, through Colonel Timothy Shaler Williams, to come to one of her "days," and to pour tea. Mrs. Flower was quite deaf. She wore very elaborate brocade dresses and wonderful opals set in diamonds.

Just after I arrived, the governor came in, accompanied by a man whom he announced as "a real Britisher." He told us that this guest had been to his office that morning, and he had invited him to come at four to the Executive Mansion.

Mrs. Flower was sitting down, as no one else had come yet, and she asked the guest to sit by her. He sat down, and immediately the chair began to play "God Save the Queen." As became a loyal subject, he rose at once, though he was bewildered as to what was happening to him.

Mrs. Flower could not hear the music, and evidently she did not remember that the chair was musical, so she did not understand why the guest stood up. Again she urged him to sit down, and again the music played.

The governor in the meantime was enjoying his joke on the "Britisher," so I thought it would be a good idea to suggest tea and rescue him. He swallowed two cups quickly, thanked me, and vanished. I wonder what he wrote home about official entertainments in the "States." . . .

In February, one of the best balls of that winter was given at Harmanus Bleecker Hall by the "Bachelors of Albany." . . . The "Washington Post" was played that night for the first time in Albany, and it was a tremendous hit. The two-step became the rage, and the waltz and polka were almost forgotten for a while.

I went down to New York quite often that winter, usually staying at the Hampden Robbs at 23 Park Avenue. I enjoyed the dances much more than the first time, when I was so overwhelmingly shy. Mrs. William Astor, who had been so kind to me on the ship the previous winter, gave what she called on her invitation "a small dance," at her house at 842 Fifth Avenue. Her ballroom was very ornate. Mr. Ward McAllister was at the height of his reign. There was a short "German" after supper.

Everything was extremely decorous and beautifully done. No doubt the present generation would call it very stiff. I can hear people say, "How typical of the gay nineties it must have been!" I suppose it was the essence of the best of that period. I am glad to have seen it, as even those then-new houses have vanished.

In contrast to Mrs. Astor's ball was the party given by [Verplanck Colvin, the "Panther"] at the Kenmore Hotel. Mr. Colvin . . . was anxious to be reappointed the State surveyor of the Adirondacks, so he gave an impressive party that none of the guests ever forgot. The invitation [sent to men only] was for eight o'clock. No mention was made of a dinner, but everyone supposed there would be one, or at least a supper later.

Everyone arrived promptly in a Kenmore parlor, and they were greeted by the "Panther" in his day clothes. There was a table near him, on which was a large white pitcher of ice water and a tray of glasses, and the "Panther" kept urging the guests to have some. But it was a cold night, and nobody wanted any.

There were about thirty men, and they stood around in groups and talked. Time passed. The men stood first on one foot and then on the other. The nine o'clock bell boomed from the City Hall tower. Everyone looked at his watch, and so did the "Panther." Each man urged the other to try to find out what was to happen. At 9:30 Judge John Clinton Gray went up bravely and said good-bye.

It worked perfectly. The "Panther" also said good-bye and thanked Judge Gray for coming. The judge in turn thanked him for the refreshment that was so cooling, and the judge stalked out, a very mad man. Then everyone else followed, and the room was left to the "Panther" and his water pitcher.

Many of the men went to the hotel restaurant for some late supper, all very cross. Four of the men took a table and had started to eat when the "Panther" came in. Just as a joke, one of the men said, "Mr. Colvin, do join us and have some supper after your hospitable labors." The "Panther" smiled, as much as he ever did, joined them, ate his share of their meal, spoke of the successful party, and let the others stand the treat.

The city rang with the tale of the "Panther's party." We told him he must include the ladies at his next one.

. . . Jimmy Cox gave me a yellow poster advertising "Hyberta Pryne," who was dancing in a theatre on 14th Street in New York. He traced the dancer and found that she came from the coast and on the way had visited friends on Eagle Street and been quite ill there. She had not decided what name to take on her way to fame and fortune until she saw my name in a paper here, as having been to some party. She had never heard of any name like it, and so she changed the spelling enough to be legal. I am glad to say she was a success.

I have one of her programs. At the same time Harry Sage gave me a small photograph he found in a box of cigarettes made by a company in Ithaca. It was a girl in tights, sitting on a table and smoking their brand of cigarettes. Underneath was printed "Bertie Pryne." They issued about twenty-five thousand boxes with the same picture in it. I wish I had kept that picture, which was quite shocking for those days but would be nothing now.

Mother and I went to Washington for the inauguration of President Cleveland on March 4, 1893. We stayed at the Hotel Arno, later known as the Gordon. It was next to the house we had rented. We had a bad time, as the proprietor was only interested in experimenting with flying machines down on the Potomac. So we had no gas by which to dress for the Inauguration Ball in the Pension building, but Marie went out and managed to find some candles.

We were very fortunate at the Senate and found seats with Mrs. Cleveland and her mother. Mrs. Levi P. Morton was also there, which was rather hard, as she was the "out-going" glory. Her husband had been Vice-President with Harrison. The new Vice-President was Adlai Stevenson.[1]

Mrs. B. F. Warder had rented the big second story front window of Cornwall's grocery store on Pennsylvania Avenue and invited us to see the parade from there. It was an excellent location, between 14th and 15th Streets, and she had a luncheon served there, so we were very fortunate. The two outstanding figures in the parade, besides the President, were General Fitzhugh Lee, the son of Robert E. Lee, and Governor William E. Russell of Massachusetts. The crowd went wild over General Lee. They cheered and shouted and ran after him as much as the police would let them. Governor Russell had almost as much enthusiasm.[2]

The Clevelands asked us to tea a few days later. It was not long before the birth of Esther in the White House — the only child of a President born there. We had a delightful ten days and intended to stay longer, but we left suddenly on the *Colonial* for Boston, as Dr. A. P. Peabody of Cambridge had died. Mother wanted to be at his funeral, as she was very fond of him, and he had married her aunt.

This was the year of the Columbian Exposition at Chicago, and Aunt Mary Corning was at the head of the New York State women's division. She had her headquarters in Albany in an unused shop on State Street, and Mrs. Ives was her secretary in charge. In May the nations of the world sent their finest ships over to pay honor to the discovery of America, and among them was the Dutch naval vessel *Van Speyk*. The Holland Society invited Captain Arriens and nineteen officers to come to Albany in special cars attached to the Empire State Express — with engine 999 — to be welcomed by the governor, and to receive from the mayor the Freedom of the City. Many of the New York members of the Holland Society also came, and Jack was of course much interested and worked at this end.

Dr. Vander Veer was the president of the Albany Branch, and Mother invited the whole party to luncheon. Included, of course, were Governor and Mrs. Flower and Mayor and Mrs. James H. Manning. It was a lovely spring day and a pretty sight to see the officers walk through Academy Park from the City Hall to Elk Street. The Dutch had taken Albany again. With Dutch descendants here, the luncheon was served for one hundred and fifty people.

Fromo greatly amused the officers. He was enjoying the fountain with his wooden ball, so I told them his name was really Van Tromp, which made quite a hit.[3] They generously distributed hat bands with "Van Speyk" in gold letters, and there were other souvenirs. Carriages came for them about two o'clock, and they made a tour of the city.

❦   ❦   ❦

Towards the end of May came the first of the wonderful spring house parties at the Robert Pruyns' new camp, "Santanoni," near Newcomb, Essex County. The invitation was from May 21st to June 2nd. Eighteen of us were to be there. I am sure that every invitation was eagerly accepted. The camp had been a subject of interest all winter, as we heard of the furnishings being taken in over the snow.

In these days of comfortable sport clothes it is hard to understand the difficulties that presented themselves as to what to wear and how to get it. May Cooper, Bessie Oliver, Mabel Sard, and I conferred seriously and made trips to the shops, both here and in Troy. When I look at the pictures of the group on the steps at the camp, I marvel that we survived, with our almost-long skirts, our high collars, ruffled shirt waists, and pointed shoes. The only sweaters to be found were very heavy and had to be pulled on over our heads, and they were stiff and uncomfortable. We bought long black leggings, with shiny black buttons that had to be buttoned by a button hook. They were very hot for walking, but they saved us from black fly bites and brambles.

We left by the D. and H. about 4:30 one afternoon, changing at Saratoga for North Creek. We spent the night at a primitive hotel, and who should appear but the "Panther." He wanted to tell us about the famous guides who could walk one hundred miles without rest or food. He gave me several cards to use in case we needed any help from them and said that any one of them would come any distance for his sake. All this was during our early breakfast after a hilarious night of laughing and discomforts in the crude hotel. The rest of the party listened while the "Panther" and I stood up and he gave me the cards.

The drive into the camp was only thirty-five miles, and now when you can breakfast in Albany and lunch at "Santanoni," it seems incredible that it took from 8:00 a.m. to 6:00 p.m. We had a stop of an hour at Aiden Lair, where we ate beside a brook from which the trout for our luncheon had been caught. We drove through a bad forest fire and crouched in the bottom of the wagon to escape the smoke. The roads were just one hole after the other, and it was not very often that the horses had a chance to go faster than a walk.

I never will forget the first impression of the camp, and how we rushed from one thing to another, full of wonder and amazement that anything so fully settled and well equipped could be at the end of the rough journey. The outside was not yet finished, but inside we had every luxury, even a piano. When we discovered that there were five bathtubs, we were lost in amazement. I believe they were some kind of papier maché and very light to carry in, but they looked like enamel on metal. We acted like birds let loose! We were encouraged by the older members of the party, who seemed to enjoy jokes on one another just as much as we did.

In the evenings we had singing by Uncle Neddy Bowditch, either in the big living room or outside at a roaring camp fire. To Dick Meneely we were indebted for introducing the charming Canadian habitant song of "O! Alouette, gentille alouette" as we marched Indian file through the woods on our way to a picnic somewhere. Another equally popular song, also introduced by Dick, was:

> For they look like men in uniform,
> They look like men of war,
> And they are clad in armour bright,
> And conquering arms they bore, they bore.

Every night when we took our candles to go to bed, we made a line — each one with the left hand on the shoulder of the one in front, while with the right we grasped the candlesticks. Uncle Neddy was leader, and each squad of us was conducted to their cabin. The procession, growing smaller and smaller, wended its way along the dark piazza, while the black forest around us looked uncanny. [It would have been easy to imagine] the bears were laughing at our antics — perhaps they were. Mabel and Bessie and I shared "Scylla," and the single men shared "Charybdis" at the other end of the five houses, all connected by a wide covered piazza.

We played "Duck on the rock," we fished, had a regatta, a fancy dress party, and were given lessons in "Wig-wag," as used then by the Signal Corps, of which Fred Kelley was a member. At dinner every night Jim Cooper and I drank to the north and south side of Elk Street. He was always "Southside Jim." . . .

We spent that summer at Bar Harbor, stopping at Boston for Class Day at Harvard. Two of the Parkers were with us, and Mrs. Goodrich had a wonderful dance at Cambridge. . . . We had a gay summer of tennis tournaments and dances at the Kebo Club, where the new waltz and song, "After the ball is over," became enormously popular. Mavroyeni Bey and his friend Diodati Thompson gave a wonderful evening party at Bar Island, with fireworks both overhead and underwater, and we canoed and went on picnics. . . .

Soon after our return to Albany, we went to the Chicago Exposition. Eleven of our family went, and we had a car to ourselves. We stayed at the Chicago Beach Hotel near the fair grounds. I believe that the University of Chicago now occupies the site.

The weather was perfect, and I never will forget the glories of the Court of Honor and the Peristyle with the inscription chosen by President Eliot, "Ye shall know the Truth and the Truth shall make you free." It marked a new era in architecture that for many years influenced all the architecture of this country. One sees in almost every city some building that is dated "World's Columbian Period."

We youngsters tried the gondolas in the artificial canals, we were wheeled about in chairs in rows laughing at everything. We went up in the ferris wheel, much to the dismay of the elders of the party, but we thought we were being punished for our sins when the wheel stopped half way around on the first round, and two of our cousins were so terrified they almost fainted.

Little live lizards were sold all over the fair. They had tiny gilt chains around them and a pin on the end [for a woman to stick on her dress], so the poor little things lay on the waist front. It seemed criminal to have allowed them to be sold this way. On the train going home Louise lost hers and everyone searched for it, but it vanished for good.

Of course we went to the Midway Plaisance and saw all kinds of fakes and some good dancing. Everywhere we went "After the Ball" was played. There was a verse that went,

> After the fair is over,
> What will Chicago do,
> With all its flimsy buildings
> Run up with sticks and glue.
> I'd rather live in Brooklyn,
> Somebody'd love me there,
> Than have to live in Chicago
> After the fair.

The fall brought several house parties. I went to one in Highland Falls at the J. P. Morgans'. They were an informal and easy family, and we went on a picnic near Storm King. Mr. Morgan led the singing in church on Sunday, and in the evening he picked out the hymns for us to sing.

On Thanksgiving Mrs. Oliver chaperoned a party of us to a hunt breakfast at the Smiths' at Ballston Spa. We started on an early train and drove to the meet in carriages. Mrs. Smith rode with her four sons and a nephew, Sidney Smith, who wore a proper English pink hunting outfit. There were many Bakers and May Potter and many more at the delightful breakfast at the Smiths' house.

We returned by an afternoon train, and I went down with the rest of the family to the Cornings' at the farm for dinner at seven o'clock. That was the night that the box of terrapin that Louis Parker brought for the Cornings slid out of the carriage in Kenwood, and they all escaped but one.

On January 23, 1894, Katharine Westerlo Van Rensselaer was married to Mr. Benjamin Walworth Arnold at Vlie House in Greenbush. Katharine Van Rensselaer, daughter of Mr. and Mrs. Killiaen Van Rensselaer of New York, and I were the two bridesmaids. . . . On the night before the wedding, there was a skating party on the "Flatts" back of the house, by moonlight, and we returned to the house for supper. There were open fires in the fine old fireplaces, and Miss Kate Van Rensselaer, who owned the old place, used her lovely china for the supper that night and for the wedding reception.

The wedding was at four o'clock the next afternoon. . . . "Vlie House," the house on the marsh, was built in 1773, and it had the lovely woodwork of that period. The stairs were quite famous. I felt, as we looked down from the landing, that we should have worn period dresses. The ceremony was in the large hall where we danced while waiting with rice and slippers, but the bride and groom escaped by a ladder from an upper window in the rear of the house. "Vlie House," with its history and fine situation on the river, and the "Flatts," where we skated so gaily, have all gone. They were engulfed in the progress known as the "Port of Albany."

Mother and I sailed for Bermuda in late February [1894], as she had a very persistent cough. We had a most uncomfortable passage on the *Trinidad*, but the arrival there was a wonderful experience, as we had left ice and snow at New York. We stayed at the Hamilton Hotel and had a delightful month of lovely weather and kind hospitality. Governor and Mrs. Lyons reigned at Government House, but Admiralty House was closed. There was tennis at Happy Valley and bathing and sailing, and in fact it was all delightful.

On returning to New York, I went to the Robbs, as Nelly, Loulie, and I were to be bridesmaids to Kate Walsh a few days later. They had ordered my dress with theirs, so I had to go at once to fit it. Mr. John De Witt Peltz and Kate were married at St. Peter's in early April, and we had a house full, mostly of the Robbs. . . .

Our dresses were of pink chiffon over pink satin, with large leghorn hats with flowers. We were supposed to wear pink silk stockings and pink satin slippers, but when we were driving down State Street to the church, Loulie Robb discovered that Lily had on black Oxford low shoes, and she almost wept. "You've spoiled the whole procession!" scolded Loulie. Lily protested that she would bend over as she walked, and cover the blight. It was too late to do anything. One of the ushers was Montgomery Rochester, and as we walked up the aisle behind him, we saw the green tag of his new Prince Albert was still fastened to his coat tail.

We all danced at the reception, and Learned Hand, also an usher, danced some wonderful single steps with so much vigor that the house shook.

We went on another glorious "Santanoni" party at the end of May. The ice was just out of the lake, and soon after our return, General and Mrs. John F. Rathbone celebrated their Golden Wedding by giving a garden party at their house, 119 Washington Avenue. It was a lovely afternoon. The lively bride and groom of fifty years led the Virginia Reel, which we danced on grass, (now part of the Institute grounds). They had their four children and many grandchildren with them. Few of the family were absent for such an occasion.

Later in June I went over with the Olivers to Jack Oliver's graduation at Harvard. We stayed at the Victoria Hotel. Harvard Bridge was a novelty, and we took the trolley on Boylston Street and went over the bridge soon after ten in the morning of Class Day. It all ended by midnight, after a hot but wonderful day. It was still in the old yard, not the Stadium, and Beck Hall was in all its glory. We had a wonderful luncheon given by Edwin Morgan at a club, and in the center of the table was an enormous cake of ice, to cool us off. How we stood the high boned collars and black patent leather shoes passes my understanding now, but then we did not know anything else.

🍂   🍂   🍂

This was the summer of the [New York State] Constitutional Convention, and Elk Street seemed to be the center of the social side. As the papers stated, "Mrs. Pruyn opened the Convention summer with a dinner given in honour of Hon. Joseph Choate and Hon. Elihu Root, who have rented the bishop's house." Mr. Choate was elected President of the Convention. His nephew, Carl de Gersdorff of New York, was his secretary, and Phillips Burgess Jr. of Dedham was Root's secretary.

It was the hottest summer ever known. Mr. John Bigelow of New York and Highland Falls rented 21 Elk Street from Mr. James T. Gardiner. His two daughters, Miss Grace Bigelow and Mrs. Harding, were with him, and also little Charlotte Harding, who was about three years old.

Quite a number of families stayed in town late, and we were very gay, as dinners were given several evenings a week. Miss Bigelow was undaunted by the heat and gave at least one dance every week. The large gas chandelier made it almost unbearable. We would quietly adjourn to our garden to hold our faces and hands under the cool spouts of the goose fountain. . . .

The Women suffragists were making an all-out effort to have the word "male" stricken from the State Constitution. The "Antwerp" was their headquarters. This was close to the Capitol, on the site of the present Telephone Building. Dr. Mary Walker was always a familiar sight in town. She sometimes came to a reception at the Executive Mansion dressed in her long Prince Albert coat, striped trousers, and silk hat. She was one of the group in Albany. Others were Dr. Anna Howard Shaw, Miss Susan B. Anthony, Elizabeth Cady Stanton, Lillie Devereux Blake, and many more.[4]

The Anti-Suffrage Association of the Third Judicial District had organized in 1894. It had a large and enthusiastic committee, of which Mother was the head. There were organizations all over the state, and New York City wanted to have their committee the head of all of them, but Mother stood firm. Albany was the capital, and the work was chiefly in the Legislature; they had a joint committee from both Chambers. To an importunate New York group Mother made answer, "You must realize that New York is only the Port of Albany after all."[5]

Nothing more was heard of this idea until after my Mother's death, when headquarters for the state moved to New York. The argument was that they had more members and more money. All this was quite true.

Our house was the headquarters for the meetings and for the sending out of literature. All the printing was correctly and promptly done by Mr. C. P. Brate. On a large table in our old playroom were piled the many pamphlets, and I have kept one of them.

Often late at night Mother would walk down the two flights from the library to the playroom, carrying her glass-shaded candlestick, and pick out the articles needed. She would get them off in large envelopes in the late mail that was collected soon after ten o'clock by a mail man in a one-horse cart with two wheels. We would hear the rattle on the stones a block away and be ready for him. There was a mail box opposite our garden under the electric light.

"The hand that rocks the cradle is the hand that rules the world," chanted the "Antis," and across the parks would come the war cry, "Are we not human beings?" The Suffragists published a "Woman's Bible." I have a paper copy of Part One. It is called the "Pentateuch."

In the preface it states:

> The object is to revise only those texts and chapters directly referring to women, and those also in which women are made prominent by exclusion.

In this we are told that,

> The paucity of light and air in this ancient vessel (The Ark) shows that women had no part in its architecture or a series of portholes would have been deemed indispensible. If Miriam had planned the journey to Canaan, it would have been accomplished in forty days instead of forty years.

The *Anti-Suffragist* was one of the publications representing New York State, and the *Remonstrance* was published in Boston. The suffragists published the *Call*. I have leaflets by President Eliot of Harvard and two by Bishop Doane. May Cooper and I and many more collected signatures of people opposed to the extension of suffrage for women. These organizations were active until the Constitutional amendment was passed.

My husband told me in later years that he had always thought that women should have the ballot, particularly if they paid taxes. He was afraid that if he ever told this to Mother that she would never allow me to marry him, so he lay very low. Even I had no idea that he felt this way. In fact I cannot remember that we ever discussed it. In looking back, I cannot see why women should not have the vote, but at that time I was naturally an anti-suffragist. The fight was hot and heavy, and now the problem is as extinct as the dodo.

That summer of the Convention this question was especially active. But in early morning rides with Carl de Gersdorff, or afternoon tea piazza talks with Phil Burgess, the issue was not brought up. We took long drives in the late afternoons and had late dinner, and often in the long evenings various members would drop in to smoke and talk on the upper piazza, known as the Bower, with its lovely view across the river.

Many of the delegates went home for weekends. There was not much to amuse them in or around Albany at that time. The Country Club was in its infancy and only available for those who had horses or rode bicycles. It had very little equipment for games and no golf yet. There was no restaurant — you had to bring your own food and picnic. So it did not enter into the life of the delegates.

Sometimes the rougher side of life thrust in. One hot night that summer, I was awakened about 2:00 a.m. by hearing loud knocking on a door of a house not too far away, and shouting of "Let me in — let me in."

From an upper window came a woman's voice, "You go back where you got that and stay!" . . .

CHAPTER 25

WHEN WE REACHED ALBANY AGAIN [in late summer 1894, from a trip to Murray Bay], I found trunks all about and discovered that Mother had taken passage for us to sail on the American liner *Paris* three days later, on Saturday. On Friday Mother had a luncheon for twenty people, for Mrs. Elihu Root, who had come down from Clinton to see what kind of housekeeping was going on at the bishop's house. Mr. Bigelow was one of the guests. He and I had become fast friends, and he gave me his *Poor Richard* with his autograph. He also gave me his photograph and extracted a promise from me that I would write to him.

With regrets and sad good-byes to Fromo, we set out again. The *Paris* was dirty and uncomfortable. We sat at a table with Bishop and Mrs. Littlejohn of Long Island. Mark Twain was a passenger. Mother had met him several times when he stayed at the Sages. He carried one small black bag for his summer trip. At the usual concert, he read his "German Papers," and we laughed until we cried, particularly when some of the German passengers left the saloon in a rage.

We went to London, and Mother was quite ill there, so we went to Paris and met the Cornings, who had been in Europe for some months. As Harriet was to come out that winter, we went on regular shopping expeditions. . . . Harriet and I took bicycle lessons in a rink. We learned to mount and dismount in good style, and then we were allowed to try our prowess in the Bois. We had an interested audience of the Cornings and Mother and the Bayard Van Rensselaers. I bought a bicycle costume of dark brownish cloth. It was tailor-made. The skirt touched the tops of the boots. Under it I wore bloomers of the same material. It had a short coat, and the hat was a small brown felt. It looked trig and as if made for business, and the skirt escaped catching in the wheel, which was the cause of many accidents. Nobody [took notice of this outfit] in Paris, but in Albany it was a sensation.

Early in October Mother and I left for The Hague to visit Aunt Sarah Boreel. We found her carriage waiting for us at the station, and we were soon at her hospitable house on the Bezeidenhout. Mother and I had two front rooms on the third floor, with a lovely view. Cousin Sarah's granddaughter, Sarah de Pallandt, was also there. She was a romantic figure to me. She was recovering from a shattering love affair. Later she married her cousin. She was very handsome and much admired, both at The Hague and in London.

Aunt Sarah had been a lady-in-waiting to Queen Sophie Mathilde and to Queen Emma, and her house was a great center. The Princess of Wied — who was a Dutch princess — was a great friend, and one afternoon she came in at tea time. She was a simple old lady, interested in Americans, and evidently regarding us as specimens. There were a few guests at dinner every evening, and we again met the various married children and others who were related. The intermarriages there are impossible to untangle.

The Alfred Boreels lived in the John De Witt house, on the Kneuterdyk, where his great collection of Delft and Lowestoft were beautifully arranged. In Holland it is always a pleasure to see the collections of china displayed in glass-fronted cases and also hung on the walls in almost every house.

Aunt Sarah was at this time a very old lady. She was a granddaughter of the first John Jacob Astor, whose daughter, Dolly, had eloped in Washington with my great uncle, Woodbury Langdon of Portsmouth, New Hampshire. We said good-bye with regrets as we felt it was a real good-bye.

We crossed by the Hoek van Holland and returned to London. A few days later we went to "Bearwood" to visit Mr. and Mrs. John Walter. There were about twenty people there for a long weekend. I met again my old friend Ralph of the nursery visit of long ago, when I had refused to give him the horse and cart he wanted. On a later visit to "Bearwood" he had let a jumping frog, which Mother had brought him, out of its box during Prayers. . . .

"Bearwood" was an enormous place with beautiful grounds, near Wokingham in Berks. There was a lovely lake, and in spring the rhododendrons were a great sight, as they were planted to reflect in the lake. Near the center of the lake there was a stone cross to mark the place where the oldest son, John Walter, was drowned on Christmas Eve. He had just returned from an educational trip to the United States and had stayed at 13 Elk Street on his way to sail for home in time for Christmas.

We returned again to London and took an afternoon train for Edinburgh. It had a dining car attached, which was a great novelty. Edinburgh is always a fascinating city, and we stayed for two or three days, just to wander about again and revel in the Mary Stuart era — an era which always dominates the city.

Then one afternoon we took the train for Dundee, where we were met at the Tay Street station by Lord Camperdown's carriage or omnibus. It was a three-mile drive out to Camperdown, where we found a warm welcome from Lady Abercromby and her brother Lord Camperdown, and tea and scones and jam and all the delicious things that made a Scotch afternoon tea. It was the first visit there for both Mother and me, as our former visits to them had always been at their English house near Warwick. The house at Camperdown was built in the Greek style with tall pillars on the front, and inside was a large hall with a gallery from which the rooms opened.

Other guests were the Speaker of the House of Commons, Lord Peel, and his son, and Mrs. and Miss Fenwick. There were guests every night for dinner, and the piper came in with his bagpipes and walked around the table making a frightful noise while we had coffee. The Fenwicks and Lord Camperdown danced reels and sword dances, and I was soon able to join them. We danced to the old air, "As I went thro' Sandgate, thro' Sandgate, etc." Reels had been quite a fad at home, and I learned several new steps.

Lord Camperdown was a good host. He took young Peel and Miss Fenwick and me over the grass roads of the park to Lundy's hill to see the fishermen net the fish in Loch Long. The trip was in two light carriages. I went in the dog cart with Lord Camperdown. The same party went to St. Andrews and carried a picnic luncheon, which we ate in the ruins of the Cathedral, on an old table tomb of one Betsy Wallace. We climbed the St. Regulus tower at the old College and watched the fish women in the High Street. And we walked around the famous golf links to watch Hugh Kircaldy. Everyone knew Lord Camperdown and touched their bonnets and said, "'Mornin' your Lordship." The women made curtseys.

Lady Abercromby was quite an artist. She had just made a portrait of the Master of Balliol — the famous Jowett. It is hung at the college. She had also completed Lord Hartington, who was later the Duke of Devonshire, and I watched her while she painted an excellent one of Gordon of Khartoum, which is now in the National Gallery. Lady Abercromby was preparing for a visit from the widowed Dutchess of Albany and her daughter Princess Alice, later Countess of Athlone. On the ground floor there was an old-fashioned suite, seldom used, and this was being aired and put in order for the royal visit. I was taken in to see the infinite detail necessary for such a visit: the arrangements for the ladies-in-waiting, their maids, and special maids to wait on the party. They were to stay a week.

We left Dundee and took the train to a place where Lady Airlie's carriage met us. Then we drove the five miles to Airlie Castle, which was the dower

house of "The Bonnie house of Airlie." The castle had been burned by the
Argyle clan in 1640 and had only been half rebuilt. It was on a high situation
overlooking the meeting of the tiny rivers Melgun and Isla, at the foot of
a steep ravine.

Lady Airlie was a born gardener, and the garden was lovely with box
and yew and ironwork gates and railings brought by her from Italy. The
castle was a mine of history and tradition, and I spent hours just wandering
about from room to room and asking questions of anyone who was around.
Griselda believed every legend and tradition and was very superstitious. She
took me on a rough walk up the glen of Isla to see the "Slugs" or waterfalls.

One day we drove to "Cortachy," which is the house lived in by the
reigning Lord Airlie. The family were away, but we had tea and saw the
heirlooms and portraits. . . . Lady Airlie's oldest son was then Lord Airlie.
He lost his life in the Boer War. The dairy there was fascinating — built
over a running brook. The gardens had been enlarged and were beautiful
during the time of the older Lady Airlie.

Another day we drove over to the famous Glamis Castle. In the distance,
as we wound along the avenue, it looked a huge pile, gloomy and frowning,
but as we neared it, it seemed more friendly. . . . I believe it is the oldest
continuously occupied house in Scotland.

The family sleep in what is called the new part. I do not know how new
that means. One of the many stories [about the castle] is that there is one
house inside the other. We were shown several secret places hidden in the
thickness of the wall.

One of the young Mrs. Bowes Lyons took us about and showed the room
where Macbeth was murdered, "Beardie's room," and Prince Charlie's room,
and the gloomy crypt chapel. My vivid imagination was fired, and I was
sure the whole castle was haunted. . . .

The large living room where we had tea was hung with tapestry over the
stone walls. It was entirely home-like and filled with the small tables, so
prevalent in the houses in Great Britain, with books and flowers and bibelots
everywhere. It was hard to imagine anything very dreadful could happen.
Lord and Lady Strathmore were at their place in England — St. Paul's,
Waldenburg, . . . where their granddaughter, Lady Elizabeth, became
engaged to the young Prince, later King George VI.

We left lovely Airlie with many regrets. One day at luncheon the conversation was about modern books. Everyone was reading Du Maurier's *Trilby*.
I had read it with great interest. I still like to read it. Lady Airlie spoke of

it and said that of course no young girl should be allowed to read such a book. She had forbidden Griselda to read it.

Griselda turned an agonized eye on me. She had told me in London that she had read it at the Russian Embassy, where her friend, Thekla de Stael, was the daughter of the ambassador. She knew that I had read it. The only difference was that Mother had allowed me to read it. Mother and I kept a discreet silence.

We went to stay at old Lady Kinloch's at "Meigle House." Her daughter Eva had come over with us to America several years previously. The son and his wife, Sir John and Lady Kinloch, lived at "Kinloch House" not far away. They had wonderful horses and were in the sporty world. All these places were close together, and now a modern motor would whisk one about without all the trains and changes at small stations and long drives. But the drives gave us a wonderful chance to see the lovely scenery in the lovely weather that we had all through the trip.

We [returned to] Edinburgh and went to stay with Sir George Warrender and his daughter, just outside the city, at "Bruntisfield House." . . . Sir George, our kind next door neighbor in Eaton Square, was quite ill, and Miss Alice Warrender was the hostess. As the Warrenders were in deep mourning, it was a quiet visit, but we took beautiful drives about the city and up to Arthur's seat, and we were glad of the open fires in the old house. Young Mr. Peel had bicycled over to Airlie while we were there, and he and his father were at Haliburton after they left Camperdown, and he turned up again in Edinburgh — a very nice attractive fellow.

We returned to London, as Mother was to be painted by Mr. Eddis. He lived at Shalford near Guildford, and we had to go down there for the sittings. His daughter, Mrs. Powell, lived there with her children. One was a very pretty daughter named Cicely. She married the poet, Lawrence Binyon, and in later years they came to Washington, where we saw them very often. The portrait was a great success and was given to the Rices. . . .[1]

While we were in London we again saw a great deal of the Danish Minister and Mme. de Bille. One night at a dinner there we met Jean de Pallandt, who later married his cousin Sarah, but at that time he was well amused with another charming Dutch lady. Lord and Lady Gough, who used to be at the Washington Embassy, were also there.

We went to Oxford to spend a weekend with Mr. George Broderick, the Warden of Merton College. . . . The Warden's house . . . was the headquarters of King Charles I during the Civil Wars. . . . The house was quaint, stone cold, and most uncomfortable, except in the charming large living room with a big fire. Young Sidney Peel was staying there, and Mr. and Mrs. Butler dined there. She was a niece of Maria Edgeworth, on whose stories we had been brought up. My dinner partner was Collis, the star football player, and others were an African explorer and Sir George Chesney.

In London I was busy at the South Kensington Museum three mornings a week, taking lessons at the Royal School of Art Needlework. We went down to lovely Knole again — a real treat. Funny old Lord Sackville was still living, but not doing any more indiscreet talking. . . .

I never will forget the full-length portrait hung over the fireplace in the dining room. Its eye seemed to follow me. I spoke of it, and they told me that there was only one eye. The place where the other should have been was a hole. There was a "priest's hole" [in the wall] behind it [a remnant of religious persecutions]. Whoever was hidden there could see and hear all that went on at the table. They found several "priest's holes" when they put in electricity. . . .

That was the era of Kipling. His *Tommy Atkins* was the favorite of the Music Halls, and was very catchy. However, it never had such a run as the old "Ta-ra-ra-boom-de-ay" of the 1892 period, when Lottie Collins swept London, and indeed the whole country, off its feet with the song and dance. There were endless verses — just as many as "After the Ball." I can only remember one.

> You should see me walk with Pa —
> Prim and most particular.
> The young men say, "Ah', there you are!"
> And Pa says, "How peculiar."
> "It's like their cheek," I say, and so
> Off with Pa again I go,
> But when his back's turned, then you know
> Ta-ra-ra-boom-de-ay!

We sailed on the *Majestic* and had a fair trip for that time of year. . . . We found Fromo in fine shape. Albany was in a great state of excitement over the Pageant for the benefit of the Historical Society, to be given at Harmanus Bleecker Hall the week of December 3 [1894]. There were to be ten tableaux in all, five given three nights and the other five the other nights.

Mr. Townsend Lansing was the president of the Society, and his brother-in-law, Mr. George Douglas Miller, was the recording secretary and the leading spirit in the rehearsals. Before we met at the Hall, we met in groups at the house of the head of a certain tableau.

Mrs. Jacob Ten Eyck, of 308 State Street, was in charge of the tableau of the famous wedding, in 1650, of Margaritta Van Slichtenhorst to Philip Petersen Schuyler. The questions of who should take ancestral parts, [and what would be] the proper dresses and [how] the groupings [should be formed with historical accuracy] had to be debated by Mrs. Ten Eyck and her committee. Mrs. Schuyler Crosby and her daughter Angelica had come to spend the winter in Albany and were [staying with Mr. Crosby's mother], Mrs. John Tayler Cooper's, at 134 State Street. . . . Angelica was a direct descendant of the marriage, so she was the bride, and the groom was Stephen Schuyler of the old house on the "Flatts" in Watervliet. . . .

Mr. Seavey was doing the scene painting, using the James Eights water colors, and *Munsell's Annals* were searched for data. In fact, all Albany was busy digging up history and ancestral garments. I took the part of Alida Van Slichtenhorst, the niece of the bride, as I was fifth in descent. Alida first married Gerrit Van Schaick and later the bridegroom's nephew, Pieter Davidse Schuyler. I wore the deep orange silk over a white brocade skirt, and Cousin Anna Vrooman lent me a lovely lace cap and embroidered veil.

The marriage was performed by the Civil Magistrate Anthonie de Hooges, and this part was taken with great success by Mr. Charles H. Van Benthuysen of La Fayette Street. Mr. Townsend Lansing was Brant Van Slichtenhorst. Mrs. I. H. Vrooman was the bride's mother, and the Patroon was represented by Mr. Bayard Van Rensselaer. Howard Van Rensselaer was the bride's brother, and the bridesmaids were Lydia and Ellen Hun, Pauline Townsend, and Susy Lansing. It was all a great spree and we had a lot of fun! The tableau called for about fifty guests, and we had only to look pleasant, lift our right hands, and shout, "Op de gezonheid van de bruid!" ["To the health of the bride!"].

Of the other tableaux, the La Fayette ball, with Mrs. Edward Hun as chairman, was one of the best. "The Reception of Washington," with Mrs. Bayard Livingston as chairman, was one of the best too, though she had a great deal of trouble about some man from out of town who was to be General Washington but dropped out at the last minute. I think Mr. Billy Barnes substituted for him.

The Civil War period had two scenes. The first was on State Street, with the old Capitol in the background, at the outbreak of the war. The next was a camp scene, and Mr. Bowditch sang "Tenting tonight on the old camp ground" to great applause from members of the G.A.R. [Grand Army of the Republic]. I believe the proceeds were satisfactory. The Hall was sold out every night. . . .

Another excitement that met our homecoming was the news that there was to be a "Dancing Class" every other Saturday night in the old Murray Hall on Pearl Street. It was a wretched place, but no other was available. The patronesses were the mothers of the buds. There were to be six dance classes, all of them cotillions. The price for all six was $12.00. Supper was ice cream, cakes, and lemonade. These dances were on the model of Mrs. Sands' Saturday evening dancing classes in New York, to which many of us had been invited as guests.

Mother gave a dinner and cotillion for Harriet Corning, with twenty-four couples, and gave favors brought from Paris. Pauline Townsend was another debutante that year, and a very popular one. She was a beautiful dancer too. Walter and Julia Wood came down from Hoosic to stay with us for the party. My partner was Rensselaer Erving. Christmas week was gay, with a dance almost every night.

❦   ❦   ❦

When the City Hall bell tolled for a fire, everyone rushed for the fire card and located the fire by its number. If it was near, almost simultaneously the front doors of our house, of the Coopers, and of the Van Benthuysens would open and slam, and May and Bessie and I would rush out. Christmas week there was a bad fire at the Kenmore Hotel, but there was no loss of life, only many rooms made unfit to use for the inauguration of Governor Levi P. Morton on New Year's Day.

But the following Sunday evening the bell rang the same number. I left the dinner table and picked up a cape in the hall. Running people shouted that it was the Delavan Hotel on Broadway! It was a tragic and disastrous fire. Seventeen of the servants who took refuge on the roof were burned to death. The origin of the fire was at the bottom of the elevator shaft, and it spread rapidly.

Mr. and Mrs. Bradley Martin were staying there. They had come from New York on business. Mrs. Martin was knitting a stocking, and had dropped her rings into it while she worked. With the alarm of fire, she dropped the stocking and it was not until she reached the street that she realized her loss. An elevator boy was brave enough to go up, and he found the stocking and rings safely. The hotel was never rebuilt. . . .

Our guests for the Inauguration were Mr. and Mrs. James Roosevelt of Hyde Park and their son Franklin; and Mr. Roosevelt's grandson, James Roosevelt, the son of James Roosevelt; and Colonel and Mrs. Archibald Rogers, also of Hyde Park. He had been appointed to the governor's staff. Mother had a dinner of twenty on New Year's Eve, and it fairly bristled with colonels, as Colonel John Jacob Astor was also on the staff, and he and Mrs. Astor also came to the dinner. Colonel William Cary Sanger had been elected a member from Sangerfield, and [he and his wife] also dined with us. Colonel Sanger was what was known as a "Goo-goo," that is a good government member. . . .

Albany did itself proud on that Inauguration Day. The sky was a brilliant blue, and the snow was heavy. Sleighs jingled their bells all day bringing people from the station to the Capitol and later to the Mansion. We were proud to have strangers see Albany. I took the two Roosevelt boys to the Inauguration. Mother went with the others and sat with the Mortons.

In the afternoon we all went to the reception at the Executive Mansion, and there was a great crowd. Aunt Kate heard two women talking. One was a stranger and asked to have people pointed out. The one, who evidently lived here, undertook to point out the golden colonels on the staff. She got them well mixed, and Herbert Satterlee of New York was called "Colonel Rogers," etc. . . . At last she came to me. . . . She looked me over carefully then said to her friend, "If my Jane had them clothes, she'd knock the spots out of her." The clothes in question was a dress from Rouff's in Paris. It was a tea rose silk with chintz flowers, trimmed with guipure lace.

In the late afternoon I took the boys coasting. My young coasting friend of four or five years back had grown tall and was at Groton, but he still loved to coast, and we had a good coasting on Elk and Columbia Streets. In the evening we went skating on the river at the foot of State Street. The Astors and Colonel Rogers joined us, and Mrs. Astor put us all to shame, as she was a beautiful skater. She wore a plain black coat and skirt, made daringly short, [only reaching] to the tops of her high laced boots, that were made especially for skating. . . .

Our good neighbor at 20 Elk Street, Mr. Leonard Kip, made a great effort to go to the reception at the Executive Mansion to pay his respects to the new governor and his lady. . . . Mr. Kip was old and lame and no doubt was also slow in the line, marching up to shake hands. Consequently, he was indignant at being told to move along by Colonel Astor in his gold braid. Mr. Kip said he had often been with his father in New York when the original John Jacob Astor was peddling his fur skins and with a strong German accent would urge, "Evey ting counts a leetle, Mr. Keep." So he felt it was impertinent for this descendant in gay plumage to treat him in so casual a manner. . . .

❦   ❦   ❦

Governor and Mrs. Morton had five daughters. The two oldest, Edith and Lena, were out, and Helen came out that winter. Lena and Helen dined with us the evening of Harriet Corning's coming out ball at Harmanus Bleecker Hall, on January 7th [1895]. It was a cotillion, and many people had guests.

My brother brought up a party from New York. One of them was Miss Louisa Ward McAllister. She had a devoted admirer, Mr. Nelson Lewis, who wore a leather bracelet watch, then considered not only a novelty, but a badge of femininity. . . .

Jack arranged for the party to have supper at the ball, in two of the large boxes at the Hall. He asked me to join them and to bring others. What I especially remember is the consternation of the good New Yorkers when they found there was no wine served. They did not like to say what they thought in front of Jack and me.

The Cornings gave an oyster roast at the farm for the three Morton girls, but I do not think they enjoyed that kind of a party. In one way I do not wonder, as many of [the guests were related to one another and had been brought up together]. Uncle Erastus led Helen out for the cake walk, and in her long white evening dress and long white gloves, I am sure she was neither happy nor at home. When Professor Van Buren awarded the cake to them, the cheering and clapping was terrific, and they had to walk around once again.

The Mortons gave a cotillion for Helen on February 8th. There were many dinners beforehand. The Speaker and Mrs. Hamilton Fish, the Billy Barneses, and the Billy Greens were among those who gave dinners. The dance invitations had said "small dance," but it turned out to be a very large one. We knew that guests were expected from New York and that Mr. Creighton Webb had been invited to lead the cotillion, much to the consternation of many matrons and to the amusement of others. His reputation was strongly disapproved.

A tremendous snow storm had raged from early morning, and the guests from New York who were coming to stay with us decided to wait until Saturday. The Mortons' guests started out bravely in a private car, on an afternoon train, and now as we arrived at the Mansion, we heard that they were stalled at Poughkeepsie. During the evening the railroad offices telephoned bulletins, which were reported to the governor's secretary, and we heard that the train was trying to push up the river.

But finally supper was served at midnight, and the storm still raged. I admit that there were murmurings among the native guests at being kept for a New York party. Soon after supper was started, an aide reported that they had arrived and were at the Kenmore, having hot baths. The heating apparatus on the train had broken down, and they were almost frozen.

They arrived just as we finished supper, six or seven of them, piloted by Colonel Astor, who had not forgotten his uniform. Mrs. Astor wore a pink satin dress and wonderful pearls, and seemingly was not tired after a delay of about six hours. Hot supper was served to them, although it was quite apparent to many eagle eyes that several had already refreshed themselves on the train.

We danced until the great Colonel Webb had supped. He looked us over and later picked out any girl who pleased his fancy and danced well. One girl gave him a glassy stare and said to her partner, "Who is this ill-mannered stranger?" Later Colonel Webb asked to be introduced to her.

My partner was Fred Kelley. We had excellent seats, but we decided to sit out two of the figures and watch all the things that were happening. It was after three before we broke up. The Mortons had sent out coffee to the coachmen waiting in the sleighs, but I fear the poor horses were the real sufferers.

Our weekend guests arrived early Saturday afternoon, in time for a dancing class that night. The next morning, Sunday, we were just started for church when a messenger arrived with a note for me from Mrs. Astor. It said that they had taken the curling ring for the morning and hoped our party would join them. It is difficult for anyone now to realize how this horrified my mother. She said not to speak of it to anyone, but it was too late. As we came out of church, we were met by the noise of the Astor party in a large sleigh, driving up State Street tooting horns, to the scandal of the churchgoers.

We had had house guests almost without a break all winter. On February 2nd, there had been a twenty-fifth anniversary of the consecration of Bishop Doane, and the house was full. Bishop Talbot came again, and also Dr. Fairbairn of St. Stephen's at Annandale, Bishop Leonard of southern Ohio, and Bishop Henry C. Potter of New York. . . .

Soon after this celebration, the dean of Rochester, England, arrived to give lectures on "Roses and Rose Gardens." I think they were for the benefit of Rochester Cathedral. He stayed at the Doanes. We had two of his party with us. One was an English artist, Herbert Olivier, and the other was Miss Pickersgill-Cunliffe. It would be difficult to forget her and her extraordinary get-up and inquiries as to our manners and customs. Other guests were Comte and Comtesse de Laugier Villars, the Whitelaw Reids, Anne Morgan, and Esther and Joe Hunt.

Harriet Corning and I went to New York for a week and stayed with the Hampden Robbs at 23 Park Avenue. Loulie Robb was to have her coming-out cotillion in the large drawing room of their new home, just built by Stanford White. Harriet and I had run through our dresses brought from Paris, so we had new ones made by Dautricourt. I never saw Harriet look lovelier than she did at that ball. The dress was plain pink satin, beautifully cut, and with a great deal of tulle of a lighter shade. Harriet and I each had a gold bead necklace, given us when we were baptized. Otherwise we wore no jewelry. . . .

There were other events that hectic week. One was a large dinner given for us by Miss Eleanor Blodgett and her brother Will before one of the "Cinderella" dances. My partner was Will Blodgett. The next night was Mrs. Edward's dancing class at Sherry's, for which my partner was Thayer Robb. Mrs. Sand's dancing class came Saturday night, and I danced with Dexter Blagden.

When Sunday came we should have stayed in bed, but each of us had a beau with whom to go to church. Afterward we lunched with Jack at the Metropolitan Club, where we had an hilarious party with Nina and Langdon Erving, Fred Delafield, and a bewildered Marquis Villa Loba. When Harriet asked him if his name meant "house to let," he became quite jolly, but he always gazed through his monocle at us. I was Jack's hostess, and we decided he was quite sweet on Nina, so we kept drinking to their healths, much to their embarrassment.

We returned to Albany with our clothes in shreds, and ready to sleep for several days. But two days later I returned to New York to stay with Mrs. Duer and Alice. We went to all kinds of parties, including a luncheon at Sir Roderick Cameron's. While we were at luncheon, Miss Anna Gould came in. She was to be married soon to Comte Boni de Castellane, and Anna Cameron was to be a bridesmaid. We went to a dance at Mrs. Pierpont Morgan's and to an Assembly after a dinner party, and then I went home again in time for a dance given by the Hamilton Fishes. . . .

As Ash Wednesday had come, we could take a rest from gaities and have time for coasting and skating. We often left a party, if it was near Elk Street, and got our sleds out, and, in evening dresses, took a few slides before returning to dance. Lena Morton organized a Lenten half-hour reading club. The members promised to read a really worthwhile book every day for a half hour, or they had to pay a fine of ten cents for every day they missed. The money went to St. Margaret's. After Lent we had a confession meeting at the Mortons', and several argued that they had not read on purpose so as to have more money to give for the charity.

In March Governor Morton said he was tired and wanted a change. There was a small hotel in the Adirondacks at Loon Lake that was open all winter, and it was arranged that we should go there. The party started out to be a small one, but by the time we started on a night train it had become quite large. There were Governor and Mrs. Morton with Edith, Lena, and Helen, Mr. and Mrs. James Roosevelt and Franklin, Colonel and Mrs. Archibald Rogers, Mr. and Mrs. Corning, and Harriet and Edwin, Mr. Walter Palmer, my mother and the Rices and myself. We had two sleeping cars and a baggage car, and we went up via Utica and the Webb Road, arriving at Loon Lake in the early morning. There were only two other people in the hotel, but our party filled it up.

We started off snowshoeing at once. The snow was deep, but there was a crust. I have several photos taken of the party, and Mr. Palmer did a small water color for my album. This original, as well as enlargements of the pictures, are in the library at Hyde Park. The older members of the party drove out in sleighs; the weather was ideal.

Then came a real blizzard. This made the railroad impassable, so we stayed two days more than we had planned. We had a candy pull in the kitchen. We had charades. I remember one was the name of Mrs. Humphrey Ward's latest book, *Marcella* (Ma was in the cellar). We sang the songs of that era, "Ta-ra-ra-boom-de-ay," "After the Ball," "The Bicycle Built for

Two," and other songs from the *Trip to Chinatown*, which was, justly, a very popular play. Selden Marvin, as the governor's military aide, was also with us, and he sang delightfully, and the two boys, Franklin and Edwin, had great disputes over their stamp collections.

One afternoon I was sitting on the top of a ladder, fixing curtains for a tableau, when the mail came in. I had a letter from Jack in New York. He wrote me in profound secrecy of his engagement, and [told] how happy he was. It was to be announced in two weeks, but he gave no name.

My guess was Nina Erving, as they were always walking together, but then he had always known her, so it might be another. It was perplexing, and I wondered, as I sat there with the tableau forgotten, if I could risk sending a telegram. With so many people about, someone might see it and the secret would be out. When I got home, there was the letter in answer to the one I had written him. It was Nina, and we all rejoiced.

At Easter in 1895, we had the women's edition of the *Argus*. That is, Mr. William McMurtrie Spear offered the publication for one day, for the benefit of St. Margaret's. Mrs. Levi P. Morton was listed as "Patron," and the Editors-in-Chief were Mrs. Erastus Corning and Mrs. Hamilton Fish. There were more than fifty associate editors, and the managing editors were Mrs. Robert Shaw Oliver, Mrs. Harry C. Cushman, and Mrs. Florence C. Ives. The latter had been on the New York State Women's Committee, and she really took charge of the office (at a regular salary) in a vacant upper floor of a shop on lower big State Street, where we reported to her. Mrs. Crannell was City Editor and there were about twenty-five reporters, of whom I was one. . . . It was published in six sections, and on the cover was a sad-looking Easter lily.

My own experiences were amusing. My assignment was to interview all the bank presidents, and Mother, in her effort to help as well as to be sure I was chaperoned, sent with me Miss Wilbur, who was secretary to Bishop Doane as well as to Mother. She took down the shorthand notes of these important interviews.

I especially remember Mr. Howard King, president of the State Bank. He was rather deaf and did not quite understand what I wanted. He began by seeming to be pleased. He thought I had come to consult him. He gave quite a list of "pet" investments, until he noticed that Miss Wilbur was jotting down all he said.

He was quite upset when, between explanations by his secretary and me, he realized this was for the benefit of one of Bishop Doane's charities and not for me. The Bishop was distinctly not one of his "pets," and he asked to have Miss Wilbur tear up the notes. He was quite rattled and could not concentrate on anything but kept repeating, "If the Republicans had charge of the government, all would be well, but now, things are different."

After turning in these interviews, I was assigned to "Society Notes" with Marguerite Read. It was a lot of fun. We let it leak out that all the fancies and foibles would be shown up without fear or favor. People spoke of the danger of libel suits, but who would be sued, the *Argus* or the committee or the bishop? We only hoped to be thought humorous. We found De Witt Walsh a great help with his ideas and suggestions. Instead of the news that families were to spend the summer at their usual place, we sent them to places that were unusual — to put it mildly — and we mixed them all up. We had a column of "Society Notes," a column about five well-known young men and numerous grinds, with a bit of fiction added to the truth.

The great day came at last. Bessie Oliver and I met at the H. G. Eyres' florist shop at 11 North Pearl Street, as he lent us his delivery wagon and horse for the morning. I have a photograph of us ready to start at 7:00 a.m. to deliver the papers that had been ordered. Our route was the center of the city — that is, the middle hill.

There were signs hung on each side of the fat horse, "Buy the Women's Argus." We had two choir boys from the Cathedral to help us. Many people had ordered as many as ten copies at fifteen cents each. The picture shows the outlandish clothes of the period — enormous leg-of-mutton sleeves and long elaborate skirts. We had our lists from headquarters, and we had to return twice for more papers.

It was just noon when we paused on the corner of Elk and Steuben Streets by the old High School. There was a waffle man there every day for the benefit of both schools, the Boy's Academy and the High School. We were tired and famished and were comfortably enjoying the waffles, surrounded by an admiring crowd of boys, when the front door of No. 1 Elk Street opened and out poured Mrs. McAlpin's Bible Class. Angelica Crosby rushed down the steps shouting to us, "I'm converted! I've got religion! But I am awfully hungry, and I want some waffles too!"

Others joined us, and we heard many comments on the social notes and what might happen to us, particularly from General Robert Lenox Banks, who was reported as being after my head. We drove down Steuben Street, wondering what came next, returned the wagon and tired horse to kind Mr. Eyres, and then walked ourselves home. We were tired, but we had the agreeable feeling that we had done a good job for St. Margaret's. . . .

In May came the third of the wonderful Santanoni parties — each one was more delightful than the last.

Mother had brought from London a complete set of costumes for the production of "Fair Rosamond," a pastoral play we had seen given at Hampstead with Lady Archibald Campbell as Rosamond. It was adapted from Tennyson's "Becket," and the date is 1160 to 1165. Mother had also bought the rights to the play for the United States and Canada. The play was to be given in June on the lawn of the Corning farm at Kenwood, but in the meantime, she started rehearsals at Drislane's Hall in April. The dramatic production was under the direction of Mr. John Malone. The music was under the direction of Mr. Tipton, the organist and choir master at the Cathedral of All Saints.

There were thirty peasants, of whom I was one. Our costumes were of brown and green — there was one original from London, and the others were copied from it. We wore caps and kerchiefs of coarse unbleached cotton. It was a tremendous undertaking. Mother said she had no trouble with the professionals, but it was the amateurs who were late, did not learn their lines, and sometimes never turned up for rehearsals.

When we returned from Santanoni, the whole affair was getting together well, but Mr. Malone insisted that there must be someone who made explanations between scenes and at the opening and ending, and he drafted me as "The Spirit of Fancy." He wrote the lines for the "Spirit." This was less than a week before the first performance, and nobody had any idea how the "Spirit" should be clothed.

Marie bought a Butterick pattern of what she thought a "Spirit" ought to wear, and it was quite funny. I was draped over and over with yards of white cheese cloth, with puff sleeves in a sort of cape, and yards of angel's sleeves. Under it all I wore the usual corsets and underwear. In these days

I would have worn sandals, and my hair should have been flowing, but instead, a gold fillet, that was not too secure as I floated around, bound it. I had to change costumes four times every afternoon, [as I was a] a peasant too.

It was a charming scene. The peasants started at the top of the hill and came dancing down, hand in hand, to the tune of "Come lassies and lads, get leave of your dads and away to the May pole hie." The musicians led us with their old instruments. The lovely trees and low shrubbery were well adapted to a stage setting, and the hill formed a natural background of great beauty. There were two bleachers built, each to hold about two hundred people.

The difficulties of transportation were many, and the trolleys ended at Kenwood, by the bridge over the Normanskill. They had to be met with all kinds of vehicles, as the hill was too long and too steep a walk for most people. Several stages were used, and the West Shore Railroad stopped a train at the Cornings' meadow both going down and returning to town. The round trip was fifteen cents. I had a buckboard, which held three people besides myself, and for several days beforehand I took people down. We carried a picnic lunch and spent the day rehearsing.

Many people did not understand about a play out-of-doors and said later on, when it was all over, that they would have gone if they had known how lovely it was, but they had thought it a rather funny idea. On the other hand, quite a few came from New York and from places on the river, and it was well written up, with illustrations, in several magazines. The costumes of principal players were historically accurate, and "Fair Rosamond's" blue was lovely. Even the chess board, at which King Henry and Becket played, had been copied from an original, table and all. In 1910 we gave the complete outfit and the rights to the play to the Dramatic Department of Mount Holyoke College.

My brother, John V. L. Pruyn, and Cornelia Van Rensselaer Erving were married at Grace Church Chantry in New York City at four o'clock on June 11th [1895], by Dr. Battershall. The Cornings, Rices, Mother, and I went down for it and stayed at the Holland House. There was no reception, so we returned to Albany on a late afternoon train with the best man, Howard Van Rensselaer, and Dr. Battershall.

CHAPTER 26

I N LATE JUNE [1895] MOTHER AND I went to Niagara Falls, and we stayed on both sides. . . . Mother was tired and liked the restfulness of the Falls. From there we went to Toronto to stay at the Grange as the guests of Mr. and Mrs. Goldwin Smith. They were very old friends and had often stayed with us, particularly in my father's time.

It was a lovely old place in the heart of the modern city. There was a brick wall about the grounds. It had been the property of the Bolton family. Mrs. Smith had been Mrs. Bolton, but after Mr. Bolton's death she had married the learned and famous Oxford professor, and they spent most of the year at this old place. . . .

The Smiths gave a Garden Party in our honor, and it was quite fascinating. I remember a very attractive young man invited especially to amuse me. We sat on a strawberry frame and ate strawberries. . . .

Later on I made a visit to the Mortons at Ellerslie, where I opened the wrong windows and started a burglar alarm late at night. After that I made another delightful visit to the Olivers at Murray Bay, and on July 24th Mother and I sailed for England on the *Majestic*. We found many pleasant friends on board, and we landed at Liverpool and went at once to London.

One afternoon we drove out to Holly Lodge to ask for the Baroness Burdett Coutts, who was very ill. We did not see her, but we did see Mr. Bartlett. It was a fine old place and was supposed to be where Dick Whittington heard Bow Bells say, "Turn back, Whittington, thrice Lord Mayor of London."

We went to Paris to leave some orders, then took the night train to Homburg, on which we met the largest flock of fleas yet encountered in our travels. I caught one and mailed it home as a specimen. We stayed at the Metropole, where we found Mr. and Mrs. Byam Stevens of New York, who had been on the ship with us. They were taking cures, and Mother started on one too. She chose a course of Swedish massage.

Bicycling was the fad and fashion. Mr. and Mrs. Stevens bicycled everywhere, and so did everyone else. Not having the costume with me that had created such [attention] in Albany, I had [a new outfit made] — a black cloth skirt lined with rose pink silk, which blew out and showed the pink as I went along. This was the fashion then, and a very pretty one.

Homburg in the season is an amusing place, and it was filled with people we knew, so the evenings were very gay. Dining on the upper terrace was the height of the gay world, and crowds walked along the lower terrace to watch those who were dining. There were all kinds of strange people from all parts of the world. From our part was Mrs. William Bliss of New York, a great-aunt of Bessie Oliver and a native of Albany. She invited us to a party for "200 poor people." They were to bring the articles they work with, such as axes, hones, scythes, or mops and brooms. But it was a gossipy place, and after the cure finished we were ready to move back to Paris and then to London and to sail again on the *Majestic*, where we found many more friends.

Home again, with Elk Street looking lovely at the end of September and Fromo well, I was happy. A few days later I went down to North East Harbour with Bishop Doane for Florence Gardiner's wedding to Prescott Hall of Brookline. The weather was lovely, and Mr. William C. Whitney came in his yacht with a gay party for the wedding. The weather was not only lovely but very hot. The ushers had told the groom that it was very cold, so he wore his winter underclothes and was most uncomfortable, to the general joy of the ushers.

William Rice had been appointed a United States Civil Service Commissioner, so they were going to Washington. They had first lived in the Field House of Thurlow Terrace but found it very far out and lonely. So they had bought the houses at the corner of Washington Avenue and Dove Streets and torn them down, and had Mr. Richard Hunt build a new house. . . . The Rices only lived in the new house a few weeks, then let it to the Chief Judge and Mrs. Andrews of Syracuse. . . .

In early December [1895] we had a visit from Elizabeth Lynch and Helen Lawrence, and it was during that visit that we went on the river on the skating party that was so nearly fatal to Bob Olcott and me. It was Lizzie's last day, and she was to be at the station at a quarter of eight in the evening to meet her father and mother on the train from New York and go on to Detroit with them. It was a perfect afternoon, and eight of us started gaily for the river. The signal on top of the Federal building had given us the condition of the ice. The other skaters were May Cooper and Bessie Oliver, Harry and De Witt Walsh, Bob Olcott, and Edward Reed.

We skated around for a while, and then someone suggested that we skate to Castleton and take a train home. The wind was behind us, and we could make good time. We did not even stop to inquire about the returning trains. Without giving anything any thought, we started off. We had been rather late in the starting, but we met several men skating up the river, and they said the ice was fine.

The afternoons were short, and we suddenly realized that the sun was dropping behind the Catskills, and we were far from Castleton. Bob and I were the third couple, May and Edddy Reed were behind us, the other four ahead.

Suddenly Bob and I were plunged into the water up to our necks, in the cold black river! Somehow in falling we had turned around and found ourselves facing up river. My long heavy corduroy skirt, with a fur border, was pulled out behind me by the strong current.

The tips of our skates struck into something hard. We dug them in! We grasped the edges of the ice, but they broke off in a discouraging way. The hole grew larger and larger.

There was a small lump of ice just beyond my reach. Bob said he would boost me, and I should try to take hold of it. Three times he gave me vigorous boosts. My right hand would almost clutch it. Then the current would sweep me off. It was like a terrible nightmare. Luckily, we both kept our heads and dug our toes harder, or we would have been inevitably swept under the ice.

Finally, I said I would yell for help, which I did. Then he did! Then both of us! We could see May and Eddy rushing towards us. Then May lost a skate, and it would have been funny if it had not been so critical.

Eddy rushed at us alone. Bob called to him to throw his coat on the ice. Perhaps by taking hold of a sleeve we could be pulled out without his going in too. Just as Eddy did this, Bob gave me a terrific boost. I grabbed the hump, then the sleeves, and was hauled out. Bob grabbed my arm and then the sleeve, and he scrambled out too.

The others had rushed back, and two men and a ladder came from the east shore. The men turned out to be Captain Staats and his son from Papsknee, or Staats' Island, where the Albany Canoe Club had its club house. As we stood up and shook ourselves, Captain Staats remarked, "Well, you're lucky! You went into the steamboat channel, and I said to my boy, 'They're gonners!'" Perhaps the Dutch settlers had given the Frisian Saint Lydwijna, patroness of skaters, special charge of reckless skaters on their river.

As we skated towards his house, the captain said the river had frozen early that year and then had broken up and frozen again. There must have been an ice jam held under the water where we fell in. They had been cutting ice near the west shore, and that fortunate jam was what gave us a footing and prevented our being swept under.

Captain Staats and his family were most hospitable. We were given whiskey and then taken upstairs and [dressed]. The clothes were much too small for me. An old-fashioned paisley shawl was wrapped around me to cover discrepancies. At the time I thought it all a huge joke, but May became almost hysterical, and the others had not much to say.

In the meantime, as there was no telephone, there was no way to let them know at home that we were all right but would be late. It was now dark, and even with the best of luck, Lizzie had small chance to catch her train. Captain Staats had a farm wagon with boards laid across for seats and a team of horses and a driver named Mike. It was pitch black as we came out from the firelight, but with the help of a lantern, we climbed on board. Bob sat up in front with Mike, and just before we left, Captain Staats whispered to him, "When you reach the city and Mike says he must speak to his uncle, you just tell him he cannot speak to anyone until he takes you all home."

The road was frozen ruts, and we had to go slowly along the six miles to the bridge. Every few minutes someone with a watch would strike a match and tell us the time, and we would speculate about catching the train. We had hardly crossed the Greenbush bridge when a lighted saloon was too much for Mike. He told Bob he had to speak to his uncle. But Bob put his hand firmly on his arm, and we jogged safely along holding on to the planks as we rumbled up the hill.

When we reached Eagle Street by the park, Eddy Reed dropped off, but the rest of us were headed for Elk Street. We found great excitement. Mother's coupe stood at the door. Mother, in her fur coat and bonnet, stood beside it talking to Helen Lawrence, Louis Parker, and Selden Marvin. The front door was open, and Christian stood on the steps. The Coopers' door was also open, and several Coopers were in the street.

As we jogged slowly over the pavement in our rattling wagon, nobody realized that we were the lost ones until we stopped just behind the coupe. There was a great outcry of joy and relief as we reported all were safe. Everyone was sure there must have been an accident. It was after 7:30, and

Lizzie was whisked into the coupe, with Selden as escort. She met her parents after all, but without any baggage. It was sent the next day by express.

Everyone was so excited about getting Lizzie off that I was able to slip in by the basement door and up to my room without meeting anyone who might remark on my strange apparel. I appeared later for dinner, but Louis, who had stayed, wanted to find out what happened. He asked uncomfortable questions, which I tried to evade. I was afraid that if Mother knew what had really happened, she would not allow me to skate on the river any more, so I tried to shut Louis off.

The next morning I pulled the clothes out from where I had hidden them the previous night, made a bundle, and sent it by messenger to the Olcott Bank, where Captain Staats was to call for them. I am sure the bank never had such a bundle consigned to its care before or since. I sent Bob a note of sincere thanks for what he had done.

Then as bad luck happened, James Newcomb, the coachman, came over from the stable to tell Mother something about the horses. He let the cat out of the bag by remarking that I had been fortunate to be saved from drowning in the river. Mother questioned him, and it seemed that a relative of James was a carpenter. He had been repairing the ice house on the west shore near where we fell in, and he saw it all. James happened to meet this man in the evening, so he had the story at first hand.

During the Christmas holidays there was usually a charity ball, and for some years, Mrs. William Barnes Jr. combined two charities with great success. She was interested in St. Margaret's Home for Babies and in the Old Men's Home on the Troy Road, so she called this ball "The Cradle and Grave Ball." Mrs. Barnes was unusually attractive and also very witty, and she managed the party and everything that went with it to make it attractive, too.

Mr. Billy Barnes owned the old *Albany Journal*, founded by his grandfather, Thurlow Weed. He was also a Republican leader for northern New York, and a potent force in his party. Their house on State Street was a real center. No trace of it is left, as that whole section was included in the park at the rear of the Capitol.

Our newspapers in those days were *The Argus* in the morning and *The Journal* in the evening, and we also took the combination *Times Union*,

New York World, and the *Boston Transcript*. For many years we had a separate weather report in the morning mail. I do not remember who issued it, but it was usually very nearly correct.[1]

The Home for Lost Dogs was started in 1895 by Bessie Oliver, Marie Sard and me. Bessie was president of this venture, I was treasurer, and Marie undertook to find homes for the dogs. After being kept in the shelter for a week and certified to be in good condition, they were ready to be placed in suitable homes. Our idea was purely philanthropic. There was no place where a lost or injured dog could be cared for. . . .

We invited an imposing list of men and women to invest $5.00 a year and become patrons. This plan was then printed and the list mailed out all over the city. The list was headed by the governor and the lieutenant governor, then the mayor and others. All responded to our appeal, and we soon had quite a fund.

We found an adequate wooden shack opposite the gate of the Ridgefield Athletic Club. We had wire yards enclosed, running from the door of the shack. Inside, it was divided into separate pens, and the Rathbone-Sard Company donated a stove to keep the place warm. An old man with a long white beard lived near there, and he owned a buggy and a cutter and an ancient white horse. We arranged to have him feed the dogs and keep the place clean, and also to respond to the calls through the telephone at the club by driving his vehicle and bringing the dogs in.

Charlie Weaver was in charge of the Club, and he was simply invaluable as he knew a great deal about dogs. He kept an eye on the place and advised us as to our problems. The sad part was that we had to install a gas box to put the maimed or very sick dogs to sleep after Dr. [David B.] Comstock had examined them. We had a dog cemetery not far away, but later a grape grower in the vicinity contracted for all the dead dogs to fertilize the grapes. For a long time I did not eat any grapes. We started with accommodations for twenty-five dogs, but in the first two weeks we had thirty-four. Dr. Comstock deserves our everlasting thanks. He practically gave his services, except for the expenses of medical or other necessary supplies.

The *Argus* published a long letter explaining the undertaking, but a few days later *The Journal* published a discouraging article, saying the work should be for homeless babies rather than for dogs. They described it as a "dog shelter erected and maintained at great expense by the society folks of this city." *The Telegram* came out with a funny article which I always thought was written by De Witt Walsh. It told of three philanthropists who first picked up all the street dogs and then gave them away. [It commented further] that there was deep feeling among many dog owners as to the philanthropic part of this business but that it looked to the writer more like dog thieves.

False calls began to come in, particularly on stormy nights. Our old white-bearded friend and his old white horse would patiently drive to some remote address and would not find any dog. One stormy night he made three futile trips. Another night six boys in succession, each carrying a dog, rang our door and deposited the dog in the hall, shouting, "Here's a dog for your home!" They vanished into the darkness, leaving some forlorn dog for us. We housed them in various parts of the cellar, fed them, and gave them a bed, but they separately and in chorus bayed and barked all night, while upstairs Fromo never slept a wink. He sat and howled, and we all had a sleepless night.

In the end the Mohawk and Hudson River Humane Society was started, principally by Dr. [William O.] Stillman. One of the bills in the Legislature was for licensing dogs. He established a shelter in a convenient place back of Harmanus Bleecker Hall and had a dog ambulance and a modern set-up. So we decided to disband after two years of our probably rather amateur efforts. I once had the statistics of how many dogs were placed, how many were cured, and how many had to be killed, but the records seem to have vanished.

After all our expenses were settled, we had several hundred dollars on hand. We thought of a brilliant scheme, to erect a horse and dog fountain in the city.

The spot we set our hearts on was in front of the Federal building at the foot of State Street, the most crowded place in the city. The Postmaster was polite but not enthusiastic. He said there was a law prohibiting obstructions in front of Federal property. This building came under the domain of the Treasury, so I took up the question with Mr. Charles S. Hamlin, just then finishing his term as an Assistant Secretary of the Treasury. He wrote that it would be a difficult job, but he would take it up with Secretary Carlisle. After some delay the permission was granted as a special dispensation.

Having obtained the consent of the subscribers to this use of the money, we ordered a plain granite fountain with two lower basins for the dogs. It was inscribed as being placed with funds left over from the Home for Lost Dogs. From the first the trouble was that the good citizens of the city seemed to consider the fountain a place for newspaper wrappers and envelopes, and the pipes were always being stopped up and water overflowing. In later years the fountain was moved further up on Broadway, and then it vanished. So ended the Home for Lost Dogs.

❦ ❦ ❦

Christmas week was not so gay as the previous winter. Edith Morton was in Colorado, Lena rather an invalid, and Helen preferred New York, but Governor and Mrs. Morton had many dinners and receptions and always delightful guests from New York or Washington. At the Edison Company in Schenectady there were agreeable young men who came down by train for the dances.

Comte de Kermel was a distant relative of the Mortons, and there was the little Italian, Marquis Serra di Cassano, introduced by Mrs. Howard Townsend. There was the young handsome Venezuelan Andrade, who fell in love with Alice Duer when she was staying with us. It happened at the dinner table between soup and dessert. He was completely bowled over.

The Dancing Class was continued, although the Crosbys were not in Albany that winter. We had the Kenmore Assemblies, and the young married people had a series of dinner dances. They also included us, and we had one dance at our house.

Harriet Corning and Jenny Wasson got up a Leap Year dance [where all social conventions were reversed] at the Odd Fellows Hall in January [1896]. . . . Each gentleman had some kind of a basket or bouquet of flowers. Mine went to Mr. Olcott. It was a basket with a tall handle. In the bottom was a stone to make it heavy, and in the top was a mass of various colored immortelles. We stipulated that the flowers must be held by them during the reception.

I have his note of thanks in which he says, "It produced some envy in the breasts of those about me, this short triumph I enjoyed, of course." I had evidently found fault with the way he had served my supper, as he goes on, "I have taken to heart and shall hereafter know in what order to serve supper to a young lady hungry after the strong exercise of dancing. It shall not be one of those hard, slippery balls of ice first, followed by hot oysters and substantials. I suppose I have followed this order of things often, but never, never again."

Harriet and Jenny had whistles, and they led the cotillion. We had let the men know that we had no partners and would dance stag and so leave them to ornament the chairs, to be, in fact, wallflowers. It was to be a severe lesson to them in the often selfish way they had left girls without partners and danced stag themselves. . . .

That was the winter that Bill Sheldon got up a set of lectures to try to uplift Albany mentally. The lecturer was the well-known Professor William Graham Sumner of Yale. He came over once a week for about six weeks, and he stayed with us. He was a brilliant and interesting guest and lecturer. The course was given in the evening, and he was generally invited out to a dinner beforehand or to a late supper. The course was, I think, appreciated, and was well attended, though Aunt Kitty Lansing, who went only once, said it was too uplifting for her — that it was way beyond her brain.

[Parker Corning had been ill, so during his vacation he and I] had gone to Washington to stay with the Rices. I stayed on after he left, but [was called home abruptly with] news of the sudden death of Katharine V. R. Arnold, leaving a baby girl only ten days old. The Arnolds lived on Ten Broeck Street, and the funeral was at the house. Everyone felt it very much. Two weeks later the other Katharine Van Rensselaer died in New York of appendicitis. It was all very tragic.

Some time that winter Mother and I spent a weekend with Mr. and Mrs. James Roosevelt at Hyde Park. Franklin was at school. There were one or two other guests. One was Mr. Will Blodgett. And I went to Hyde Park again for ice boating at Colonel and Mrs. Archibald Rogers.

Colonel Rogers owned the fastest iceboat on the river, the "Ice King," and we had some wonderful sails. The river was dotted with ice boats, and many of them waited by the tracks to catch the wind made by the fast trains. Colonel Rogers had fun for himself by heading for the cliffs on the opposite shore. Then, just as it seemed that a crash was inevitable, he would suddenly veer off. He said later that he was waiting for me to scream or say something. At last I did so, and he stopped. We had really almost touched.

One lovely day we sailed far down the river, jumping the cracks in some miraculous way, a wonderful sensation. The three little Rogers boys each had his own boat, and one of them was thrown out with a big whack, but Colonel Rogers was not disturbed. He said they had to learn.

My bicycle outfit brought from Paris the previous year would have been just the right thing to wear for ice boating, but there had been such a fuss about it that I gave it up. Several newspapers wrote it up, and older people like Mrs. Evans protested to Mother about it.[2]

We kept our bicycles at a repair shop on Willett Street and started from there on the asphalt of Madison Avenue or in the park. Sometimes we went out in the evenings and had supper later at some house, just as we had done in the toboggan era. A good bicycle then cost $100, and there were clubs all over the country. They even managed to run over the hopelessly bad roads from one city to another, with great enthusiasm. The road to the Country Club was half plank, and that made it possible to use a bicycle in going home, but when it was the first club in the sand plains, you had to walk from the main road and push the wheel.

That spring of 1896 Mother and I went to St. Augustine for a change and stayed at the Ponce de Leon. We were comfortable but very hot. The climate was very enervating. Mr. Sard was there, and we bathed every day, and we went to a cake-walk with a party of friends. It was very amusing to see a real cake-walk. Toward the end of April, Louise Parker and Harry Sweny were married one noon at St. Peter's by Dr. Battershall. Just the family and a few friends were there, and there was no reception.

Mother and I had stopped in Washington to visit the Rices on our way home in early April. The Misses Riggs . . . gave an old fashioned reception with dancing and invited us. . . .

Miss Janey Riggs introduced Assistant Secretary of the Treasury, Mr. Charles S. Hamlin to me. He invited me to dance. It was a waltz. He said later that when we got once around the drugget, I stopped and said to him that I thought he had better say that he did not dance. He decided that was good advice and was interested that I had been so outspoken.

When the Rices had told me they were going to Washington and I must visit them, I had said that I would come if they would find a new beau for me. When they returned for Christmas, they told of meeting a very attractive and able young man from Boston who was an Assistant Secretary of the Treasury and was living on Massachusetts Avenue with his two sisters. [A full year had passed before the introduction took place.]

In May we went on the last of the four famous Santanoni parties. . . . None of us had any idea that it would be our last, but the next spring Mrs. Pruyn was very ill, and only several men went up for fishing. Two years later Mabel Sard and I were both on the verge of our weddings.

On June 6th Mother had a cable telling of the birth of John V. L. Pruyn Jr. at Florence, Italy. Later came a letter from Jack asking me to be the godmother, which pleased me greatly. I was a bridesmaid in June to Cornelia Battershall, who married Dr. Harry Pearse at St. Peter's. . . .

🍂   🍂   🍂

That was the summer of the Democratic Convention in Chicago. Mr. Hamlin stopped over at Albany, but I was at the Mortons' at Ellerslie for the Fourth of July. He stopped again on his return to tell us the details of that disastrous convention, which was carried away by the "Cross of Gold" speech of William J. Bryan. Mr. Hamlin, as well as many others, bolted the ticket and formed a Gold Party ticket at Indianapolis a few weeks later, with Palmer and Buckner for their candidates.

That summer of 1896 we spent at the Pearl Island camp on the Upper St. Regis Lake. The Cornings rented a camp on Spitfire Lake between the upper and lower St. Regis Lakes. The Mortons took the Twombly camp, and the Archie Rogers took one close by, the big Stokes island camp. The Whitelaw Reids were across our lake.

We went by night train and got off at the Lake Clear station, where buckboards met us and took us to the landing, and we were rowed over from there. Our camp was picturesque, and in wet weather it only leaked a little bit. We all slept in tents. There was one bedroom over the boat house, which was kept for guests.

We entered the tents by a rear flap, so in front there would be a small piazza overlooking the lake. It had steps down to the water, so it was most convenient for bathing. The tents had wooden platform floors and a closet for hanging clothes. The main house had a living room with a large picture window and a dining room with a window framing St. Regis mountain. In the rear was a pantry and a kitchen.

Mr. Larom, the rector of Saranac Lake, had engaged a guide named Lowell Brown. His wife was the cook, so we lived mostly on pies, pancakes, doughnuts and fried foods of all kinds. Lowell considered us all "city suckers." He told us the most awful lies! He had always just seen an extra large deer or fish or bear. He rushed in one day and begged us to row hard to the landing, where a man he knew had just shot an enormous wildcat. The man was from the Hoe camp, and the animal was a large skunk. . . .

The Mortons' camp was more like a large country house. One evening we had a play there . . . for some charity. . . . Grace Parker and I had quite big parts, but we did not take it seriously and did not learn our lines, much to the exasperation of Lena Morton. She was getting it up and had invited the neighboring camps to come over and buy tickets. We made up as we went along. In the places where we forgot the lines, we got gales of laughter, and the governor laughed too, and we had an hilarious evening, so it ended well.

Dr. and Mrs. Morgan Dix and their family had a cottage at Paul Smith's. We saw a great deal of them, and the doctor and I became warm friends. We also saw Dr. Trudeau and his family, particularly Ned, who gave Grace a big rush. When we went to the Rogers' island or the Reids' camp, we were welcomed by a footman in full uniform who helped us out of the boat as it docked. Mother and I dined with the Reids and he told us of his pleasure in "roughing it" for a few weeks. Our "rough" dinner consisted of five courses with champagne and other wines, with a butler and two footmen to serve us.

We had guests all summer, of course, and one who occupied the boat house room was Charles Hamlin. He had been greatly shocked by the sudden death of Governor Billy Russell of Massachusetts while vacationing at a camp. Many felt that [Russell] should have been the candidate for the Presidency that year. Mr. Hamlin called formally on Governor Morton with his official card. Behold, the next day the kindly governor, rowed by two guides, came quickly, in great style and a silk hat, to return the call on a Federal official. Politics was the great topic of conversation, even in camp. The Republicans had nominated McKinley and Hobart, and it was a foregone conclusion that they would win against our split party.

The leading event of that summer was our trip to rough camp. Aunt Mary Corning had talked about it all summer, and at last we were to go. The place picked by Lowell Brown was on St. Regis pond. We rowed to a landing a mile across from our camp, and from there we walked.

Anna Parker carried a copy of Hugo's *Les Miserables*. Edwin had a small bag of worms for bait. I carried a blueberry pie, a mince pie, and ginger cakes. We all carried tooth brushes, and there were several brandy flasks. I was the only one who brought a nightgown, and the heat was intolerable to the others, who somehow thought you had to sleep in your clothes.

We had a night of it. Lowell had built two beds of boughs with hemlock, spread over with rubber and blankets. They were hot and uncomfortable. Aunt Mary and Harriet had the small one, while Miss Scofield, Anna Parker, and I had the larger one.

Rain started about one. It poured in torrents, and it leaked in! Anna and I had a puddle between us, and the midges were thick. Harriet got up and said if we hurried we could get home for breakfast. In the meantime she played "Idiot's delight" on a stump.

In the morning Miss Scofield, Edwin, Otie Peckham, and I went bathing, all stopping to brush our teeth in the shallow water. After another meal of heavy biscuits, Edwin and I went fishing with Lowell Brown for several hours, in the rain. When we returned to camp, we found the party all stretched out and determined to go home. Edwin and I wanted to stay. We said the first night was the hard one, and we argued, but to no purpose.

After another hopeless meal we packed and departed. The rain came down in torrents all the way, and we were a bedraggled-looking lot when we reached home. Mother chuckled at our rough camp experience.

We left Pearl Island in late September with many regrets. Mother and I went to Montreal for a week or so, as she was very tired.

Harriet Corning and Rufus W. Peckham Jr. had been engaged for some months, and their wedding was planned for October [1896]. Aunt Anna French and I had offered to direct the invitations, and we used the top floor library at the Cornings' house at 87 State Street. We worked there in the mornings and afternoons for about two weeks.

I went down to stay at the Mortons' for Alida Chanler's wedding to Christopher Temple Emmett. . . . We all drove over in an omnibus to the wedding at the little church in Red Hook, and then we drove to "Rokeby" for the reception.

It was the loveliest day possible. Mr. Stanford White had taken charge of the decorations and had hung tapestries from the windows on the front. The tables were on the piazza and the lawn. . . . It was a radiant scene with the Catskills standing out in the distance across the river. I wanted to take an early train from Barrytown, as Harriet's wedding was the next day, but Willy Chanler forgot to get one of the carriages to come for me. Langdon tried to fix it, but in the end I returned with the Mortons and went up to Albany on a late train.

Harriet's wedding was at noon in the choir at the Cathedral. She looked very handsome in her white satin dress made by Lodaux. We sat in the stalls, and there were just enough people to fill them well. . . .

Some years before this Harriet and I had had a bet. I do not remember what the bet was about, but I lost. The bet was that whoever lost should give a toothbrush to the winner. I bought a small brush, labeled on the handle "Papa's Pet," and Harriet did not like this at all.

She gave it back to me in some way, and we kept up this back and forth game. I had managed to tie it into the wedding bouquet, and after that she kept it until my wedding, when she managed to sew it into the hem of my wedding dress. I have the old brush in its silver case. . . .

Mother and I were in New York in early December. We had always stayed at the Holland House ever since it was opened in the winter of 1892. It was a marvel to everyone with the latest in hotel comforts, and it was a great contrast to the old hotels like the Cambridge, Brevoort, or Buckingham. One of the inventions was a "Teleseme." This was a flat disk set in the wall of every room. It had a long finder, and you could order about one hundred different things, including many kinds of food, drinks, a messenger, newspapers, cigars, etc.

One warm April morning Mrs. John Erving was to come to see Mother at eleven o'clock. When she arrived, she said she was very hot and would like a glass of water. Mother immediately put on her glasses and went to the teleseme and pointed at "Ice Water." She pushed the red button to call attention to the order downstairs, and a buzz answered it. The two old friends sat there talking about modern inventions and how this new one did away with the nuisance of bell boys.

Then, suddenly, Mother realized that the ice water was long overdue, and she went to the teleseme again. Just then there was a commotion in the hall, the sound of voices, and a knock on the door. On opening it, [she found] two waiters with a large table covered with a white cloth. Reposing on the center was a metal bucket of ice with the neck of a champagne bottle standing out. Mother had made the mistake of ordering champagne instead of water for two respectable Victorian ladies at eleven in the morning!

On this particular visit in December of 1896, we went to a musicale at the Miss Dunhams', to hear the Adamowskis. A most memorable evening it was. The Blodgetts were there, and Will Blodgett went on with us to the Assembly Ball given at the Waldorf, the newest and most famous of hotels, on the corner of Fifth Avenue and 34th Street, on the site of the William Astors' house. Mrs. William Astor herself received the guests. . . . We had supper in the main dining room, which seemed a mass of overpowering and over-decorated marbles and woods. . . .

We had had great interest in the election in November, although we had all felt that McKinley would be elected on account of the bolt from Bryan. But it took the Republicans a large sum of money and eighteen thousand speakers to beat Bryan, who really fought his fight almost alone, as far as speaking was concerned. Mrs. Henry Cabot Lodge in a letter to Sir Cecil Spring Rice tells just what a close fight it was.

During the campaign little Bill Rice was staying with us, and I thought to please him very much by making a pumpkin lantern for him. I brought home an extra large one and decorated it with a fierce black mustache with the blacking sponge, also black eyebrows and hair. I was pleased with my attentions to my nephew as I lighted a candle in it and placed it by the head of the stairs, where it would burst on him when he went to bed. He had his supper downstairs and came into the library with his nurse to say good night. As I sipped my tea, I waited for the shouts of joy.

But alas. What we heard were shrieks and howls and a patter of feet on the stairs as he ran sobbing into the library. Indignant grandmother and nurse took a long time to pacify the child, while I was sternly told to take the lantern away — anywhere.

My work was quite a success, and why destroy it? Just at this moment I saw Mrs. Farnsworth and Emma going up the street. Here was a chance to place the lantern in their small bow window, which commanded a view of the whole street.

I carried it over, and Katy opened the door. I explained it to her. She was friendly but not enthusiastic. However, when I showed her how well it looked, she agreed.

In a few minutes we heard the sound of a band. It was coming over Hawk Street towards the viaduct. The leader saw the bright light of the pumpkin, and there were shouts, "Three cheers for Bryan! Give them a serenade!"

In a moment the street was filled with the procession and many other people. "There's a hot time in the old town tonight," brought everyone to their windows. Between times, the leader shouted, "Three cheers for the peerless Bryan — sixteen to one!"

But at this point Mrs. Farnsworth appeared from somewhere. She called out, "Down with Bryan! This is a McKinley house! You should be ashamed not to support the man who went to the Albany Law School!" She rushed in, picked up the unlucky pumpkin, and threw it into the street. "There's Bryan, where he belongs!"

Katy was called in and asked where the pumpkin came from, but she was loyal and kept quiet. Finally I emerged to save her from any blame. The band and crowd vanished, and all was quiet as I made my way home.

The Rices came up from Washington for Christmas, and Hattie and I gave a small german at Graduates Hall for Harriet Parker. Mother had a dinner, but she had not been well and did not feel up to giving a large dance, such as she had given Anna Parker at Odd Fellows Hall the previous winter.

Governor Morton did not run again. He and Mrs. Morton and two of their children came to stay with us over the New Year and the transition period of moving out of the Executive Mansion and the inauguration. The new governor was Frank Black of Troy. The new lieutenant governor was Timothy L. Woodruff of Brooklyn.

The Woodruffs took the Sweny house at 5 Elk Street. Everyone on the block was interested to see all their beautiful horses and turn-outs and the lieutenant governor's fancy waistcoats. In the evening he wore white satin with jeweled buttons or else black satin with gay buttons. In the day time the waistcoats were of plaids and stripes, and sometimes in the late afternoon, of dark brocades. His sports clothes were baggy trousers, or rather knicker-bockers, with coat and vest of the same material, usually plaids or loud checks. The golf stockings were something to see, while the caps over one ear brought all Elk Street to their windows.

It was for Mrs. Paul Fenimore Cooper to discover the real sensation, however. Mrs. Cooper sat by a window looking over the Academy Park and lower Elk Street. She sat there with her sewing or knitting, and one could recognize the white lace cap with a pink or blue bow watching all comers.

She became much interested in the appearance of the Woodruffs' English coachman. He wore the very smartest English outfits and had the air of being most distinguished himself. In some way known only to herself, Mrs. Cooper found out that Elk Street was harboring the former coachman of the "Jersey Lily," Lily Langtry, then only too famous all over the world [as an actress and woman of extraordinary beauty]. What had Elk Street come to in such degenerate days, and what to do about it? The lieutenant governor had brought this on Elk Street, and to make it more exciting, the coachman was said to have a large photograph of the fair Lily in the stable on Spruce Street, and the only uncertain item was whether or not she had signed it. Mrs. Cooper said that many people had suddenly developed an interest in Spruce Street but would not own up to it.

Mrs. John Clinton Gray was always a woman of action. She was deter-mined to find out about that photograph, so she drove to the stable and found the coachman. He was proud to show her the photograph, with "Yours Sincerely, Lily Langtry" signed on it.

Mrs. Gray had the facts, but still there was a fluttering indecision on Elk Street. What should be done about further hospitality? Miss Barnard said the name of the Lily was not to be mentioned in her house. Mrs. Doane and her sister Miss Condit had a heart-to-heart talk about whether to invite the Woodruffs to a dinner already planned.

It was sad, in those degenerate days, that many people thought this incident funny and others had no thoughts on the subject at all. It was "Fin de Siecle," so many queer things happened — this accounted for all. Clothes, furniture, food, and usual parties were all given this label for several years.[3]

On a cold Sunday afternoon in January, Catherine Walsh Peltz was baptized at St. Peter's. Nelly Robb was a godmother. She was staying with us. About thirty people, relations and friends, were there.

Everything happened according to schedule until Dr. Battershall said "Name the child." Nelly gave the name and handed the baby up to the doctor, who perched her nicely on his left arm while he started to dip his right hand fingers into the water in the font. . . . Now, just at the wrong moment, the sleeve of Dr. Battershall's surplice caught the chain of the stopper, and out went the water with a whir-r-r-r. The doctor looked gravely at the empty bowl and handed the baby back to Nelly, who sank down on a bench.

Bridgeford, the sexton, was seen approaching at a run down the side aisle from the choir door, carrying a large white pitcher, and the ice in it rattled. The water, ice and all, was poured into the bowl, and the service proceeded as before. Then the same thing happened again; the water ran out.

By this time most of us were ready to collapse. I took refuge in a pew far enough away so as not to have my feelings show, and Nelly and the baby returned to the bench. Another pitcher of water was brought, without ice this time. The water was poured in, and everything went well until the end. . . . The baby was a girl, but Dr. Battershall said, "May he grow up to an unholy but righteous life, Amen." . . .

It was during that winter that the Junior Friday Morning Club was started. I think it met on another day at first, but Friday seemed to be more convenient. Mrs. Chauncey P. Williams's Friday Morning Club had been in existence for about ten years and was very successful. In fact we looked up to the members with awe and admiration, feeling sure we never could be one of the chosen ones, or at least not for many years. Lily Read came over to our house one afternoon full of plans for starting a new club. She had talked it over with Mrs. Wallace, the wife of Judge Wallace and her neighbor on State Street, and she had a list of names of persons to be invited.

Everyone thought it a good idea, and we soon started meetings. May Wasson, Daisy Pruyn, Bessie Oliver, Marie Sard, Emma Rathbone, and Sarah Lansing, were some of the founding members, and more were elected the second year — like Emma Farnsworth. I think Lily Reed was the first president and had the first meeting. I was a member for the two years before I married. . . .

CHAPTER 27

I SPENT A GREAT PART of that winter [1897] in Washington. My sister was a very strict chaperone, even in that time. When a busybody reported to her that I had been seen walking cross-lots at Boundary in order to reach 16th Street, accompanied by the Assistant Secretary of the Treasury, she took me severely to task. I must walk on sidewalks or stay at home. She would not be responsible for me otherwise.

When I returned to Albany, it was Lent. We did not keep Lent so strictly any more. In my childhood we were not allowed to take a meal outside the house except on Sundays, and we had either stewed prunes or baked apples for dessert every night. We ate no cake or candy or even drank soda water, and my sister tried her soul by cutting buttonholes in heavy pieces of cotton and sewing them, as a Lenten penance. She never cared for sewing, so she made these buttonholes in cotton, silk, and wool.

Mother read to us in the evenings in the library. Several of the books I remember were Miss Mulock's *John Halifax, Gentleman*, *The Schoenberg Cotter Family*, *Angelica Kauffman's Life*, and delightful *Quits*.[1] I usually sewed my dolls' clothes. We had an open fire, and there was a gas light on each side of the mantelpiece, with very poor light, according to present standards.

During Holy Week we went to church with the school. On Holy Thursday we went to the Cathedral of the Immaculate Conception on the first hill to hear the beautiful "Tenebra" service. Then came Good Friday, and in the afternoon we were allowed to eat Mrs. Maidment's delicious hot cross buns with sugar crosses. Grandmother always ordered ten dozen of them to give away, mostly to the grandchildren.

But somehow these strict Lents oozed out as we grew older. The new Lenten gaiety was started with the arrival of the two representatives of the L. P. Hollander Company of Boston, Miss Hyde and Miss Lane, showing their spring and summer fashions at Stanwix Hall on Broadway.[2] The exhibition lasted three days, and all Albany flocked to it. We tried on a dress, and if it was what we wanted, our measurements were taken very carefully, and the dress, made in Boston, arrived in about a month.

Fitting a dress at that time was a difficult matter. The boned collars and the leg-of-mutton sleeves were hard enough to get right, even when you had two or three fittings. Then there was always trouble about the length of the skirt, and how it hung, and where the pocket should be placed (for looks — never for convenience, as they were always hard to find). So this system [of the Hollander Company] never worked very well, but we kept trying it year after year.

Bustles were another difficulty. If not properly adjusted, the dress sagged badly, and no matter what they were made of, bustles were hot and uncomfortable. Lily Read wore very large ones. One day she dropped [her bustle] on State Street, and a man picked it up and said as he handed it to her, "Fine feathers make fine birds!"

I have an old newspaper description of a surprise party we gave for Rensselaer Erving during that Lent. He was staying in my brother's house, 270 State Street, while Jack and Nina were at Lakewood with their baby, who was not at all well. We sent Bill Sheldon to have dinner with Rensselaer, so that he would not go to the club. We gathered at Dr. Ward's house across the street, at 281 State Street. There were about fifteen of us. Several had arrived in fancy dress, and others wore black masks.

We crossed the street together, and as the door latch had been left open, we burst into the house with terrific noises of howling and hooting, and we all ran all about. Rensselaer came down from the library, and in his polite and courteous way bade us welcome and even added that he was glad to see us. Fred Kelley started a game of "Going to Jerusalem," which proceeded fast and furiously, while Mrs. Dunkin Van Rensselaer Johnston sang "The Lost Chord." We had charades in the hall and took the word "Rensselaer." Learned or B. Hand was a wren. He was dressed in a heavy winter undershirt of my brother's put on upside down, that is, his legs were in the arms, and he picked up crumbs from the floor and made queer noises.

We had pooled our funds and hired a hand organ man to play for three hours without stopping. He earned five dollars. The tunes were "Darling I am growing old," "In the gloaming, O' my darling, when the lights are dim and low," the "Blue Danube," and "Dolce Napoli." No doubt some of the neighbors tried to stop the music, as we heard the telephone ring over and over, but we had no time to answer it. We spied a policeman in the street after the door bell had rung frantically. He talked to the organ grinder, who shook his head over and over.

We had ordered a large block of ice cream, with a cat sitting on it, from Mason's. The cat had blue glass eyes. We cut off the long curled tail for Rensselaer and the head for B. Hand. Grace Parker and Sue Ransom had provided a large bag of peanuts, and we gave six at a time for prizes for answering questions. We asked Jim Cooper, "Did you have a grandfather?" Bessie Oliver and I felt that the newspapers deserved to have this story of Lenten gaiety, so we telephoned each of them and gave the names of the self-invited guests, [noting] that the James Fenimore Coopers were the chaperones and that the supper consisted of ice cream and peanuts. One paper published an article, with a sarcastic comment as to the strange doings of modern "society." Anyway the party was a complete success, and we carried a supper out to the faithful organ grinder to refresh his energy so he could carry on to the end.

As a contrast to this noisy evening, I will tell of another evening to which I was "promoted" when I was seventeen. This was the wedding anniversary of dinner at Mr. and Mrs. Theodore Townsends' at 39 Elk Street, every June 15th. Mr. and Mrs. Townsend had given the matter of inviting me much thought, but they evidently decided that I would soon put away childish things and forbear to "black up." . . .

So I had a note from Mrs. Townsend, inviting me for seven o'clock. On the morning of the fifteenth Miss Julia Treadwell drove up, in a Harris hack, from her house on Broadway, to spend the day with Mrs. Townsend. She had been her bridesmaid. Mrs. Treadwell was dressed in white, and Mrs. Townsend, also in white, had a blue bow on her lace cap. The two old friends sat in the front room upstairs and talked of the past and especially of the wedding. I used to join them for a few minutes, bringing some of our garden flowers, and so it came about that I was invited to the annual dinner. I used to wonder, as I ran home, if I ever would be married for so many years and would sometime celebrate my wedding anniversary in this way. It seemed far off then. . . .

As we sat at dinner in the June evening the windows were open, and we could hear the clopping of the horses on the viaduct close by. When dinner was over, the ladies adjourned to the front room, leaving the dining room to the men. We talked of summer plans — the Townsends always went to the Adirondacks, — of the plans of the neighbors, of the Gardiner children's latest clothes from London, and what Bishop Doane had said to his friend the Archbishop of Canterbury. Dr. Battershall saw me home when the party broke up a little after nine. The Harris hacks had already come to convey the Thachers to tree-lined South Hawk Street, and Miss Treadwell to Broadway.

❦   ❦   ❦

We were greatly saddened by the death, after weeks of illness, of little John V. L. Pruyn. His illness was at first thought to be from his teeth, but complications arose. There were no baby specialists in Albany at that time. I always thought that if he had been hurried to Dr. Holt in New York, he would have been saved.[3]

❧   ❧   ❧

Mother and I sailed on the *Majestic* again [June 1897], and Langdon and Rensselaer Erving and Langdon Marvin came to see us off. Mr. and Mrs. Byam Stevens had reserved a table for ten. Besides Mother and me, some of the others were Mr. George Morgan, Mr. David Bishop, and his son Cortland, and Miss Davidge. The Harvard crew was on board, going over to race at Henley. . . .

We arrived in London in the early afternoon of a lovely July day and went to the Bristol Hotel, Burlington Gardens. As I stood in the window watching the passing crowds, I was attracted to an open Victoria with two gay-looking older women sitting on the back seat. It stopped at the hotel, and to my astonishment Mrs. Doane and Miss Amy Townsend of New York got out, and in a few minutes they came up to our sitting room.

The Doanes and Miss Townsend were guests of Mr. J. P. Morgan at his house in Prince's Gate. It was the year of the Pan-Anglican Conference, and the Doanes had sailed as soon as the St. Agnes Commencement was over. Bishop Lawrence of Massachusetts was also a guest there, and the house was in charge of Hans, who had for many years been with Mr. Morgan.

Bishop Doane came in later. They were all enthusiastic about the crozier that Mother had had made at Child and Child's in London. I had never been told about this "Holy Stick," as we irreverently called it. Mother liked a secret.

She had ordered it over a year earlier. When the Doanes reached London, Mr. Child delivered it at the Morgans' house. Mother had received a mysterious cable one morning about three weeks before we sailed, and I had never known what it was about, but now it could be told to me. The cable was sent by Bishop Doane to thank Mother for her surprise gift. It was a beautiful piece of workmanship, and it was beautifully cared for in a large box made especially for it. Later Mother had a book made at the Merrymount Press in Boston, with a picture and description of the crozier, but I never could see much good in it.

Two nights later we dined at Mr. Morgan's, and Mrs. Doane presided. I sat next to Bishop Lawrence, and he was delightful. . . . He told a funny story about a young curate at the meeting at Lambeth that morning. The curate was in charge of the commissary department for the Conference, and in the midst of questions of worldwide importance, he asked for time and read a long report about sour bread that had been furnished by the London Aerated Bread Company and their many excuses. We were the only ones who laughed at the [bishop's] very clever imitation of the little curate's voice and manner. The others looked solemn. In fact, Miss Townsend never spoke all through dinner. . . .

After dinner Miss Townsend asked me to walk with her in the garden in the late English twilight. She wanted a friend. She told me about the dinner a few nights before, when Mrs. Doane had forgotten how many bishops and their wives she had invited. First she counted in Miss Townsend, then when she was dressing, she sent word that she had better have her dinner sent up, as they were short of places. Then when her dinner had been sent up and she was in a tea gown reading comfortably, Mrs. Doane sent word that a bishop had arrived without a wife, so would she please come down. But that was too much, and she went to bed. I laughed so hard that finally she saw the funny side and felt better. . . .

We were sorry to leave, but we crossed to Paris and the delights of an entresol at the Bristol. In Paris we gave our orders for clothes and left by the day train for Basle. From there we went to Lucerne to see Mrs. Franklin Delano, who was now a very old lady, and to spend a few weeks at the Schweitzerhof. Mrs. Delano was most kind and hospitable but given to long drives in the hot sun and the dust of those days. Mother drove with her in a Victoria. Her great nephew, Jean de Steurs of Holland, who was younger than I was, and I drove in a huge, heavy landau. We were almost eaten by horse flies.

One night when we were dining with Mrs. Delano and Jean, the chaplain of the American Church, Rev. Mr. Allen of Boston was also a guest. He was most abusive of everything American and said really terrible things about his native land. I was hot and tired and a bit cross over the horse flies, and I raged at him. I was impertinent enough to ask if he did not receive an American salary. I also said I was going to report him to Bishop Doane, who at that time had the care of our churches in Europe. Luckily Mrs. Delano was deaf, but Mother gathered me up as soon as she could, and the next day, Sunday, we went to the English Church.

Mrs. Delano seemed to be glad to have us. She said she was very lonely. The day she left for Bayreuth, we went to Vevey. We stayed some time at the comfortable Grand Hotel, where our balcony overlooked the lake. I went bathing every morning while Mother had a good rest, and in the afternoons we usually took a drive. I will always associate hours of reading two of Sienkiewitz's books with that balcony and with that last trip to Europe that I made alone with Mother.[4]

I was sorry to leave the peace and quiet of Vevey, but we moved on to the Beau Rivage at Ouchy, and the following day we took a boat across the lake to Evian-les-Bains, in Savoy. From there we drove to the Chateau de Marclaz to visit Marie Read de Foras, my old friend. Mrs. Meredith Read was Miss Pumpelly of One Elk Street. She was also there as well as Meredith and Mr. and Mrs. Harmon Read.

It was a quaint and roomy old place, and Mrs. Read had done a great deal to modernize it in the way of plumbing. Marie had a little girl of her own, Huguette, and also a stepson. The place was full of relatives and the Vicomte de Waldaon with his phaeton. The old Comte and Comtesse de Foras lived not far away at the Chateau de Thuiset, with its lovely gardens.

One day all of us except Mother and Mrs. Read went in a large brake up the Valley of the Durance — a wild and beautiful drive. We had our luncheon, with delicious omelette, at the Auberge de Montbelliat. We went down into the Gorge du Diable, a rather perilous trail with slippery wooden stairs, rocks to climb over, and a wild river racing below us. Harmon Read lost his hat over the gorge. He started to try to get it, but Max de Foras pulled him back just in time.

We spent several days with the old friends. Then we returned to Ouchy and on to Geneva, where we were lucky enough to see Mount Blanc in the sunset, with snow glistening and a moon rising — a glorious sight!. Who should turn up but Dean Sage with Rex Finck of Utica! I was certainly glad to see them. They dined with us, and I went sailing with them. We took lovely drives to Coppet and Ferney and many other places, and then we returned to Paris.

From Paris we went down to Orleans, stayed at the "Univers" at Tours, and drove all through that lovely country, stopping to see the various chateaux. It is simple and easy now to see the Loire country, but then the horses were poor, the harness apt to be broken, and the dust heavy. While at the Chateau d'Usse, a man on a bicycle joined us. We knew at once that he came from Boston by his accent. He also spoke excellent French.

We drove on to Azay-le-Rideau, with the Indre flowing about it so charmingly — a lovely spot outside, but inside it was a disappointment. The Bostonian turned up again. It is almost useless to try to describe all those wonderful chateaux. We ended the tour by deciding that probably Blois was the most fascinating of all.

We returned to Paris and found it full of friends. Mother saw in the *Paris Herald* that Judge Fiero of Albany was in Paris, but the paper gave no address. There was an alarm of fire, and from the noise and confusion, we knew it must be close by. I told Mother that if she would only let me run out, I was sure I would find Mr. Fiero, because anyone who lived in Albany always went to fires.

I ran after the crowd on the Rue St. Honore, and although the fire turned out to be a small one, and the hose not nearly long enough to reach the third storey, there, sure enough, was Mr. Fiero. I brought him back to the Bristol in triumph. . . .

The last morning that we were there I came late to breakfast and told Mother I had had a most vivid dream. We seemed to be arriving at Albany. The carriage met us, and as we drove up to the house, Aunt Mary Corning came down the steps with her hand out in a welcoming gesture that was very characteristic. But she was dressed in the deepest mourning and wore a heavy veil thrown back from her face. It was very real to me, and I was bothered, but Mother laughed and said I must have been over-tired or have eaten something that disagreed with me.

We went over to London to the Bristol on Burlington Gardens. We had our return passage for September 15th, on the White Star liner. . . .

I had several commissions to do for Uncle Erastus Corning. He and Aunt Mary had come to say good-bye to us [the afternoon when we left for Europe]. . . . He had seemed sad and depressed, but he asked me to buy a certain kind of pipe and overcoat and several other things for him in London. I had found them all, and they were packed.

The de Billes had taken a place called "The Hall" at Finedon, and we went down there for the weekend. . . . The next morning, while I was dressing, Marie came to my room and said that Mother wanted me at once in her room. Mother handed me a cable from Parker Corning, saying his father had died suddenly Sunday night. The dream came back to me. That was the warning and the reason for Aunt Mary's deep mourning.

We left at once for London. Mother's one idea was to try to get on the *Teutonic* sailing the next day, as she was greatly upset and distressed. Mother took one list of steamer agencies and I another, but it was the crowded season, and it looked as if we would have to wait until the 15th until I went in to tell the Mortons. The governor told me he had the refusal of an extra deck room on the *St. Paul*, for Saturday, when he and Lena and Helen, were to sail. I rushed back to tell Mother, and she was very grateful. We had only two days left but managed to get some black clothes altered or made at Jay's.

The last afternoon everyone was busy, and Marie was at home with her daughter, so, as a great concession, Mother allowed me to go out alone to do some necessary errands. Just as I came out of the Burlington Arcade on Piccadilly, I saw a horseless carriage — as motors were called then. I waved it to a stop, and a crowd collected at once. I felt embarrassed and was sure that Mother never would trust me again. I spied Phoenix Ingraham in the crowd and made him come with me. We went along Piccadilly, past Hyde Park corner, beautifully. The motor was an old four-wheeler, made over, and the man sat up in front.

We stopped to show off to the Mortons. The governor was a good sport, and in spite of violent protests from his family, he came with me. The Morton family crowded on the balcony to watch us try this mad invention. The governor had on a silk hat, and we went along smoothly through Knightsbridge, when suddenly the seat reared up, and the governor had his hat crushed flat against the roof. Something had gone wrong in the machinery, which was evidently under us. There were awful noises.

The governor held his squashed hat and called out to the man to return at once, but he could not turn. He said he always had to go either ahead or to the right. Finally, we did turn slowly to the right and had to go across Hyde Park and around by Park Lane before I could land the governor safely. Phoenix Ingraham joined me again and we went slowly but safely to the Bristol, where we found Mr. Samuel Thayer, former Minister to Holland, having tea with Mother. We persuaded them to try the new contraption — which they did, for a tour around the block, and they said it made noises and never could succeed.

We sailed on the *St. Paul* from Southampton, and the first person we saw as we went on board was the young man of the Touraine trip. I bowed cordially, but he rushed over to Mother and said he must introduce himself properly. His name was William K. Richardson and, as we had guessed, from Boston. Mother then introduced him to me in correct style, and all was Victorian again.

The ship was uncomfortable, and the trip was rough. The deck rooms had no bathroom, and you had to go downstairs and through the saloon to find one. . . . The Mortons and I had a very nice time, with our chairs up in front in the sun where other people joined us.

Another passenger was Captain Oberlin Carter, lately attached to the Embassy in London. He was a handsome man with deep blue eyes. He said he had been cabled to return home and report, and he had no idea what it was about. The Mortons did not like him, but I rather did.

We arrived off Quarantine on a perfect September afternoon, and later a full moon rose as we steamed up the harbor. We were met by Mr. John Palmer, who had been Secretary of State of New York, and Mr. Corning, who was attached to the Customs service. In those days the courtesies of the port meant something.

As I went to find my handbag in the stateroom, I saw Captain Carter leaning against the stair rail. He looked ghastly white, and thinking he must be ill, I went over to him. He stared blankly at me, muttered that he had had the most terrible news, that he must go to Washington to clear himself, and that he was thankful that his wife had been spared. He was shaking and saying over and over, "It's untrue! It is untrue!" I stood by, hoping I could help him, but in the confusion of landing I lost sight of him.

I never saw him again, but in a few days the sad story was published, and it attracted wide attention. Captain Carter was accused of defrauding the government in the construction of projects in Savannah harbor and several other projects. He was sentenced to five years at hard labor in Leavenworth and a fine of $5,000. He has often been called the American Dreyfus. He came from Ohio, and at West Point had a record second only to Robert E. Lee.[5]

For forty-five years Captain Carter fought to have his name cleared, but it never was. He died in 1944, aged 83, always to the last claiming his innocence. In talking it over many years later, an army officer said to me, "He was as guilty as hell!"

We went home the next day. Uncle Erastus had been out driving on Sunday afternoon with Parker and Rensselaer Erving. They had been going to Mr. Sage's in Menands. He had been taken ill in the carriage, and as soon as they could reach the Sages, he had been carried into a bedroom on the ground floor. He had had a stroke and died that night.

We had several English guests that fall. Among them . . . were the Bishop of Rochester, England, and Mrs. Talbot. Mr. and Mrs. Byam Stevens had come over from Lenox, and after dinner Mrs. Talbot and Mrs. Stevens and

I were talking together.

Mrs. Talbot was quite deaf. She was evidently curious to find out why I was not married. I told her that both Mother and I had done our best, but I had proved to be a drug on the market. Now Mother had bought me some more new clothes in Paris, and I had promised to make some effort. I felt sure that Mrs. Talbot had a nice young curate in mind at home, and that she was ready to urge me to return to England with her, and she would help me. . . .

❦   ❦   ❦

In October Mother and I went with the Doanes and Mary Spring Gardiner to Saratoga to have luncheon with Mr. and Mrs. Spencer Trask at "Yaddo." Although Mrs. Trask was an invalid, she was also very energetic, and she wrote plays and poetry. She had a tower room filled with Browning souvenirs. She had planned an historical dinner that night, and she asked me to stay over and be an icicle. She said she would have yards of white cheesecloth wound over my black dress, and all I would have to do would be to stand against a pillar in the hall.

I fortunately could plead a dinner engagement for that night. To be truthful, being wound with cheesecloth on a rather warm evening did not sound too promising. Mr. Trask was to be Pericles, Mrs. Trask, Faustina, and Mr. George Parsons Lathrop was to be Marcus Aurelius. I never found out where an icicle fitted in with such a group, but Mary Spring was delighted to stay over and take the part. I can think of no family in the world who had more troubles than the Trasks, losing their four children, and yet [they always stepped forward] to give help to all who chanced to pass their way. Few people have such a record of good deeds behind them.

We rejoiced that October when Erving Pruyn was born at 270 State Street. Mother was in New York with Uncle Tuy Marvin, but when Jack telephoned me the good news, I rushed up. Jack was so excited that he was trembling. I saw the baby when he was an hour old. Later he was christened at the house by Dr. Battershall, and the godparents were Fred Townsend, Robert Pruyn, and Mrs. Erving.

I made several visits that fall. One was to Brookline to stay with the Prescott Halls. Mr. Hamlin had been to Japan that summer as special commissioner on the subject of a treaty with England, Russia, Canada, and the United States for the protection of the seal herds that were being rapidly wiped out by the Pelagic sealing. He had had a most interesting experience and had returned with several of the Japanese commissioners. His sister Harriet had gone with him. Later on he told me that if I had been in this country in August, he would have gone straight to Albany to ask me to go with him. So I never went to Japan.

Jack gave me a large, brass ball from India for Christmas. The idea was that the bridesmaids at a wedding were supposed to light the small lamp in it and roll it by turns. The one who succeeded in rolling it the farthest without its going out would be the next bride. He wrote on his card that he hoped I would try it soon. He thought that I should have someone better to care for than a dog who showed signs of rheumatism.

When I was in Boston, Mr. Hamlin had dined with the Halls and had invited us to go to the theater. The play was called "Never Again," and to Mr. Hamlin's horror, it turned out to be risqué — according to the Victorian standards of that day, and Florence, my chaperone, insisted that we must leave. Probably now the play would be considered very slow. So we departed and went to another play, but that seemed to be even worse, and I got to laughing; it was so ridiculous.

It was only about nine by the time we had exhausted the two plays, but Mr. Hamlin found a carriage and insisted we must come to the club for supper. He had a conference with the steward, and the result was that after we had waited for a long time, a large platter of fried whitebait was served. They were considered a great delicacy, but they looked like the thousand leggers that used to infest Washington houses, and I could hardly swallow them. This dish was followed by canvas-backed ducks, so rare they must have been just carried through the kitchen. I did my best, but the evening could hardly have been called a success. The host left for Montreal later that evening.

The holidays were very gay, and I went to a dance every night. The skating and coasting also were fine. December and January both brought visits from Charles Hamlin, on his devious way to Montreal. A blizzard came up while we were on a walk, and he froze one ear but was too polite to say so. It seemed to me he might be discouraged by the things that seemed to go wrong whenever we met, but he always came again.

Mother was far from well. Her heart was in bad shape, and I felt that she should not be left alone in that large, old house with none of the family to live there with her. She did not feel this way at all. She had become very fond of Mr. Hamlin and admired him and his ability.

She gave me quite a scolding about my lack of seriousness and love of having a perpetual good time. She said Mr. Hamlin was not the man to be treated casually, that I had a happy way of putting him off, and I must decide one way or the other and be fair and square. This was the only time that Mother had ever said anything like that about anyone who had hung around, so I knew it meant a great deal. But I felt very strongly about Albany. I was rooted in the life there, and to live anywhere else held no attraction for me.

William Rice's term as Civil Service Commissioner was coming to an end. It had not been a full term, as [he had been appointed only to complete] the term of Mr. Theodore Roosevelt, who had resigned to become Police Commissioner in New York. So the Rices were at the Arlington until it was time to leave, and [young] Bill was in Albany at our house. I went down to Washington to join [Hattie and her husband] for a last visit.

We decided to take a short trip to Virginia, although January is not a very good month there. We went down to Charlottesville especially to see the University and Monticello. From there we went to Richmond, to the Jefferson Hotel, where we found Mr. Hamlin waiting for us. I do not know just where he came from. After two days there we went to Williamsburg, a very different place from what it is now. We drove out to Jamestown over an almost hopeless road. That was before the Jamestown restoration and the fair, so it was in a ruinous condition.[6]

We then returned to Richmond and went down to Old Point Comfort and stayed at the old and dirty Chamberlain Hotel. Mr. Hamlin and I took a short walk on the piazza in the evening, but it was indeed short. The vigilant sister came out after me and spoiled our chance for a tete-a-tete undisturbed. We crossed by the Cape Charles route and went to New York and home.

Our next excitement was the blowing up of the *Maine* in Havana harbor. This caused the most intense excitement, and Albany was particularly excited when the news told us that the Captain of the *Maine* was Sigsbee, an Albany boy. He received a great ovation later on. Trouble had been brewing for a long time. President Cleveland had refused to send any naval ship down there, as he feared some disaster in Cuban waters.

In the meantime Mr. Hamlin and I had become engaged. It was just as Mother told me: he would not be treated in any casual way. His heart was in it and I must realize that it was a serious thing. He even told me that he was not only amazed but also discouraged at my lack of decision. It is funny now to look back on, but nobody realized how much I cared for Albany, Elk Street, and the old way of life so familiar to me.

He wasted no time. He went to New York at once, already armed with a letter of introduction to Mr. Kuntz at Tiffany's from Dr. Augustus C. Hamlin of Bangor, a great collector of jewels and the owner of Mount Mica in Maine. He returned with a card for fitting the right size ring and departed again for New York — this time returning with the lovely diamond ring in a blue velvet box.

It then came over me what this meant. I was really pledged. I do not think I ever had thought of myself as being engaged. Life was full of fun, and why settle down? My cousin Elizabeth Cooper Pruyn had announced her engagement lately to Mitchell Harrison of Philadelphia, and now Mabel Sard was engaged to Arthur Amory of Boston, so at last Albany girls were being snapped up.

In March we went to Virginia Hot Springs. Aunt Mary Corning was not well, and Mother thought the cure there would do her good. Edwin had his Groton holidays just then, so we took the night train from New York.

Charlie came over to see us off and intended to come down for a weekend, but owing to some mistake about a room, he never came. He was very upset and provoked about this. It really was not my fault, although it seemed so, owing to misinformation given to me by a room clerk, which I had passed on to him. I told him that he blew up like the *Maine*.

CHAPTER 28

THE DAY SET FOR THE ANNOUNCEMENT of our engagement was Saturday, April 16th [1898]. We each had written dozens of letters. On Easter Eve I went down to St. Peter's to help with the [Easter] decorations. When they were about finished, I sat down in the front pew to look at them with Dr. Battershall, and I told him of our engagement. I do not know whether he was surprised or not. Like most of those affairs, the news got around somehow. When I wrote Mrs. Farnsworth, she replied that she was never so surprised in her life. Perhaps this was because so much of the courting had been done in Washington.

The day of the announcement was lovely. A light breeze blew the nursery curtains. Flowers poured in by express and from in town, and letters, telegrams, and special deliveries [arrived]. Relations and friends ran in and out the whole day and most of the night. I expected some awful jokes to be played on us, as it was often predicted in ominous tones, "Wait until your turn comes!" But nothing other than nice things happened, and everyone said lovely things about everyone.

Charlie's relatives wrote ecstatic letters about him telling me how fortunate I was. It was hard to make adequate replies. One in California wrote, "Our glorious Charles is altogether lovely." What could I reply to that? I kept it with me to read to everyone.

Bishop Doane wrote a poem and presented it with a bunch of arbutus.

First fragrant flower of the warming earth,
Pushing thy pink lips up, to catch the kiss
Of the spring sun, and, with thy fragrant breath,
Telling the hoarded memories of the bliss
Of summers past — while thy own beauteous birth
Foretells the joys of summers yet to come;
Thou art both herald and historian too,
Binding in one, remembrance of the past
And hope of future joys; I hail thee true
Prophet of all my prayers; that time may cast
One only shadow, on the years to come
Of this dear child; remembrance of the life
Of the dear home, whose Light she is; to be

> The spicy fragrance of sweet memory,
> In the rich happiness of the wedded wife.
>
> W.C.D., April 16, 1898

In our guest book are two entries for April 16th. One is Goldwin Smith of Toronto, and he writes, "The day of a happy announcement." The other is signed Charles S. Hamlin, and it runs,

> She is my own, and I as rich
> In having such a jewel, as twenty seas,
> If all their sands were pearl —
> The water nectar, and the rocks pure gold.[1]

Our dear old friend Mr. James C. Carter of New York wrote, "I hope, I know you will be very happy in it, for you have a fine, noble fellow for a lover, whom it will be a delight to love. Every pleasure to you." Dear Mr. Bigelow at Highland Falls wrote, "I beg you both to receive an old man's blessing — Your faithful friend yesterday, today and forever — John Bigelow." Another letter from him says,

> I have sent you a picture of a venerable and saintly gentleman who made a profession of shedding tears for people. He is to be your mascot — such was my purpose in sending it — and is to shed all the tears for you during your married life which you might otherwise feel called upon to part with in the progress of your future acquaintance with the tyrant sex. When you come to look upon this venerable Saint always wiping his eyes, you may infer my hope and expectation that he will do wiping enough for both of you for the rest of your days and my earnest prayer that no tears but tears of joy shall stain those eyes and cheeks of yours, which none have ever looked upon but to admire — none named but to praise — as always your affectionate friend,
>
> John Bigelow.

Dr. Morgan Dix wrote, "I am really very happy to think that you are so happy and shall look forward with impatience to telling you so in person." Mr. Dean Sage wrote in his usual amusing vein — "I hope it is safe to assume that your engagement results from the awakening of the sacred emotions of undying affection rather than from yielding to the matrimonial mania now raging in these parts, etc., etc."

The gem of the several hundreds we received between us was from "Professor" Van Buren, the . . . banjo teacher who had played for the Corning oyster roasts.

Miss Huybertie L. Pruyn.

Dear Lady: Mrs. Van Buren joins me in congratulation. The high, the low, the young and old unite to do you honor. Like the Sunbeams, your kindness radiates upon all. When the dignity of Madam has mantled your form, we know that it will hang in gracious folds from your shoulders. May your husband be as the immortal Charles Sumner — an ideal, faithful, incorruptible, public man and serve to hold the standard higher, in domestic life. "The heavens forbid but that your loves, and comforts, should increase even as your days, do grow."

Your humble Friend, Charles M. Van Buren.

One morning I met the Van Burens in Myers's. They showed me their incubator baby and gave me the details as to his size and weight when born. I said I hoped they would come to our wedding, and they said they would bring the baby, so that he would always remember such an event.

In the meantime war had been declared against Spain in early April. Immediately our neighbor Meredith Read organized the "Read Rangers." They paraded all through the spring in the late afternoons and presented arms in front of Mrs. Kidd's house, as she was supposed to be the fairy godmother who equipped the men. The Coopers complained that the noise and dust made it impossible to sit on their stoop. Meredith looked very handsome in his decorated uniform, and we enjoyed the martial spirit on Elk Street. But in the end the authorities proved to be hard-hearted and did not accept them. The papers said it was from lack of funds.

News from the "Rough Riders" filled the papers to the exclusion of other affairs, and the great casualty of those early days was when "Rough Rider Woodbury Kane burned his hand while scrambling eggs over a camp fire."

At that time there was a very high opinion of the strength of the Spanish fleet under Admiral Cervera, and Europe showed unmistakable signs of sympathy with Spain. They insisted that our fleet was weak, that no captain could train his sailors as they were of such mixed nationalities, and that when orders were given, few knew enough English to obey, so discipline was poor. It was soon strange for us to look back on all this, particularly the panicky rush to send all valuables to inland cities for safekeeping, in case the Spaniards bombed or were able to hold coast cities. Men, before joining up, moved their families away from the coast into the hills or mountains. Later, after it was all over, no one would own up to this panic, or [admit] that they had feared the rotten Spanish fleet. Trips planned for

Europe in the summer were abandoned in April, but the great victory of Admiral Dewey, on May 1st, at Manila, settled the question, and nerves were restored. The April panic vanished with the power of Spain.

Cables reported that Sousa's march "El Capitan" was played on Dewey's flagship, and so it became the rage. It never attained the popularity of "There's a hot time in the old town tonight," but the Cubans were convinced that it was the national anthem and played it on every occasion. There was great talk about the welcome to be given Dewey on his return, and puns were made on his name, such as "There is the girl who kissed the grass because it was dewey."

Then came the Richmond Pearson Hobson brave effort to blockade the harbor at Havana.[2] It failed, but that did not take away from the bravery of the man. However, the newspapers made a fool of him by publishing stories of his always having kissed every girl he met — hence the candy at Huyler's called "Hobson's Kisses" which sold for years.

With breathless interest we followed the *Oregon* around Cape Horn. This long trip for the much-needed ship led to the serious consideration of the need for the Panama Canal. After that came the victory in the Caribbean, and the endless controversy as to whether Admiral Schley or Admiral Sampson should have the laurels for smashing Spain's other fleet. The yellow fever scourge in the Cuban camps, the typhoid in our own camps, the shiploads of food sent down to Cuba but never unloaded, Secretary of War Alger and the "Bully Beef" scandal, and the perpetual excitement about Colonel Roosevelt, particularly the controversy over whether he led the "Rough Riders" up San Juan or Kettle Hill — all these excitements belong to the weeks of our engagement.[3]

The Dooley letters were a wonderful contribution to that era. They were written by Finley Peter Dunne. Dooley and his friend, Mike Hennessey, settled every question. The White House cat, "Brother Abner McKinley," and how Rosenfeld or Roseford fought "alone in Cuba" were discussed; and Mark Hanna, Bully Beef, and what Dewey said to Gridley were [considered] witty beyond words.[4]

We were invited out to many dinners on Saturday nights, when Charlie could come over for the weekend. Several parties were shared with Elizabeth Pruyn and Mr. Harrison, who were to be married on Wednesday, June 1st. We were well chaperoned throughout. When we dined out, we drove to the dinner in the coupe. It had a light, controlled by the coachman, over the seat. We must have resembled Cinderella's pumpkin coach.

When we drove out in the spider phaeton, we had a footman in the rumble, so that every word was overheard. Our drives with Mother were most circumspect, as Charlie had to sit on the back seat of the Victoria, facing Mother and me, and the noise of the tireless wheels on the stones drowned out any conversation. When we sat in the conservatory, the Coopers had many eyes on us and knew to a second just how long we had sat on the window seat talking. When we went for a walk, the windows were a thousand eyes. Katy at Mrs. Farnsworth's announced, "The man from Boston ain't no dude — like as some others Miss Bertie has walked out with."

During these weeks we had a funny and also a vexatious experience about the portrait done of me by Mr. Percy C. Nicholson the previous fall. The story dates back to the pageant at Harmanus Bleecker Hall in December 1894 [when] I took the part of Alida Van Slichtenhorst. . . .

[Mr. Skinner], who had often done work for Mother . . . wrote to [her] that he had a nephew who was an artist. He had studied in Paris and in Boston and now had returned to live in Albany, provided he could get orders for portraits. He had seen the pageant and would like to paint me in the orange dress, not as an order, but merely as a starter. He said that Mother would be under no obligation whatever.

Mother was the most kind-hearted woman in the world. So she said if I did not mind, she would like to help this young man. Mr. Nicholson came in one afternoon to see me, the dress, the lace and jewelry, and Mother gave him a photograph taken at full length. He left, thanking us profusely and saying that he would not need a sitting and would write to Mother when the portrait was finished. All this sounded simple, and we really did not think much about it.

After several weeks Mr. Nicholson wrote to Mother that he would like us to come to his studio to make suggestions or criticisms. Mother, Jack, and I went there and were amused, and rather aghast, at the full-length exhibited on an easel. It was about four feet high and done on heavy paper — not on canvas. It looked like a cheap advertisement of some fancy picture. There was very little to praise.

Unluckily, Jack was very outspoken in his comments. He said it had been cheaply done and was posed from the photograph, that it was in fact an enlarged copy of it and badly colored. Mr. Nicholson said that a friend of his from the west, who had only seen me in a sleigh, recognized the likeness at once and thought it a remarkable piece of work. Mother got very nervous and feared something worse might be said, so she hastily bade Mr. Nicholson good-bye, and we departed.

　. . . Mother asked Mr. Walter Palmer to look at it and give his opinion. He reported that the artist seemed to have cast a shadow on the paper, enlarging the original photograph, and then had colored it. Mother was perplexed what to do about it. Mr. Palmer said the artist was in an ugly mood, and he feared he might sell it to some conspicuous place, like a saloon, and that the well-known dress would be easily recognized. He advised Mother to write and offer Mr. Nicholson $25, so as to get it in her possession. Mr. Nicholson was very angry at this offer and stated in his reply that the picture was worth $1,000, and that the "artist" sent by Mother was evidently jealous of outside talent coming to town.

At this point Uncle Amasa Parker stepped into the story and said he would settle it so that we would have the portrait and no publicity. In the rush of my engagement we forgot all about it and consequently were amazed to have Uncle Amasa drop in at breakfast two mornings after our return from Hot Springs. He told us to be at the City Hall at ten o'clock and to have Hattie come too, as the portrait case was coming up before Judge Myers, who was an old friend. We had never heard there was to be any case. We could not make it out, and Uncle Amasa never asked us any questions about it.

We found it was quite a serious affair, with all the court room paraphernalia, a solemn-looking judge and an expectant-looking jury. Uncle Amasa was quite deaf. He had his office clerk with him — a Mr. Hughes — who sat by Uncle Amasa and all through the ridiculous proceedings kept leaning over and, in a loud whisper, correcting dates and other mistakes. Amasa Jr. and Louis Parker turned up, having heard what was happening. Then, one by one others dropped in, and before an hour passed, the room was crowded with friends to see the fun.

The portrait was hung near me for all to see. Harry Peckham, B. Hand, and Rensselaer Erving all arrived, anxious to learn how to try a case like this one. Reporters swarmed. We knew our clothes were being written up. As it was all funny, we knew we were in for ridicule. But there we were and had to go through with it.

Mr. Nicholson had a clever lawyer. Mr. Palmer was a witness, but he had not prepared for it. Pirie MacDonald was called as a witness. He looked particularly jaunty that day. He was asked if he was a photographer, and he said that he was not. Everyone gasped, as he was then the popular photographer. He was delighted with the sensation he had created. He was

asked to state his profession and he replied, "I am an artist in photography."
A roar of laughter led by Harry Peckham greeted this. Pirie described the
difference between just taking photographs and his art, and he testified that
he never would have recognized the so-called portrait nor could libel me by
finding any resemblance.

Mother was put on the stand and made an awful mess of it, as she was
completely rattled. To every question she would say, "I do not know. I have
no recollection whatever. No. No. I never ordered any portrait. Yes. Yes. I
showed him the clothes. I wanted to help him."

Mr. Cass, the lawyer for Mr. Nicholson, would say patiently, "Now, Mrs.
Pruyn, please say only yes or no," and Mother would begin all over with
the confused replies.

It was really excruciatingly funny, and the courtroom rocked with sup-
pressed laughter. I wished so much that I had had a chance to answer these
questions. It would have made such a difference if it had been made clear.
The shrewd lawyer only asked me two simple questions. He could have
made it disagreeable for me, by having me dress up in the costume, but
he knew that would create sympathy for me, so he treated us all most
courteously. Hattie was put on the stand. She had been away and knew
nothing, but she answered clearly the questions put to her.

Charlie stood in the rear, by the door, but I did not know it. He had
arrived unexpectedly from Montreal, and at our house had been informed
by Christian that we were all in court at the City Hall. This was most
surprising information, and he walked over to investigate. He arrived in
time to hear it all.

He was disgusted at the performance and was not surprised when the
jury, after half an hour out, returned a verdict for half the amount asked
by the artist. He had started by asking $1,000, but had lowered his claim
to $500, so the judgment was $250 for Mother to pay. Charlie always said
we were lucky, that he had heard the testimony, and he thought Mother
had certainly encouraged the artist. He felt that Mother was known to the
jury as a kind and generous citizen, and so they had halved the claim.

Louis Parker took out a large knife and, hacking violently, cut the portrait
from the bars on which the paper was stretched. Then he came over and,
bowing low, presented it to me without a smile. He was very angry.

On the following Sunday the *Albany Telegram* published a very witty
account of the whole affair. It was headed: "Huybertie does not like her
face — says it is that of an old woman, and she is a young girl." None of

us seems to have kept this choice clipping.

As we walked across Academy Park to our house for luncheon, Louis silently trudged along carrying the hapless portrait. We found C.S.H. sitting glumly in the conservatory. After expressing our surprise at seeing him so unexpectedly, he and Louis started on the morning's performance, and each told his version of how it should have been conducted. Finally, we all got hysterical, because it was so funny.

Mother and I went to New York for some shopping and then to Boston for me to meet my future in-laws, which was very frightening to me. We dined with the George Lymans and the Richard Olneys, and we looked at houses but did not decide on any one of them. We saw quantities of people, old and new friends, and I felt totally inadequate.

[When I was] once again at home, the Parkers had a fancy dress dinner for me, and Grace sent her father and Louis to the club. There were ten of us, and we had a grand evening of fun. We ate some remarkable new dishes, told fortunes by a Ouija board, and Grace danced on the table without tipping over anything.

Charlie was very musical. He set to music the poem by John G. Saxe, "Do I love her, ask the bee?" From a small photograph I had taken of the view across the river from the nursery window, he had a cover made for the music, and it was published by Oliver Ditson. The two towers of the North Dutch Church stand out in the foreground. He published five songs in all. I have them in a leather cover.

We had selected Wednesday, June 8th, for our wedding, but on consulting Mr. Rogers at St. Peter's, we found that Mabel Sard had already chosen that day, so we decided on Saturday, June 4th. At that time Saturday was an unusual day to select, but it turned out to be a perfect day, cool and lovely, whereas June 8th, we heard later, was a fiery furnace. "Town Topics" called the three weddings, "Bonds, Brains, and Beauty." Mr. Mitchell Harrison was "Bonds," Charlie was "Brains," and Mr. Amory "Beauty."

Before I had finished notes of thanks for engagement notes and flowers, the wedding presents began to arrive. The nursery table was soon covered with them, and extra trestle tables were brought in. A large bookcase was emptied of books to make room for presents. But they were soon piled on the floor in their boxes, and it was a job to try to keep up with the notes.

One morning about eleven, I was unpacking some gifts that had just arrived, and Mother was watching. I was attracted by a small box marked from Tiffany's, and as I had had very little jewelry, I said perhaps this would be something nice. It was beautifully packed, and I finally reached a red leather box with gold tooling. Inside there was a twisted gold bracelet. On one end was a large diamond and on the other a large pearl. I slipped it on my wrist and said to Mother, "I wonder who sent me a fake. It must be one of the cousins trying to be funny."

The telephone rang in the hall and I had to know who it was. Then a box of flowers arrived in the lower hall, and I ran down to see it. As I stood at the front door, May Cooper came over, and although she was supposed to be nearsighted, she at once spied the gleaming bracelet. She looked at it carefully, and I said it was just a joke, but May said, "Who sent it?" I said I had not looked at the card.

May said a sure test of a diamond was to write with it on glass. If you could write with it, it was a real one, and she thought this looked real. Our lower windows had bars, and so we went across the street to Mrs. Farnsworth's basement window, which was just the right height. I started to write my name and it worked perfectly. May said, "I knew it! Now let's see the card."

Just then Mrs. Farnsworth opened the window above us and asked what we were doing. I told her and held up the bracelet and said that May was sure it must be real. She asked why we chose to experiment on her window, as we had plenty at home. I said hers was much better, but this did not placate her. She told me to leave at once and then to let her know who sent it.

We went up to the nursery, where Mother was still busy rearranging the presents. She said, "Here is the card that was with the bracelet. You will be able to decide whether it is real or not." On the card was written, "With love and best wishes from Mr. and Mrs. J. Pierpont Morgan." I telephoned Mrs. Farnsworth, and she said, "I knew it was real all the time. Now, if you get another, write on your own window."

We had wonderful presents, about five hundred in all. Everyone was so generous. One morning Grace Parker, Sarah Sage, and Ruth Pruyn came in to see them and offered to write some of the notes of thanks for me. I was very grateful and left them in the library with plenty of paper and the lists. They said they would do twenty notes between them, and I went out. They did write them, but luckily Mother overheard them laughing, and she was suspicious that something was wrong.

So Mother offered to take them and have them stamped and mailed, but they never were! They were the most awful trash. One of them was to one of Mr. Hamlin's best clients, Sir William Van Horne of Montreal, who had sent a Tiffany vase. These Tiffany lamps and vases and bowls were then all in fashion. I am glad they soon ceased to be on the market, as they were extraordinarily twisted and ill-shaped.

The Custom House telephoned that the box of clothes from Mme. Lodaux in Paris had arrived. They brought it up, and it was opened in the office in the basement. Lodaux always packed her clothes beautifully. I think her husband did that part and arranged for the shipping. Marie said I must not try on the wedding dress, as it would be bad luck, but I had to know how it looked and fitted, so it was carried to Mother's dressing room, and a sheet was laid on the floor in front of her long mirror in the library door.

It was a beautiful dress of the softest satin, embroidered gracefully with pearls in love knots, with some brilliants scattered in. The sleeves were long and tight and covered with thin tulle ending in a puff at the shoulder. The collar was high and of tulle pleated over satin, and in front there was a square yoke of tulle, with pearls embroidered about it. At the belt there was a small bunch of artificial orange blossoms. The long train was plain, but beautifully hung from the waist belt. The waist and skirt were separate, according to the fashion of that time.

The veil was of tulle, with a tiny wreath of orange blossoms for the front. I cannot now imagine why I did not wear Mother's real lace veil over the tulle, as she offered to get it out for me. With the dress was a lovely under-petticoat of white brocade, with two chiffon flounces edged with tiny lace and chiffon ruffles. The slippers were white satin with embroidery. I had bought them in London the previous fall but had never worn them. It seems unbelievable now when I say that the bill from Lodaux for this wedding outfit was only $130.

She also sent several other dresses. One was particularly striking, and I am sorry I did not keep it. It was a soft plaid silk with black, light red, and a fine yellow line, on a dark background. It was piped with black taffeta at the seams, and had a wide flounce on the skirt of the same material piped on. It was a rather conspicuous dress, but everyone admired it [with its] white lawn and lace vest, and the belt of black satin [with] a paste clasp. With it I wore a plain black straw hat with some ostrich tips. (The wedding dress is in the Albany Institute.)

There were eight bridesmaids. Four were Jane Hamlin, Bessie Oliver, Nelly Robb, and Lena Morton. They all wore white made at Mme. Frank's in New York.

The dresses were fine white French muslin, with lace insertions and edgings, and beautifully finished. They had girdles of white satin ribbon, with a bow and sash ends in the back, and the satin ribbon collars were high and boned. They had slight trains and were very full in the skirts. The sleeves were long and tight to the top, where there was one big puff. The slippers and stockings were white, and the hats, made by Helen Lawrence, were white open-work straw, with a cluster of white ostrich plumes on the left of the front. The hats now look in the photographs like trimmed soup plates turned upside down.

Little Elinor Hamlin, aged seven, had written me a special delivery letter saying she too wanted to be a bridesmaid, so she and Billy Rice, who was about the same age, walked together but declined to take hands. The bridesmaids carried bouquets of Easter lilies, and the ushers had lily-of-the-valley boutonnieres. The groom gave the bridesmaids brooches from Howard and Company in New York. They were like an old-fashioned crown with pearls set in, and the ushers had scarf pins like them, but much smaller.

Jean Rowell had charge of sending out the invitations, and the upper library was given over to this job. There were about six thousand sent out. They were engraved here by Gavit and Company and read differently from other invitations, as my father had always insisted that guests were invited as witnesses.

Mrs. Pruyn
requests your presence
at St. Peter's Church,
Albany, N.Y.
on Saturday, June fourth, eighteen hundred and ninety eight,
at twelve o'clock
to witness the marriage of her daughter
Huybertie Lansing
to
Charles Sumner Hamlin.

Enclosed were cards for the Church and for the reception at the house.

With the house like an express office and a railroad station combined, I wanted to be with Fromo as much as I could. I felt apologetic to him. He had his usual Saturday morning bath and his teeth and coat brushed regularly, as he had his own china and brushes in the playroom.

He played with his wooden balls in the fountain, while I lay in the hammock under the chestnut tree, reading and trying to realize that my old usual life was almost over and that I was going to live away from Albany — away from the relatives and friends with whom I had been brought up. It was not like going off for a few months and then going home again. It was a forever break. I would have to make new friends and find new interests, and I was so terribly shy with strangers.

Louis came to luncheon almost every day, as he was to be head usher and we had to settle about the seating. I insisted that the Spruce Street children must be well placed, and he asked how he should know them. I said they would tell him who they were. Then there were the St. Agnes group and the Shakers, and the Van Buren family must not be forgotten.

The best man was to be Josiah Quincy, mayor of Boston, and the ushers were George Hamlin from Boston, Frank Hamlin from Chicago, John T. Wheelwright of Boston, and William E. Curtis of New York, and four of my cousins. Parker Corning was to have been one, but owing to the death of little Gertrude Corning, Langdon Marvin took his place. Ned Pruyn was asked to be an usher but, owing to Harvard examinations, he could not come. Marvin Selden and Rensselaer Erving were the other two.

There was no *Capital Chips* to give amusing descriptions of the wedding. The *New York Herald* published two unrecognizable pictures of me; we never knew where they found them. Many other papers wrote or telephoned for pictures, but were refused as a matter of course. The idea still prevailed that a woman's name should only appear in print with the announcement of her wedding and her death.

But in spite of all that, the *Boston Globe* described me as,

> . . . a brunette of slender and graceful figure and of medium height. She is of a vivacious disposition and possesses a refreshing indifference to some of the stilted conventionalities of "Society." This trait shows itself to some extent in her dress, which while tasteful and becoming, is simple to a degree. Her family belongs to an exclusive set and she is much sought after therein, especially on account of her pre-eminence in out of door athletics, notably equestrianism, golf, and tennis.

This was amusing, as I did not play golf at all, rode only passably, and played a most uneven game of tennis. However, it really did not matter. My scrapbook has clippings from many papers — Washington, Baltimore, Boston, New York — besides our own here.

Elk Street never looked lovelier than it did that May. The old elms met in a long archway, and the Coopers on their stoop sat in their shade and watched everything that came and went at our house. The Kidd and Townsend dogs yapped playfully from the lower end, while the Johnston dogs frisked next door. The awnings shaded our side windows looking over the garden. The vines were at their best. The wisteria bloomed in large clusters over the glass roof of the conservatory, and in the garden the old Syringa bushes looked like snow.

On Wednesday, June 1st, Elizabeth Pruyn was married to Mitchell Harrison at noon at St. Peter's. Our old Newport neighbor, Dr. Jack Mitchell, was best man and stayed with us. There was a small reception at the house at 62 South Swan Street.

The next day, June 2nd, Charlie arrived with his brother, George, and they stayed at the Parkers. On Friday, Harriet and Jane Hamlin, who had just returned from a trip around the world, came over from Boston with the Edward Hamlins and little Elinor. The latter three stayed with the Rices. At our house, besides Harriet and Jane, were Jack and Nina Pruyn, Nelly Robb, and Lena Morton.

Mr. and Mrs. Byam Stevens stayed at the Kenmore. Mr. Robb and the Goodhue Livingstons stayed at the Farnsworths. Mr. W. E. Curtis stayed at Mrs. Hand's, and at the Fort Orange Club were Mayor Quincy, Mr. Wheelwright, and Frank Hamlin. Governor Morton and Helen, Bessie Curtis, and Mr. John Jay Chapman came up on the Empire State Express for the day, as did also Mrs. W. E. Rogers and Nelly from Garrison.

While Mother did not approve of rehearsals for weddings, she agreed that with such a large wedding party we should meet at St. Peter's late on Friday, about five, and get some idea as to where everyone was to stand. It was an entirely decorous performance — no laughing or jokes. The procession was soon straightened out, and the two children were impressed with their responsibility for doing just what they were told to do. Bill Rice looked suspiciously at Elinor and seemed doubtful about walking with her.

After that was over, I went home with the Parkers, and we had tea and hot buttered toast and jam on the piazza, just like old times. We talked over the wedding plans and the favorite presents. They assured me that they had sewed up the pockets, sleeves, and button holes of everything in the groom's trunk. Even his slippers had been glued together, and so had his brother's. Grace Marvin and Harriet Peckham were also there.

I ran home through the garden and by the back way, down the dusty unpaved upper Elk Street, and managed to get in without being stopped. I was late, and I knew I would be missed and the groom would imagine I had eloped with someone else at the last minute. I remember how fresh and lovely the Linden looked in front of the nursery windows.

We had dinner at seven, as Mother had invited all the visitors and the wedding party to come at nine to see the presents, have supper, and dance. The Prescott Halls were at the Doanes', and the bishop asked me to come and sit by him and go over the service in order to be sure he would pronounce my name the right way. He used the name with great emphasis and effect in the service. I asked him to give the lovely blessing used at the closing of the Cathedral service at Commencement. We had quite a talk in a corner.

Then I went up to the library to go over the seatings with Louis, as many more people had come from outside Albany. Mr. Edward Davis and Lily from Worcester, and Mr. James C. Carter from New York, and Mrs. Reed from New York were only a few. We tried to squeeze in everyone, and I made cards for many to come in by the back entrance, so as to avoid crowds. Charlie came after me to meet some more friends. Dr. Battershall wanted to sit down quietly and talk it all over. He was very sweet and hoped I would always be happy, but for him Albany would never be the same.

Christian broke in with a special delivery letter from Mr. Joseph Choate. He was so sorry to be unable to come up as he had planned. He said, "I wish you all the joy you can hope for in your married life, a true appreciation of all its blessings, and a brave heart for all its trials." I have often thought of that letter.

Louis stood by patiently, waiting to work out the pews, but I was too tired. I was almost ready to cry. Then Jack came nobly to my rescue. He said that if I promised not to comment on any arrangement, he and Louis would do the best they could. People had come and gone. It was after 10:30. Nelly Robb, who was a night owl, tried to stay and talk to me, but Mother ran her off, leaving me with Fromo, who curled up on the foot of my bed.

Just as I was settled, Mother came in and sat down in the little white rocker and began to cry. This frightened me. The only time I had seen her really cry was when Aunt Cora died, many years ago. She said I had been all the world to her, that no one was good enough, even Charlie, whom she liked so much.

I laughed at that, but she did not smile. She felt life alone in that big house was not worth living. I was sorry. I did not know what to say to comfort her. I was afraid I might cry too, and that would be so dreary, and anyway it was all very late in the day.

Fromo solved the problem. He gave a wide and noisy yawn and then rolled over and fell out of bed with a thump. Then he ran off and curled up on a rug in the nursery.

I was so tired that I slept well that night, and it was Fromo's cold nose that woke me up. Then Marie appeared with red nose and eyes, as she had evidently been weeping. First Fromo was combed and brushed, every snarl pulled out. Then a wide white ribbon was tied to his collar. He objected to this ornament. He was shut up in the playroom so as to be kept clean, but in the confusion of open doors, he escaped. Jack remarked at breakfast that he hoped I would take as good care of my husband as I had of my dog.

It was a lovely day, with soft cool breezes from the south and a few light clouds drifting about. More presents, more flowers, and then the house grew quieter and quieter as everyone went to their rooms to dress. There seemed to be a hush over everything. Harriet Hamlin came into the nursery to look at the latest presents, and we had quite a talk. Loulie Livingston ran in and then Emma Farnsworth came to help adjust the veil. My hair, with its two cowlicks, was not suited for any head dress.

Mother came in ready to go ahead down to the Church. She wore a lovely black chiffon and lace over white, and white in her little bonnet, and her pearls, and a brooch set in diamonds. She looked very handsome.

Charles telephoned and insisted on speaking to me. He seemed worried and asked me if I was frightened and sounded disappointed when I assured him I was not. I said that I had slept and eaten normally and hoped he would not lose the ring. I knew he never would own up that he was terribly nervous.

In the meantime Elk Street became crowded. The awning had a policeman on either side, and carriages rushed up and down. I saw the Theodore Townsends walk down arm in arm, and Miss Lou and Miss Laura walking in front, just like Sundays. Mr. and Mrs. Leonard Kip, also arm in arm, were turning into Academy Park. Miss Barnard and Miss Walsh, from No. 25 Elk Street, were walking by Steuben Street, as they were going in by the rear door. It seemed strange to think they were going to my wedding.

Nina Pruyn, with Harriet Hamlin, and the bridesmaids in the house, and Mother, drove down in two carriages. Aunt Mary Corning was to meet Mother in the choir room, and they would stand just inside the chancel, as Mother was to give me away.

I was ready ahead of time. . . . I had a good-luck pin to wear. This was for "something old." I borrowed a lace handkerchief from Mother, and I wore a blue garter. Marie had found a four-leaved clover in the garden, after long search, for the heel of my slipper. My dress was the "something new." The bishop had given me a white Prayer Book to carry. I had no gloves or bouquet. This was a great innovation.

Yes, I was all ready. The servants were waiting in the hall to see me. Jack was in the lower hall. He was not so excited as he had been for Hattie's wedding. Jack sang out that it was ten minutes to twelve. Then I think it all swept over me. . . . I realized that when I returned to the nursery, it would be as a bride with a new name. It seemed overwhelming for a moment.

Marie arranged the train over my left arm and the exclamations of the maids followed me down. There was no need of a wrap. Jack and I went out the door and faced the crowds, pressed around the awning and standing across the street in front of the Academy fence. James Newcomb, the coachman, and Leon, the Swiss footman, wore immense boutonnieres of white flowers, and the horses had white cockades by each ear and white head bands. The landau was closed, but we must have presented a gay appearance.

The doors and windows in Elk Street were crowded, and the Academy boys at play crowded to the edge of the park to shout and join in the fun. I began to laugh too and enjoy the excitement. It would be the one time of my life in which I would be the center; why not make the best of it?

We speeded off and soon reached the head of big State Street where we were stopped by several policemen and asked to wait a moment so that they could hold back the crowd. Jack looked at his watch and said it was two minutes to twelve. He had thought that this time we would be prompt, but we were bound to be late.

The crowd was badly handled. Two women managed to stand on the steps on either side of the carriage. The horses cavorted about. We finally reached the church awning after one more stop. Police said later that they had had to clear the awning so that we would have a place.

The chimes were playing gaily above the street noises, as we emerged onto the crimson carpet and walked quietly up the steps. Louis met us in the vestibule. He looked as if he had been through a street fight. He was moping his face, and his collar was melted. He tried to tell us, in whispers that grew louder and louder, how he had found all Spruce Street wedged under the awning, and he could not get anyone else in until he let them in. The "Professor" Van Buren family were in the front pew of the side aisle reserved for St. Agnes. But I did not listen.

We were in the church, and it seemed to me that I never had seen anything so lovely as the aisle. Mr. H. G. Eyres had had charge of it. Tall Easter lilies were fastened to each pew end, and the banks of white and green in the chancel looked like fairyland.

The wedding party was gathered in the tower room. Everyone had had trouble in reaching the church, and all whispered at once. The two children in white grasped lilies in their hot hands, and Grace Parker gave them last touches. Elinor was enjoying her importance, but Mr. "Cuffy" Rice looked bored.

Our old Biddy was in the last pew, and beside her sat a forlorn-looking usher, Mr. Jack Wheelwright. As he mopped his brow, he murmured that he was looking for the hair of the dog that bit him at the club the previous night. He was barely able to limp up the aisle. The other ushers looked fresh and busy, but many people had to be left unseated, as there were not enough seats. Some who had special seats reserved had come too late. People stood on the seats and clung around the pillars.

But now the choir was coming down the west aisle singing the Lohengrin Wedding March, and it sounded as only St. Peter's choir could sing it. Dr. Battershall, with his assistant, followed the choir. Then Dr. Fairbairn, the Warden of St. Stephen's at Barrytown. Dean Robbins came next with his long lip, and then Bishop Doane, rolling along with his peculiar gait, and wearing his Cambridge hood.

At this point the ushers appeared from everywhere in proper two and twos. It seemed miraculous, for only a moment before they had been running about distractedly. Then came the two children, with Grace and Anna Parker close behind them to see they went straight.

After the last two bridesmaids started, Jack gave me his arm without any further words, and we followed on. It all seemed strange to me. I kept saying to myself,

> "So I am being married.
> This is my wedding.
> How lovely everything is!
> What a lot of trouble everyone has taken!
> I must watch out.
> This is my wedding.
> Somehow I am not frightened.
> That's funny.
> A bride ought to cry.
> Now where is the groom?"

As we neared the chancel, the groom managed to struggle through the crowd that had packed against the choir room door as soon as the choir had marched out. The best man was no good at this. Charlie had had to call at the club for him and keep the ring himself. He told me later that it was like a nightmare. They could hear the procession coming nearer and nearer, and they had to punch and squeeze to make way. Nobody believed them when they said they were the groom and best man.

But what a changed groom! He wore a high collar and looked hot and uncomfortable. Mr. William Curtis was at the bottom of this. He said it never would do to wear a low collar. So he produced a high collar and insisted the groom must wear it.

Dr. Battershall began the service. It seemed absolutely unreal. I could not believe I was being married at last.

It had always been fascinating to watch Dr. Battershall. When he would say impressively, "If any man can show just cause...," he would search the church with an eye that seemed to say he would kill anyone who interfered. Then in the mildest tone he ended, "... or else hereafter and forever hold his peace." Nobody stood forth. No protests were heard, and the service proceeded.

Mr. Rogers played the organ enchantingly. We moved up to the rail where the bishop, in all his gorgeousness, was waiting. Mother was there too, with Aunt Mary Corning just behind her. The altar with its flowers was lovely, and the windows shone in the June sunlight. The colors blended and glistened.

Mother took my hands. I knew it was a hard moment, and I smiled reassuringly. Charlie put on the ring, and it has never been taken off.

The bishop gave the blessing "The Lord preserve thy going out and thy coming in until that coming in from which there shall be no going out forever, Amen." The organ pealed the Mendelssohn march. Mother threw back the veil, and we turned around.

It seemed funny to take Charlie's arm and face that crowd. Everyone smiled and looked happy. We had the wide aisle to ourselves, with the procession trailing behind. When we were about half way down, the chimes blended with the march. They were playing,

> Now you are married, you must obey.
> You must be true to all you say.
> You must be kind, you must be good,
> And help your husband chop the wood.

It sounded gay and cheerful as we came out under the awning.

The carriage was waiting, with Leon at the door. Just as we got seated, the old policeman, Captain Oliver, reached in his hand and said, "First shake, Miss Bertie, and don't get arrested in Boston!" Leon jumped on the box, James touched up the horses with his decorated whip, and off we started.

But we did not get far. A mass of young men and boys stopped us. They wanted to unharness the horses and draw the carriage themselves. The police had to interfere, and we finally escaped, the horses trotting along Eagle Street.

Mother and Aunt Mary were already at the house. Aunt Mary waited to give us each a kiss and wish us well, and then she slipped off. Mother stood in the drawing room. The bridesmaids stood in line into the conservatory, and we stood at the north end under a bell of white lilies with one large lily as a clapper.

The reception was great fun. Whenever some elderly lady approached, I would whisper to Charlie to be sure to kiss her. He did his duty — to the amazement of many of the guests.

Our table was at the north end of the dining room piazza. The whole wedding party sat at it, and the cake was in the center. We each had a silver gilt wager cup for drinking the healths in champagne. Governor Morton and Bishop Doane, Mr. James C. Carter, Governor Black, Lieutenant Governor Woodruff — wearing one of his magnificent waistcoats — the mayor of Boston, and Dr. Battershall made speeches. There was great clapping and laughing when some particularly good hit was made.

Then Louis Parker made the best speech of all. He gave a graphic description of his morning's work at St. Peter's, telling about the Van Buren family, the Spruce Street families, and the lady from Cohoes who had come down on purpose. She told Louis to get her "a view of a real swell function" and offered him luncheon for two later if he would just walk her up to a "first-class, top-row seat near the families." He held up his split gloves, torn cuffs, and empty buttonhole, and his wilted collar told its own story. It was the masterpiece of the day. We toasted Louis and drained our wager cups in his honor.

In the garden were the other tables for four, each with a glass vase of lilies. It looked so pretty. Fromo pursued his ways, having several wooden balls in the fountain, which had been cleaned in the morning, hoping it would stay so — but Fromo managed to get ahead of us. Pirie MacDonald came and took the photographs, which I treasure. They give a good idea of the dresses and hats of that period, and how the procession looked. In one of them Fromo lies at my feet, kept there with difficulty. Bill Rice — or

Mr. Cuffy as we called him — convulsed the party, who were trying to look dignified, by suddenly announcing, "I was the only bridesmaid what wore pants."

Gioscia and Gartland's orchestra played under the maple tree, my old Greenwood tree of Robin Hood days. We were patriotic in those days, and in addition to repeated calls for "There's a Hot Time In the Old Town Tonight," the orchestra gave us "The Red, White and Blue," "Columbia the Gem of the Ocean," and of course "The Star Spangled Banner." People did not treat the national anthem as reverently then, in our fifteen-weeks war, as they do now, after the two world wars. "The Bowery" and "Ta-ra-ra-boom-de-ay" were still popular, as was also "After the Ball," now changed to "After the War is Over, What Will Our Teddy Do?"

Jim Cooper and I drank to the north and south side of Elk Street and we danced a jig in the garden. It was a lovely party. I made the best of being the centerpiece of the occasion. A bridegroom never has much of a show at his own wedding.

I was loathe to leave and stood with Cousin Charlotte Pruyn in the conservatory to take a last look before going up to change to my going-away suit. She said it had been a most lovely wedding in every way. I thought so too.

The train for Saratoga left about three, so we both departed to array ourselves in the going-away clothes, about which there was almost as much fuss as about the wedding dress. Several of the bridesmaids stood about in the nursery, talking it all over, and Marie kept handing me things and urging me to hurry. Bessie said there was nothing more that anyone could do about a wedding; this had been so perfect. She helped me decide which of the lovely brooches I would wear with my resada green suit, and we selected William Rice's. I had a small green straw hat, and I pinned it on with the two amethyst hat pins given me by Mrs. Dean Sage.

Then Bessie reported that an impatient groom was waiting in the hall. We expected a gauntlet of shoes and rice. I gave Mother a flying kiss. There were crowds everywhere.

We rushed out with a hailstorm of stuff hurled at us and cheers and laughter as we jumped into the carriage and started off for the station. The Frederick Townsends' balcony was crowded with people. They were in mourning. They had not come to the wedding.

It was just there that I missed my old handbag, which Mother had said was too shabby to use. As we stopped, Owen was running after us with the bag. So we kept on down Steuben Street to the old Delaware and Hudson Station under the main station.

Mr. Horace Young, the president of the Delaware and Hudson Railroad, had very kindly lent us his private car, and we fully expected to find it elaborately decorated. It was a wonderful chance, but nothing had been done — this showed a lack of enterprise.

We got off for Saratoga without any excitement. We heard later that our friend "Angel" Booth had had a big crowd upstairs. It was thought we were going to New York to sail for Europe, but we were on our way to Santanoni, which had been lent to us for our honeymoon.

I have a copy of an old-fashioned book, published in England, called the *Queen of the County.* The heroine writes her reminiscences at the end of sixty years. I once thought that was a long time. I have changed my mind as now I have written a record with much of it more than sixty years [past]. Our golden wedding would have been celebrated this coming June 4th, but there will be no celebration. I am alone.

"Perhaps sometime it will be a pleasure to recall these things."

MAPS AND REFERENCES

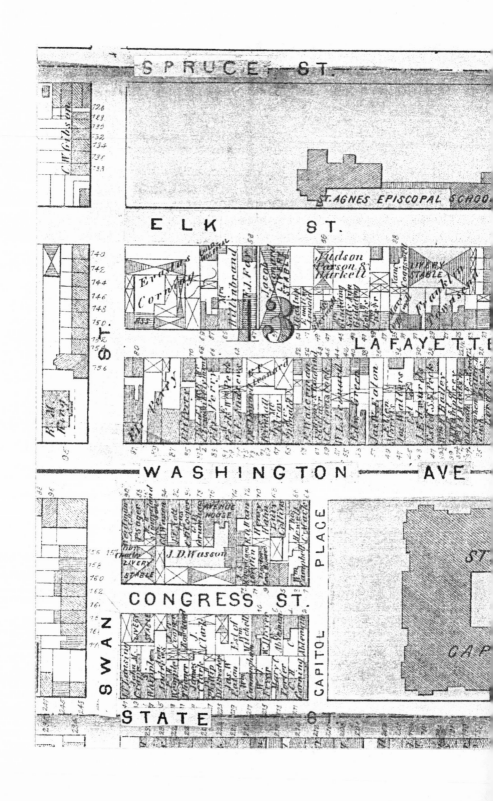

ACADEMY PARK

PARK ST.

ST.

EAGLE ST.

STATE HALL

CITY HALL

Est. R. Hun

Them Hun

BISHOPS HOUSE
The Croswell
Doane

Bernard

D.P.
Bernard

M. Howard
Tennsend

J. V. L.
Pruyn

H. Miller
Buckler

Jas Kidd

S. H.
Madison

Fredrick

ALBANY ACADEMY

E. D.
Palmer

Est. of R. H. King

Dr.
Hood

Butler

J. A. Saunders

P

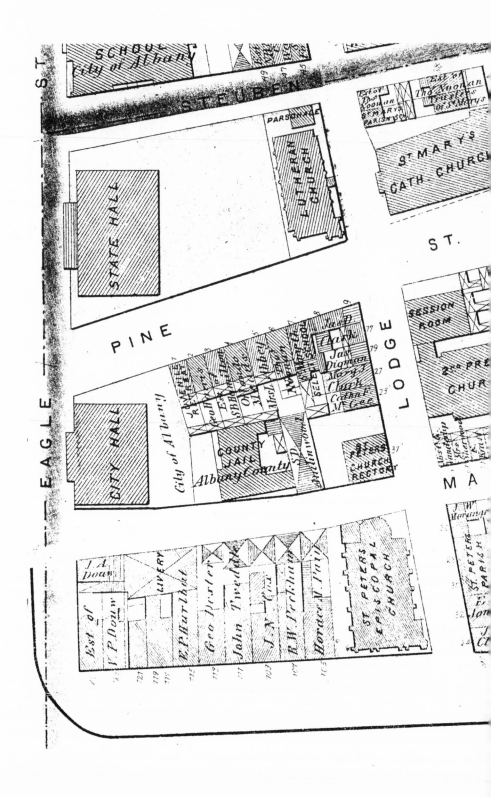

LIST OF ABBREVIATIONS

ACD   *Albany City Directories.*

A.I.H.A.   Albany Institute of History and Art.

Chronicles   Reynolds, Cuyler. *Albany Chronicles.*

DAB   *Dictionary of American Biography.*

DNB   *Dictionary of National Biography, 1912–1921.*

Harsha   David Addison Harsha. *Noted Living Albanians and State Officials.*

HMGFM   Reynolds, Cuyler. *Hudson-Mohawk Genealogical and Family Memoirs.*

H.P.H.   Huybertie Pruyn Hamlin.

NYSM   Hill, Frederick S. *New York State Men: Biographical Studies and Character Portraits.*

WBD   *Webster's Biographical Dictionary.*

WWW   *Who Was Who.*

NOTES

Notes to In Memoriam

1. Wendell Tripp, "A Memory of Alice Kenney," *New York History,* 66, 2, April 1985.

2. William Rowley, "Celebration, Grief for Alice Kenney," *Times Union*, Feb. 5, 1985.

Notes to Introduction

1. The author's first name appears throughout family documents with various spellings — *Huybertie, Huybertje,* and *Hibertie.* In this edition her name is spelled as it was on her christening certificate and in her mother's will — *Huybertie.* (The McKinney Library has cataloged the material by the spelling the author most often used as a signature — *Hibertie.*)

2. William Kennedy, *O Albany!* (New York and Albany: Viking and Washington Park Press, 1983), 15.

Notes to Prologue

1. "Purely Personal and Thirteen Elk Street," Hamlin Papers, Box 21, Folder 152.

2. Here and throughout text, editorial changes introduced to make material more readable are signaled by brackets and ellipses.

Notes to Chapter 1

1. The Albany Academy, founded in 1813, opened in 1817 in a building by Philip Hooker north of the Capitol; Academy Park was completed in 1833. The first principal was Theodorus Romeyn Beck (1791–1855), a doctor who published in 1823 a book on medical jurisprudence which became a standard text. This school, attended by generations of Albany patricians, moved in 1932 to its present quarters, designed by Marcus Reynolds, on Academy Road. The old building, restored in 1935 by Reynolds as a W.P.A. project, is now the Joseph Henry Memorial, the headquarters of the City Board of Education. James H. Manning, *Albany's Historic Street* (Albany: National Savings Bank, 1918); see also Cornelia Brooks Gilder, ed. *Albany Architects: The Present Looks at the Past* (Albany: Historic Albany Foundation, 1978), articles on Reynolds, 19, Hooker, 2.

2. J. V. L. (John Van Schaick Lansing) Pruyn (1811–1877) was an eminent citizen of the city and the state. He was descended in the sixth generation from Frans Janse Pruyn,

a tailor who had come to the Hudson Valley when it was still ruled by the Netherlands. Frans Janse's descendants worked hard, lived comfortably, and won the respect of their neighbors. All their wives were of Dutch descent, some daughters of substantial families, though the colonial Pruyns did not themselves become members of the group of wealthy merchant patricians who guided Albany's civic affairs. J. V. L. Pruyn's father was David Pruyn (1771–1843). His mother, Huibertje Lansing (1773–1855), was noted for her strong and benevolent character, particularly for her efforts in founding Sunday schools in the early nineteenth century, when poor children had few other opportunities to learn to read. John, named for his mother's father, John Van Schaick Lansing, was the youngest of their eleven children, of whom only one sister and one brother survived early childhood.

When he was thirteen, John entered Albany Academy, which had been founded in 1813 to provide a good education for the young men of prominent families in Albany. After graduating, John studied with a prominent Albany lawyer and was admitted to the bar in 1832, after which he practiced for twenty years, most of them in partnership with a fellow student, Henry H. Martin.

Early in his career he perceived the promise of railroads, and in 1835 became director and counsel for the Mohawk and Hudson between Albany and Schenectady, one of the first lines in the United States. This brought him into close business and personal contact with Erastus Corning (1794–1872), then rising from hardware merchant to iron master to president of the Utica and Schenectady Railroad. In 1840, John married Corning's niece, Harriet Corning Turner (1822–1859). In 1853, he drew the legal instrument creating the New York Central System. Pruyn now retired from his legal practice to devote his time to the railroad. He remained until 1866, when Cornelius Vanderbilt secured control of the road. Pruyn also traveled repeatedly in Europe with his wife, who died in 1859, after the birth of their youngest child, John.

Pruyn now began a career in public office. During his term in the New York State Senate (1861–1863), he served as chair of the Public Works Committee, which supported legislation to authorize the building of a new Capitol. In 1863, he was sent to Congress to complete the second term of Erastus Corning, political activities which brought him into close association with long-time Democratic leader Judge Amasa J. Parker, whose daughter Anna became Pruyn's second wife on September 7, 1865. After their honeymoon in Europe, he was again elected to the U. S. House of Representatives, serving from 1867 to 1869. Their elder daughter Harriet Langdon, named for Anna's mother, was born on January 31, 1868.

Pruyn held no public office after 1870. He used his leisure for European travel and enjoyed his home and his growing children. He noted Huybertie's birth, in 1873, in his diary. Although sixty-two when she was born, he remained vigorous enough to give his younger daughter one memorable ride on his shoulders. His health was failing, however, and he died on November 27, 1877 at sixty-six.

3. Elkanah Watson (1758–1842) came to Albany from Rhode Island in 1789. A journalist and promoter, he advocated many city improvements, including the paving of streets and the building of what became the Erie Canal. His best known campaign sought to cut off the long water spouts which carried rain water from steep Dutch roofs to gutters in the middle of the street because they interfered with vehicular traffic. Dutch housewives who found that the water then poured back into their cellars became so enraged that they pursued Watson down the street with their brooms. After 1817 Watson sought greener

pastures in Berkshire County, Massachusetts, where he pioneered in agricultural societies and county fairs. See Winslow C. Watson, ed., *Men and Times of the Revolution; or Memoirs of Elkanah Watson*, 2nd ed., (Elizabethtown, N.Y.: Crown Point Press, 1968); and Hugh M. Flick, *Elkanah Watson: Gentleman-Promoter, 1758–1842* (New York: Columbia University Press, 1947).

4. Harmanus Bleecker (1779–1849), descended from an Albany Dutch fur trading and merchant family, was admitted to the bar in 1801 and practiced law in Albany until 1838. He was elected to Congress in 1811 and to the New York State Assembly in 1814 and 1815. Deeply interested in preserving the city's Dutch heritage, he was a leading member of thé St. Nicholas Society.

J. V. L. Pruyn became acquainted with Bleecker as a young lawyer, and through the St. Nicholas Society. In 1839 Bleecker asked Pruyn to take charge of his affairs. Pruyn eventually became trustee of the fund Bleecker had left to the citizens of Albany, which was used for construction of Harmanus Bleecker Hall. Bleecker's story is told in detail in Harriet L. P. Rice, *Harmanus Bleecker: An Albany Dutchman* (Albany, 1924).

5. The New York Central Railroad, organized in 1853, combined eight existing lines spanning New York State and two "paper" lines which had never been built into the corporation and was capitalized at $23 million. Erastus Corning was elected president, Dean Richmond of Buffalo vice-president, and J. V. L. Pruyn secretary and treasurer. Pruyn also served for a number of years as attorney for the road. Corning and Pruyn worked together closely to maintain control of the road until Corning retired as president in April 1864, after which Corning's power declined. In January, 1867, Cornelius Vanderbilt seized control and succeeded in throwing Corning's supporters off the board of directors in December, 1869. Irene G. Neu, *Erastus Corning: Merchant and Financier* (Ithaca, N.Y.: Cornell University Press, 1960).

6. Pruyn, who had long advocated a more impressive Capitol, was a member of the Senate when the Legislature authorized the new structure on April 24, 1863. He was appointed to the original Capitol Commission, which on December 7, 1867, accepted plans by Thomas Fuller, an English architect who had designed the Canadian Parliament building in Ottawa. Excavation began immediately, the first stone being laid on July 27, 1869, following an oration by Pruyn, then a Congressman. C. R. Roseberry, *Capitol Story* (Albany: State of New York, 1964), 16, 24–25.

7. The New York State Board of Regents, established in 1784 as the governing body of the University of the State of New York, was empowered to supervise secondary and higher education. In the mid-nineteenth century its members made periodic visits of inspection to academies and colleges, and were also responsible for the State Library and the State Museum; after about 1890 they also had authority to license members of all professions except law. Though the position was unpaid, it carried great prestige, and those appointed were distinguished leaders in public service. Pruyn was a member from 1844, and Chancellor from 1862 until his death, the longest term in the history of the Board. "Board of Regents" in Alexander C. Flick, ed., *History of the State of New York* (New York: Columbia University Press, 1937), IX: 16–21.

8. The Albany Institute, formed in 1824 by consolidation of two existing organizations, had divisions of physical science and natural science, and a new division of history and literature. During Pruyn's presidency (1856–1877), the Institute developed an interest in local history. In the 1870s it held field meetings at historic sites, thereby combining an educational experience with a fashionable social occasion. After Pruyn's time, however, control of the Institute reverted to professional scientists who did not seek to build a broad popular base of support. By 1900, when it merged with the Historical and Art Society, the Institute had a venerable tradition, a valuable library, and little forward impetus. James H. Hobbins, "Shaping a Provincial Learned Society: The Early History of the Albany Institute," in *The Pursuit of Knowledge in the Early American Public: American Scientific and Learned Societies from Colonial Times to the Civil War*, ed. Alexander C. Olsen and Sanford C. Brown (Baltimore: Johns Hopkins, 1973); James H. Hobbins, "The Albany Institute and Resistudes in the Learned Culture" (unpublished, May 1975).

9. The St. Nicholas Society, formed in the early nineteenth century, was a benevolent organization to "keep the peace of St. Nicholas" and to assist poor and needy persons of Dutch descent. It was particularly noted for its annual banquets on December 6, St. Nicholas Day, but these ceased after 1850. The Society was still listed in the *Albany City Directory* as meeting monthly in the chapel of the Reformed Church, until 1891. Rice, 70–71.

Notes to Chapter 2

1. "When I was about seven, the Chandlers had laid up enough money to retire, and wanted their own home. It was a sad day when they left us, with their canary bird, and drove off in our carriage to the apartment they had taken at 463 Central Avenue. . . . Thither we often journeyed to see them." H.P.H., "Purely Personal and Thirteen Elk Street," 20–21.

2. Dr. James W. Cox (1828–1896), born in Otsego County, graduated from Albany Medical College in 1852. Choosing to practice homeopathy, he developed an extensive practice, helped found the Albany Homeopathic Hospital, and was a leader in societies of homeopathic medicine.

3. Dr. Cox and three other homeopaths organized their own dispensary in 1867, and the Albany Homeopathic Hospital was started in 1872. A building at 123 North Pearl Street was purchased and remodeled in 1875, and the hospital remained there until 1906, when it moved into new facilities at 161 North Pearl Street. In 1923, when the distinction between homeopaths and regular doctors had largely disappeared, the name was changed to Memorial Hospital, and in 1957 it moved to its present site on Northern Boulevard. "A Tribute to Long Service," *Knickerbocker News*, November 16, 1968.

Homeopathy was a medical system based upon the theories of Samuel Hahnemann (1755–1843), a German physician who observed that some drugs produced the same symptoms in a healthy person that they relieved in a sick person; he also believed that diluting a drug increased its potency. Allopaths, or "regular doctors," followed traditional concepts about the efficacy of drugs. In the late nineteenth century, most American homeopaths had moved away from strict adherence to Hahnemann's theories, and many, like Dr. Cox were "eclectics," dissatisfied not only with the inability of orthodox medicine to relieve much suffering, but also with the violence of some of its treatments. Many patients, particularly wealthy and socially prominent people, thought homeopathy was safer, and were also impressed by its vogue among European nobility and upper classes. E. Richard Brown, *Rockefeller Medicine Men: Medicine and Capitalism in America* (Berkeley: University of California Press, 1979), 64, 88, 110.

4. The City Hall, across Academy Park from the Pruyn home, was built by Philip Hooker in 1829, and destroyed by fire on February 10, 1880. The jail behind it was used from 1854 to 1904. The new City Hall, designed by H. H. Richardson in Romanesque style, was completed on the same site in 1883 and is still in use.

5. Several sources indicate that the correct date of this accident was May, 1882.

6. Benjamin Franklin Stevens (1833–1902), born in Barnet, Vermont, held various antiquarian and library positions in the United States before moving to London in 1860 to join his brother, Henry, in the book-selling business. After a brief partnership, he struck out on his own, serving as agent for many American libraries and private buyers. He had a lifelong interest in indexing and publishing facsimiles of documents relating to the American Revolution. DAB, IX, pt. 2, 606–607.

7. Anna Sewell (1820–1878) wrote *Black Beauty: Autobiography of a Horse* (1877), her only book, to encourage humane treatment of animals.

Stella Austin, an English author, wrote a score of books between 1873 and 1892, dealing "both pleasantly and with considerable understanding with small children's everyday dreams." They included *Somebody* (1875), and *Pat* (1880), and though popular in their time, were inferior in literary quality. Roger Lancelyn Green, *Teller of Tales* (New York: Franklin Watts, 1946).

Maria Edgeworth (1767–1849), a contemporary of Jane Austen, is best known for her novels of fashionable life and of Ireland. The *Parent's Assistant* (1796), her first attempt at fiction, was a collection of stories.

Rev. J. Erskine Clarke founded the magazine *Chatterbox* in 1866 in England to raise the moral level of periodicals available to children. It included stories, biographical and scientific articles, and many pictures. There was an American edition, but it was read far more in America as an annual.

8. Baroness Elizabeth Martineau des Chesnez's *Lady Green Satin and Her Maid Rosette* (1902) is a story about Jean Paul, a boy who travels from his home in the Pyrenées to Paris with his trained white mice to earn money for his mother and sisters.

Captain Frederick Marryat's (1792–1848) *Children of the New Forest* is a story of the English Civil War, in which four orphaned children of a cavalier are hidden in the New Forest by a gamekeeper who brings them up as his grandchildren.

Juliana Horatia Gatty Ewing (1841–1885), the daughter of a Yorkshire vicar, as "Mrs. Ewing" wrote a number of children's books, including *Lob Lie-by-the-Fire* (1873) and *Jackanapes* (1884).

Charlotte M. Yonge (1823–1901) wrote *The Heir of Redclyffe* (1853), and followed it with 160 books for children, many of them historical novels about England and France. As editor of the *Monthly Packett* (1851–1889), a magazine for young people, she was one of the leading authorities on children's literature in late nineteenth-century England.

Bertha M. Clay wrote *Queen of the County* under the pseudonym Charlotte Monica Braeme. It was eventually reprinted in New York in 1901. The same is presumably true of *Margaret and Her Bridesmaids*, by the author of *The Valley of a Hundred Fairies* (New York, 1897). See *U.S. Catalogue, 1902*; *English Catalogue of Books* (London, 1890).

9. Jacob Abbott (1803–1879), author for young people and teachers, was particularly noted for the Rollo books and the Franconia series (1850–1853).

Thomas Bailey Aldrich (1836–1907), a writer from Portsmouth, N.H., published in 1870 *The Story of a Bad Boy*, said to be his best piece of prose. Editor of the *Atlantic Monthly* from 1881 to 1890, he was well known for short stories such as "Marjorie Daw" (1873).

Susan Bogert Warner (1819–1885) of Constitution Island, near West Point, N.Y., wrote several novels, of which *The Wide, Wide World* (1850) and *Queechy* (1852) were the most popular. The first, a best seller for years, concerned the intellectual and spiritual growth of a young girl after the death of her parents, and included vivid scenes of rural life in the lower Hudson Valley.

Louisa May Alcott (1832–1888) wrote a number of successful books after *Little Women* (1868–69).

10. Ann McVicar Grant (1755–1838) lived in the Albany area for ten years, 1758–1768, while her father, Captain Duncan McVicar, served in the French and Indian War. Returning to Scotland, she married Rev. James Grant of Laggan (died 1801), by whom she had eight children. She drew on her Albany experiences in *Memoir of An American Lady* (1808).

James Fenimore Cooper (1789–1851) wrote, among his many novels about American history, the Littlepage Trilogy on the mid-nineteenth century in the Anti-Rent controversy. The first two volumes, *Satanstoe* (1845) and *The Chainbearer* (1846), contain vivid scenes in colonial and post-Revolutionary Albany.

There is no reason to believe Domine Theodorus Frelinghuysen Jr. (1759) wrote any history of Albany; H.P.H. may have confused him with Rev. E. P. Rogers, D.D. whose *Historical Discourses on the Reformed Protestant Dutch Church of Albany* (NY: R.P.D. Church Board of Publications, 1858) discusses his career.

Joel Munsell (1808–1880), born in Northfield, Mass., settled in Albany as a young man and became an editor, genealogist, and antiquarian. Most significant of his many publications on local history are *Annals of Albany* (10 volumes, 1850–60), and *Collections on the History of Albany* (4 volumes, 1865–72).

11. Jessie Fothergill's (1851–1891) *The First Violin* was reprinted in Chicago in 1893, but the English edition was evidently considerably earlier.

12. Kate Greenaway (1846–1901) became noted after 1879 for her illustrations for children's books.

Gilbert and Sullivan's *H.M.S. Pinafore* was first produced in Albany at the Leland Opera House, February 17, 1879, and was a great success. *Chronicles*, 696.

13. This play must have taken place between 1882 and 1884, when Frau zum Busch, a member of the St. Agnes faculty, taught German at the school. St. Agnes Archives. *ACD*.

14. The Albany Female Academy, in the early nineteenth century the principal school for patrician girls, was founded in 1814 and moved in 1834 to the west side of North Pearl Street, where it remained until 1892, when it removed to 155 Washington Avenue, next door to Harmanus Bleecker Hall. Its present location is on Academy Road.

15. J. Mollinard, professor of French at Albany Academy and Albany Female Academy, lived at 2 Park Place.
Jenny Lind (1820–1887), the "Swedish Nightingale," sang in Albany in 1851 while on her American tour, 1850–1852.

16. Beautiful blond Eliza Brown married in 1804 Stephen Jumel, a New York wine merchant who amassed a considerable fortune. In 1833 she married Aaron Burr, but divorced him a year later because she feared he would run through her fortune. Aaron Burr (1756–1836) studied law and practiced in Albany from 1781 to 1783, before his term as Vice-President (1801–1805), his trial for his duel with Alexander Hamilton (1804), and his acquittal of treason charges (1807); after 1812 he resumed his law practice in New York City. Mr. and Mrs. Jumel were friends of Joseph Bonaparte. During his sojourn in America (1815–1832), he visited them at their mansion at Washington Heights in New York. Joseph Bonaparte (1768–1844), eldest brother of Napoleon Bonaparte, reigned as King of Naples (1806–1808) and King of Spain (1808–1813). He visited Albany August 15, 1822.
Charles Dickens would have visited the Jumel mansion on his American tour in 1842; *Great Expectations* was published in 1860–61.
Anna Parker's visit to Madame Jumel was in 1862. She wrote an account of it which was published in a history of the mansion by its curator.

17. Anne Grant observed that it was an old Dutch custom to plant a tree at the birth of a member of the family. Quoted in Helen Wilkinson Reynolds, *Dutch Houses in the Hudson Valley Before 1776* (New York: Tayson and Clark, Ltd., 1929; reprint Dover, 1965), 55.

18. The Pruyn Library at North Pearl Street and Clinton Avenue was torn down in 1968.

19. David Pruyn and his family were members of the Second Reformed Church. It split with the First Reformed Church about 1800. J. V. L. Pruyn remained affiliated with that congregation until after the deaths of his mother and his first wife, although Harriet Turner Pruyn and the Corning family were Epicopalians. He joined St. Peter's Church in 1859, but until the end of his life attended New Year's services in the Dutch Reformed Church.
St. Peter's Church, founded as an Anglican mission in 1715, served the British garrison, English settlers, and the Iroquois Indians throughout the colonial period. Rev. Henry Munro came to St. Peter's in 1768 and remained until 1773 or 1774. During the Revolution it was held together by Patriot laymen, including Albany's first Revolutionary mayor John Barclay, who read the service occasionally. The membership was much diminished, but

Aunt Catherine's memories of imprisonment and persecution are overstated. Joseph A. Hooper, *A History of St. Peter's Church in the City of Albany* (Albany: Fort Orange Press, 1900).

Early in the nineteenth century the highway to Schenectady was called "The Bouwerie" because it passed among Dutch farms. The name was changed to Central Avenue July 15, 1867. By this time it had become the main street of a working class district, many of whose menfolk were employed in the New York Central Railroad stockyards at West Albany. William Kennedy, *O Albany!* (New York: Viking, 1983), 142.

20. John Lansing Jr. (1754–1829) was an Albany lawyer who served in the Revolution, was mayor (1786–1790), and a delegate to the U. S. Constitutional Convention. An anti-Federalist and follower of George Clinton, he was Chancellor of New York State 1801–1814, after which he returned to the practice of law. *DAB.*

Thurlow Weed (1794–1882) was editor of *The Albany Evening Journal* 1833–1863, after which he moved to New York City. The story about Lansing's disappearance is related in Thurlow Weed Barnes, *Memoir of Thurlow Weed* (Boston: Houghton, Mifflin and Co., 1884), 33–35.

Richard M. Blatchford (1798–1875) and Hugh Maxwell (1787–1873) were New York City lawyers, long time associates of Weed in Whig and Republican politics. *DAB.*

Modern scholars have learned little more about the disappearance of Chancellor Lansing. Joseph R. Strayer commented, "Weed always refused to give more precise information, and descendants of Lansing who investigated his story were satisfied that it had no basis of fact. The most likely solution of the mystery is that Lansing, who was seventy-five at the time of his disappearance, missed his footing on the dock or the gang plank in the dim evening light, fell in the river, and was swept out to sea. Another possibility is that he was robbed and murdered on his way to the boat." Joseph R. Strayer, ed., *The Delegate From New York* (Princeton: Princeton University Press, 1939), 3–4. Glyndon G. Van Deusen, *Thurlow Weed: Wizard of the Lobby* (Boston: Little, Brown and Co., 1947), does not mention this incident and nothing has been added since.

21. The long-standing boundary dispute between New York, Massachusetts, and Connecticut originated because the Dutch had claimed the Connecticut River as the eastern boundary of New Netherland, while Massachusetts and Connecticut claimed all the land extending westward between stated latitudes to the Pacific Ocean under their "sea-to-sea" charters. In 1683 Albany Dutchmen bought from the Indians land along the Hoosatonic River, and assembled Dutch families were living near present-day Great Barrington when the first New Englanders arrived about 1720. By the mid-eighteenth century, local farmers and landowners and provincial governors were disputing titles to the territory between the Berkshire and Taconic hills, and violent episodes erupted in 1755, 1757, 1762, and 1766. In 1773 an intercolonial commission proposed a boundary acceptable to all sides, but the survey was not completed until 1787, by congressionally appointed surveyors. Ruth Piwonka of Kinderhook, New York, former director of the Columbia County Historical Society, provided this information.

Outbreaks of violence between Indians and frontier settlers were exacerbated by wars between the settlers' homelands, England and France. The Schenectady massacre, 1691, set off ten years of warfare whose devastating effect on both French and English Indians prompted a tacit agreement between Albany and Montreal to suspend hostilities in 1701, but despite efforts by Albany leaders, New England was not included, and raids continued there. Infiltrators in both colonies believed that those of the other took advantage of events to increase their profits, and some New Englanders asserted that materials from raids on their homes turned up in the market in Albany. Thomas Elliott Norton, *The Fur Trade in Colonial New York, 1686–1776* (Madison: University of Wisconsin Press, 1974), 129–230; Douglas Edward Leach, *The Northern Colonial Frontier 1607–1763* (New York: Holt, Rhinehart, Winston, 1966), 121. Philip J. Schwarz, *The Jarring Interests* (Albany: SUNY Press, 1979).

22. On February 8, 1690, after the outbreak of King William's War (the War of the League of Augsburg) between France and England, French and Indians from Canada slipped through the woods and destroyed Schenectady. Perhaps one-third of the inhabitants were killed and one-third carried away. Symon Schermerhorn (1658–c.1696) rode sixteen miles through the snow and bitter cold to warn Albany. Others in nineteenth-century Albany shared Aunt Catherine's sentiments about the historic significance of his heroism. Joel Munsell described the event in *Annals of Albany* 2nd ed., Vol. IV, 226–259; Alfred B. Street's poem "The Burning of Schenectady" (1842) gave Longfellow some competition, and a mural by David Lithgow illustrated the event. See "Symon Schermerhorn's Ride," *Dutch Settlers Society of Albany, Yearbook* Vol. 46, (Albany, 1977–79), 5 and, for a picture of the mural, McEneny, *Albany: Capitol City on the Hudson: An Illustrated History* (Woodland Hills, California, Windsor Publication, 1981), 53.

23. The long-standing custom of allowing hogs to run at large in the streets of Albany, where they served as garbage collectors, was characterized by New York City journalist Nathaniel P. Willis, in an often quoted — and much resented — observation of 1830 as "more Dutch than decent." A custom appropriate in a community of three thousand in 1790 did in fact become a nuisance as the population grew eight-fold by 1830, and redoubled to over 50,000 in 1850. Many of the newcomers, however, came from rural districts in Ireland where the family pigs not only contributed to diet, but their butchering and sharing was an important social ritual. The cholera epidemic of 1832 prompted an ordinance that pigs be confined, but it was not always strictly enforced. Finally in 1853, after another cholera epidemic, a final ordinance prohibiting the keeping of hogs was passed, and 15,000 porkers were banished, some of them found in cellars and attics, and even under the beds, of poor citizens. *Chronicles*, 483.

24. Marie Joseph Paul Yves Roch Gilbert Du Motier, Marquis de Lafayette (1757–1834), a French officer who volunteered his services to the American Revolution in 1777, was stationed in Albany in 1781. On his tour of the United States in 1824–1825, he visited Albany three times, September 17, 1824, June 11–12, and July 1, 1825. The grand ball occurred on his first visit. *WBD*.

Notes to Chapter 3

1. As Bertie looked out from the nursery window, she might see the Doane family taking their Sunday constitutional. William Croswell Doane (1832–1913) assisted his father in the work of the diocese of New Jersey, where he was bishop, and succeeded him

as rector of St. Mary's Church, Burlington. In these years he married Sarah Catherine Condit of Newark, New Jersey, and had two daughters, Eliza and Margaret. After a pastorate in Hartford, Connecticut, he was called to the rectorship of St. Peter's Church, Albany, in 1867. Some older members found his High Church innovations outrunning their capacity for change, and his incumbency was stormy. In 1869 the newly created Diocese of Albany elected him its first bishop, and some of his more ardent supporters followed him to his new cathedral, but the Pruyns, while remaining warm personal friends, remained at St. Peter's.

2. The Episcopal Diocese of Albany, comprising 19 counties from Columbia, Greene, and Otsego north to the Canadian border, was set off from that of New York at a convention in September 1858. At the first convention of the new diocese, in December 1868, William Croswell Doane, the thirty-five year old rector of St. Peter's in Albany, was elected bishop, though not without some opposition. The diocese grew phenomenally with the opening up of the Adirondacks, to which many wealthy vacationers brought their Episcopal communion. Hooper, 20–21.

3. William West Durant was the son of an early promoter of railroads into the Adirondack region. To attract attention of New York millionaires, he built Camp Pine Knot on Raquette Lake in 1879, and followed it by several others which he sold to his wealthy friends. Pine Knot passed into the hands of California railroad magnate Collis P. Huntington, but was abandoned after his death in 1900. In 1948 it became the property of the State University of New York at Cortland, which has used it as a recreational and environmental center. On October 18, 1983, fire destroyed three of the thirty original buildings and the many valuable artifacts and antiques they contained. "One of the Adirondack luxury sites hit," *Albany Times Union*, October 19, 1983. See also Craig Gilborne, *Durant: The Fortunes and Woodland Camps of a Family in the Adirondacks* (Sylvan Beach, N.Y.: North Country Books in cooperation with the Adirondack Museum, 1981), and Harvey H. Keyser, *Great Camps of the Adirondacks* (Boston: David R. Godine, 1982).

Walter H. Larom (b. Brooklyn) was ordained in 1884 and served various parishes before going to Saranac Lake, where he remained 1889–1909. *Lloyds Clerical Directory*, 1898.

4. Dr. Edward Livingston Trudeau (1848–1915) was compelled by a lung ailment to move his practice from New York City to the Adirondacks. In 1884 he founded the Adirondack Cottage Sanitarium for treatment of incipient consumption in working men and women, the first institution for open-air therapy in the United States. In 1894 he established the Saranac Laboratory, the first research facility for the study of tuberculosis in America. *WWWA*, 1897–1942.

5. This incident, which must have taken place betweem 1867 and 1869, is not mentioned in the history of St. Peter's Church. The "Queen Anne Silver" consisted of two communion services presented by that sovereign to the Iroquois sachems who visited her in London in 1710. That given to the Mohawks was used by them in their chapel at Hunter and taken by them to Canada after the Revolution. The other, intended for a chapel among the Onondagas that was never built, remained at St. Peter's, which was

the official mission to the Five Nations throughout the colonial period. This Onondaga delegation, which must have come from one of the reservations in western New York, did not succeed in obtaining the six massive pieces, which are still among the church's treasures. Hooper, 481.

6. Dr. Thomas Hun (1808–1896), his sons Dr. Edward Hun (1842–1880) and Dr. Henry Hun (1854–1924), and his grandson, another Dr. Henry Hun (1893–1972).

Two other sons, Marcus Tullius Hun (b. 1845) and Leonard Gansevoort Hun (1848–1891), were lawyers. As allopaths, the Huns were, of course, opponents of Dr. Cox; they staunchly supported the new cathedral parish and were leaders of an independent reform movement in city politics which leaned toward the Republicans. As a consequence, the Pruyns were less intimate with them than with some of their other neighbors.

Notes to Chapter 4

1. J. V. L. Pruyn's funeral took place on November 23, 1877. H.P.H. was four and a half. The details of the service are presented in Jack's sketch of his father in *HMGFM*.

2. An eleven-foot wooden statue of Themis, the Greek goddess of Justice, stood on the dome of Philip Hooker's Capitol (1804–1883). One tradition tells how a young newspaper man, going home in a wind storm in 1880, heard a crash and discovered that the scale of Justice had fallen. A recent history of the present Capitol has it that the statue itself blew down shortly before the building was demolished in 1883. Manning, 35; Roseberry, 13, 19.

3. Erastus Corning Pruyn (1841–1881), the eldest son of J. V. L. Pruyn and Harriet Turner, was compelled by ill health — probably tuberculosis — to live in a warm climate. He settled in Teneriffe, in the Canary Islands, in 1871, and married Maria Delores Velasquez in 1872. He died there on February 1, 1881. This date suggests that H.P.H. misremembered her age at the incident of the red dress, which must have taken place during the preceding summer, 1880, when she was seven.

4. H.P.H. tells more details elsewhere about the coming of Frieda Wagner: "Aunt Mary Corning found her crying in the hall of the United States Hotel at Saratoga. She wore her peasant dress, and her bundles and clothes were piled around her. Aunt Mary's maid, Marie Hoffman, extracted her story from her and took her in charge. She had been brought from Strasbourg by an eccentric old lady from New York, who was now tired of her, and for some trivial offense had discharged her, bag and baggage, but she gave Frieda a good character. After keeping her some time and finding her satisfactory, Aunt Mary turned her over to us, and she stayed about five years." H.P.H. "Purely Personal and 13 Elk Street," 19.

5. The First Lutheran Church was built at the northwest corner of Pine and Lodge Streets, across the street from St. Mary's, in 1871; Rev. Irving Magee, who resided at 9 Lodge Street, was pastor until 1883, when he removed to Kingston, New York. James B.

Keene was a watchmaker at 35 North Pearl Street, home 240 Lark Street, until 1881. *Chronicles*, 648; *ACD*.

6. Grover Cleveland (1837–1908), a Buffalo lawyer and reform mayor, was elected Governor of New York in 1882 and won the Democratic nomination for President in 1884. His running mate was Thomas A. Hendricks (1819–1885), of Indiana, who died soon after the inauguration. The Republican candidate was James G. Blaine (1830–1893). In the course of a long political career as Congressman 1862–1877, Speaker of the House 1869–1875, Senator 1877–1881, and Secretary of State 1881, he had become involved in a bitter rivalry with New York Republican boss Roscoe Conkling. *DAB*.

7. General Farnsworth, a Republican, must have been one of those so incensed by Conkling's high-handed boss rule that they supported Cleveland for Governor in 1882 and then for President in 1884. The local political situation was equally ambiguous. Both parties were split, and Albany's first Irish mayor, Democrat Michael N. Nolan, 1878–1883, had recently been unseated when Republicans won a court challenge to his 1882 re-election on the grounds of vote fraud. Their candidate, Dr. John Swinburne, was then installed, and was in office during the 1884 campaign. Irish-Americans generally favored Blaine, whose sister was the mother superior of a convent, until late in the campaign, when one of his supporters, a Protestant clergyman more zealous than tactful, referred to the Democrats as the party of "Rum, Romanism and Rebellion." See William E. Rowley, "Albany: A Tale of Two Cities, 1820–1880" (Unpublished Ph.D. Dissertation, Harvard University, 1967).

8. William Morris Hunt (1824–1879), brother of architect Richard Morris Hunt, studied in Paris and became a leading painter of his time. His Capitol murals, "The Discoverer" and "The Flight of Night," depicted the accomplishments of Columbus and the concept of Enlightenment.

9. The Assembly Chamber ceiling, the widest stone vault ever constructed, demonstrated almost from the beginning that it was too heavy for the building's foundation. In 1888, when stones began to fall, a commission of architects recommended that it be removed and replaced with a lighter flat ceiling, which was completed in time for the session of 1889. Though there were many charges of speculation and overcharging, no one was ever indicted for fraud. Roseberry, 46, 83–89.

Notes to Chapter 5

1. William Waldorf Astor (1848–1919), son of fur merchant John Jacob Astor, married Mary Dahlgren Paul. He served in the New York Legislature, 1878–1881, but moved to England in 1890. In 1893 he purchased the *Pall Mall Gazette*, in 1899 became a British subject, and was raised to the peerage in 1916.

2. John Walter (1818–1894) inherited the proprietorship of the *London Times* from his father, its founder. A graduate of Oxford, he raised the literary and ethical tone of

the paper, and in 1859 introduced the Walter Cylindrical Press. He had two sons, John Balston (d. 1870) and Arthur S. (H.P.H. must have misremembered the name), who succeeded him at the *Times*.

3. Arthur Penrhyn Stanley (1815–1881), after completing Rugby and Balliol College, entered the Church of England, becoming a leader of the Broad Church Party. His *Life and Correspondence of Dr. Arnold*, his mentor at Rugby, was published in 1844. In 1864 he was appointed Dean of Westminster Abbey and made his tour of the United States in 1878.

Sir George Grove (1820–1900) started his career as a civil engineer, but later became an organist and musicologist. He is best known for his editorship of *Dictionary of Music and Musicians*, still a standard authority.

Dr. Gerald Harper (d. 1929) was a London physician, associated with hospitals for poor clergy and for women. A close friend of Dean Stanley and Sir George Grove, he contributed to their biographies.

4. Charles Loyson, "Père Hyacinthe" (1827–1912), was ordained a priest in 1851, but was excommunicated for heterodoxy in 1869. Married in 1872, he continued to profess his Catholic faith, serving as pastor of a liberal Catholic church in 1873–1874, and in 1879, as rector of a Gallican Catholic church in Paris. (The Gallican Church is the national church of France, which asserts its independence from the Vatican in certain matters of principle.) He was also the author of several works expounding his religious ideas.

5. The Van Rensselaer Manor House (1765–1893), on the north side of Patroon Creek near Broadway, was a Georgian style building, remodeled in 1840 by Richard Upjohn, and wings added in 1847. Then the neighborhood changed drastically, and after the death of Harriet Bayard Van Rensselaer in 1875, the house was no longer used as a residence. In 1893 it was demolished, Marcus Reynolds supervising the transportation of the facade to Williamstown, where it was reconstructed for a fraternity house at Williams College. The site was then used for railroad tracks and other commercial purposes, and is still so used.

6. The *ACD* for 1876 is the first to show the new numbers for Elk Street.

7. The portraits of Anna Parker Pruyn, Erastus Corning, and Mary Parker Corning painted in 1885 by Felix Moscheles (see Chapter 13, Footnote), are now in the Albany Institute of History and Art (A.I.H.A.).

8. In 1910, after Anna Parker Pruyn's death, a large collection of Pruyn pictures, china, silver, glassware, and books — the list required two printed catalogues — was auctioned by American Art Gallery in New York City. The only Pruyn china pieces now at A.I.H.A. are the large Chinese export punch bowl, one round 9-½" blue and white Delft plate (probably — not documented), and two large French vases. A.I.H.A. Curatorial Records.

9. Mr. Pruyn was not the first Minister to Japan, but the second. He followed Townsend Harris.

Notes to Chapter 6

1. There is no mention in the *ACD* of John Eytal, suggesting that this may have been sobriquet for "the Italian," and that his name was something else.

2. The west end of Capitol Park was laid out about the same time that the Alfred E. Smith building was erected in 1926. To make room for Lafayette Park in 1908, about thirty houses, including those of Erastus Douw Palmer, Leonard Kip, and James Parsons, were demolished. *National Register.*

3. This dollhouse, with its furnishings, is now in A.I.H.A.

Notes to Chapter 7

1. H.P.H. was five years old. In 1878 Albany had the nation's third working telephone exchange, with one hundred subscribers. In 1879 a commercial telephone company was organized, and in 1883 the Hudson River Telephone Company. McEneny, 21.

2. The group photograph was taken in early 1878, when H.P.H. was five years old.

3. Billings Learned Hand (1872–1961) was the son of Samuel Hand, a leading Albany lawyer and great nephew of William Law Learned. After earning his B.A. and M.A. from Harvard in philosophy, he graduated from Harvard Law School in 1896 and joined the firm of Marcus T. Hun. In 1902 he moved to New York. His opinions were so widely respected he was often called the tenth member of the U.S. Supreme Court. *DAB.*

4. Lancers was a form of square dance for eight or sixteen couples, whose five figures were performed at a brisk walk in strict tempo. The polka was a nineteenth century dance for couples in 2/4 time, characterized by a hopping "polka step"; the "heel and toe" polka had a heel and toe step. By the late nineteenth century, both versions resembled a vivacious waltz. Schottische was a round dance for couples in 2/4 time or 6/8 time, which resembled a slow polka. W. G. Raffe, *Dictionary of the Dance* (New York: A. S. Barnes and Co., 1964).

5. Walton W. Battershall (1840–1920), born in Troy, graduated from General Theological Seminary and was ordained in 1866, then served in various charges including five years in Rochester, 1869–1874. He was called to St. Peter's, Albany, where he remained for the rest of his career. He was married in 1864, but his wife died in 1872, leaving him with three children, Fletcher, Cornelia and Anna. Frederick S. Hill, *New York State Men: Biographical Studies and Character Portraits* (Albany: Argus Co., 1906).

6. The "Overslaugh," a bar in the Hudson River below Coeymans, was so difficult that captains often had to wait until high tide to get over it. After the Civil War it was improved by a series of dikes and dams designed by federal engineers, and was finally removed in 1916. McEneny, 25, 85.

7. The jingle, which throws light on the pronunciation of this name of French origin, was "Dear Mr. Pumpelly / fell down in the jelly / right up to his belly / oh helly, oh helly!" Harmon Pumpelly was very wealthy, having made a fortune in land investment. After the death of his first wife, he traveled in Europe in great style, in a coach with four outriders.

8. H.P.H. states elsewhere that Gilbert Wilson was closely associated with her father in the New York Central and dates his suicide in 1865. It was therefore certainly not related to the failure of four Albany banks in May 1861, in the financial uncertainty at the outbreak of the Civil War which strained the resources of many Albany patricians and may well have prompted the sobriquet "Church of the Holy Bankrupts." The phrase gained added pungency because there was in Albany a Church of the Holy Innocents, founded in 1850 by a wealthy citizen in memory of his four children.

Notes to Chapter 8

1. Having a farmers' market in the center of the city *was* unusual for that era. The farmers' market was removed to Hudson Avenue in 1888.

2. The Albany Railway Company was organized in 1863, and its horsecars began operating in 1864. The granite blocks for the foundation of the new Capitol, some of which weighed four tons, were quarried in Hallowell, Me., shipped by water to the Capitol Commission's own dock, then drawn up the hill on the street railway tracks to a spur built into the Capitol grounds. Roseberry, *Capitol Story*, 24, 91.

3. Samuel J. Tilden (1814–1886), who led the destruction of the Tweed Ring in New York City, was elected Governor of New York, 1875–1876, and ran as the Democratic candidate for President in 1876. He won more popular votes than Republican Rutherford B. Hayes, but Hayes was declared the victor in the Electoral College. *WWW.*
Horatio Seymour (1810–1886), of Utica, married Maria Bleecker, an Albany patrician, and resided in Albany during his long public career, which included terms as governor, 1852–1854 and 1862–1864. He was the Democratic candidate for President in 1868, but was resoundingly defeated by Ulysses S. Grant. *WWW.*
Roscoe Conkling (1829–1888) was the New York State Republican boss and U. S. Senator, 1867–1881. He was particularly noted for his ruthless and corrupt use of patronage to maintain the power of his machine and for his opposition to Civil Service reform; he finally resigned from the Senate during a dispute with President Garfield over appointments to the New York City Customs House. *WWW.*

4. The Second Presbyterian Church, at Chapel Street and Maiden Lane, was erected according to designs by Philip Hooker in 1813. It was remodeled into a theater after 1918, and demolished in 1972. The weather vane in the form of a fish and pumpkin, supposed to symbolize Massachusetts and Connecticut respectively, and thus indicating early nineteenth-century Yankee influence, was then removed to the Albany Academy in 1922.

5. A turf speedway, one mile in length, on Washington Avenue between Quail Street and Manning Boulevard was opened on July 4, 1895. For sleigh racing on Western Avenue in the winter, see Chapter 15.

6. The Tweddle Building, named for wealthy merchant John Tweddle, was built in 1860. It had stores and offices on the lower floors, and on the top floor a public hall, noted as a concert hall. The Tweddle Building was destroyed in a spectacular fire on January 16, 1883, but it was rebuilt and continued in use until 1895, when it and the Corning house next door were demolished for the Ten Eyck Hotel. This in turn was replaced in 1982 by the present Hilton Hotel.

7. John Barker Church was a well-born Englishman who came to the United States incognito during the Revolution and eloped with Angelica, eldest daughter of General Philip Schuyler. He engaged in various business ventures and land speculation in America and later returned to England, where he became a member of Parliament. His son, Walter, who purchased the Van Rensselaer leases in Albany County after the Anti-Rent War, spent the rest of his life in extensive litigation to collect back rent. Bennett, 78.

8. Geological Hall was known as Agricultural Hall in 1858, when the specimens assembled by Professor James Hall in his pioneer geological surveys were deposited there. In 1870 this collection became the nucleus of the New York State Museum.

Notes to Chapter 9

1. Bertie's family circle met in many gatherings of sixteen first cousins, grandchildren of Judge and Mrs. Amasa J. Parker. Son of a Connecticut minister, Amasa J. Parker served as principal of an academy in Hudson and graduated from Union College before he was twenty. He then studied law with an uncle in Delaware County, was admitted to the bar and practiced there, and served a term in Congress when he was barely thirty. Appointed a justice of the New York State Supreme Court, he conducted the 1845 trial of an Anti-Rent militant charged with the murder of the sheriff of Delaware County, and his even-handed fairness did much to reduce the tension of this explosive situation. Active in Democratic politics, he was his party's candidate for governor in 1856 and 1858, both years of Republican landslides, and thereafter practiced law actively until his death. Of the eight children born to him and his wife, four survived to become Bertie's mother, uncle, and two aunts.

2. Cookies played an important part in the Dutch tradition, from which the word has entered the English language. St. Nicholas cookies, used in celebrating his feast day on December 6, represented the figure of the saint, a foot or more high, and frosted in various colors. They were shaped in elaborately carved molds, originally brought from the Netherlands. *Dood koeks* were very hard wafers, four to six inches across, bearing the name and date of death of the deceased, distributed to mourners at funerals and treasured as mementos. J. J. Schilstra, "Dutch 'koekplanken' of the Seventeenth and Eighteenth Centuries," *de Halve Maen*, v. XLII, No. 3, 17. *Nieujahrkoeks* were flat

cookies like *dood koeks* made in a wafer-iron. *Olykoeks* were balls of raised dough with fruit in the middle, fried in oil or deep fat, like jelly doughnuts.

3. Edna Lyell was the pseudonym of Ada Ellen Bayly (1857–1903), an English author of numerous novels with religious overtones.

4. The Hudson River State Asylum at Poughkeepsie, now the Hudson River Psychiatric Center, was founded in 1867.

5. The word "stateroom" originated from the fact that rooms of state in palaces or castles were so called. It was then applied to individual apartments in steamboats or railway cars. The practice of naming such rooms for states instead of numbering them seems to have been limited to the Mississippi River, except for the "Texas," which was given to the large bow apartment that on some western vessels was used by the boat's officers. Fred Irving Dayton, *Steamboat Days* (New York: Tudor, 1939).

6. Brigadier General Richard Montgomery (1736–1775) was field commander of the Continental army invading Canada. In 1775 he captured Montreal, but was killed in the unsuccessful attack on Quebec. In 1773 he married Janet Livingston (1743–1828), a sister of Chancellor Robert R. Livingston of Clermont. Barrytown is nearby.

7. Perhaps H.P.H.'s memory of four summers spent at Newport was inaccurate, or perhaps they were not consecutive, because events which took place there may be dated in 1880, 1881, 1883, and 1884.
S. Wier Mitchell (1829–1914) was a prominent Philadelphia neurologist, author of several books on medical subjects and the novel *Hugh Wynne, Free Quaker. WWWA.*

8. Zara Malcolm Freeborne (1861–1906) was the artist of an 1884 portrait of Huybertie and Harriet Pruyn, 17-^{15}/$_{16}$" x 14-^{1}/$_{16}$", oil on canvas, which was given to A.I.H.A. after H.P.H.'s death but has deteriorated and is no longer in existence.

Notes to Chapter 10

1. The Albany Gaslight Company had begun lighting the streets on November 1, 1845, and supplying residents soon after. The Albany Electric Illuminating Company contracted with the city for street lighting June 21, 1881. H.P.H. was eight years old.
The paving of city streets with granite blocks began in the 1870s on principal thoroughfares, and by 1885 there were four miles of paved streets to thirty-four miles of cobbles. *Chronicles.*

2. Harriet Gaylord (1824–1905), niece of Edwin Croswell, long-time editor of *The Argus*, for many years kept a private school at Catskill, attended by sons of a number of Albany patricians.
St. John's School, Ossining, New York, was founded in 1869 and remained in operation until 1948.

3. John T. Hoffman (1828–1888) was a Tammany Hall politician who served as mayor of New York City from 1865 to 1868 and governor from 1868 to 1872. His election as governor was assisted by large scale vote fraud in New York City, and when public sentiment turned against Tammany, his political career was ruined, despite his effort to break with the machine. He then returned to his New York law practice.

4. Roswell P. Flower (1835–1899) began his career in Watertown, N.Y., then moved to New York City, where he became a financier and acquired considerable wealth. This was his principal asset in several attempts to gain the Democratic nomination for governor, in which office he served from 1892 to 1895. *BDGUS.*

Notes to Chapter 11

1. In the mid-nineteenth century the Hudson Valley took from Boston the lead in the business of cutting ice for use in the brewing and meat-packing industries as well as for homes and hotels. In the winter large blocks of ice were cut from the river, its tributary creeks, and ponds constructed for the purpose, and stored, protected by layers of salt hay, in large ice houses on the river banks. In summer the ice was shipped on barges to local consumers, to New York City (where most of it was used), and even as far as the West Indies. At its height, ice-harvesting employed about 20,000 men, (many working in brick yards during the off seasons), 1,000 horses, and filled 135 ice houses between Albany and New York, a considerable number of them in Albany County. About one year in three, thaws ruined the ice crop. Bennett, 77.

2. After two centuries of private supply, the city of Albany established a public water system in 1850, building a reservoir at Rensselaer Lake (now the Six Mile Water Works) on a branch of Patroon Creek. But this source proved insufficient for the growing population, and after 1873 water was also taken from the river. That supply, however, was increasingly polluted by sewage discharged from towns upstream. It was observed during an 1891 typhoid epidemic that only 2 of 203 cases came from the districts served by the reservoir. The situation was much improved by a filtration plant for river water opened in 1899. *Chronicles*; McEneny.

3. St. Agnes Cemetery, the Catholic burying ground on the Menands Road next to the Albany Rural Cemetery, was opened in 1867.
St. Mary's. the oldest Catholic church in Albany, founded in 1797, was in H.P.H.'s childhood housed in its third and present building, a Romanesque structure at Pine and Lodge Streets where it has been since 1869.

4. The United Society of Believers of Christ's Second Appearance, founded by Mother Ann Lee (1736–1784) in Manchester, England, came to Niskayuna in 1774 and established a community which survived until 1930. Called Shakers by outside observers of their worship, which included vigorous group rhythmic movement akin to dancing, they were noted for their simple, disciplined life, their dedication to industry as a religious exercise, and their adherence to celibacy. At their height in the mid-nineteenth century, the Niskayuna community was home to perhaps 350 of the 6,000 Shakers in the United

States, who achieved economic success with a wide variety of crafts, such as high quality agriculture, production of seeds, and manufacture of furniture which is now valued for its simple, functional beauty. But their numbers could increase only by conversion and adoption of orphans, and as these sources fell off, they declined. Their cemetery and other parts of the Niskayuna site are now on the National Register of Historic Places. Bennett.

5. A Mrs. J. Somers, hairdresser, was listed at various addresses, 1893–1900.

Delia Guardinier, 206 Livingston Avenue, was listed until 1882 as a dressmaker, after that as a cake maker.

6. Alfred Booth, 160 Livingston Avenue, was a grocer until 1891, when he was listed as doorman at the New York Central Depot, and so remained for the rest of the century. Evidently he so impressed local travelers that H.P.H. misremembered him as on duty during her childhood. *Chronicles*, 800.

Notes to Chapter 12

1. There was an excellent school within a block of Bertie's home. Bishop Doane, whose father had been a leader in education, especially of young women, began his Episcopate by founding St. Agnes School in 1870. After two years in a house on Columbia Place it moved into its own building at the northeast corner of Elk and Swan Streets, with a hearthfire ceremony that became a school tradition. Its curriculum included a thorough grounding in languages — Bertie eventually studied French, German and Latin — basic mathematics, and general literary, historical, and religious knowledge. It also adopted such then pioneering innovations as kindergarten, which Bertie attended, and physical education. Its reputation spread and besides day students from Albany, boarders came from considerable distances.

2. Mother Helen was Helen Dunham, who, after a broken romance, joined the Sisterhood of the Holy Child Jesus, a diocesan organization founded in 1873 by Bishop Doane, and became its first Mother Superior. She had come to the school in 1872, a teacher of illuminating and watercolors. Sister Eliza was Mrs. Lewis, who, after the death of her husband on their honeymoon, joined the sisterhood and in 1902 became Mother Superior. She taught literature and history and was in charge of the junior room. Members of the sisterhood lived at the school and supervised the boarding students.

Ellen Wright Boyd, born at Winsted, Connecticut, came to St. Agnes in 1872 as a teacher and served as headmistress from 1873 to 1900. H.P.H., "Memories of St. Agnes School 1878–1891, by an Old Girl," H.P.H. Papers, Box 23, Folder 170.

Notes to Chapter 13

1. H.P.H. had gone to Europe when she was six, her mother having been sent to Dieppe for a cure.

2. Sir Laurence Parsons, fourth Earl of Rosse (1840–1908), of Birr Castle, Parsonstown, Ireland, was the eldest son of William Parsons. An astronomer, he investigated the radiation of heat from the moon and wrote a book on the great Nebula of Orion.

3. Mathilde Grauman Marchesi (1826–1913), the wife of Italian baritone and composer Salvatore Marchesi (1822–1895), was a noted singer and voice teacher, who, about 1881, organized the École Marchesi in Paris.

4. Charles Frederick Worth (1825–1895), born in England, moved to Paris in 1858, and established his own fashion house, in which, as couturier to Empress Eugenie, he became the unchallenged arbiter of style.

5. Dame (Alice) Ellen Terry (1847–1928) was a noted actress and an intimate friend of Charles Dickens. After her role as Portia in 1875, she became England's leading Shakespearean actress, dominating the stage from 1878 to 1902. *Chambers*. Her partner was Sir Henry Irving (1838-1905), the first English actor to be knighted.

John Lawrence Toole (1832–1906) was a popular comedian who played throughout the United Kingdom, the United States, and Australia and for many years managed Toole's Theater in London.

Henry James (1843–1916), grandson of wealthy Albany merchant William James, was born in New York City, but passed his first few years in Albany. In 1876 he settled in London, becoming a British subject in 1915. Among his many novels were two depicting perceptions of Europe by young women from the area, *Daisy Miller* (1878) and *The Portrait of a Lady* (1881). He recounted some memories of Albany, including his aunt on Elk Street (Ellen James Van Buren) in his autobiography *A Small Boy and Others* (1913).

6. Junius Spencer Morgan (1813–1890) was a banker, the founder of J. S. Morgan & Company, which his son John made into a major firm.

Oliver Wendell Holmes (1809–1894) was a physician of Boston, professor at Harvard Medical School 1847–1882, and Dean 1847–1853. He was also a literary figure, a founder and contributor of many essays to the *Atlantic Monthly* (1857), and author of much-loved poems, including "The One Hoss Shay."

Notes to Chapter 14

1. The translation of this poem is as follows:

> St. Nicholas good holy man,
> Put your best tabard on,
> Travel therewith to Amsterdam.
> From Amsterdam to Spain,
> Where the oranges
> And the pomegranates
> Roll through the streets.
> St. Nicholas my good friend,
> I have served you always.

> If you will give me something now
> I will love you all my life.

Charlotte Wilcoxen, *Seventeenth Century Albany: A Dutch Profile* (Albany: Albany Institute of History and Art, 1981), 120–121. Translation into English and into seventeenth-century Dutch by Dr. Charles T. Gehring.

2. The Albany custom of New Year's calling survives in the annual open house at the Governor's Mansion.

Notes to Chapter 15

1. Ridgefield Athletic Club was organized in 1884, and its facilities in the undeveloped areas south of Madison Avenue and Partridge Street were opened in 1885; the toboggan chute was built in 1886. Horse shows were held there in 1894 and 1895, and the club house was built in 1897. Later the club became the Ridgefield YMCA.

2. Old Harmanus Bleecker Hall was at 527 Market Street (Broadway).

3. Long & Silsby (James Long and H. W. Silsby), carriage and sleigh manufacturers, 352–362 South Pearl Street, throughout the period.

4. An "Albany Cutter," a swell-bottomed sleigh with a gracefully curving outline which could take four to six passengers, was one of the most beautiful American sleighs. Cutters were manufactured by James Gould (1879) and by several other families. Bennett, 52.

5. Western Avenue was begun in 1789 as the Great Western Turnpike, which eventually extended to Syracuse and Buffalo. The Washington Park Commission acquired title to all the land on both sides of Western Avenue as far out as Manning Boulevard.

6. Little's pond would have been at Forest Hills, the estate on the Menands Road. Charles W. Little was a member of a firm of law book publishers.

7. *The Express* was a morning Republican newspaper, which in 1889 was purchased by William Barnes Jr. and eventually consolidated with *The Press* and *The Knickerbocker* to form *The Knickerbocker News*.

8. Sloan's Hotel, a three-story brick building built in 1830 and destroyed by fire in 1900, was operated by Henry Sloan and his sons, for which family the crossroads of Sloansville was named. The hotel was located in the village of Guilderland.

9. Washington Park Lake, a dammed-up portion of the Ruttenkill, was excavated in 1873, and the Lake House built in 1875; it was replaced by the present one in 1925. The ice palace was built for a winter carnival in 1886–87.

10. The Capitol City Rink Company, S. M. Hickey, manager, Lark near Spruce Street, is listed only in 1885.

11. John Boyd Thacher (1847–1909), eldest son of George Thacher, railroad car wheel manufacturer, graduated from Williams College in 1869 and went into the family business. He followed in his father's footsteps as mayor, serving in that office 1886–1888 and 1896–1898. Among his accomplishments were building the public market square on Hudson Avenue and sponsoring the first winter carnival south of Montreal, for which the ice palace in Washington Park was built. He was also a collector of rare books and manuscripts, particularly about Columbus. After his second term as mayor was cut short by a sudden illness during a civic crisis, he lived in retirement, writing a three-volume work about his Columbus manuscripts which is still regarded with respect by specialists. His summer home was the "Indian Ladder" tract of the Helderbergs, which in 1914 his widow donated to the state as John Boyd Thacher Park.

Notes to Chapter 16

1. Joseph Chamberlain (1836–1914), a British radical reformer and a member of Parliament, prompted the organization of the Liberal Party in 1876, and served in the second and third Gladstone cabinet. In October 1887, he was selected chairman of a three-man commission to resolve differences over the Newfoundland fisheries which had been at issue with the United States since the Peace of 1783. After the negotiations were completed, he married Mary Endicott on November 15, 1888.

2. Daniel Scott Lamont (1851–1905), of Dutchess County, brought to Albany by Governor Tilden in 1874 as Deputy Clerk of the Assembly, also served on *The Argus* as a reporter in 1875, and was later managing editor. He became private secretary to Governor Cleveland in 1883 and to President Cleveland in 1885, and Secretary of War in 1893. Thereafter he returned to private life as a financier.

3. Thomas Francis Bayard (1828–1898), of Pennsylvania, served in the U. S. Senate from 1860 to 1865, as Secretary of State from 1885 to 1889, and as Ambassador to Great Britain from 1892 to 1897.

4. Edmund Charles Genet (1763–1834), whose father was in Louis XVI's foreign office and whose elder sister, Mme. Henrietta Campan, was first lady-in-waiting to Marie Antoinette, was a brilliant student who learned several languages and shared his family's enthusiasm for the American Revolution. He joined the French foreign service and after serving in several courts was then sent to the U. S., where he attempted to stir up support for France's war with Britain and commissioned some privateers, prompting Washington's 1793 Proclamation of Neutrality and a demand for his recall. During the Terror, Genet requested asylum, and in 1794 married Cornelia Clinton (1775–1810), daughter of New York Governor George Clinton. After some years on Long Island, they moved to Rensselaer County, about five miles below Albany. After Cornelia's death, Genet married Martha Osgood, daughter of Washington's paymaster general. He fathered eleven children by his two wives.

George Clinton Genet (1824–1904), born in East Greenbush, was the youngest son of Citizen Genet. He was a lawyer and held the office of Corporation Counsel in New York City.

The house in Schodack which Governor George Clinton purchased from Henry K. Van

Rensselaer and sold to Edmund Genet in 1802 was built by Colonel Van Rensselaer's father Kiliaen in 1742 for his bride, Arriantje Schuyler. The Genets lived there for several years before building a new home, Prospect Hill, on the ridge to the east, which would have been the house where H.P.H. visited.

5. Henry Burden was president of the Rensselaer Iron Works on the Wynantskill, the principal rival of Erastus Corning's iron works on the same stream. In the following generation the two firms were consolidated as the Albany-Rensselaer Iron Works.

6. Beverwyck, a seventy-two room mansion on a hill a mile above the present city of Rensselaer, was built for William P. Van Rensselaer, an heir to the manor land east of the river. Even his contemporaries thought it overly ambitious. The Van Rensselaers' interest in the family land was wiped out by the Anti-Rent clauses of the Constitution of 1846, and about 1850 he sold the house to Paul Forbes, a New York tea merchant. Many legends grew up about it, such as a romantic fiction that said it was haunted by the ghosts of Richard and Alice Forbes, killed in a midnight duel with her rejected lover on New Year's Eve, 1799 — many years before the house was built!

The property was opened as a picnic area, Van Rennselaer Park, in 1905. It passed into the hands of the Franciscan Order in 1911 and became Mount St. Anthony. J. M. Frazer, "Beverwyck Manor: St. Anthony's on the Hudson," *Golden Jubilee Book*.

7. Joseph K. Emmett (1841–1891) originated German dialect comedy, including graceful dancing, sentimental and comic songs, and yodeling. He first presented his character "Fritz" in Buffalo in November 1869, but the real beginning of his great success was a two-week stand in Albany the following month. About 1882 he bought property on Van Rensselaer Boulevard and erected "Fritz Villa."

8. New York governors lived in rented quarters until the present mansion, built about 1850 by Thomas W. Olcott, was rented by Governor Samuel J. Tilden in 1874 and purchased by the State in 1877. In the late 1880s, Governor Hill decided it was too small and had it remodeled in the then-fashionable Queen Anne style, as it appears today.

9. The Albany Rural Cemetery, begun because the former burying ground in present-day Washington Park was full, was incorporated in 1841 and consecrated in 1844. Over 40,000 bodies were transferred from the former burying ground in 1869, when Washington Park was being constructed. On the Menands Road, halfway between Albany and Troy, the Albany Rural Cemetery eventually comprised about 400 acres and was landscaped with lakes, carriage roads, and many trees, shrubs, and other plantings. Its monuments, many by noted artists such as Erastus Douw Palmer, came to be a treasure house of late nineteenth-century memorial sculpture. As was common at the time, it served as a public park, a favorite destination for an afternoon drive. Its records are still among the best sources for nineteenth-century Albany genealogy.

10. Dean Sage (1841–1902), born in Ithaca of a family which contributed much to Cornell University, graduated from Albany Law School 1861 and went into the family lumber business. He was a lover of salmon fishing and a collector of books, particularly on that subject.

11. Tradition has it that the Treaty of Tawasentha was concluded in 1618 by Jacob Elkins, acting for the New Netherland Company, the first Dutch company to trade for furs in the Albany area, and the Mohawk Indians, but there is no documentary support for this. Elkins did build a fort on Castle Island in 1614, and when it was washed away by a freshet in 1617, probably rebuilt it at the mouth of the Normanskill, though no archaeological evidence remains. The neighboring Indians at the time, however, were the Mahicans, an Algonkian tribe who, after fighting with the Mohawks between 1626 and 1629, gradually moved into western Massachusetts, where they were kown as the Stockbridge Indians. The Mohawk, easternmost of the Five Nations of the Iroquois, were then moving into the region from the west, and in 1642 they made the Great Chain of Friendship Treaty with Arent Van Corlaer, a compact inherited by the English and maintained with great ceremony throughout the colonial period; folklore evidently condensed these two agreements into one. Other sites also claimed the Treaty of Tawasentha, such as one on the upper Normanskill, Schenectady County, which is identified by a roadside historical marker.

12. Captain William Kidd (circa 1645–1701), a New England ship owner and sea captain, with his wife owned considerable property in New York. He became acquainted with various merchants and officials, including Robert Livingston. In 1896 they commissioned him (whether it was to pursue pirates based in Madagascar or to engage in trade with them is in dispute). He turned pirate, for which he was tried and hanged in London in 1701. His career captured popular imagination. As the subject of many broadsides, ballads and folk tales, he became the most famous pirate in English literature.

Notes to Chapter 17

1. The Loan Exhibition in the chapel of the Albany Academy opened on July 6, 1886. The celebration centered upon church services, a parade, and special events sponsored by many civic organizations during the week of July 22, the 200th anniversary of the Dongan Charter. It displayed memorabilia, furniture, silver, portraits, and other heirlooms treasured in old Dutch families.

2. Herman Melville (1819–1891) was a son of Maria Gansevoort Melville, the only daughter of Peter Gansevoort. The literary significance of his novels was not recognized until the 1920s, and for the latter part of his life he worked in the New York Customs House. Captain Gansevoort Lansing visited frequently at his New York City home until 1876, when their two hair-triggered tempers clashed and these visits and correspondence between them ceased. This account is the first suggestion that Melville visited at 115 Washington Avenue later. See Leon Howard, *Herman Melville* (Minneapolis: University of Minnesota Press, 1961); and Alice P. Kenney, "Herman Melville and the Dutch Tradition," *New York Public Library Bulletin* (Spring, 1976).

3. Anthony Augustus Peebles (1822–1905), a second cousin of Aunt Kitty Lansing, inherited a large estate at the junction of the Mohawk and Hudson Rivers, where he bred fine horses, and was also a founder and for many years a director of the Peebles National Bank of Troy. His wife, Mary Louise Parmalee, was the author of a number of novels.

His estate included Peebles Island, now the home of the New York State Office of Parks, Recreation and Historic Preservation.

William H. Van Schoonhaven (b. 1849) was a lawyer and bank president in Troy. He was unmarried.

Both were descended from the Van Schaick family of Van Schaick's Island, near Cohoes, grandsons of a brother of Catherine Van Schaick, wife of General Peter Gansevoort, and therefore second cousins of Catherine Gansevoort Lansing.

4. Captain Steward Dean (1746–1836) was master of the 60-ton sloop *Experiment*, which sailed directly from Albany to Canton in 1784 and returned two-and-a-half years later, in April 1787. At that time the Pruyns were of modest status, not among the thirteen wealthy patrician families, including the Gansevoorts and Lansings, who ordered sets of porcelain dinnerware.

5. General Nelson Miles (1839–1925) fought in every major battle of the Civil War but one, rising from captain of infantry to major general of volunteers. In later years he won a reputation as an Indian fighter; his troops captured Chief Joseph of the Nez Perce in 1877 and the Apache Geronimo in 1886. His friendship with Kitty Lansing's beloved brother, Colonel Henry Gansevoort, developed between 1866–1868, while both were stationed at Fortress Monroe, Virginia.

6. The Albany Railway Company introduced electric trolley cars in 1890 and sold 200 horses. This company was consolidated with the West Shore Railroad Company to form the United Traction Company in 1899.

Notes to Chapter 18

1. Sir Lionel Sackville-West, second Baron Sackville of Knole (1827–1908), was unmarried but had two sons and three daughters by a Spanish lady. A career diplomat, he was British minister in Washington from 1881 to 1888, but was asked to leave because of the Murchison letters. H.P.H.'s description of the Murchison letters incident is essentially accurate.

2. The sequence of events in construction of All Saints Cathedral are as follows: The land was donated by Erastus Corning Jr. on April 1, 1872. The western portion (at Swan Street and Elk) was intended for St. Agnes School and the eastern portion (Hawk Street at Elk) for the cathedral. On November 1, 1872, the cathedral chapel was consecrated in the former Townsend machine shop at Hawk and Elk. On March 27, 1873, the legislature granted a charter to the Dean and Chapter of All Saints Cathedral, the first American Cathedral to be independently organized on the English model. On June 30, 1882, acquisition of land for an alternative site, on the southeast corner of Elk and Swan, was completed. On June 3, 1884, land was dedicated and the cornerstone laid. On November 20, 1888, the building was dedicated.

3. Lillian Price Hamersley (d. 1909) was the daughter of Commodore Cicero Price. In 1879 she married New York millionaire Lewis Hamersley (d. 1883). Then in 1888, she

married the Duke of Marlborough (d. 1892), and finally in 1895, she married Lord William Beresford (d. 1900). She had one son, William Warren Beresford. The reredos was promised in 1884, at the time of the laying of the cornerstone.

4. Marie Louise Cecilie Emma, née Lajeunesse (1852–1930), daughter of a music teacher in Chambly, near Montreal, was a soloist in St. Joseph's Church before her operatic career as Madame Albani at Covent Garden, London, 1872–1896. She returned to Albany on tours in 1883 and 1896.

Notes to Chapter 19

1. This incident probably took place in early 1889, when Roosevelt had just turned seven and H.P.H. was going on sixteen, as the following winter she was in England. "Ratty" would probably have been much nearer his age, but Franklin's behavior as H.P.H. recalls it, seems precocious. There is no record of this visit in the papers of James Roosevelt or Sarah Delano Roosevelt at Hyde Park, or the early correspondence of Franklin Delano Roosevelt at the F.D.R. Library, Hyde Park, N.Y.

Notes to Chapter 20

1. Lady Selkirk, born Cecely Louisa, daughter of Sir Philip de Malpas Grey Egerton, tenth Baronet Egerton, married James Dunbar, sixth Earl of Selkirk and one of the Representative Peers and Keeper of the Great Seal of Scotland.
The other lady who visited Mrs. Pruyn in Albany was probably the Dowager Countess of Shrewsbury; the Pruyns visited the Shrewsbury seat at Alton Towers on their wedding trip in 1865.

2. Estes Park, Colorado, though accessible only by exhausting rides on stage or horse-back, began to attract tourists from Denver in the early 1870s, when the state's first dude ranch, renting cabins and providing horses and guide service, was established there. British visitors and investors were attracted by the efforts of wealthy Lord Dunraven in establish-ing private hunting preserves. In 1877 he opened a first-class English resort hotel, which burned in 1911.

Notes to Chapter 21

1. The Hawk Street viaduct, bridging Sheridan Hollow from Arbor Hill to Capitol Hill, had been proposed for some time, but had been bitterly fought for ten years by two mayors, two common councils, and a number of prominent Hawk Street patricians, who evidently feared it would damage the quality of their neighborhood. Efforts to secure authorization from the legislature were defeated in 1882 and 1885, then in 1887 passed by the assembly but weakened in the senate by amendments pressed by Amasa J. Parker

Jr. This situation was reversed in 1888 by a new city administration headed by Albany's second Irish mayor, Edward A. Mahar, and supported by both the Irish and by construction and utilities magnate Anthony N. Brady, who had held many contracts for paving city streets with granite block and had now secured that for the stone work on the viaduct. *The New Albany*, vol. 2:5 (1892) 139–43.

2. Ezra Ripley Thayer (1866–1915) was admitted to the bar in 1891 and, after practicing with several law firms, became professor and dean of Harvard Law School from 1910 until his death.

3. About 15,000–17,000 years ago, when the most recent glacier was melting, water was discharged down the Mohawk and Hudson valleys. Where the two rivers joined, a shallow body of water collected, held in the basin formed by the Helderbergs, Taconics, and the Mayfield Hills; geologists called it Lake Albany. The deep center of this bed formed the Sand Plains. Though many Indian relics have been discovered there, buffalo were not customarily hunted in the eastern forests — H.P.H. simply reflects the popular ethnology of her youth, which extended to Indians in general the cultural features characteristic of the Plains Indians.

4. The shad running up-river to spawn were so conspicuous every spring that sturgeon was popularly known as "Albany beef."

5. H.P.H. observed that both she and Louise Parker were too poor in their book work to have any delusions about medals, and one or the other of them was certainly at the bottom of the class, but they never could be sure which. Nevertheless, the bishop made a splendid speech when presenting their diplomas about his pleasure of having the daughters of two old friends graduate. H.P.H.'s valedictory address was entitled "The Last Word," playing on the double meaning of the last word as the woman's prerogative and as "good-bye." H.P.H., "Memories of St. Agnes, 1878–91, by an Old Girl," Box 23, Folder 170, 90f, A.I.H.A.

Notes to Chapter 23

1. Mr. Cavendish Bentinck would have been a member of the family — perhaps the younger son — of the Duke of Portland.

2. Sir James Matthew Barrie (1860–1937) became even more famous for *Peter Pan* (1904).

3. Emma Eames (1865–1952) was an American operatic soprano who made her debut as Juliette in Paris in 1889, and appeared thereafter in London and New York. She married portrait painter Julian Story in 1891, but was divorced from him in 1907, and in 1911 married baritone Emilio De Gorgorza. Though her photograph may have been widely sold, she was not technically one of the "Professional Beauties," who were women of high social position.

Notes to Chapter 24

1. Adlai Ewing Stevenson (1835–1914), grandfather of the twentieth-century statesman of the same name, was a congressman from Illinois 1875–1877 and 1879–1881, assistant Postmaster General 1885–1889, and Vice-President 1893–1897.

2. Fitzhugh Lee (1835–1905), son of Commodore Sydney Smith Lee and Anna Marie Mason, was a Confederate general and later Democratic governor of Virginia 1886–90 and U. S. Consul in Havana from 1893 till the outbreak of the Spanish-American War. H.P.H. has confused him with William Henry Fitzhugh Lee, son of General Robert E. Lee, who died in 1891.

William E. Russell (1857–1896), a Massachusetts lawyer, served as mayor of Cambridge 1884–1887 and governor 1890–1892, but returned to private practice in 1894. Because of his defense of Cleveland, he was considered for the Democratic presidential nomination in 1896, but he died suddenly in July of that year while on a fishing vacation in Quebec. His influence helped launch Charles S. Hamlin, a personal friend, on his political career. *DAB.*

3. There were two admirals Van Tromp, both noted for victories over the British navy in the seventeenth-century Anglo-Dutch wars. Maarten Harpertszoon Tromp (1597–1653) defeated a Spanish fleet in 1639, and a British fleet under Admiral Blake in 1652, but was killed in action against the British in 1653; Dutch vessels in these wars henceforth carried brooms at their masthead, in memory of his sobriquet "besom" who swept the British from the sea. His son Cornelius (1629–1691), also an admiral, won victories over the British in 1673 and became lieutenant admiral of the United Provinces in 1676.

4. Dr. Mary Walker (1832–1919) received her physician's certificate from Syracuse Medical College in 1855, served as a nurse in the Civil War for three years before being commissioned and assigned duty as a surgeon in 1864, and after the war practiced in Washington, D.C. She was a zealous activist for improving women's lives, and her preference for male attire caused her many problems with both men and women.

Dr. Anna Howard Shaw (1847–1919) was in 1880 the first woman ordained by the Methodist Protestant Church, lectured widely on women's rights, and was very active in the Women's Christian Temperance Union.

Susan B. Anthony (1820–1906) organized in 1869, with Elizabeth Cady Stanton, the National Women's Suffrage Association, and thereafter devoted her life to this cause.

Elizabeth Cady Stanton (1815–1902), daughter of a New York State Supreme Court judge, married in 1840 Henry B. Stanton (d. 1882), an anti-slavery activist. In 1848 she called the first Women's Rights Convention at Seneca Falls, N. Y., served as president of the National Women's Suffrage Association 1863–1893, and advocated women's property rights and suffrage.

Lillie Devereux Blake (1835–1913), left a widow with two children 1859, married Grenfill Blake in 1866 and later became active in the women's suffrage movement, serving for eleven years as president of the New York State Women's Suffrage Association. She also advocated women's economic rights, particularly in such novels as *Fettered for Life, or Lord and Master* (1874).

5. Anna Parker Pruyn's anti-women's suffrage activities included a meeting, co-chaired by Bishop Doane, at 13 Elk Street, April 11, 1895. The Albany Anti-Suffrage Association of the Third Judicial District of which she was president opened its offices at 125 State Street in 1896. A woman's suffrage amendment to the New York State Constitution was rejected by the voters in 1913 and 1915 but passed in 1917; the national amendment was adopted in 1919. For more about Anna Parker Pruyn's part in this organization, of which she was president 1894–1900, when it had about 8,000 members, see H.P.H., "Diary of Anna Fenn Parker," 56–58.

H.P.H. collected considerable material on anti-suffrage activities in New York State, which would make an interesting paper in its own right. The subject is recommended to a historian on the women's movement. See H.P.H. Papers, Box 39, Folder 289. I am indebted to Mildred Zimmerman for locating these materials.

Note to Chapter 25

1. This portrait is in the Pruyn Room, devoted to Albany history, in the Albany Public Library.

Notes to Chapter 26

1. Weather reports at this time were the charge of the U. S. Signal Corps. The Albany station, which was opened around the year 1870, was located at the Dudley Observatory.

2. Bicycling was introduced in the 1880s and clubs were formed in Albany in 1880 and 1886. The early "penny-farthing" bicycles, with their large front and small rear wheels, were difficult to balance and inappropriate for riders wearing skirts. Women had to wait for the "safety bicycle" in the 1890s, with two equal-sized wheels and structure stable enough to dispense with the horizontal rod connecting the stearing shaft with the seat.

3. It is difficult to understand what H.P.H. means here. It does not seem in character for her to have taken offense at the presence in Albany of the coachman of a European actress. She does imply a belief in strong spiritual forces at work in society at the end of a century. In this she was not alone. "The end of the century" was often viewed as an explanation — or excuse — for the reputed decadence of the 1890s.

Notes to Chapter 27

1. Dina Maria Craik (1826–1887), "Miss Mulock," married in 1865 to George Lillie Craik, partner in the Macmillan publishing house, was the author of forty-six novels of which *John Halifax, Gentleman* (1857) was the best.

2. Stanwix Hall, on the lot at the southeast corner of Broadway and Maiden Lane, which had been owned by the Gansevoort family since the 1670s was, with the Delavan

House, one of the city's leading hotels. Built in 1833 by Judge Peter Gansevoort on land the family had owned for five generations, it was one of Aunt Kitty Lansing's principal assets until her death in 1918; it was demolished in 1932 to make way for the post office which now stands on the site. *Chronicles*, 504.

3. Dr. Luther Emmett Holt (1855–1924), of New York City, a pioneer in American pediatrics, was, after 1898, in charge of the Babies Hospital of New York City, and 1901–1924 at the College of Physicians and Surgeons of Columbia University. His works included *The Care and Feeding of Children* (1894), a widely used manual for parents, and *The Diseases of Infancy and Childhood* (1896), which became the standard text in this field. *DAB*.

4. Henryk Sienkiewicz, pseud., Litwos, (1846–1916), was a Polish novelist noted for colorful historical tales, such as *Quo Vadis* (1896). He received the Nobel Prize for literature in 1905. *WBD*.

5. Carter claimed this was political reprisal for his refusal to recommend the Nicaragua over the Panama route for the canal. In 1939 the House Military Affairs Committee voted to invalidate the court-martial, but the Senate did not concur.

6. In 1897 Monticello was the home of a family named Levy, who respected its historic significance and cherished many relics of Jefferson while adapting it to their own use as a private residence. Visitors were therefore their guests.

The University of Virginia was then in the midst of rebuilding after a disastrous fire in 1895 that had severely damaged the rotunda and destroyed several other buildings designed by Thomas Jefferson. Architect Stanford White and his firm, McKim, Mead and White, reconstructed the rotunda and designed three classroom buildings which are still at the heart of the greatly expanded campus.

Jamestown Island had been in agricultural use by several private owners since the seat of government was moved to Williamsburg at the end of the seventeenth century. At the end of the nineteenth century there were two structures on the island, an eighteenth century house and the mid-seventeenth century church tower, as well as a 1790 brick wall around the graveyard near the tower.

Notes to Chapter 28

1. William Shakespeare, *Two Gentlemen of Verona* II:iv:159.

2. Richmond Pearson Hobson (1970–1937) was a naval officer 1889–1903 whose principal work concerned the stability and fire power of vessels in action. He was awarded the medal of honor in 1933 for sinking the *Collier Merrimac* in 1898 in Santiago harbor.

3. Russell Alexander Alger (1836–1907), a lumber merchant who had been Governor of Michigan and a favorite son candidate in 1896, was Secretary of War 1897–1899, but he proved inept in the Spanish-American War, when unwise appointments and inefficiency

in procurement and transportation of supplies resulted in many unnecessary losses from disease among the American troops. *DAB*.

Theodore Roosevelt was a member of the U. S. Civil Service Commission 1889–1895 and by his vigorous activity did much to put into effect the reforms the law intended; when he resigned to become New York City's Police Commissioner, William G. Rice was appointed to complete the remainder of his term. In 1898, Roosevelt organized the first volunteer regiment, U. S. Cavalry, known as the "Rough Riders," becoming its colonel. Later in 1898, after the war, he was elected Governor of New York, and in 1900 Vice-President, becoming President in 1901 on the assassination of William McKinley. *DAB*.

4. Finley Peter Dunne (1867–1936) served on the editorial staff of Chicago newspapers 1893–1897 and as editor of the *Chicago Journal* 1897–1900. His humorous Irish characters of Mr. Dooley and his friend Hennessey appeared in a number of books, including *Mr. Dooley in Peace and War* (1898).

Marcus Alonzo ("Mark") Hanna (1837–1904), a Cleveland industrialist, was an astute political organizer who managed McKinley's campaign in 1896, then became Senator from Ohio in 1897 and a respected advisor of President McKinley and Theodore Roosevelt, but did not hesitate to use his position for personal gain. *DAB*.

Charles Vernon Gridley (1844–1898) served on various ships and posts 1844–1897, when he took command of the *Olympia*, flagship of the Asiatic squadron. Dewey's famous command, "You may fire when you are ready, Gridley," giving him the responsibility for starting action against the Spanish fleet, was considered a high compliment. He died on his way home to the U. S. afterwards. *DAB*.

BIBLIOGRAPHY

Albany City Directories.

Albany Institute of History and Art. Curatorial Records.

Albany Institute of History and Art. Manuscript Collection.

"Albany Parks, Washington Park." Exhibition Project No. 178. Vertical file, Albany Institute of History and Art.

Albany Rural Cemetery Records.

Albany's Historic Street. Albany: Albany Savings Bank, 1918.

All Saints Cathedral Booklet. Albany: All Saints Cathedral, n.d.

"A Tribute to Long Service." *Knickerbocker News,* November 16, 1968.

Barnes, Thurlow Weed. *Memoir of Thurlow Weed.* Boston: Houghton, Mifflin and Co., 1884.

Bennett, Allison. *The People's Choice: History of Albany County in Architecture.* Albany: Albany County Historical Association, 1980.

Biographical Directory of the United States Executive Branch, 1774–1977.

Blackburn, Roderic. *Cherry Hill.* Albany: Historic Cherry Hill, 1975.

"Board of Regents." *History of the State of New York.* Ed. Alexander C. Flick. New York: Columbia University Press, 1937.

Bonney, Catherine Van Rensselaer. *A Legacy of Historical Gleanings.* 2 vols. Albany: J. Munsell, 1875.

Brown, E. Richard. *Rockefeller Medicine Men: Medicine and Capitalism in America.* Berkeley: University of California Press, 1979.

Chamber's Biographical Dictionary. Rev. ed. New York: St. Martin's Press, 1968.

"Charlie Ross Revived: Today the Eighth Anniversary of the Abduction." *Philadelphia Record,* June 30, 1882.

Christman, Henry A. *Tin Horns and Calico.* New York: H. Holt and Co., 1945.

De Mille, George E. *Pioneer Cathedral*. Albany: Diocese of Albany, 1967.

Dictionary of American Biography. 17 vols. New York: Charles Scribner's Sons, 1964.

Dictionary of National Biography. 22 vols. London: Oxford University Press, 1882–1953.

Doyle, Brian, ed. and comp. *The Who's Who of Children's Literature*. New York: Schocken Books, 1968.

Dutch Settlers Society of Albany Yearbook.

Edelstein, David S. *Joel Munsell: Printer and Antiquarian*. New York: Columbia University Press, 1950.

Ellis, David M., James A. Frost, Harold C. Syrett, and Harry F. Carman. *A Short History of New York State*. Published in cooperation with the New York State Historical Association. Ithaca, N.Y.: Cornell University Press, 1957.

English Catalogue of Books. London, 1890.

Flick, Hugh M. *Elkanah Watson: Gentleman-Promoter, 1758–1842*. New York: Columbia University Press, 1947.

Frazer, J. M. "Beverwyck Manor: St. Anthony's-on-the-Hudson." *Golden Jubilee Book*. Albany: St. Anthony's-on-the-Hudson, 1962.

Gilborn, Craig. *Durant: The Fortunes and Woodland Camps of a Family in the Adirondacks*. Sylvan Beach, N.Y.: North Country Books in cooperation with the Adirondack Museum, 1981.

Gilder, Cornelia Brooke, ed. *Albany Architects: The Present Looks at the Past*. Albany: Historic Albany Foundation, 1978.

Grant, Anne. *Memoir of an American Lady*. London: Longmans, 1808.

Hamlin, Huybertie Pruyn. "Diary of Anna Fenn Parker." Box 7, Folder 48, Hamlin Papers. Albany Institute of History and Art.

————. "Elk Street and Its Neighbourhood." Box 21, Folder 156, Hamlin Papers. Albany Institute of History and Art.

————. "Memories of St. Agnes School, 1878–1891, by an Old Girl." Box 23, Folder 170, Hamlin Papers. Albany Institute of History and Art.

————. "Purely Personal and Thirteen Elk Street." Box 21, Folder 152, Hamlin Papers. Albany Institute of History and Art.

Harsha, David Addison. *Noted Living Albanians and State Officials*. Albany: Weed, Parsons and Co., 1891.

Hill, Frederick S. *New York State Men: Biographical Studies and Character Portraits*. Albany: Argus Co., 1906.

Hoadley, John C., ed. *Memorial of Henry Sanford Gansevoort*. Boston: Rand, Avery & Co., 1875.

Hobbins, James M. "The Albany Institute and Resistudes in the Learned Culture." May, 1975. Unpublished.

_____ . "Shaping a Provincial Learned Society: The Early History of the Albany Institute." *The Pursuit of Knowledge in the Early American Public: American Scientific and Learned Societies from Colonial Times to the Civil War*. Ed. Alexander C. Olsen and Sanford C. Brown. Baltimore: Johns Hopkins University Press, 1973.

Hooper, Joseph A. *A History of St. Peter's Church in the City of Albany*. Albany: Fort Orange Press, 1900.

Howard, Leon. *Herman Melville*. Minneapolis: University of Minnesota Press, 1961.

Kaiser, Harvey H. *Great Camps of the Adirondacks*. Boston: David R. Godine, 1982.

Kennedy, William. *O Albany!* New York: Viking Press and Washington Park Press, 1983.

Kenney, Alice P. "America Discovers Columbus." *Biography*, Spring, 1980.

_____ . "Herman Melville and the Dutch Tradition." *New York Public Library Bulletin*, Spring, 1976.

_____ . "The Holland Society's Compleat Angler." *de Halve Maen*, 2 parts, October, 1974; January, 1975.

Leach, Douglas Edward. *The Northern Colonial Frontier, 1607–1763*. New York: Holt, Rhinehart, Winston, 1966.

Lloyds Clerical Directory, 1898.

Manning, James H. *Albany's Historic Streets*. Albany: National Savings Bank, 1918.

McEneny, John J. *Albany: Capital City on the Hudson: An Illustrated History*. Woodland Hills, California: Windsor Publications, 1981.

Meigs, Cornelia, et al. *A Critical History of Children's Literature*. New York: Macmillan, 1953.

Miller, Ellen, and Paul Stambach. *Selected Receipts of a Van Rensselaer Family, 1785–1835*. Albany: Historic Cherry Hill, 1976.

Morison, Samuel Eliot, and Henry Steele Commager. *Growth of the American Republic*. New York: Oxford University Press, 1962.

Munsell, Joel. *Annals of Albany*. 10 vols. Albany: J. Munsell, 1871.

Neu, Irene G. *Erastus Corning: Merchant and Financier, 1794–1872*. Ithaca, N.Y.: Cornell University Press, 1960.

Norton, Thomas Elliott. *The Fur Trade in Colonial New York, 1686–1776*. Madison: University of Wisconsin Press, 1974.

"One of Adirondack Luxury Sites Hit." *Albany Times Union*, October 19, 1983.

Pearson, Jonathan. *Early Records of the City and County of Albany and Colony of Rensselaerswyck*. 4 vols. Albany: J. Munsell, 1869.

_____ . *Genealogies of the First Settlers of Albany, From 1630 to 1800*. Baltimore: Genealogical Publishing Co., Inc., 1976.

Plaza Row. Albany: Historic Albany Foundation, 1979.

Raffe, W. G. *Dictionary of the Dance*. New York: A. S. Barnes and Co., 1964.

Reynolds, Cuyler. *Albany Chronicles*. Albany: J. B. Lyon Co., 1906.

_____ . *Hudson-Mohawk Genealogical and Family Memoirs*. New York: Lewis Historical Publishing Co., 1911.

Reynolds, Helen Wilkinson. *Dutch Houses in the Hudson Valley Before 1776*. New York: Tayson and Clark, Ltd., 1929; reprint Dover, 1965.

Rice, Harriet L. P. *Harmanus Bleecker: An Albany Dutchman*. Albany, 1924.

Roseberry, Cecil R. *Capitol Story*. Albany: State of New York, 1964.

_____ . *Flashback: A Fresh Look at Albany's Past*. Ed. Susanne Dumbleton. Albany: Washington Park Press, 1986.

Rowley, William E. "Albany: Tale of Two Cities, 1820–1880." Ph.D. diss., Harvard University, 1967.

Schilstra, J. J. "Dutch 'Koekplanken' of the Seventeenth and Eighteenth Centuries." *de Halve Maen*, 42:3.

Servier, Christine. *History of the Albany Cathedral of the Immaculate Conception*. Albany: Weed, Parsons and Co., 1891.

Strayer, Joseph R., ed. *The Delegate from New York*. Princeton: Princeton University Press, 1939.

"Symon Schermerhorn's Ride." *Dutch Settlers Society of Albany Yearbook*, vol. 46. Albany, 1977–79.

The New Albany. Albany: Brandow Printing Co., 1891–1893.

Van Deusen, Glyndon G. *Thurlow Weed: Wizard of the Lobby*. Boston: Little, Brown and Co., 1947.

Van Olinda, Edgar S. "Quality Row." *Times Union*, May 2, 1941; May 7–8, 1942.

————. "Tattletales of Old Albany." *Times Union*, April 26, 1942.

Watson, Winslow C. *Men and Times of the Revolution*. New York: Dana & Co., 1856.

Weise, Arthur James. *The History of the City of Albany, New York*. Albany: E. H. Bender, 1884.

Who Was Who. 7 vols. New York: St. Martin, 1941–1961.

Who Was Who in America. 10 vols. Chicago: Marquis.

Who Was Who in America, Historical Volume, 1607–1896. Chicago: Marquis, 1963.

Wilcoxen, Charlotte. *Seventeenth Century Albany: A Dutch Profile*. Albany: Albany Institute of History and Art, 1981.

Worth, Gorham. *Random Recollections of Albany From 1800 to 1808*. Albany, N.Y.: J. Munsell, 1866.

INDEX

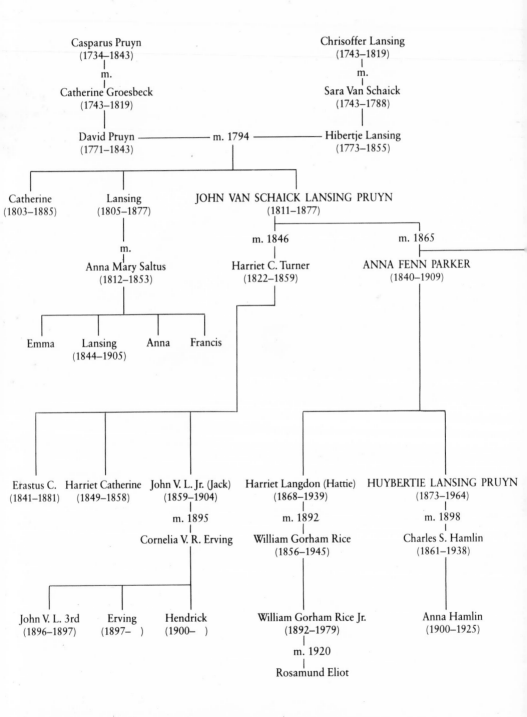